Also by Mark Derr

Dog's Best Friend: Annals of the Dog-Human Relationship

The Frontiersman:
The Real Life and the Many Legends of Davy Crockett

Over Florida

Some Kind of Paradise:
A Chronicle of Man and the Land in Florida

A Dog's History of America

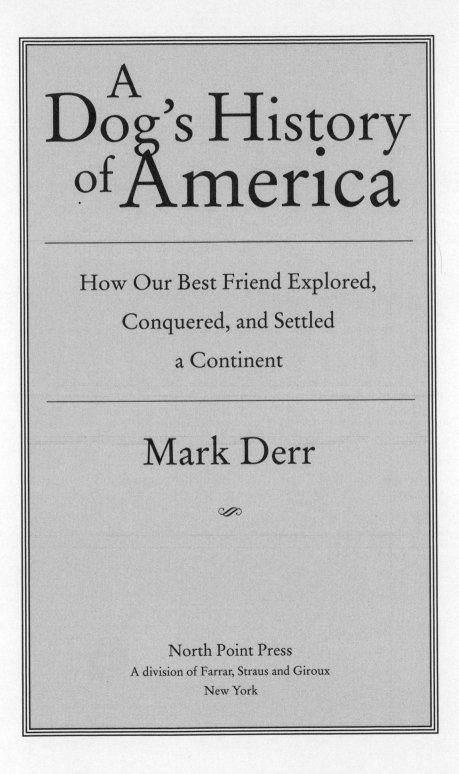

A Dog's History of America

How Our Best Friend Explored,

Conquered, and Settled

a Continent

Mark Derr

North Point Press
A division of Farrar, Straus and Giroux
New York

North Point Press
A division of Farrar, Straus and Giroux
19 Union Square West, New York 10003

Grateful acknowledgment is made to Jessica Dunbar Dorn for permission to reprint lines from Recollection of Gran Apacheria by Ed Dorn.

Grateful acknowledgment is also made to the following for permission to reproduce the images throughout the book: University of Miami Archives and Special Collections for the images of the Hare Indian dog and the Esquimaux dogs, and for George Catlin's painting of the dog fight (taken from Letters and notes on the manners, customs, and conditions of the North American Indians: written during eight years' travel amongst the wildest tribes of Indians in North America. In 1832, 33, 34, 35, 36, 37, 38 and 39, by George Catlin, London, 1841); Library of Congress, Prints and Photographs Division for the stereograph (left half) of Custer, for the photograph of the Aroostook County dog (Farm Security Administration Office of War Information Collection), for the lithograph of the sheepdog and shepherd, for the chromolithograph of the pug, and for the photograph of the Alaska prospector (Frank and Frances Carpenter Collection); the Collection of the New-York Historical Society for the drawing of Union troops (accession number 1945.58); the National Gallery of Art for the detail of the boy and his cur from the painting The Grave of William Penn; the Florida State Archives for Frederic Remington's drawing of the leopard cur, for the photograph of the woman with her gun, for the photograph of the bird-hunters, for the photograph of the African-American handlers, and for Remington's drawing of the grizzly bear; the Ohio State University Archives, Papers of Admiral Richard E. Byrd, for the photograph of the dog sleds; and the National Archives and Records Administration for the U.S. Marine "Raiders" and their dogs.

Library of Congress Cataloging-in-Publication Data
Derr, Mark.
   A dog's history of America : how our best friend explored, conquered, and settled a continent / Mark Derr.—1st ed.
      p. cm.
   ISBN-13: 978-0-86547-631-8
   ISBN-10: 0-86547-631-4 (alk. paper)
   1. Dogs—America—History. I. Title.

SF422.6.A3D47 2004
636.7'00973—dc22

                                                                                    2003071069

Designed by Abby Kagan

Frontispiece photograph: Cirques Emmy TDI,
certified therapy dog for twelve years, by Greg Goebel

www.fsgbooks.com

1   3   5   7   9   10   8   6   4   2

For the Dogs

Contents

⌘

Preface

୶

TOURING THE OZARKS in 1818, the young mineralogist Henry Rowe Schoolcraft noticed that every hunter—meaning every settler in that rugged country—had six to twelve dogs. "A very high value is set upon a good dog," he said, "and they are sought with the greatest avidity." Schoolcraft thought the hunters he met a lazy lot for ignoring agriculture and their livestock, allowing whatever they might have in the way of horses, cows, and hogs to forage unattended in the forest, while seeking meat for themselves and their hounds. But at the same time, he had stumbled upon a signal truth: the long hunter could not have blazed the trails that opened the frontier or survived in his isolated cabin without his dogs. Schoolcraft had learned firsthand the futility of trying to hunt a black bear without a dog to tree it. He understood as well that a dog was needed to roust a bear from its den, to track it or other game when wounded, it fled, or to hold it at bay so the hunter, fresh out of shot, could kill it with his knife or a spear. That same dog served as a sentry around the camp and house. It was no wonder people remembered their favorite dogs and frequently told stories late into the night about their courage, the tone of their cry when striking a trail, their talent and sagacity, as if they were valued members of the family.[1]

At one time or another during the past 15,000 to 20,000 years, virtually all of America was a frontier for someone, and the dog played an essential role in its settlement, one that standard histories have overlooked or mentioned only in passing. Often dogs do not even appear in the indexes of early histories, although they occasionally leap from the text. They were ubiquitous, and invisible, taken for granted like beer and rotgut whiskey, cooking pots, the labor of women and children, the diseases that regularly ravished people and animals, even the lives of slaves and indentured servants. Truth be told, it has also long been considered more important for historians to focus on the grand sweep of events—the wars, famines, revolutions, political machinations, social and economic structures—that affect the lives of people. But times change, and over the past thirty to forty years historians have focused increasing attention on the daily lives of people as a way to gain clearer understanding of the past. It seems appropriate, then, to give dogs their book, one that recognizes their contributions to the settlement of America by successive waves of immigrants. Yet because dogs do not exist independently of human society, their story is finally our story as well.

IF DOGS DID NOT COME with the first people to enter North America from Siberia, they were not far behind, and by all appearances they have accompanied every explorer and settler since, except Columbus on his first voyage. For 10,000 years or more, dogs were the only domesticated animals in much of the Americas, and they were invaluable, their primary duties shifting according to the needs of their people. They were guards, hunters, fishers, food, pets, and commonly beasts of burden, sharing the weight of moving the camp and hauling firewood and meat with the women. At least one tribe raised them as foot warmers for arthritics, and another kept them, like sheep, to provide hair for weaving. Some Native American women valued their dogs more highly than their children; indeed, a tribe's survival sometimes depended on dogs. Not surprisingly, the dog figures in the creation myths of a number of tribes and frequently serves as a guide to the spirit world.

Bringing dogs on his second trip to the Americas, Columbus loosed them in the first pitched battles of the Conquest, and his successors never released them. Much is made of the Spanish advantage in arms, armor, horses, and ruthless devotion to destroying anything that stood in the way of their quest for riches. But they possessed as well dogs such as the Native Americans they encountered had never seen, fell beasts trained to attack and maul, to terrorize. Later, the heirs of the conquistadors turned the descendants of those dogs to tracking African slaves, creating in the process a tradition and breed that became prized in the antebellum American South.

English colonists learned from their Spanish competitors to bring mastiffs to the New World, but although they flirted occasionally with the notion of deploying them against Indians in the Spanish fashion, they invariably stopped short of doing so. African slaves were a different matter. Dogs figure every other way in the settlement of North America, and because the record is so rich, and their roles so varied, I have focused on that region, and more precisely on what became the United States, with some essential forays south and north, especially to the poles. Whenever possible, I have relied on firsthand accounts, contemporary news reports, and histories to provide a sense not only of the types of dogs present but also their uses and people's views of them. Uniquely among animals, the dog has accompanied people through all stages of history, changing in form and purpose—I should say, changed often by humans—to meet the demands of new circumstances. Thus, with the rise of agriculture and the domestication of sheep and cattle, the proto-dog of nomadic hunter-gatherers split into several types in the Old World—mastiffs, herders, companions, sight hounds, and various curiosities with dwarf legs, hairless bodies, and other mutations. In the New World, divisions appear in many cases to parallel geographic and tribal boundaries, but the operative word is *appear*.

Through what Darwin called conscious and unconscious selection, people around the world created dogs that suited their desires and needs, and the dogs, in turn, helped transform those societies by assisting in the domestication and husbandry of livestock and in hunting game for the table and other predators for protection. The trend accelerated in the late eighteenth and early nineteenth centuries, when men began actively "improving" types of dogs and creating new ones through "scientific" breeding, bestowing on the creations value and powers far exceeding those of their rough-born forebears. With expanding industrialization, that trend became even more pronounced, and by the middle of the nineteenth century, coincident with the rise of the Fancy in England and the United States, people began arguing that the time had come to "civilize" the dog, to make it suitable by virtue of its pedigree, bearing, and behavior for proper urban bourgeois society. Dissenting voices were raised in celebration of basic dogs, just as they were, in support of the poor, of workers, slaves, women, children, and ultimately Nature. In effect, the dog came to embody the conflict between city and country, rich and poor, white and black, civilization and the wild, to assume an ambiguous position as an intermediary between worlds.

Those contradictions continue to this day, although dogs have been fenced, leashed, and corralled to such a degree that many of them leave the confines of their human house and home only for periodic trips to the veterinarian, if that. Professional trainers and certified animal behaviorists are available to help dogs and people adjust to the stresses of isolation and bad genetics—the result of too much inbreeding and sloppy overbreeding of purebred dogs. People seeking to keep their dogs exercised in a world of diminishing public open space frequently clash with their human opposites over off-leash walking or the establishment of "bark parks." These parks are often small, poorly maintained, flea-and-tick-infested canine ghettos that provide local park administrators with the illusion that they have done something positive to end the continuing conflict between the people who share their lives with dogs and those who fear and loathe them. The real need, of course, is for more large urban and suburban parks for dogs and people. But that runs well ahead of the story, which I have allowed dogs and people to tell.

The history also indirectly addresses several controversies regarding dogs. It has become popular of late to dismiss the dog as a "social parasite," a camp scavenger who ingratiated itself with a band of human suckers 15,000 or more years ago—in some versions, women were the suckers—and has been tagging along ever since. Even a cursory look at the role of dogs in human affairs, beginning with the first Americans, should lay that view to rest. Territorial protection and hunting are innate in the dog, as they are in the ancestral wolf. Once trained to carry a pack or haul a travois or sled, the dog had no choice but to transport goods. Dogs certainly had no more to say about going into the pot than did any other animal that humans chose to put there, and although some tribes did not eat them, others considered them a delicacy. Surprisingly, early European settlers and explorers, most famously Meriwether Lewis and all the Corps of Discovery except William Clark, readily developed a taste for dog, often, it must be said, of necessity. Some wolves and humans got together in Asia or Europe—not the Americas and probably not Africa—perhaps as early as 135,000 years ago, because they could help each other, and the tame wolves became dogs through a process that is still not understood. The species have been together ever since, although it appears that dogs have often gotten a raw deal.

While showing persistence over time and across cultures, attitudes toward dogs and the uses to which their talents are put have changed dramatically with the destruction of indigenous societies, the opening and closing of the frontier, the rise and demise of plantation slavery, and the transformation of America from a predominantly rural to an urban and suburban society. The types of dogs have changed, too. The Native American dog is gone, killed or mixed with those from Europe. Occasionally someone suggests that a few of the originals exist in a remote Arctic village or an isolated Andean valley, but probably all that can be said with certainty is they resemble the old type physically. The dogs who came with the first waves of European settlers are gone, too, long ago thrown into the general gene pool that produced, I believe, the big all-purpose cur and smaller feist of the frontier and various crossbred hounds. Following World War II, the demand for purebred dogs soared among the flourishing middle class that suburbanized America, until in 2000 they represented approximately half of all dogs. Today the Labrador, the golden retriever, various small dogs, and retriever–German shepherd mixes have become as numerous as the cur and feist were a century ago. Following their human companions, they have developed weight problems; an estimated 40 percent of American dogs are considered obese, and countless more are overweight.[2]

Inherited from the wolf, the dog's basic talents and personality traits have remained remarkably unchanged, although they have been reshuffled through intensive artificial selection in certain breeds; other breeds are so mutated physically that they cannot perform a full range of behaviors. The basenji does not bark, while poodles and American Staffordshire terriers appear limited in the types of barks they can make. In the mid-nineteenth century, breeders began to associate floppy ears with enhanced trainability and a desire to serve, which they wanted in their gun dogs. The Labrador, preferred for contemporary detection work because of its hunting drive and tractability, was created from that mold. Breeders also selected eyes set more forward and domed heads, as well as shortened noses, in an effort to make their dogs look more "civilized" and childlike, as the dog became an urban pet. The resulting brachycephalic dogs—bulldogs, pugs, and boxers, for example—have difficulty breathing in the heat.

I HAVE STITCHED *A Dog's History of America* from historical events and the accounts of people living at the time—most commonly people doing something with their dogs or observing those of others. The story tracks through time and space, like a hound on scent, beginning with the first Americans and moving through the Spanish Conquest into the English Colonial period. From there, I look at the age of Revolution and Enlightenment; early Western explorers, Lewis and Clark foremost among them; travelers with their dogs, like Audubon, and the Oregon and California pioneers; dogs

in the Cotton South; the Indian Wars and the destruction of the
buffalo, featuring that notorious dog lover George Armstrong
Custer; the closing of the frontier and the range wars at the end of
the nineteenth century; attempts to civilize the dog while civilization shattered in World War I; the Roaring Twenties and the Depression; World War II through Vietnam; and now. Each chapter is
subdivided, with major events and players briefly described to provide context, but I also attempt to focus on ordinary people and
their dogs.

The last chapter constitutes a journalistic essay more than a history because the background noise is too high, the fat of opinion
too thick, to make sound judgments about the relative merits of
events. The eras of Vietnam, the Cold War, and even World War II
still exist within the living memory of many readers of this book,
and their recollections will cast a different emphasis on those events,
but at least they can be viewed as having discrete ends—the abandonment of Saigon, the fall of the Berlin Wall, surrender. Much as
people would now like to make the events of September 11, 2001, a
turning point in history, it is too early to tell. Certainly what has
followed politically appears to be more of the same, especially the
failure of the world's governments to address global warming, the
near-catastrophic collapse of fishing stocks in every ocean and sea,
the continuing loss of habitat and extinction of plants and animals,
and the imbalance of wealth between rich and poor. But some trends
stand out, especially the use of dogs to detect everything from land
mines to termites, to find victims of natural and human catastro-
phes, to track endangered species in an effort to preserve, not kill,
them, and to improve the health and quality of people from all
walks of life. As always with dogs, problems also persist, primarily
those associated with the overbreeding of dogs for show and profit
and with canine aggression.

For those reasons, I have attempted in closing to tie together
some loose ends and point to developments and trends, providing
both a summation and a conclusion while avoiding many judgments
and pronouncements that are bound to be wrong. Some readers will
doubtless have a favorite historical anecdote that I have missed, a

relatively easy thing to do, given the ubiquity of dogs and the often obscure texts reporting on them. I hope nonetheless to have provided enough evidence to give these remarkable animals their due. The one thing of which I am sure is that dogs will be around if we are. They are too valuable in all regards to give up. They are too much a part of who we are.

A Dog's History of America

1

First People and Dogs Settle the New World and Finally Are Lost:
Reassembling the Scant Bits and Pieces of the Vanished

❦

THE INUIT HUNTER'S DOGS, hitched in a fan formation to his sled, caught scent of Nanuq, the polar bear, and broke into a run across the rough snow-sheeted ice. Cawing like a raven, he urged them forward. As they drew within sight of the big white bear—a demon waiting to cause them harm—the hunter reached across his sled and unloosed one dog. Closing on his prey, he unloosed another, then the third and the fourth, so that he was dashing forward now on foot, spear in hand. His cousin joined him and soon they were upon the bear, brought to bay by several growling, snarling dogs, pumped full of rage and fear, dodging his massive paws. Snapping at his rear, other dogs prevented Nanuq from turning on the men. As one hunter feigned an attack from the bear's right, the other in a quick motion thrust his spear up under the demon's ribs and deep into his heart before somersaulting away. The bear died almost instantly, and after appropriate observances to appease his spirit, the hunters butchered him. The dogs hauled the meat and hide back to camp.

That same day, thousands of miles to the south, a small group of

Assiniboin hunters on the Great Plains, near the confluence of the Missouri and Yellowstone rivers, hitched their dogs to sledges and sent them toward a herd of bison. Drawing near, the dogs broke into a sprint, sending the bison into a stampede. It was a dangerous, bone-rattling ride, requiring balance, skill, courage, and luck—or good medicine, derived from proper observance of bison hunting ceremonies. Kneeling in the sledges, dependent on the steadiness of their dogs, the Indian hunters shot their arrows into the flanks of the bison, bringing down a score before they were done. Soon women, dogs, children, and wolves—the bison's "shepherds," Meriwether Lewis called them—came to the field, to slaughter and feast. Battles ensued, as women beat back their dogs from stealing the prime slabs of bison. After hauling the meat home on their backs, the dogs raced to join their cousins the wolves in scavenging what remained.[1]

These were versatile, often abused animals, according to many European chroniclers, who reported that the dogs shared a life of toil, drudgery, and mistreatment with women—only they got less to eat and were beaten more frequently. Among the Inuit, Athabascan Indians, Plains Indians, and several other groups, women managed and trained the dogs, packing the household goods on their backs or on the sledges or travois they pulled as they moved in search of prey—be it seal, walrus, caribou, polar bear, or, on the plains, bison. In many cases, they knocked out or broke the shearing carnassial teeth of their dogs to prevent them from chewing precious harnesses and leads.

A Plains Indian village on the move was a riot of sound, motion, and color. Women loaded the dogs who would carry a pack or pull a travois, exempting puppies and assorted adults never broken to work. Then, shouldering their own heavy burdens, the women would drive their dogs forward, keeping them in line and breaking up fights, while the warriors walked or, after the arrival of the horse, rode as guards, guides, and hunters. Dogs were beaten to make them move or to break up fights. The whole column pressed forward for hours, sometimes an entire day, before resting, with dogs that bore no packs darting in and out of the fray to the amusement of children and warriors, the consternation of the dog drivers.

A dissenter from the view that the dogs were sorely abused was George Catlin, who in a remarkable span of seven years, 1832 to 1839, visited, by his estimate, forty-eight Indian tribes with a combined population of 400,000 people. Along the way, he produced more than 500 paintings, providing the most complete visual record of the Indians of the United States at a time when war, whiskey, religion, and smallpox were decimating entire tribes and cultures. Catlin sought to create something permanent against their destruction, which accelerated over the next fifty years. "The dog, amongst all Indian tribes, is more esteemed and more valued than amongst any part of the civilized world," Catlin observed. "The Indian who has more time to devote to his company, and whose untutored mind more nearly assimilates to that of his faithful servant, keeps him closer company, and draws him near to his heart; they hunt together, and are equal sharers in the chase—their bed is one, and on the rocks and on their coats of arms they carve his image of fidelity."[2]

In his search for a Northwest Passage across the continent, which took him, through bad navigation, to the Arctic Ocean in 1789, Alexander Mackenzie encountered the Athabascan people and dogs along the Mackenzie River (named for him), between Great Slave Lake and Great Bear Lake to its north. At one landing—he doesn't specify the location or the tribe, because both were unknown to him—he killed a dog that was getting into his baggage and threatened to kill more if the people did not tie up the dogs. The woman who owned the dog became distraught after its death, "crying bitterly, and said she had lost 5 children last winter for whom she was not so sorry as for the Dog." Mackenzie appeased her with "a few Beads and an Awl."[3]

Early European travelers frequently accused the Inuit—whom they called Esquimaux, or Eskimo—of abusing their dogs despite relying on them for pulling speared walrus and seals from the water before they could sink, for hunting polar bears, and for hauling their goods from camp to camp. Most of those travelers were abusing themselves, dogs, and natives—literally starving to death in many cases—in what the Inuit saw as a mad quest for a Northwest Passage and the North Pole, and so should have understood the harshness of Arctic life. But they did not. Few noticed that the Inuit would sometimes bring puppies or nursing females into their homes as pets, or fathomed the interdependence of dogs and people.

These different views of the relationship of Indians and their dogs are explained in part by the biases of the observers and by variations between cultures and tribes in the treatment of dogs—not to mention people, horses, and wildlife. But it is also true that the treatment of dogs varied within tribes and from season to season. When winter lay long and cold on the land and food grew scarce, Indians and dogs suffered. Along the upper Missouri, a favorite stopping-off place for travelers wanting a "wilderness adventure," winters grew more lean during the 1830s because of the steady depletion of game to feed the markets for fur and food, as well as the unending flow of whiskey and smallpox that killed thousands of people. The dogs were left to fend for themselves.

Into the Americas

No one knows when dogs first came to the Americas, or even whether they arrived by land or sea. Suggested dates range from roughly 35,000 to 12,000 years ago, with most experts contending that the first immigrants crossed the Bering land bridge, called Beringia, the 55-mile-long, 1,000-mile-wide expanse of tundra—not unlike that found today in the far north—linking Siberia and Alaska. Periodically exposed during the Pleistocene from 1.6 million to 10,000 years ago, Beringia served as a convenient mixing zone for plants and animals passing from Asia to North America and back—the way the gray wolf returned to its ancestral home after migrating to Asia and Europe. At the height of the Ice Age, glaciers reached south to the Ohio River and east to Long Island, while covering western Canada, Alaska, Washington, Idaho, and Montana.

Sea levels were some 300 feet lower, making for much more extensive coastal plains than exist today.

The best guess among some experts, based on linguistic, genetic, and archaeological evidence, is that the "first" Americans crossed Beringia in two to five migrations, which could each have lasted several years. They moved south along the coast, meaning whatever record they left of their presence now lies underwater; or, spreading south and east, they followed inland game routes between ice sheets. Within several thousand years, one group, broadly referred to as American Indians, passed from Beringia to Tierra del Fuego, the tip of South America. Na-dene speakers, usually called Athabascans, probably crossed into North America around 10,000 years ago in another wave of migration and settled inland in the Arctic and sub-Arctic. Some 6,000 years ago, the Inuit and Aleuts island-hopped the Bering Strait in their skin kayaks and settled along the coasts of the far north, to southern Alaska for the Aleuts and to Greenland for the Inuit.

Even with the powerful tools of genetic analysis, considerable disagreement remains over the origins of Native Americans. Some American Indians appear to be related to the Ainu (the aboriginal people of the Japanese island of Hokkaido), ancient Polynesians, and ancient Australians, while others have much in common with the ancient people of southern Siberia, near Mongolia. The Aleut and Inuit still have counterparts in northeastern Siberia. Whatever their origin—and there is still much to learn—the bet here is that all of these newcomers traveled with dogs.

A decade ago such a notion would have been dismissed as heretical fantasy. But some controversial genetic evidence has pushed the split of dogs from wolves to around 135,000 years ago in perhaps as many as four different locations. More recent studies have placed the origin of the dog in southern China and Southeast Asia, somewhere around 40,000 to 15,000 years ago, a spread that points to the crudeness of current genetic dating. On the whole, the dates indicate that dogs were probably abundant at the time of the first migrations to the New World, because of their usefulness to hunters and gatherers as companions, guardians, food, beasts of burden, and hunters.[4]

The transformation from wolf to dog is still locked in the canine genome and the archaeological record, which have recently disagreed over timing. Absent facts, we are left to conjecture. I subscribe to the notion that for many thousands of years dogs closely resembled wolves, breeding freely among themselves and probably with wolves, although the extent of that is open to debate. We can surmise that these wolfdogs, or proto-dogs, were more social and less fearful around people than "wild" wolves. Sometime around 15,000 to 10,000 years ago, when some groups of nomadic hunters became more sedentary, establishing semipermanent villages, their wolfdogs became genetically isolated and, through inbreeding, began to change physically—becoming slightly smaller and developing greater variations in coat color and a curled tail. Behaviorally, they might have become more tame and tractable, which would have increased their value to humans. In much of the New World, those few physical and behavioral changes remained the most significant differences between wolves and dogs until the arrival of Europeans. But even in the New World, with the development of agriculture and more organized societies, the gap between domesticated and wild wolves became larger, as different cultures began to raise their own types of dogs, including, it appears, some with floppy ears.

Despite tantalizing evidence that dogs and humans began arriving 35,000 to 20,000 years ago, the archaeological record has largely remained silent about the first Americans and their dogs until about 12,000 to 11,000 years ago, when they appear in Paleo-Indian sites in Alaska and Wyoming. These wanderers probably began crossing Beringia around 15,000 years ago, with their dogs and lethal weapons, including the atlatl, for throwing spears accurately and far. Whether they had bows and arrows is far less certain. Some archaeologists argue that the bow and arrow was invented around 20,000 years ago, while others hold to a much more recent date. In the New World, the oldest evidence for that weapon currently dates to around 11,500 years ago and was found in Alaska, but it is unclear how widespread the technology was. Conventional archaeological wisdom places adoption or independent invention of the bow and arrow in the New World sometime after 8,000 years ago.

The question is far from academic, since the weapon would have significantly improved the Paleo-Indians' hunting abilities. In any event, people and dogs arrived at the end of the Ice Age, when North America was in the throes of a dramatic climatic change that transformed ecosystems across the continent and coincided with one of the greatest mass extinctions in the world's history.

In 1967, University of Arizona ecologist Paul Martin proposed that Paleo-Indians hunted to extinction many of North America's big herbivores, especially mammoths and mastodons and *Bison antiquus* and *Bison occidentalis*, as well as giant rhinoceroses, cave bears, giant ground sloths, camels, flightless rheas, tortoise-shelled glyptodonts, and the indigenous horse, in a Stone Age "blitzkrieg." In the last several decades that theory has gained more adherents, in part because of contemporary observations of how destructive humans are. Extirpation of these large grazing animals, the adherents of this theory argue, triggered the collapse of whole ecosystems and the extinction of other species, including the pumped-up predators—saber-toothed cats, giant lions, and dire wolves—who, along with humans, fed on them.

No one knows with certainty what happened, but it is hard to imagine that Paleo-Indians were so ruthlessly efficient with their stone, bone, and wood weapons (even if they had bows and arrows) that they destroyed animals ranging all the way to the tip of Florida, as much a winter resort during the Pleistocene as it is today. More plausibly, the Paleo-Indians helped nudge populations stressed by rapidly changing climatic conditions over the edge, by consistently targeting juvenile and breeding-female mammoths, for example, and by driving herds of bison off cliffs or into arroyos. There is also some speculation among scientists that new diseases and parasites, some brought by dogs, wreaked havoc among the larger animals, in much the same way smallpox would among Native Americans thousands of years later.[5]

HABITAT DESTRUCTION is the greatest cause of extinction for many populations of animals, and the Pleistocene extinctions coincided

with changes in ecosystems across much of North America. As glaciers retreated, the climate grew warmer and sea levels rose, reconfig-
uring coastlines and flooding Beringia. Ecosystems were transformed.
Steppes and grasslands turned into forests. The inland sea of North
America, with its lush marshes, dried into high desert. New lakes,
marshes, and swamps appeared. Large, specialized animals could not
adjust and perished, whereas their smaller kin and species that were
more adaptable survived and ultimately flourished.

Certainly between 15,000 and 6,000 years ago, the flora and
fauna of North America were transformed into the mosaic of ecosystems we recognize today. Around 8,000 years ago bison vanished from the Great Plains because the draining of glacial lakes and
quick shifts from a cool, wet climate to a warm, dry, windy one and
then to cool, dry winters and warm, wet summers brought a transformation in vegetation. Lush, nutritious grasses gave way to less
nutritious grasses and sagebrush. The climate changed again around
7,500 years ago to its current pattern of "warmer" winters and
cooler, wetter summers, but bison did not return to the Plains for
another 2,500 years. These were *Bison bison*, the "smaller" animal
we know today, and with them came new groups of hunters, with
their dogs.[6]

The (Nearly) Ubiquitous Dog

Before Columbus's voyage, dogs appear to have flourished everywhere in the Americas, with the exception of a few individual tribal
territories and possibly the Amazon. Sadly, only fragmentary evidence of those dogs exists until European contact, when chroniclers
began to report on the civilizations they were destroying. Urban-
ized Mayan, Aztec, and Incan societies provide the most records,
but they are far from comprehensive and are not representative of
less centralized cultures. These fragments form a series of cross sections that, when flipped through quickly, create a flickering, ghost-
like film of the evolution of different tribal groups, cultures, and
civilizations over the thousands of years of human history in the

Americas. Yet the images are often so faint that the viewer has to conjure details and points of connection, an act of creative interpretation subject to constant revision and only partially satisfying.

Many of those bits and pieces come from a painfully incomplete archaeological record—in part because a sixty-five-mile swath of western North American coastal plain, an ice-free region where humans would have settled, now lies under several hundred feet of water, and because nomadic hunters and gatherers leave few traces that remain for thousands of years. But the sites that have been excavated show clearly that human cultures, like the ecosystems they inhabited, changed after the Pleistocene extinctions. In much of North America, a transition began around 8,000 years ago from the big-game-hunting nomadism of Paleo-Indians to a more settled Archaic culture that relied on a variety of plants and other animals to survive. Lasting until around 2,000 years ago, the Archaic culture marked the beginning of permanent settlements and agriculture, the creation of pottery, and, according to prevailing theories, the widespread adoption, if not invention, of the bow and arrow. The Olmec civilization—apparently the first in the Americas to breed dogs for food, to carve colossal human heads from limestone, and to develop a basic form of writing—rose and fell along the Gulf of Mexico in Central America during that time. Big-game-hunting nomadic cultures persisted on the Great Plains, in the Arctic, in Patagonia and Tierra del Fuego, and other game-rich areas, but even they changed over time.

After the dawn of the current era, the cultural and tribal divides of the Americas found at the time of European contact began slowly to take shape. Clearly, ideas and goods moved throughout much of the Americas in ways archaeologists can piece together from ceremonial pipes and ceramics, tool and weapon design, and in some areas earthworks, petroglyphs, and cliff dwellings, as well as the more elaborate cities, temples, and hieroglyphics of civilizations in Central America and the Andes. Often these routes followed rivers and coastlines.

The dog remained the sole domesticated animal of many Native American groups for all that time, its central role enhanced by myth and ritual, memorialized in art. Dogs also migrated with their people and were traded, allowing some types to spread widely and new ones to arise. Around 1,400 years ago, for example, a group of Athabascan people lashed their few possessions on the backs of their big, wolflike dogs and began a long, slow walk from their ancestral homes in the Pacific Northwest, around what is now southern Alaska, down the spine of the Rocky Mountains to the high mesas and shimmering pueblos of the Southwestern desert. There, this group of immigrants became Apaches and Navajos. Whenever they moved their camps, they lashed thirty- to forty-pound packs onto the backs of their dogs and set off through the rugged country, often driving trains of more than a thousand dogs. Bands of Apaches continued that practice long after they adopted horses from the Spanish in the seventeenth century, as did many Plains Indians a century later. In camp and on the trail, women supervised the dogs, but once the band was settled, men would use them to hunt birds and small game. From the Spaniards, the Apache and Navajo adopted not only horses but also sheep and goats and the method of raising dogs to escort and guard them.

NO ONE CAN SAY WITH CERTAINTY what the very early dogs did for their human companions, but it seems unlikely that they were merely camp-following scavengers. At the least they were companions, fellow travelers, and camp guards. European visitors often recorded that the dogs they encountered among various tribes were uncivil to strangers, attacking them and their horses with such persistence that they had to be beaten off with sticks and stones. Maximilian, Prince of Wied, a fifty-year-old world traveler and self-taught naturalist, witnessed dogs attacking and killing one of the distinctive white wolves that stalked bison along the upper Missouri River. For native people in the Arctic, there was no suitable alternative to the dog for transport until the snowmobile became widely available in the 1960s. The Plains Indians relied on the travois, two poles crossed over the dog's shoulders, which was well adapted to travel across flat terrain. Sledges appear to have been a later invention, but that, too, is unclear.

In 1769, Samuel Hearne, a young Hudson's Bay Company officer, sent from the Prince of Wales's Fort on the west shore of the bay to search for precious metals and the Northwest Passage, spent time among the Chipewyans, an Athabascan people of the Canadian Plains, and the Algonquin-speaking Cree of southern Canada and observed their cultures and dogs. What he saw applies to many Athabascan groups who used dogs for transport. Tents, kettles, and firewood "are always carried by dogs," Hearne said, "which are trained to that service, and are very docile and tractable. Those animals are of various sizes and colours, but all are of the fox and wolf breed, with sharp noses, full brushy tails, and sharp ears standing erect. They are of great courage when attacked and bite so sharp, that the smallest cur among them will keep several of our largest English dogs at bay, if he can get up in a corner." Although the dogs were adept at hauling sledges, he added, the men generally refused to make them, and so the women lashed packs to their backs. Invariably, the women hauled more than their share.[7]

The Chipewyans among whom Hearne found himself did not use their dogs for hunting, but the Cree trained their dogs to bay up moose, so they could more easily kill them. Many other tribes had dogs that were accomplished and productive hunters. Studies conducted in the late 1960s showed that !Kung San bushmen of the Kalahari Desert who hunted with dogs regularly brought home 75 percent of the animal protein their band consumed. Anyone familiar with the hunting prowess of dogs would be hard put to imagine ancient people who lived by hunting big game, like moose, elk, bears, and even seals and walruses, not using them to track and bay their prey, or to help carry the meat to camp. Bison are largely excepted from this view. Assiniboin hunters on the Plains used dogs when pursuing bison, but how common that was among other tribes is unknown. There is also no direct evidence that dogs were used to stampede bison, a common way of hunting them before the bow and horse allowed Indians to ride directly into the herd.[8]

Most Indian dogs could forage for themselves, either stealing food or bringing down sometimes large animals. Tucked in the accounts of many travelers are unadorned remarks about a dog killing a baby elk or a bison calf by itself, underscoring that they were more than abused, skulking curs. Rather, they were basic dogs, capable of serving and living with humans while retaining some of their wolfish skill as hunters.

Alvar Núñez Cabeza de Vaca, one of only four survivors of the ill-fated expedition through Florida of Pánfilo de Narváez in the late 1520s, found his way to the banks of the Rio Grande, where he observed Coahuiltecan Indian women throwing newborn girls to their dogs, who promptly consumed them. They told him that they did so because when their daughters were old enough, they would have to marry men from one of the neighboring tribes, all of which they were at war with, thereby increasing the number of their enemy. Whether that was a practice specific to a time of war or a long-standing custom of the Coahuiltecan, we have no way of knowing, but they were considered a warrior people and were renowned for their endurance and their use of mescal and peyote.

A NUMBER OF INDIAN MYTHS suggest the centrality of dogs in the people's lives, and some of those tales doubtless originated far back in time. During his stay among the Chipewyans, Samuel Hearne recorded their creation myth, according to which the first person of Earth was a woman. She had been alone for some time when one day, on her search for berries, her only food, she encountered a dog who followed her back to her cave. "This dog, they say, had the art of transforming itself into the shape of a handsome young man," said Hearne, "which it frequently did at night but as the day approached, always resumed its former shape; so that the woman looks on all that passed on those occasions as dreams and delusions." But they were no delusions, and the woman soon became pregnant. With that, "a man of such surprising height that his head reached up to the clouds, came to level the land, which at that time was a very rude mass." After creating lakes, ponds, and rivers with his walking stick, he seized the dog, tore it into pieces, and threw the guts into the lakes and rivers, ordering them to become fish. He threw its flesh over the land, commanding it to become animals. He threw its skin into the air, turning it into birds. He gave the woman and her offspring the power to kill and eat the creatures he had created for their use and then vanished, never to be seen again.[9]

In other myths, the dog is also the progenitor or the facilitator, present at or near the creation of the world and its denizens, just as it was integral to the lives of many people. Plains Indian tribes were often divided into societies, or groups, that performed various duties—acting as camp police, for example—and were named after powerful totem animals. Among the Cheyenne and several other tribes the bravest warriors—the Dog Soldiers—belonged to the Crazy Dog Society.

WIDE CULTURAL DIVIDES appeared between groups of people when it came to eating dog. Among a number of tribes in eastern North America and on the Plains, dogs were sacrificed and eaten amid great ceremony to solidify alliances, welcome important visitors, appease angry spirits, cure the sick, and prepare for the hunt or war. The Sioux, for example, began eating dog out of respect for the Great Spirit, having promised during a severe famine in the remote past that if it brought them food, they would throw a feast for the dogs. In a peculiarly human transference, because the dogs ate human food and embodied great spiritual power, according to anthropologists William K. Powers and Marla N. Powers, they became food for humans—on special occasions. The Sioux always prepared dog for honored guests, as many Anglo-American travelers discovered, some to their disgust, others to their unexpected delight at the taste. The Powerses report that dogs were also sacrificed and eaten to cure illnesses and on feast days for the society of clowns, a group of men who, having dreamed of thunder and lightning, were required to walk and talk backward and act the opposite of what was considered natural—call it ritualized idiosyncrasy. It is difficult to determine how much mythification and ritual are covers for necessity,

but from a practical standpoint, dogs represented fresh meat in the
lean times of winter, when the people were running low on dried
meat and roots—or starving. Rituals surrounding the practice probably served to limit consumption and guarantee the survival of dogs
in the camp.[10]

Many thousands of years after the arrival in the Americas of their
forebears, the Olmecs and Aztecs of Mexico and Central America
raised dogs for market and regularly ate them as a source of animal
protein. The Maya appear to have consumed them on ceremonial
occasions alone. The Taino of the Caribbean Islands hunted hutia, a
large rodent, with their small, generally spoiled dogs, which they
also ate on ceremonial occasions. Other dogs were killed to accompany their dead humans to the spirit world.[11]

There were also tribes that found dog eating abhorrent, no matter how hard-pressed they were. The Nez Percé, for example, traded
dogs to the Corps of Discovery of Lewis and Clark while looking
upon the white men as debased for eating them. In North America,
as a rule, Athabascan-speaking Indians of inland Alaska and western Canada, but also including the Apache and Navajo, did not eat
dog, says Marion Schwartz in her book *A History of Dogs in the
Early Americas*. Similarly, the Inca of Peru maintained strict taboos
against eating dog, although indigenous people along the coast
indulged. It is a subject that takes on more significance with the
arrival of Europeans, who culturally condemned the practice but
in many cases became prodigious consumers of Native American
dogs.[12]

Even if not eaten, dogs were often sacrificed to ward off illness
or evil spirits and to accompany, if not lead, their dead humans into
the afterlife. Walking along the Missouri on April 20, 1805, Meriwether Lewis came upon the corpse of a woman laid out on a scaffold with two dead harnessed dogs. At the foot of the scaffold lay
the body of a large dog, apparently killed when the body was laid to
rest. Lewis thought that "this was no doubt the reward, which the
poor dog had met with for performing the friendly office to his
mistress of transporting her corps to the place of deposit." The
Assiniboins, Mandans, and Hidatsa sacrificed dogs and horses be-

longing to the deceased, as did other tribes, believing a person should not undertake the journey into the next reality alone.[13]

VIRTUALLY ALL early European observers of North American Indians' dogs comment on their wolfish appearance, although the dogs were sometimes smaller than the local wolves and had tails that tended to curve over the back, while those of wolves tended to hang straight. Differences between types of dogs were largely in size, coloration, coat, and muzzle shape. They generally had prick ears, thick, double, multicolored coats, and a lupine demeanor. It is generally assumed that, with few exceptions, tribal groups did not consciously breed dogs to achieve certain characteristics, but at least some did cull unwanted females and castrate selected male puppies. Those acts limited the gene pool and helped preserve a general look, but the remaining intact dogs were allowed to breed according to their own rules. Variations also reflected the different waves of human migration to the Americas, and the relative isolation of groups of people and dogs. The hairless dogs found in Mexico and coastal Peru were among a small number of exceptions, but they were products of both a particular genetic mutation and human efforts.

Exploring the upper Missouri in the 1830s, Maximilian, Prince of Wied, regularly commented on the dogs he encountered, including those of the Sioux, the largest and most powerful tribe in the region. "In shape they differ very little from the wolf," he said of the Sioux dogs, "and are equally large and strong. Some are of the real wolf colour; others black, white, or spotted with black and white, and differing only in the tail being rather more turned up. Their voice is not a proper barking, but a howl, like that of the wolf, and they partly descend from wolves, which approach the Indian huts, even in the day time, and mix with the dogs."[14]

By the time Maximilian visited the Sioux, the Plains Indians had possessed horses for less than a century; indeed, because most of them lacked a word for *horse* in their language, they referred to it as a big, magical dog. European dogs were already crossbreeding along the upper Missouri with those of the Mandan and Hidatsa, just as they did with Indian dogs in the rest of what is now the United States mainland. Before then, dogs were the only domesticated animal for Plains Indians, as they were for tribes throughout the Americas, with the exception of the Central American Indians, who had turkeys and guinea pigs, and the Andean Indians, who had llamas and alpacas.

Native American Dog "Breeds"

Summarizing available written and fossil records in 1920, Harvard University zoologist Glover M. Allen identified three major types of Native American dog—the wolflike Eskimo dog, smaller wolflike dogs, and much smaller dogs found in the Southwest, southern Mexico, South America, and the Caribbean. He subdivided those into seventeen distinctive types, cautioning that at the time of his writing it was "too late to find purebred American Aboriginal dogs" because of extensive mixing over several centuries with European dogs.[15]

Working at a time of great interest in establishing different breeds of dog, Allen tended to subdivide his major groups too finely and overlook the fact that among nomadic tribes particularly, dogs were interbreeding within and between tribes, with the result that the dogs came in a wider variety of coat colors and sizes than most twentieth-century breeds. It is possible that the Sioux dog, a large wolflike animal; the Plains Indian dog, a medium-sized animal with "ocherous tawny," "whitish tawny," or a black-and-gray coat; and the common Indian dog, a larger black or black-and-white animal, were basically the same. Core populations of these dogs might have existed, but outside those isolated areas they must have mixed, because they had overlapping ranges, extending from Alaska through Canada and the Great Plains to Florida, and down the West Coast into Mexico.

In *Sea of Slaughter*, his account of the exploitation of fish, birds, and marine mammals in eastern Canada beginning in the fifteenth century, when Basques and other Europeans first started heavily fishing those waters, Farley Mowat argues that the Beothuk Indians of Newfoundland had a large "black water dog" that followed them around and helped with their fishing and hunting. The common view among archaeologists is that the Beothuk did not have dogs, but Mowat has found written accounts to the contrary from early European visitors and suggests that this dog is the primary precursor of the Newfoundland and Labrador retrievers. The Beothuk were Algonquian speakers who apparently migrated to Newfoundland around 50 B.C., and it is likely they possessed the black common Indian dog. Certainly that dog figured in the creation of the Newfoundland, who became renowned in the late eighteenth and nineteenth centuries for its sagacity, tenacity in the water, courage, and devotion. But it was a markedly different animal—smaller, more robust and active—from today's Newfoundlands.[16]

Glover Allen's other types of Native American dogs are more clearly defined. He called the wolflike Eskimo dog "transarctic" and observed that everywhere it was found—from Siberia to Greenland—it was essential to the survival of its people. "It should be kept in mind," Allen said, "that since the advent of Europeans much attention has been given to increasing the size and strength of these northern dogs for draught purposes. It is likely that the larger wolf-like Eskimo dogs now common in the North, are considerably different from the original stock found by the early Arctic explorers." They are even more different today.[17]

The Klamath dog, named for the Indians occupying the Klamath River valley of northern California and southern Oregon, was a medium-sized brindled animal that served as companion, guard, and perhaps beast of burden.[18]

A short-legged Indian dog that had straight, not bowed, legs was found from the Columbia River across Canada to New England. With his idiosyncratic grammar and spelling, Meriwether Lewis described this dog in his entry from Fort Clotsop on Sunday, February 16, 1806: "The Indian dog is usually small or much more so than the common cur. they are partly coloured; black white brown and brindle are the usual colours. the head is long and nose pointed eyes small ears erect and pointed like those of the wolf, hair short and smooth except on the tail where it is as long as that on the cur-dog and straight. the natives do not eat them nor appear to make any other use of them but in hunting the Elk as has been before observed."[19]

The Clallam dog was bred and maintained on islands in the Puget Sound and near Vancouver Island that were kept free of all other dogs to prevent interbreeding. Clallam women carefully main-tained these dogs for their thick, woolly black-and-white hair, which they wove into clothing and blankets until the arrival of the Hud-son's Bay blanket in the nineteenth century brought the demise of that craft. The Clallam dog vanished.[20]

Allen also identified a small Indian dog that was either black, black and white, brownish, or yellowish and about the size of a fox. This all-purpose dog ranged from central and southwestern North America into northwestern South America. A small, short-nosed black-and-white Indian dog appeared from Virginia to Southern California. These two animals may well have been variations on the short-legged Indian dog.[21]

Around Canada's Great Bear Lake and along the nearby banks of the Mackenzie River, Hare Indians raised a "small, slender dog" that was "white with dark patches" and had broad webbed feet that helped it cross snow, to bay up moose and other large game for hunters. The dogs, as Alexander Mackenzie discovered on his transcontinental journey, were more highly valued in some ways than children, proba-bly because a good dog meant the difference between eating and starv-ing and was not easily replaced. Other Mackenzie River Athabascans, like the Slavey, Beaver, and Dogrib, had similar dogs. John Wood-house Audubon painted the Hare dog for *Quadrupeds of North America*, by his father, John James Audubon, and James Bachman, but for all its worth, the dog did not survive the onset of modernity, and it, too, disappeared from history.[22]

The Tlingit, Tahltans, and other Pacific Northwest tribes also employed a small hunting dog, this one black and white, that the hunters carried with them in baskets until their large dogs bayed a bear. Then the hunters would release the agile dogs to harass and dis-tract the bear while they moved in for the kill with their spears.

Glover Allen missed the Tahltan bear dog, perhaps because it was not substantially different from the small Indian dog or the Hare dog; such are the difficulties involved in trying to sort these animals.

Another terrier-sized hunting dog, with a grayish coat and "webbed" feet, hunted otters with the Yahgan of Tierra del Fuego, the tip of South America. Hunters carried them from island to island in their canoes and unloosed them to pursue wounded otters. The coastal Chono people in Patagonia trained their dogs, probably the same type, to drive fish into nets. They also spun the dogs' hair to make clothes, like the Clallam thousands of miles to the north. The dogs ate mussels, cracking the shells with their teeth.[23]

In mountainous inland Patagonia, a wolflike, foxhound-sized, wiry-haired dog hunted guanacos, a kind of wild camel, and the flightless rhea with its people. The rhea are gone, and the guanacos are now imperiled. The dogs long ago hybridized with European breeds. Curiously, some of the evidence for the entry of people into the Americas 30,000 to 40,000 years ago comes from Patagonia.[24]

On the high plateaus of the south-central Andes, Paleo-Indians hunted alpaca and llamas, probably with dogs. For reasons that might relate to the cultivation of plants, as well as other cultural changes, hunting turned into herding of both animals around 6,000 years ago. It is fair to imagine that the dog was party to the transformation. Thousands of years later, when Spanish conquistadors under Francisco Pizarro were raping and pillaging the Inca Empire, men were hunting with an animal that resembled a small collie. Its taller, long-haired cousin guarded the children, herds, and village. Glover Allen also identified a Peruvian pug-nosed dog from the Andean highlands, making that rugged region south to Tierra del Fuego something of a hotbed of ancient dog diversity.[25]

The most unusual dog in the Americas was doubtless the slate or reddish gray hairless animal the Colima appear to have isolated in what is now western Mexico around 250 B.C. The peyote-eating Colima, who flourished for some 700 years, immortalized their wrinkled, sometimes mottled animals in elaborate ceramics, and their successors kept them alive. At the time of European contact, the dogs were found among the Aztec and the people of coastal

Peru, having arrived by sea about 1,250 years ago, according to anthropologist Alana Cordy-Collins. The dogs also seem to have been traded in parts of the Caribbean and elsewhere in South America. Called *xoloitzcuintli* in Mexico, the hairless dog appears in miniature, small, and medium sizes and apparently was used as a natural treatment for a variety of ailments—it would sleep on humans' arthritic joints—and as a sacrifice to break droughts.[26]

Mystery surrounds these animals. The dominant genetic mutation for hairlessness also causes dogs to have an incomplete set of teeth—sometimes nearly no teeth—and is lethal. Embryos abort if they inherit two copies of the gene—one each from the mother and father. For these reasons, the nude dogs, found in Asia and Africa as well as the Americas, are always rare and their breeding is uncertain. Enamored of them, the people of Central and South America appear to have helped nature along, as indicated by the presence of the fossil record of hairless dogs with complete dentition, and at least one report from an early Spanish conquistador. Glover Allen says that some of the dogs "were rubbed with turpentine from early youth, causing the hair to fall out." The artificially created hairless dog might not have even been related to those with the genetic mutation.[27]

When the cultures of Europe collided with those of the Indians, the dogs of the Americas fared no better than their human companions. The crossbreeding with European dogs and the actual destruction of native dogs that began with Columbus had run their course, except perhaps for a few isolated areas, by the time Allen compiled his catalog in 1920. There were no longer any full-blooded Native American dogs. Recent genetic analyses of ancient New World dogs supports Allen's assessment; the lineages are lost. Sadly, despite the wishful thinking and hard work of many breeders, they cannot be "reconstructed" or "re-created" in any but an imaginary sense—we know too little about them, their behavior, and their cultures.[28]

2

Deadly Encounters: Dogs of Mayhem and Slaughter
Take the New World for Spain

❧

CHRISTOPHER COLUMBUS and his crews on their first voyage may have been the only people to visit the Americas without at least one dog in tow. At the least, dogs were amusing company on what could be a long, tedious voyage, and if they were large enough, they guarded the ship while at anchor. In addition, they intimidated natives ashore and tasted food at the local banquet. Columbus and his men doubtless encountered the spoiled small dog, or *aon,* of the Taino people on Cuba and Hispaniola, who howled, chortled, and whistled but did not bark. They may even have observed that some of the dogs were castrated and fattened for the pot, while others were employed in the hunt for hutias and iguanas. But the *aon* clearly failed to make Columbus think "dog," the way the natives failed to impress him other than as prospective slaves. In fact, Columbus would have neglected to carry dogs on his second voyage, in 1493, had not the bishop of Burgos and patriarch of the Indies, Juan Rodríguez de Fonseca, who outfitted the fleet, added twenty greyhounds and mastiffs as weapons of war.

Spain at the time was fixated on the concept of blood purity, *limpieza de sangre*, which its soldiers and priests applied to humans as well as animals. In the decades just before Columbus's first voyage, inquistors sought to root out the impure of spirit and blood, investigating and condemning Jews and Moors who had converted to Catholicism to escape expropriation, expulsion, or death. Having cast them out, the inquistors then turned on those who remained true to the faith of their fathers and mothers. The same concept was applied to breeding livestock, horses, and dogs—*lebrel*, a fast chase dog sometimes associated with a greyhound; *mastin*, or mastiff; *sabueso*, a bloodhound; and *alano*, or wolfhound, a rough combination of the two types—with different monasteries or nobles maintaining their own lines. These divisions were based on size, coat coloration, and use: by tradition, light-colored mastiffs were used to guard flocks, in the belief that they would not scare the sheep, and dark-colored ones to guard homes and to fight, because they terrorized people. They were not "breeds," as they are known today, divided by registries and close adherence to standards. Eventually all of these dogs, as well as spaniels and settlers, made it to America, along with the concept of blood purity, but the most significant were the *lebrel*, *mastin*, *alano*, and *sabueso* and crosses involving them that ultimately became known as the Cuban bloodhound, a fearsome, long-legged dog with size, endurance, strength, and a mastiff's crushing jaws, used to track down and kill slaves.[1]

The forebears of these dogs, and their handlers, had learned the art of *la monteria infernal*, the infernal chase, in the Canary Islands in 1480, when they literally ran to ground, maimed, killed, and devoured the natives. But the fell beasts were even better known for feasting on children abandoned at the doors of churches and mosques by their desperate parents during Ferdinand and Isabella's successful campaign to seize Granada from the Moors. That victory came just months before Columbus's first voyage; a few of these dogs or their offspring were doubtless on his second trip.

Running Amok in the Indies

Unlike his first, small exploration with the *Niña*, *Pinta*, and *Santa Maria*, Columbus's second voyage entailed a fleet befitting the Admiral of the Ocean Sea—17 ships, 1,500 sailors and colonists, seeds, wine, horses, mules, sheep, pigs, and those twenty dogs. Financed by the crown with wealth stolen largely from expelled Jews and Moors, the expedition was charged with bringing back even greater riches from the inhabitants of the new lands. Columbus wanted as quickly as possible to relieve the garrison he had left at La Navidad—his first settlement at Cape Haitian, Hispaniola (then Espanola)—and start the process of extracting gold from the newly found lands. It mattered to him not at all that the virtually naked (the women sometimes wore short grass skirts), relatively peaceful Taino had not a clue about the yellow metal that drove the white men wild.

Before the arrival of the Spaniards, the people of the Caribbean appear to have lived largely in village groups under an elder—a cacique, the Spanish called him—fishing, collecting sea turtles and their eggs, and hunting. They grew squash, maize, bananas, and manioc, or cassava, which they made into bread. While not unknown, war was uncommon. The islands were not paradise, to be sure, but they provided what the people needed for a relatively healthy existence, especially when compared with the plight of people in other parts of the world, including Europe, where starvation and pestilence were the rule among the urban poor. The Taino, in short, were unprepared for the single-minded, brutal, licentious, greedy Spaniards.

At the end of 1493, Columbus found La Navidad ruined, its garrison slaughtered after making sex slaves of the locals' wives and daughters. Sharing wives with visitors was a common practice among some Native Americans, but there is no clear evidence that the Taino did, although their attitudes toward sex and nudity were alien to the Spaniards. Believing the Taino existed to serve them in all respects, the Spaniards misread every cultural cue and sought only to fulfill their own sexual pleasure, by rape and enslavement if necessary. They also demanded ever larger quantities of food, being too lazy to fish, hunt, or even farm on their own—not that their seeds would grow. The local Taino soon rose in disgust and anger and attacked the Spaniards, destroying their fort and leaving their bodies to rot under the sultry Caribbean sun.

Columbus laid out another settlement on Hispaniola, naming this one La Isabela, for his queen, and soon thereafter went exploring to Cuba and Jamaica. In their comprehensive *Dogs of the Conquest*, the historians John Grier Varner and Jeannette Johnson Varner argue that the first confrontation between Columbus's dogs and Native Americans took place at Puerto Bueno, Jamaica, in 1494. Judging the local Taino hostile when he went ashore, because they did not fall on their faces before him, Columbus attacked with crossbowmen, swordsmen, and a dog that did more than the soldiers to rout the natives.[2]

Columbus pressed on in search of something more substantial than an island and ended up in Cuba, where, sick and hungry, he and his men ate iguana and dog. They quickly came to prefer the tender, sweet meat of the dog and soon were eating all the *aon* they could barter or steal from the local people on whatever island they occupied. On Hispaniola, the Spaniards who arrived on Columbus's second voyage ate virtually all the native dogs within a few years, and subsequent waves of Spaniards continued the practice wherever they went. Markets in Central America became stocked with hundreds of dogs, large and small, sold and butchered for immediate consumption along with and often preferred to turkeys, pigs, and other livestock. Some markets also sold butchered Indians as dog food. In fact, there is a stronger case to be made for the Spaniards eating the native dogs into extinction than for the Paleo-Indians hunting large mammals into oblivion at the end of the Pleistocene. When the Spaniards ran out of native dogs and still faced starvation, they ate their own dogs in a peculiar form of cannibalism, since those animals had fed on the flesh of native people and were treated better than most Spanish soldiers, not to mention Indians.

That is not saying a lot, since brutality toward other living things was the rule rather than the exception in Europe at the time, with most peasants and urban poor living in squalor and misery. Indeed, the New World attracted the poor as soldiers and sailors precisely because it represented an opportunity, at least in their imagination, to attain untold riches and freedom from social constraints. For the same reason, it drew the second, third, and fourth sons of aristocrats and merchants, who were prevented by the rules of primogeniture from inheriting the estates and businesses of their fathers. In the New World, they could establish their own estates, over which they would have total control, and not have to lift a hand for their own upkeep—as long as they enslaved the local infidels.

A year after his Jamaica attack, Columbus revealed the full might and fury of his dogs on Hispaniola, on the Vega Real, a broad plain. He and his colonists had continued to alienate the local people with their incessant demand for maize, and the Taino had responded by refusing to plant more, choosing to limit themselves to the bread they made from pounding manioc, a bitter root with toxic juice, rather than feed the invaders. In turn, the colonists captured a local cacique, or chief, Guatiguaná, and a number of his people and prepared to ship them back to Spain for sale in the Seville slave markets, which at the time also featured Africans, Turks, and eastern Europeans. Guatiguaná escaped and rallied his people to drive the invaders into the sea.

Columbus marched to war, meeting Guatiguaná on the plain on March 27, 1495. There, he commanded Alonso de Ojeda, a veteran of the Granada campaign, to unloose the dogs of war, according to Bartolomé de Las Casas, who chronicled the annihilation of the Indians of the Caribbean and Central and South America in excruciating detail in his classic *Brevísima relación de la destrucción de las Indias* (A Brief Account of the Destruction of the Indians) and the more comprehensive *Historia de las Indias*. Las Casas said that men, women, and children were cleaved by swords, skewered on pikes, and run down, disemboweled, torn to pieces, and consumed by dogs. In all, he reported that Columbus's 20 dogs killed 100 Taino in an hour—sometimes the passage is interpreted as saying that each dog slaughtered 100 men in an hour, an improbable number. Not long thereafter, because the Indians would occasionally manage to kill one of their tormentors, the rule of Spanish vengeance became 100 dead Taino for every dead Spaniard.[3]

After their first victories, Columbus and his subalterns and successors regularly deployed dogs. Dogs were loosed on caciques or children by "accident" or in sport, and the deaths that followed inevitably led to greater conflict. The Taino struggled against their enslavement and the constant demands for more food, more women, more gold. They fled to the mountains and were hunted down with dogs. Once found, they were hanged or slowly roasted to death in the name of "our redeemer and his apostles," and fetuses were ripped from their mothers' wombs, Las Casas said. Enslaved, lashed, dogged, the Taino were called dogs so frequently that the word became a foul insult, banned by the Law of Burgos of 1512, which was promulgated by Ferdinand to regulate relations between Spaniards and Indians. But insults were the least of the problem, and the law was toothless.[4]

By then, dogs were being specifically bred and trained to hunt down and disembowel Indians, as the conquistadors pursued their quest for gold and other riches. Conditions in the gold mines of Hispaniola were so depraved early in the sixteenth century that slaves joined with dogs in scavenging bones under their masters' tables. In despair, people committed suicide, often by drinking the toxic juice of manioc. Malnourished nursing mothers stopped producing milk, and their babies perished. In 1516, 14 Dominican priests on Hispaniola, including Las Casas, complained to the Spanish imperial court about the abuses. Spaniards—Christians, as they were then called—had ripped a nursing child from his mother's teat and, laughing, thrown him to their dog for food. Christians regularly made enslaved Taino carry them and their dogs in hammocks—the Taino's distinctive furniture—for vast distances. If the slaves tried to escape, the dogs killed them. Nothing was done until the adoption of the New Laws of 1542, which outlawed Indian slavery and restored some rights to the indigenous people. The laws, largely the result of the agitation of Las Casas and other priests, doubtless saved thousands of lives on the mainland, but they came too late for the Taino, who had become virtually extinct in the Caribbean. The dogs continued to terrorize the growing number of African slaves, brought in to replace the vanishing Indians and to work the sugar plantations that ultimately produced more riches on Caribbean islands than all the gold ever found on them.[5]

In addition to their dogs and horses, the Spaniards brought pigs, sheep, goats, and cattle to the New World, which, along with the sugar monoculture, transformed entire ecosystems. On the Caribbean islands and finally throughout the Spanish colonies, dogs and hogs, especially, were left to forage on their own. In some areas, free-ranging dogs became so numerous that they depleted populations of wild game and livestock and contributed to constant food shortages. Laws were promulgated to handle stray dogs, but, like most such laws, they were enforced only erratically, if at all.

The Spaniards brought with them multiple pathogens, including smallpox in 1518, which historians now think killed more people than did war and enslavement combined. No one knows with certainty how many people died during the Conquest. Las Casas put the number on Hispaniola at around 3 million, with an equal number lost on Puerto Rico, Jamaica, and Cuba. At least 12 million died in all, he said, and maybe as many as 50 million. Historians continue to argue the case heatedly, often basing their choices more on ideology than fact, with those who want to emphasize the extent of the slaughter of innocents on paradisiacal islands choosing the higher numbers. It is sad enough to say that millions of people died in what can only be called genocide, and that dogs had a hand in it.[6]

China, Mongolia, India, Japan, the Middle East, North Africa, and Europe—all had long traditions of using dogs in war to great effect, in large measure because to a dog a human is just another form of prey and because large fierce dogs could sow panic among all but the most disciplined troops. The Egyptians used dogs resembling mastiffs some 5,000 years ago, according to hieroglyphics. The ancient Greeks tied pots of burning oil on the heads of some of their assault dogs so they could terrorize and burn the bellies of opposing horses. The Greeks, Romans, and Celts used spiked collars on their dogs, and the Celts were said to have large beasts similar to wolfhounds that could catch and hold a horse by its nose or pull its rider to the ground. Roman legionnaires feared the wolf dogs of the Germanic tribes, and many people found the Roman molossus, perhaps the forebear of the European mountain dog, or mastiff, a frightening sight. Tens of thousands of dogs have regularly been deployed in battle in Europe, up to our own time, but never with the systematic intent to terrorize, maim, and kill applied by the Spanish in the New World.

LAS CASAS AND A FEW OTHER PRIESTS—though many priests actively participated in the genocide—became indefatigable defenders of Indians, and although he did not save them from extinction, he bore witness, and his books were translated throughout Europe in the sixteenth century, exposing Spanish atrocities, Spain's Black Legacy, and giving England, France, and Holland ample excuse for breaking Spanish hegemony in the New World. Although the date of his birth is in question, Bartolomé de Las Casas was the son of a merchant from Seville who sailed on Columbus's second voyage and was wealthy enough to educate his son in law and theology at the University of Salamanca. Las Casas arrived in Hispaniola in 1502 with the fleet of Gonzalo Fernandez de Oviedo and so was witness to many of the events he recorded. The chronology is confused, but he appears to have become a priest in 1510—the first ordained in the New World, according to legend—and to have been with Diego de Velázquez in his conquest of Cuba a year later.

Hatuey, a Taino cacique, had fled to Cuba from another island and led an uprising there against Velázquez, Cuba's new governor, a butcher fond of feeding captives to his dogs, often while they were alive. Velázquez quickly suppressed the rebellion, captured

Hatuey, and ordered him roasted alive. Just before the fire was lit, Las Casas reported, a priest asked Hatuey if he would accept the Lord, so he could die in a state of grace and go to Heaven. Hatuey asked whether Spaniards went to this Heaven and, when told they did, he replied that he would rather go to Hell and refused conversion. He was tortured while he roasted. By some accounts, Las Casas himself was the priest, but in any case, for his efforts he was awarded an *encomiendo* in Cuba—a land grant complete with all the Indians living thereon. His disgust at the abuse of the natives eventually overwhelmed him, however, and he returned the Indians, if not the land.[7]

Las Casas then became a campaigner against the brutality, and in 1516, after pleading the Indians' case in Spain, he was named priest-procurator of the Indies by Cardinal Francisco Jíminéz y Cisnerós. In 1520 he founded a community devoted to Christian ideals in Venezuela that ultimately failed because of attacks from his fellow Spaniards, unwilling to give up their iron grip on the native people. Yet in one of those contradictions that often mark the lives of even the most moral people, Las Casas supported the importation of "Christianized" African slaves, believing them better suited to heavy labor than the Indians, until the atrocities against African slaves became too great to ignore and he turned against that, too. He was the conscience of the Spanish Conquest, recording atrocities one by one, and although he has occasionally been accused of exaggeration, it appears that the charge springs more from a desire to obscure than to reveal the truth.

Becerrillo and Leoncico Rise Above the Pack

As the conquistadors wore out Hispaniola, they moved on to Jamaica and Puerto Rico, then called San Juan Bautista, or, by the English, St. John, in 1509, where, Las Casas said, they used tactics perfected on Hispaniola. The conqueror of Puerto Rico was the intrepid Juan Ponce de León, who had explored the island in 1508, discovered gold, and hustled back to Hispaniola. He had Diego Columbus, Christopher's son and the island's governor, declare him governor of Puerto Rico, and set out with men and dogs to become rich. The leader of Ponce de León's pack was a powerful, somewhat stocky, reddish brown chase dog with a reputation for ferocity and sagacity, named Becerrillo.

It is significant that chroniclers named and described Becerrillo and his son, Leoncico, who helped Balboa cut a trail of blood through the rain forests of the Isthmus of Panama, because nearly all other dogs of the time remained anonymous. If the accounts are true, they were long-lived superdogs, active and vital, courageous and terrifying when they were eight or more years old—ancient for war dogs, especially in a tropical climate that fostered parasites and infection. Most likely they were largely legendary animals, their stories embellished, however unconsciously, to counter charges of unbridled atrocities and to personalize the fell beasts, to create dog heroes and thereby prove the worth of all dogs in Spain's Conquest. To a degree it worked, for they are the representative dogs of the Conquest in many popular histories.

Becerrillo's origins are obscure, but it seems almost certain that he was born in the New World, perhaps in the kennels of Ponce de León, a veteran of the campaign against the Moors, who, like Las Casas, probably arrived on Hispaniola in 1502. Becerrillo in turn sired Leoncico, who as a puppy fell into the hands of Vasco Núñez de Balboa, then an indebted swordsman looking for a chance to make his fortune. These dogs were said to embody the concept of *limpieza de sangre*, and the belief in their purity and nobility shines through in accounts of their endeavors. When it came time at the end of a campaign to divide the spoils, Becerrillo was awarded half again the share of a crossbowman, while Leoncico earned double the average share of the spoils in gold, silver, slaves, and other booty—high for war dogs but not for horses. Of course, the spoils went directly to their owners.

At various times, Diego de Salazar and Sancho de Arango, two of Ponce de León's most trusted and brutal captains, handled

Becerrillo, and the dog repeatedly showed himself the greater noble than both. Fresh from a victory over rebellious Indians, Salazar ordered Becerrillo to kill an old Indian woman captive he had just sent off with a "message" for Ponce de León, then on his way to the battlefield. The woman fell on her knees and begged the dog to let her go and deliver her message to the "Christians." Becerrillo aborted his attack, sniffed at her, and then urinated on her prostrate body, convincing the men that God was at work and leading Ponce de León to order the woman spared because, great though the dog was, by definition he could not be more noble and true than a Christian.[8]

If a slave fled, Becerrillo reportedly would track him to his village and find him amid all his people—a feat that no dog has been shown to perform with any reliability. If the runaway did not resist, Becerrillo would take him back to camp, the Varners said in *Dogs of the Conquest*, but if he fought back, Becerrillo would kill him instantly. He could, they said, "distinguish between friend and foe, fierce Carib and docile Arawak [Taino]." The Spanish guard dogs were known to walk straying sheep gently back to the fold, but they were protecting animals they viewed as their own kin. It is difficult to imagine that a dog trained to maim and kill Indians would be able to exercise such judgment.[9]

After Diego Columbus decided that Puerto Rico offered far more riches than played-out Hispaniola, he persuaded the king to name him governor and officially usurped Ponce de León. The deposed warrior then secured his own grant, to find and conquer a reportedly rich island named Bimini, said also to have a fountain with the power to reverse aging. He set sail in 1512, leaving Becerrillo in Puerto Rico, under the care of Arango. On Easter Sunday, April 3, 1513, Ponce de León "discovered" la Florida, only to be greeted with a shower of arrows that drove him off. Shortly thereafter he arrived in Bimini, but neither peninsula nor island held gold, silver, or a fountain of youth. He landed in what is now Tabasco, Mexico, site of the defunct Olmec empire, three years later, and then, with dogs, suppressed Indian slave rebellions on Guadeloupe and Dominica before returning to the southwest coast of Florida in 1521. There Calusa Indians, enraged at incursions of Spanish slavers, managed to drive an arrow through Ponce de León's armor, and his men carried the old warrior to Cuba, where he died. His fate paralleled that of the dog he never saw again after leaving Puerto Rico.

During an attack on Puerto Rico one morning in 1514, Caribs from the nearby island of Vieques wounded and seized Arango, apparently intent on carrying him off as a hostage or sacrifice. Becerrillo led the counterattack and forced his handler's release. Then he pursued the attackers attempting to flee in their dugout canoes—made from a single tree, the largest of these craft could hold twenty or more men. Alone in the water, Becerrillo became an easy target, and the Caribs shot him full of arrows, according to Gonzalo Fernández de Oviedo y Valdés in his 1535 *Historia general y natural de las Indias, islas y Tierra Firme del Mar Océano*. The Varners said that a Carib shot him with a "poisoned arrow" and that Becerrillo killed his assailant before swimming to shore, where he showed Arango and his men the wound. Becerrillo always wore a padded vest, an *escaupil*, in battle, the Varners reported, but whether he was protected on that fatal night is unclear. The men cauterized the wound to no avail, and the dog was given a secret burial. Regardless of whether his death was this dramatic, Fernández de Oviedo makes clear that the Spaniards mourned the dog more than their fallen comrades.[10]

By force of will, cunning, and courage, Balboa became governor of Antigua, in what is now Panama, in 1511, and there his legend grew along with that of Leoncico, reddish brown, like his sire, Becerrillo. Also like his sire, Leoncico reportedly could distinguish between "good" and "bad" Indians, showing charity toward the former and unrelenting ferocity toward the latter. Leoncico achieved enduring fame when, on the way across the isthmus, he reportedly tore off the head of the cacique Torecha, who dared to stand with his people in Balboa's way. Many of the estimated 600 victims of the massacre that followed were thrown to the dogs. Not long after, Balboa sacked the village of Torecha's brother and fifty other men because they were "sodomites"—apparently transvestites living in

peace. Balboa committed other atrocities with his dogs, while earning the reputation, at least among Spanish chroniclers, of someone
who treated the Indians fairly, becoming violent only when they offended the laws of nature, God, or Spain.

According to the Varners, Leoncico was a great protector of
Balboa's favorite concubine, Caretita, the daughter of a compliant
cacique. In 1516 the dog helped her fight off an attempted rape by
Garabito, another Spaniard and "friend" of Balboa. Outraged and,
doubtless, humiliated to have been bested by a dog and an Indian
woman, Garabito poisoned Leoncico and then helped Balboa's
father-in-law, Pedro Arias de Avila, better known as Pedrarias
Davila, prosecute Balboa for insubordination and ultimately be-
head him in 1519—not that Pedrarias needed much excuse to dis-
pose of a rival. Free of his rival, Pedrarias began holding gladiatorial
games between his dogs and Indians, earning for such deeds the
nickname El Furor Domini, the Wrath of God.[11]

Hitting North America

Las Casas observed that the atrocities of the Spanish conquerors
grew in magnitude as they moved first to Cuba and then to the
mainland, foremost among them the practice of bringing along on
any campaign chained Indian slaves as food for the dogs. When
feeding time came, handlers would butcher one or more Indians and
trade or sell body parts among themselves to conserve their supply.
Diego Columbus used his dogs to hunt down Indians as if they were
prey when he was governor of Hispaniola in the second and third
decades of the sixteenth century, and other Spaniards in other
colonies did the same. Other conquerors and governors, like Pedrarias Davila, sponsored contests between dogs or, more to their
liking, between dogs and Indians and rebellious African salves. On
the few occasions when the Indians struck back and killed dogs, the
Spaniards exacted vengeance with more brutal killing. The dogs
went everywhere, sweeping with their masters through Mexico and
into what is now the southwestern United States; running amok

through the mountains, valleys, and jungles of South America, even into the Amazon, where tribes that may never have known dogs eagerly adopted them as hunters and companions; and probing through Florida and up the Mississippi River. As they had on the islands, the conquistadors obliterated cultures, people, and animals; they changed forever the way survivors lived and altered entire ecosystems by introducing horses, cattle, sheep, goats, pigs, and dogs and by extracting mineral wealth and timber. Although the role of the war dogs nearly vanished from memory until the Varners resurrected their sordid history in 1983, their legacy was strongly felt well into the nineteenth century, through their notorious descendants, especially Cuban bloodhounds. Probably crosses between mastiffs and greyhounds, the bloodhounds first earned their reputation for ferocity for their role in suppressing in one year Jamaica's long-running Maroon Rebellion of 1655–1739. They were equally renowned as trackers and abusers of runaway slaves.

The veteran Indian killer and slaver Juan Ponce de León doubtless had dogs on board when he first landed in Florida in 1513 and again in 1521, when he attempted to renew his claim and instead met death. But the lore of terra incognita—to the Spaniards, Florida included virtually all of North America and was nothing but a blank on the map—was too powerful for the ambitious subalterns of the conquerors and governors of Central and South America, out to increase their own power and prestige, to ignore. Some among them were also seeking a Northwest Passage above the Americas. Ponce de León added to the attraction of Florida in another significant way: for his explorations of 1512 and 1513, he had marked the Gulf Stream, thereby helping chart a course for the treasure fleets bound for Spain through the Straits of Florida and the Bahama Channel. The route was fast but deadly because of coral reefs and foul weather, not to mention pirates, so Havana became the most significant port in the Caribbean, home to troops and wreckers looking to protect and salvage ships. Florida stood just ninety miles north.

Pánfilo de Narváez was the first to mount a major expedition into Florida. As lieutenant governor of Cuba under Diego de

Velázquez, Narváez had earned a reputation for brutality surpassed by none. Eager for riches, he had gone to Mexico in 1520 to arrest the rogue Cortés, only to lose an eye, the battle, and, for three years, his freedom. Released, he returned to Spain and persuaded Charles V to award him the patent to conquer Spain's provinces from the Rio Grande to the tip of Florida. He sailed from Spain in June 1527, with the colony's new treasurer, Alvar Núñez Cabeza de Vaca, who chronicled the ill-fated expedition. After a series of misadventures, including the loss of a third of his men to mutiny and drowning and the sinking of a ship in a hurricane near Cuba, Narváez anchored in Tampa Bay in April 1528.

Arrogant and stupid, he ignored the advice of Cabeza de Vaca and decided to take an overland route north in search of the gold of the Apalachee, a tribe centered around Tallahassee. He ordered one ship to return to Havana and the others to trace the Gulf coast and meet him at what is widely assumed to be Pensacola Bay, thereby sending his men and ships, as Cabeza de Vaca warned, from one unknown place to another by an equally unknown route. But Narváez was determined. Ucita (sometimes called Hirrihigua, a confusion of names common among Europeans meeting American Indians for the first time), a Tampa Bay cacique, had directed him to the Apalachee after convincing the fortune hunter that his people had no gold of their own. As thanks, Narváez reportedly cut off Ucita's nose and unloosed his war dogs on the cacique's mother.

As Cabeza de Vaca recounted in his *Relación y comentarios*, first published in 1542 in Zamora, Spain, the natives and the environment, for a change, rejected the invaders—chewed them up and spit them out. On the journey north, Narváez and his 300 men, 40 mounted, managed to incite to battle every group they met because of their brutality and their incessant demands for food, women, and gold. Nearly starved at various points, forced to consume many of their own dogs because they were incapable of hunting, they nonetheless arrived in the panhandle territory of the Apalachee in a famished state, only to find none of the promised gold and silver. Moreover, the Apalachee were big, well-proportioned, and strong, capable with their short bows of driving their red arrows home through Spanish armor.[12]

Narváez made his last advance to the village of the Aute on the headwaters of the St. Marks River, believing that there at last he would find treasure. But forewarned of the hostile intentions of the intruders, the Aute had abandoned and burned their village, leaving only their fields of beans, maize, and pumpkins. Settling in, the Spaniards feasted by day. But the villagers attacked at night and inflicted so much damage that the invaders fled down the St. Marks to Apalachee Bay.

Narváez had lost a third of the 300 men who had set off from Tampa Bay six months earlier, and the survivors were reduced to eating the remaining horses and raiding the Aute for maize while they patched together boats caulked with palmetto and rigged with horsehair ropes and sails made of their own clothes. They shaped uncured horse hides into water bags and, heavily laden, pushed off for the Gulf and the rendezvous with their ships. They floated for thirty days without finding their boats, drawing a little freshwater from the mouth of the Mississippi and subsisting on short rations of maize, before Narváez declared that every one of the five boats was on its own.

Two boats sank not long after, and the remaining three ran aground along the Texas coast. The boat carrying the ruler of Florida washed back into the Gulf before he disembarked and vanished from history. The survivors ate one another until only four were left from the shipwrecks. Each was rescued by a different group of Indians and held for eight years. They eventually found themselves in the same place, and Cabeza de Vaca engineered an escape to Mexico, where Indians were systematically dogged and tortured. It is a curiosity of colonial history that charges of the native people being savage cannibals often came from those adventurers whose savagery and cannibalism, even toward their own people, were unsurpassed; of course, they argued that they were doing it out of dire necessity to survive, while the natives did it habitually for pleasure.

CABEZA DE VACA RETURNED TO SPAIN to apply for his own commission to conquer Florida, but the king settled ultimately on Hernando de Soto, Francisco Pizarro's top captain in the destruction of the Inca. Before joining Pizarro and earning a fortune in plunder, de Soto had become addicted to *la monteria infernal* while serving with Balboa and Pedrarias in Panama and Nicaragua, then part of Castilla del Oro, earning there the nickname Child of the Sun because of his fondness for dawn attacks. As the newly appointed governor of Cuba, he had access to top dogs for his voyage to Florida, where he planned to exercise his title as *adelantado*, or territorial governor and military chief, and find the Northwest Passage.

In May 1539, de Soto left Havana and landed in Tampa Bay with nine ships, 600 men, two women, more than 200 horses, uncounted dogs, long-legged pigs bred specifically for herding, and provisions that proved inadequate for feeding an army on the move. Among the dogs was de Soto's favorite greyhound, Bruto. In addition to greyhounds, there were probably guard dogs and herding dogs, to help with the pigs, and Cuban bloodhounds.

Upon landing, the Spaniards found a deserted village of eight huts, with the cacique's hut at one end and a temple at the other, both built on mounds. They took food and pearls, and soon thereafter an advance party found a sunburned, tattooed man, as naked as the natives, who signaled that he was a Christian. The Knight of Elvas, a Portuguese nobleman who had signed on with de Soto and become one of the chroniclers of the expedition, reported that the man, named Ortiz, had arrived in Tampa Bay in 1528 as part of a search party sent by Narváez's wife to find her lost husband, but he had fallen into an ambush set by the vengeance-seeking Ucita. Ortiz was staked out for roasting over a barbecue pit when Ucita's daughter intervened, arguing that having a Christian in their midst would bring honor to the village. Her love healed his wounds, and, like all captives who were not sacrificed, he became a slave, albeit much better treated than Indian slaves of the Spaniards. Ucita's daughter saved Ortiz again three years later when her father was preparing to sacrifice him after his defeat by a neighboring cacique. Warning Ortiz, she set him on a course for the village of the rival,

Mococo, where he lived until the cacique sent him to de Soto, believing that his return would buy some goodwill. (The story has
clear parallels to Pocahontas's rescue of Captain John Smith from
her father, Powhatan, nearly eighty years later in Virginia, and some
historians have suggested that Smith borrowed liberally from the
account of Ortiz's ordeal.)[13]

Armed with an interpreter, albeit one who had never traveled
more than thirty miles from his village, de Soto set out for a rich
country that Ortiz had heard lay to the north, under the rule of
Paracoxi. Along the way he and his subalterns unloosed their dogs
on various Indian men and women who offended or betrayed them
in some way, with Bruto often leading the charge. He caught and
killed in a slow-flowing Florida river an Indian who had leapt from
the scrub to stab a Spaniard and then tried to swim away. On
another occasion, he tackled four Indians trying to escape from
de Soto's force and kept them pinned to the ground until he was
relieved.

De Soto planned to winter in a village called Acuera, near the
Withlacoochee River, but instead ended up in a neighboring village,
Ocale, sometimes called Cale. Both were associated with the Timucua confederation, a warlike group stretching from the Atlantic
Ocean to the Gulf of Mexico across the northern third of the peninsula, and they consistently fought the invaders. After initially hiding from de Soto, the cacique of Ocale crossed the Withlacoochee
and promised to build a bridge if the Spaniards would leave his village. While scouting a location, he and de Soto came under attack
from villagers hiding across the river, and Bruto, following his
habit, broke loose from his handler to do battle. But once in the
river, he was an inviting target for the Timucua archers, who filled
him with arrows.

The Spaniards had more dogs and continued to loose them on
guides and other Indians as they trudged north through the pine
flatwoods and swamps of the west side of the Florida peninsula,
aiming for Apalachee territory. In most cases they followed existing, well-used Indian trails. The Knight of Elvas said that not far

north of Ocale, at a village named Mala-Paz, de Soto and a detachment from his main force encountered an Indian who presented himself as the cacique and exchanged himself as a hostage for some prisoners. The next morning the cacique attempted to flee into a group of his warriors, but a "bloodhound" who had already bitten him charged through a crowd of Indians and grabbed him at de Soto's command. The Spaniards later learned, or were convinced, that the Indian was not the cacique. Whether he was or not, he ended up dead.

From Mala-Paz, the expeditionary force moved on to the village of Anhaica, near present-day Tallahassee, the heart of Apalachee territory, and occupied it from November 1539 to May 1540, with the Indians ambushing them the entire time. By the time they reached the village, the Spaniards were starving, despite the abundance of the land. The Knight of Elvas observed that the Indians were excellent hunters, always able to bring down deer, turkeys, rabbits, and other game with their bows and arrows, whereas the Spaniards, for all their vaunted dogs and fighting skills, were hapless. They were always on the move, and in any event, they feared that if they left the main force to hunt, the Indians would ambush and kill them. By the time de Soto and his men reached Anhaica, the men were so starved for meat that they promptly slaughtered and ate the twenty to thirty village dogs they discovered.

Finally forced from Anhaica, the Spaniards moved along the Florida panhandle to what is now Alabama. While there, they engaged in a fierce battle at Mauilla, in which some 2,500 Indians were killed, according to the Knight of Elvas, along with about a dozen Spaniards. Worse, to de Soto's mind, all his pearls and other booty were lost. Determined to replace them, he decided to miss the planned rendezvous at the end of 1540, even though his ships were anchored not far away, in Pensacola Bay, and marched his tired and disgruntled men north in search of gold, pillaging fields, enslaving and slaughtering Indians—occasionally in pitched battles—and spreading diseases that wiped out even more, long after the invaders had left. Although their precise path is subject to debate, they traveled at least as far north as Lookout Mountain in Tennessee before turning west and finally crossing the Mississippi River into what is now Arkansas. Approximately half the Spaniards, including Ortiz, died on that long, pointless march. De Soto himself became ill and died in June 1542 near the confluence of the Mississippi and the Red rivers, after signing his command over to Luis Moscoso de Alvarado.

In 1543, Moscoso and 322 members of the expedition, plus 100 Indian slaves and the remaining horses, floated out of the mouth of the Mississippi and sailed along the Texas coast to Mexico, losing ten more of their party along the way. They landed at Auche, now San Augustine, Texas, and were led in circles before Moscoso ordered dogs to kill their treacherous guide. The survivors finally straggled into Mexico. But the Knight of Elvas, who actually made the entire journey, said nothing about dogging a guide, nor does he mention dogs being loaded onto the boats in the Mississippi.

Some of the pigs broke free along the way and flourished, and for years there have been rumors that some of the spotted, blue-eyed greyhound-mastiff mixes did as well. Crossing with Native American dogs, they reportedly became the basis for the leopard cur that, by the nineteenth century, was being used in Florida and around the Gulf coastal plain to roust cattle out of the scrub and swamps. (In 1979, Louisiana named its version of this animal, the Catahoula leopard dog, the state dog and proclaimed itself the place of origin.) The stories sound far-fetched, but no one knows, and the leopard dog certainly dates to colonial times. But the Spanish dogs at its root, like the Spanish tradition of raising herding dogs, more likely dated from the mission period in Florida in the late sixteenth and seventeenth centuries.

Desert Delusions

Spanish dogs, sheep, goats, and, most important, horses took hold in the Southwest and on the Great Plains in the decades following Francisco Vásquez de Coronado's expedition in search of the "seven cities of gold," from 1540 to 1542. As usual, the Indians played a role in the misdirection of the governor from New Galicia in northwest Mexico. But the main culprit was Friar Marcos de Niza, a priest sent north from Mexico to seek gold, following Cabeza de Vaca's return and his report on the Narváez expedition. Friar Marcos took with him two greyhounds and a hyperactive imagination, all three of which received abundant exercise, and he returned with tales of Cibola, the greatest of the seven cities of gold.

With 300 men, upward of 1,000 Indian slaves, dogs, horses, and livestock, Coronado stopped first at Cibola, a Zuni pueblo devoid of gold. Rather than turn around, he sent the lying Friar Marcos back to Mexico in disgrace and pressed onward. His captains "discovered" the Grand Canyon and the petroglyphs of the Acoma in New Mexico, little suspecting that their expedition would be traced in rock as well. As he pushed north and east, Coronado continued to find cities not of gold but of mud, adobe pueblos carved into rock faces or built on mesas, and occupants hostile to his presence. Responding with dogs and brutality, he earned the enmity of all he encountered, from the Rio Grande through Arizona and New Mexico, into the north end of Texas and the heart of Kansas. The constant attacks wore him down, until he returned to Mexico with just 100 men.

But, as in Central and South America and Florida, missionaries eventually followed in the Southwest and in California. They Christianized and enslaved the Indians but also taught them to raise livestock and guard dogs and horses. Taken from their mothers at birth, newborn puppies were weaned on a sheep's teat and raised solely with the flock, virtually independent of human interaction. As a result, they thought of the sheep as their kin and were devoted to their well-being and protection, ferociously defending them against any threat. These big dogs earned a reputation as sheepdogs that reached far into North America well into the nineteenth century, when a number of sheep ranchers argued that they were far superior to any of the English or Scottish herding dogs.

Josiah Gregg, a northeasterner who traveled to the Great Plains in 1831 for his health and became a trader, hauling goods into Santa

Fe and Taos, described the Spanish dogs in his *Commerce of the Prairies*: "The well trained shepherd's dog of this country is indeed a prodigy; two or three of them will follow a flock of sheep for a distance of several miles as orderly as a shepherd, and drive them back to the pen again at night, without any other guidance than their own extraordinary instincts." The dogs were so devoted that when Apaches would rustle a flock and drive them off a ranch—even after they killed the shepherds—the dogs would follow along with their charges, unless they, too, were killed.[14]

Writing in the *American Agriculturist* in 1844, during a period when people in the United States were working to improve their sheep and therefore demanding better protection from predators, J. H. Lyman recommended the Mexican sheepdog as superior to half the humans he knew and far better at guarding and more gentle in handling sheep than any other dog. He recognized them as the mountain mastiff brought from Spain, primarily by the priests, at the time of the Conquest and said they would as easily attack and kill wolves, bears, and marauding dogs—then, as now, the most prolific killers of sheep. If a sheep strayed, the dog would gently take it by the ear and lead it back to the flock.[15]

Used extensively on the missions of the Southwest, these dogs were lost to American history with the defeat of the Navajo and Apache in the late nineteenth century. Although the Navajo continue to use sheepdogs raised in the traditional Spanish way, they are small mutts—just as effective but not as physically imposing. Many Anglo-American ranchers have in the past thirty years employed large European guard dogs, probably all related centuries ago to the Spanish dogs, to protect against coyotes and marauding dogs, more than a century later following the sage advice of Lyman. Dogs or not, there was little environmental benefit to sheep, cattle, and horse ranching in most of the West, but there was considerable financial profit to be gained from the animals, timber, and minerals. The drive to exploit these resources often led in centuries to come to open warfare—between miners and nearly everyone else, for example, or between sheepherders and cattle ranchers. Brutal though those battles were, they did not match the atrocities committed by the conquistadors and the dogs working at their behest. In most of North America, colonization and conquest, though ultimately no less destructive of native cultures and people, did not involve the use of war dogs.

3

The English Take Hold, Spread Out

❧

B Y THE TIME Columbus sailed, the colonization of the
Americas was an event waiting to happen. The Vikings had
planted a colony on Newfoundland under Leif Eriksson
nearly 500 years earlier, and they might have visited periodically in
the years after its failure. In the decades before Columbus reached
the Caribbean, Breton, Basque, and Flemish fishermen and whalers
scooped tons of cod and marine mammals out of North American
waters and seasonally occupied fishing camps from Newfoundland
to Cape Cod. They must have traded, fought, and fornicated with
the natives. Following in Columbus's wake were Portuguese,
French, English, Dutch, Swedish, even Finnish seafarers and fortune hunters. Most, if not all, of the newcomers had dogs, first as
ships' mascots, and then, after the example of Columbus and the
conquistadors, for intimidating the natives and for hunting. The
European dog, like the European people, had come to stay—to replace and in some cases to mingle with the indigenous animals to
create distinctive new types, like the Newfoundland, and perhaps

the spotted leopard dog of the Gulf of Mexico coastal region and the ubiquitous "yellow dog," or cur, of the frontier.

When Sir Walter Raleigh selected his 109 colonists for their trip to Virginia in 1585, he included artisans and craftsmen, hunters, rabbit catchers, masons, and farmers. He chose greyhounds to kill deer, bloodhounds to trail wounded game, and mastiffs to kill wolves, bears, and human predators, if necessary—all at the urging of Richard Hakluyt and his nephew and namesake—although it is unclear how many actually boarded a boat. The Hakluyts were geographers and chroniclers of New World expeditions, as well as promoters of colonization, and they were part of Raleigh's brain trust as he sought to settle Virginia in honor of Elizabeth, the Virgin Queen, his benefactress. Ralph Lane, a veteran warrior known for his fortification of Ireland against an anticipated Spanish attack, was designated to lead the colony to be established on Roanoke Island, off the northern coast of what is now North Carolina. The painter John White and the polymath Thomas Hariot (sometimes spelled Harriot) were aboard to record the settlement's history and catalog the country's "bounty." Hariot was also the only Englishman capable of speaking the local Indian dialect, having learned it from Manteo, an Indian captured the year before by raiders sent out by Raleigh to scout sites for his colony and to bring home a native to learn English.

Hariot reports that too many of the colonists were city dwellers and adventurers incapable of living off the land in England, much less in an unfamiliar country whose people were unknown to them. Their odds for success were further diminished when the ship *Tyger*, carrying the bulk of the seeds and provisions that were to sustain the colonists in their first months, broke apart crossing the sandbar into Pamlico Sound. The ship was salvaged, but nearly all the provisions, including the beer, were ruined. The settlers' prospects spiraled downward from there. Wherever the English went, they spread diseases, killing friend and foe alike, often decimating whole villages. The result, Hariot says in *A Briefe and True Report of the New Found Land of Virginia*, was that the Indians came to view the fatalities as the work of the Christian god operating through the English, and to see the English themselves as demonic creatures existing somewhere between gods and men. The colonists hurt their cause even more with their incessant demands for food and directions to the precious metals they knew existed somewhere.[1]

Lane sent groups exploring soon after the settlement was established and the flotilla, under Sir Richard Grenville, had returned to England for more supplies. Hariot and White went into the southern end of the Chesapeake Bay, where they spent part of a hungry winter before returning in March. Lane himself took forty men, Manteo, horses, and two mastiffs up the Roanoke River in search of Indians who were said to plate their houses with copper. For two days the English adventurers rowed hard against a fast current, seeing fires at night but no natives—certainly not the guide that a local weroance, or chief, Menatonon, had promised to send them. Their meager rations of one and a half pints of corn a day were exhausted, said Lane in his report to Raleigh, when they heard Indians calling from the shore. Manteo said they were Mangoaks planning an attack, so Lane ordered his light horsemen to disembark, but before they could, the Indians showered them with arrows. Although no one was injured, the Englishmen beat a retreat down the river, along the way turning the mastiffs into "Dogges porridge" seasoned with sassafras leaves. Among its other virtues, sassafras was believed to cure syphilis.[2]

Despite the dog porridge, the men were once again famished when they reached the river's mouth, so they stole fish from the Indians' weirs to fuel their return to Roanoke Island. The situation there deteriorated, then seemed to improve, then deteriorated again. At the end of May, Lane learned that Wingina, the weroance of the neighboring Roanoke Indians, who had alternately helped and hindered the settlers, planned to attack. Lane launched a preemptive strike against Wingina's village. The weroance fled into the forest, with two English officers in pursuit. They caught, killed, and beheaded him. Almost simultaneously, the colonists spotted Sir Francis Drake's fleet, fresh from the sacking of St. Augustine, lying off-shore. A hurricane scattered Drake's ships, but they soon regrouped, and the colonists—at war with the local Indians, their supplies exhausted, their hunger a constant ache, their morale shot—decided to head home with the privateer on June 19, 1586, Manteo included.

The only indication of what might have happened to the remainder of the dogs comes from Hariot, who included in his bestiary of Virginia an oblique reference to dog eating: "The inhabitants sometime kill the <u>lyon</u> to eat him: & we sometime as they came into our hands of their *wolves* or *wolvish Dogges*, which I have not set down for good meat, least that some woulde understand my judgement therein to be more simple than needth, although I could alleage the difference in taste of those kindes from ours, which some of our company have become experimented in both." In short, the English dogs were eaten, along with whatever of the Indian dogs could be caught.[3]

Although in their haste to flee, the colonists dumped many of the samples of plants and animals they had collected, along with written records, Hariot kept his notes and some tobacco, known through the Spanish and English privateers but still rare in England. Among its other medicinal virtues—it was said to cure constipation, for example—it was believed to be an antidote to gluttony, then a growing problem among English men and women with enough money to buy food. That habit repeatedly set the English aristocrats who came to North America apart from many of the Indians, who regularly fasted and accepted that the height of the winter would bring lean times. Hariot also correctly foresaw that tobacco could be an important commodity for future colonies.

In 1587, John White led 120 new colonists, including women and children, to Roanoke Island, along with assorted dogs, horses, pigs, sheep, and cattle. Before the year was out, he returned to England for additional supplies but could not then make it back to Virginia for another three years because of war between England and Spain. When White finally returned, the entire settlement, including his granddaughter, Virginia Dare, the first English child born in the New World, had vanished without a trace, leaving an enduring mystery. Giles Milton, in *Big Chief Elizabeth*, argues that a small group of colonists assimilated with the local Indians while a larger contingent made their way into the Chesapeake Bay region where Wahunsonacock, weroance of the Powhatans, obliterated them soon after the arrival of the Jamestown colonists, in 1607. Perhaps that happened, but it is also possible that Indians, fed up with beggary and brutality, attacked the settlement, killing many of the men and enslaving the survivors, especially the women and children. They ultimately would have become assimilated into the tribes, some even marrying and producing offspring, but no one knows for sure.[4]

James Cittie

The English next sent colonists to Virginia in 1607, two years after Spanish priests founded Santa Fe and four years after the death of Elizabeth and the ascension to the throne of James I, who thought Indians verminous and was not too keen on colonies. Apparently having learned little from the failure at Roanoke—Raleigh and his experiences were imprisoned in the Tower of London—the directors of the Virginia Company sent a party of about 104 men to build James Cittie, as it was first known. Approximately half of them were aristocrats out to gain instant wealth without working; the rest were craftsmen or laborers from the cities, not the poachers, fishermen, and farmers needed to gather and produce food in the new land. On the voyage across the Atlantic, internal dissension fractured the group, and at least one of its captains—John Smith—was locked in chains when debate over the direction of the settlement veered dangerously close to combat. Of course, Smith's role as a member of the governing council was unknown until secret orders were unsealed upon the flotilla's arrival; he was then promptly, if grudgingly, unchained.

Despite the best efforts of its feuding gentlemen to wreck it, Jamestown ultimately succeeded, in large measure through destruction of the Indians and heavy exploitation of indentured servants, convict laborers from England, and, after 1619, African slaves. The culture that sprang up in Virginia, Maryland, and other Southern colonies also relied heavily on dogs for hunting, sport, and tracking runaway slaves, and it persisted largely intact for more than three centuries, with vestiges apparent today. Just six years after the founding of Jamestown, Alexander Whitaker, minister to the settlement at Henrico, a plantation seventy miles upriver, complained in a message home: "The Prodigall men of our land make hast to fling away Gods treasures ... spend yearly an hundred pounds, two, three, five hundred and much more about dogs, hawkes and hounds and such sports." They also indulged, he said, in building fancy homes for their "whores," gambling, and drinking, rather than helping the poor or the colony at large. Some of these men had faced starvation and still refused to labor to produce their food or build their homes, preferring instead to maintain their social position in the face of all adversity and to rely on indentured servants and slaves. When those impressed and abused laborers ran away, as they often did, they were sometimes tracked with dogs. When the colony was still sparsely populated, many simply escaped.[5]

The colonists faced four problems: the choice of a location for their colony; ignorance of how to plant, hunt, and gather food; an unwillingness to work or even to learn how to care for themselves; and gluttony. Within months of their arrival, the 104 colonists had consumed nearly all the food they had brought with them. Having neglected to locate their settlement near good, fresh water, they became sick from the fetid, stagnant water of the James River and began dropping like flies. By the time the local Pasapegh Indians, part of the Powhatan confederation, brought them fresh supplies from their autumn hunts and harvests, only forty settlers remained. The provisions were enough to enable Smith and fifteen men to go raiding for more, especially corn, and bring it back before setting off again in search of Wahunsonacock, the leader of the confederation, and whatever information he might have on the lost Roanoke colonists. In a typical bit of confusion, the English mixed up the name of the leader with that of the people, so to them and to history, Wahunsonacock became known as Powhatan, a name I use hereafter. The Powhatan confederation itself occupied the whole of eastern Virginia, from the Chesapeake Bay inland to what are now Richmond and Fredericksburg.

After rowing some distance up the Chickahominy River, Smith and his party took off overland but were almost immediately ambushed and seized by Opechancanough, Powhatan's half brother and eventual successor. All but Smith were killed, and he was taken to the great weroance himself. The chief's many wives, his dignity, and his calm majesty impressed the red-haired English adventurer, who nonetheless was marked for death. According to Smith's second version of his captivity, Powhatan's favorite daughter, Pocahontas—also known as Matoaka—a young girl of twelve or thirteen, intervened just as the executioner was about to bash in his head. Faced with such a clear message from the gods, sent through his precious daughter, Powhatan adopted his captive as a son and sent him back to Jamestown, Smith wrote in *The Generall Historie of Virginia, New-England, and the Summer Isles*, which he published in 1624. Pocahontas herself made frequent trips to the settlement throughout 1608, helping Smith save its remaining colonists from starvation. It is popular of late to suggest that Powhatan arranged the whole thing as part of an elaborate plan to win the colonists' allegiance, but there is no proof of that.

Not long after his near-death and adoption as a vassal, Smith turned the tables on Powhatan. He and Captain Christopher Newport, who had arrived from England with fresh settlers—still too many gentlemen—and orders to crown Powhatan as a king subservient to James I, went to the weroance bearing gifts and a crown. Among the luxuries was a white greyhound, perhaps the first used in the New World for diplomacy rather than brutality. The greyhound also became a symbol of the Englishmen's treatment of the Indians, and the treatment of dogs in general became in Virginia a measure for how well poor people were treated, much as it was in Spain's colonies: to be called a dog was insulting, to be treated worse than a dog was to be considered subhuman. The coronation of Powhatan turned into farce when Newport attempted to force the weroance to kneel. Believing that he should submit to no one, especially one of his own vassals, Powhatan resisted, and it was only by placing their full weight on his shoulders that Newport and Smith forced him to stoop enough to receive his crown. After the coronation, it was clear that Powhatan continued to believe that the newcomers owed tribute to him, while the colonists were equally certain that he owed allegiance to his and their king. The struggle continued for more than a decade, with the Powhatans falling to disease, the colonists succumbing to starvation and illness, and both periodically killing each other.

Smith earned the enmity of most of the remaining colonists because he sent them out to forage for nuts and acorns and to hunt so that they could survive. If they did not work, they did not eat. Finally, in the summer of 1609, they rebelled and removed him from his position as president of the governing council. A short while later, just after the arrival of a flotilla with new settlers and supplies, Smith was severely burned in a gunpowder explosion—possibly an assassination attempt—while in a canoe on the river, and he was forced to return to London for treatment. At the time, there were around 500 colonists in Jamestown, stocked with provisions, hogs, a few horses, chickens, goats, sheep, dogs, cats, and a fresh harvest of food.

Following Smith's departure, Powhatan cut off the flow of food and went to war, ambushing the few settlers who ventured out to hunt or gather nuts and roots. The new president of the council, George Percy, could do little more than attempt to maintain his sartorial splendor and record the dissolution of the colonists into a collection of cannibals that grew less numerous by the day. The "starving time," as it was known, descended on the colonists with the winter of 1609; it was hastened in large measure by their refusal to work and their profligate consumption of food—matched in some cases only by the voraciousness of the rats that had traveled with them.

By the end of autumn, according to Percy, the colonists had eaten their horses, goats, sheep, chickens, and hogs, forcing them to turn in winter to their dogs, cats, rats, mice, snakes, toadstools, horse hides, boots, and shoes. As the food dwindled, they began to die, and they kept dying, while the survivors exhumed and consumed Indians they had killed—and sometimes, it appears, their own dead—and drank blood from the open wounds of the living. One man "murdered his wyfe Ripped the childe outt of her woambe and threw it into the River and after chopped the Mother in pieces and salted her for his foode," said Percy. Before the wife eater could finish all the evidence, he was caught, tortured, and executed; Percy does not say whether the murderer was eaten in turn. Only seventy of close to 500 colonists remained when Percy discovered in the spring that a small group at a satellite fort had plenty to eat—he offered no explanation for not having checked there earlier. Before Percy could act on the knowledge, Sir Thomas Gates, the colony's new lieutenant governor, arrived from Bermuda with 140 more people but scant supplies, having lost most of them in a hurricane that had wrecked several ships.[6]

After surveying the dismal scene, Gates decided to abandon Jamestown. The colonists had reached the Chesapeake Bay when they were intercepted and ordered back by Lord De La Warr, the new governor, just sailing in with more colonists and provisions. He imposed draconian discipline on the colonists and instituted a reign of terror—including the killing of women and children—to subdue the Powhatans. De La Warr developed scurvy and left the following year, but the battles continued until Pocahontas again, and initially not voluntarily, rescued the colonists from their own folly.

Following Smith's departure, the young princess married an Indian and settled down until she was kidnapped in 1613 and hauled back to Jamestown as a hostage to be exchanged for English prisoners held by Powhatan. While negotiating the exchange, the colonial authorities moved Pocahontas to Henrico, where Alexander Whitaker taught her English and converted her to Christianity. There she also fell in love with John Rolfe, who a year earlier had begun planting Caribbean tobacco, hoping it would become a cash crop for the colony. Within five years, Rolfe was shipping tobacco to England, and the colonists were planting it everywhere, to the exclusion of food crops.

In 1614, Rolfe begged the governor, Sir Thomas Dale, and Powhatan for permission to marry Pocahontas, who had been baptized as Rebecca, rather than have her exchanged for hostages. The marriage created an alliance that brought some peace to the colony for eight years, enough time for the monoculture of tobacco, based on African slave labor, to take root in Virginia's soil, but Pocahontas did not live to see it. She traveled to England with Rolfe and an emissary of her father, Uttamatomakkin, known to the English as Tomocomo, a wise man charged with counting all the people in England and generally learning the truth about the place because, as he told John Smith, Englishmen "will lie much." Tomocomo tried to count by notching a stick for each person he saw but gave up before leaving Plymouth, where the ship had anchored, because there were too many people. Lady Rebecca was a hit with all but the Indian-phobic King James; nonetheless, Smith helped arrange for her and Tomocomo to attend a royal reception after the Twelfth Night opening of Ben Jonson's *Masque of Christmas*. As usual, the shabby, unprepossessing James barely recognized his guests, and they had no idea such an unmagnetic person could rule anything. Later, Tomocomo reproached Smith for failing to introduce him to the English king. Convinced at last that he had, indeed, seen James, Tomocomo said, "You gave Powhatan a white Dog, which Powhatan fed as himselfe, but your kind gave me nothing, and I am better than your white Dog." Pocahontas died before her ship left for home, it is believed from pneumonia or tuberculosis, and was buried in England. For some years after, her people were even denied English dogs.[7]

By 1619 the tobacco-obsessed colonists were accusing the Indians of being profligate destroyers of game, and taking steps to prevent them from hunting near Jamestown and its outlying settlements. Meeting that year, the Virginia Assembly, created to govern the fast-growing colony, passed a law forbidding the sale or presentation of "any English dogs of quality, as a mastive [mastiff], greyhound, bloodhounde, lande or water spaniel, or any other dog or bitche whatsoever, of the Englishe race, upon paine of forfeiting 5s[hillings] sterling to the publique uses of the Incorporation where he dwelleth." Because the dogs were so helpful in hunting and in guarding, the colonists feared that if the Indians obtained them, they would become even more efficient. Given that the Indians were killing large numbers of game to trade the meat and hides to the colonists, the complaint seems largely to have come from the gentlemen who were having increasing difficulty finding game near their plantations to pursue for sport with dogs and hawks. The list of banned dogs also indicates that they were abundant and fully integrated into the lives of the settlers, as, with the exception of the starving time, they had been from the start. It also appears that the Indians, whose own dog was the typical small, wolflike common Indian dog, wanted the English canines for their physical abilities and, perhaps, their trainability. Tribes in other parts of the Americas felt the same. Bans against trading dogs to the Indians ended with their defeat by force and disease, and by the late seventeenth century relict Indians and settlers were swapping dogs, livestock, and goods at sites in more established parts of the colonies, like the market in Fredericksburg, which operated until the Revolutionary War and then went into hiatus until resurrected in the 1920s as the Fredericksburg Dog Mart.[8]

Trade in women was also regulated, as the Virginia Company, looking to increase the population, shipped ninety women to Jamestown to become "wives" of colonists. They cost 150 pounds of "best leafe Tobacco."[9]

Despite such ploys and the continuing influx of settlers, the Virginia colony's survival remained uncertain for many years. In 1622 the Powhatans, under Opechancanough, who had become weroance after Powhatan's death four years earlier, rose up and killed more than a third of the 1,000 English colonists. They also destroyed the colonists' crops, once again threatening their survival. The situation became so desperate, according to Smith's history of the colony, that stray dogs caught foraging in the fields were hanged—a not uncommon fate for stray dogs found bothering livestock. But Virginia had few food crops and little livestock—the obsession being tobacco—and there is no record of how many dogs were killed. By that time, the French and English were in Canada and New England, and the New World was on its inexorable way to becoming European, despite continuing efforts by the Indians to wrest back their land.

The hunting to which the Reverend Whitaker referred in his 1613 report from Henrico became a deeply ingrained part of the culture in Virginia and the rest of the slave states, for food as well as sport, and all types of dogs were used—blooded hounds for the plantation-owning gentry, hardworking curs for the common people. Other dogs were employed throughout the colonies, as in England and Europe, for turning spits in cooking, for catching bulls and other animals, for herding, and for companionship, but it was the hunt and hunting dogs that ruled in places where settlers lived off game—eating the meat, rendering the fat, of bears especially, for oil, trading the hides. Often, too, the curs—of the yeoman farmer, squatter, homesteader, and laborer—served triple duty as hunters of large and small game; finders and herders of feral cattle, sheep, and horses; and protectors of the home.

IN HIS *History of Virginia*, first published in 1705, Robert Beverly reports that the English colonists hunted rabbits with "swift dogs" that either ran them down, caught and killed them, or forced them into a hole or tree hollow. The hunters then smoked the rabbits out of their most secure hiding places for the dogs to seize. The colonists also hunted raccoons, opossums, and foxes, often at night, with "little curs" that would tree the game and then wait while the hunter climbed up and threw the animal to them. The dogs, which came to be known as feists, tore their prize to pieces—it was a long cry from starving time. Beverly says that the hunters always took their "great dogs," their mastiffs and greyhounds, with them on these excursions to guard against wolves, bears, panthers, and wildcats. Meanwhile, young people in many settlements hunted the growing population of feral horses with dogs. Wild, fast, and scrawny, the ponies were not worth much for meat or hide; killing them was simply sport.[10]

Bears were a different story, and their killing quickly became, and remained for nearly 300 years, the measure of a hunter and his dogs. In 1705 an anonymous young sailor, who set out from bustling Plymouth, England, with an eighty-ship flotilla bound for Virginia and Maryland, arrived on the shores of the Chesapeake Bay after a six-week voyage that included a fleet-scattering hurricane. He described in a brief narrative finding peach trees and peach brandy and an abundance of game at the table—venison, turkey, ducks, geese, and partridges. But the high point of his visit was a successful black-bear hunt behind "three large mastiffs" just before he sailed back to England.[11]

Massachusetts Bay

Coming upon Cape Cod on November 15, 1620, the *Mayflower* dropped anchor and sent out its landing party not far, it is assumed, from where the English trader and explorer Martin Pring stepped ashore seventeen years earlier and terrorized the natives with his "great and fearefull mastives," Foole and Gallant. The Wampanoag Indians might have remembered Pring's visit, for the group that Myles Standish, William Bradford, and their cohorts saw took flight, as if they had seen ghosts. The natives' dog lingered until they whistled for it to follow. The Indians had reasons to be wary of the strangers. English seafarers and adventurers had been stealing people from the Cape for several decades, and between 1616 and 1619, smallpox had decimated the New England tribes. On another exploration, the Pilgrims, with their dogs, found a village that the Indians had abandoned upon their advance, and helped themselves to the food they found inside while ignoring several pieces of venison curing in the hollow of a tree, judging it "fitter for the dog than for us." They coasted the Cape Cod shoreline for another five weeks, taking corn and beans from deserted villages or from graves, where it had been left to fuel the dead's journey to the spirit world.

Finally they turned up the coast and, after finding a safe harbor toward the end of December, began building their homes.[12]

Unlike other Europeans, who came to the New World to establish colonies to exploit resources, the Pilgrims—and the Puritans after them—arrived with their families, intent on creating permanent communities, like the ones they had left behind. Only in the New World they hoped to worship in peace, free of persecution and what they saw as the corrupting influence of the Church of England. But the weeks of exploration had depleted their supplies and damaged their health, and in the first months of that first winter in New Plimouth, as they called it, fifty of the original ninety-nine colonists died of starvation, illness, and exposure. Living on shipboard, struggling to lay out their town and build homes, they were grateful for whatever fish they caught, birds they downed, or deer carcasses they scavenged from wolves or Indian snares. Desperate though they were, the Pilgrims, unlike the Jamestown colonists, appear to have avoided eating their dogs, not to mention the corpses of their brethren.

They believed that the Lord sometimes intervened to avert disaster, and the accounts on several of those occasions show how integral dogs were to the community. Thus *Mourt's Relation*, an account of the colony's first two years believed to have been written by the governor, William Bradford, with Edward Winslow and Robert Cushman—the title comes from a bastardization of the surname of George Morton, who wrote the preface to the 1622 London edition—reports that on Friday, January 12, 1621, John Goodman and Peter Brown took their meat from their midday meal and went for a walk with a "great Mastiffe bitch" and a spaniel. Not far from the plantation, the dogs took off after a deer, with the unarmed men trailing behind. They got lost and, unable to find their own people, Indians, shelter, or food, they decided to park themselves under a tree they could climb should one of the panthers they heard roaring in the distance attack. They held the mastiff by the neck to prevent her from charging into the night after the roaring cats, so she could protect them in the event of an attack. Thus, they spent a wretched, freezing night in the dark and the snow. They finally found their way home the next night, suffering from exhaustion, hunger, and exposure. Goodman's feet were so badly frostbitten that his boots had to be cut from his swollen feet— fortunately he kept his toes. The next night the settlement's "rendezvous house" burned to the ground. Several days later, Goodman was hobbling toward the water to go aboard the *Mayflower* so his feet could heal when two wolves charged his spaniel. The terrified dog sought protection between his master's legs. The unarmed Goodman seized a stick and threw it, hitting one of the wolves. They retreated, then returned, and Goodman found a board with which to defend himself, but the wolves were content to sit on their tails and watch, "grinning at him, a good while," before ambling off.[13]

The Pilgrims were "rescued" by English-speaking Indians in late February and March, particularly by the man they called Squanto, more properly Tisquanto. There are multiple, contradictory versions of his early life, but it appears he was taken from the area of the new Plymouth Plantation while a young man by English adventurers, offered for sale in the slave markets of Malaga, Spain, and rescued and educated by priests there. He finally made his way to England and ultimately back to his homeland around 1619, only to find that he was literally the last Patuxet Indian, the rest of his tribe having died in the smallpox epidemic of 1616–19. In fact, the numbers of New England Indians were so reduced that shortly after his arrival in the Massachusetts Bay Colony in 1630, John Winthrop, the Puritan leader, observed that the epidemic was God's way of clearing the Puritans' title to the land. A second epidemic, from 1633 to 1634, killed 50 to 95 percent of the remaining Indians. The first Great Migration to North America—this involving the Puritans—was under way at the time, and the rapidly expanding English population put intense pressure on the declining Indian population, forcing tribes to surrender their land or strike back against superior numbers and weaponry.

AN ESTIMATED 20,000 TO 25,000 English immigrants arrived in New England between 1629 and 1642, and they wanted land for towns and farms. They also demanded ever increasing quantities of natural resources, both to meet their needs in Massachusetts and as trade goods to secure necessary supplies from England. From the Indians they obtained furs, including the pelts of Indian dogs and doubtless stray English dogs, and game for their tables. The newcomers also whaled, fished, logged, farmed, and engaged in the growing slave trade. But to succeed, they had to take land and resources from the Indians and predators, especially livestock-killing wolves, and keep them from people—heretics, they were called— who disagreed with the prevailing theology, lest the dissenters gain enough followers to take power. From the start, Indians and wolves were discussed in much the same language, as wild, brutal, savage, uncivilized creatures blocking the advance of Christian civilization. The Indians could be converted, and Roger Williams and a few other colonists sought to do so, although Williams himself was later banished from the Massachusetts Bay Colony for his beliefs. But no one appears to have publicly offered a defense of wolves or other predators.

The settlers used dogs to guard their homes and manage their livestock, to kill wolves, to hound Indians; to turn wheels that powered spits, wells, machinery, bellows, and churns; to keep their feet warm during Sunday services; and occasionally to save them from their own folly. Dogs pulled carts, killed rats, and drove livestock, once it became more abundant, to market. Some dogs were mourned nearly as deeply as if they had been valued members of the community. Recounting to friends in England the illness, death, and bad weather that shadowed the voyage across the Atlantic in 1629 of the first five ships bound for the newly chartered Massachusetts Bay Colony, Reverend Francis Higginson, one of the Puritan leaders, reported sadly that Thomas Goffe's "great dog"—probably a mastiff— fell overboard from the *Talbot* and was lost in midocean on May 26. Once landed, the English sometimes used dogs for barter; Roger Clap traded a "little Puppy-Dog" to an Indian for a peck of corn.

Later, as we have seen, the colonists periodically sought to keep English dogs away from Indians.[14]

In the journal and letters of John Winthrop, the colony's first governor and one of the founders of Boston, livestock, wolf, dog, and Indian matters are interwoven with theological disputes involving Roger Williams, John Cotton, Anne Hutchinson, John Wilson, and Winthrop himself; arguments over the place of women in society, with Winthrop and his allies believing women should not read and write or concern themselves with business or politics; and battles over centralized versus local authority in politics and theology, church and state being intertwined. The theological debates often involved antinomianism, the belief held by Hutchinson and her followers that humans were saved by faith in God's grace alone, as opposed to believing and following the scriptures and commandments in all behavior. Great attention was paid as well to policing people's sexual proclivities—"perversions" being punishable by branding, expulsion, or death—and even the behavior of their dogs.

MANY OF THE PURITANS' cattle, goats, sheep, and horses died on the first ships sent to the new colony, so the survivors were such precious commodities that they could not be killed for food. Only pigs reproduced fast enough to be slaughtered, but in some areas they were prime wolf prey, along with goats, sheep, and calves. Because of the shortage of domestic stock, which persisted throughout the 1630s, even with ships arriving regularly from England, the colonists relied on game for their meat, but they complained that wolves were also suppressing deer populations.

These wolves were so ubiquitous that I suspect some of them must have been misidentified Indian dogs that had reverted to the wild, or become feral, after their humans had succumbed to war or disease. Virtually every early chronicler commented that the Indian dogs they encountered closely resembled wolves in size, coloration, appearance, and vocalizations—they howled but did not bark. Certainly the East had a large population of wolves—called red wolves in the South and timber wolves in the North—but there were probably even more dogs, and they were allowed to breed and wander freely, often foraging on their own. As the Indian population crashed, still more of those dogs were left to find food wherever they could, and any number of them could have survived for a while, at least. Colonists would have classed them by appearance, predatory behavior, and habitat—ranging freely along the edges of settlements—as wolves.

From the start, the Puritans placed bounties on wolves' heads, and they ordered wolf-killing greyhounds from Ireland, deemed the best in the world. On August 12, 1633, John Winthrop, Jr., received a letter from Edward Hawes in England, telling him that "3 woolfe doggs & a bitch with an Irish boy to tend them" had been shipped to him. Unlike other Irish, Hawes wrote, this boy is "honest." John Winthrop the elder recorded the arrival in his journal on October 11, and not long after interjected in a letter to his son, who had returned to England to recruit new immigrants: "Rich came in and told me the dog had killed an old wolf" on their land. The dogs and human hunters were effective; livestock populations steadily expanded while wolf populations declined. But losses still occurred, and bounties were periodically imposed and rescinded. In 1648 the Massachusetts Bay Colony authorized its towns to purchase as many wolfhounds as they needed to obliterate the remaining wolves. By the end of the eighteenth century, wolves were effectively extirpated from southern New England, remaining only in the less populated northern regions of Vermont, New Hampshire, and Maine. By the Civil War they were rare east of the Mississippi, with pockets along the Texas-Louisiana border and in Canada. After that, the most intense fighting against Indians and predators occurred in the West.[15]

A persistent irony concerning dogs is that they are as efficient at killing livestock as they are at herding and protecting it, and that was evident from the earliest days of every American colony. In colonial New Amsterdam, free-roaming dogs harassed sheep being driven to market with such intensity that the drives had to be suspended periodically. In Massachusetts, the first dog-control laws were passed in Salem in 1635, making it a crime for dogs to kill sheep and pigs, harass horses and cattle, eat fish, or enter a meeting-house. The last proscription was passed despite the fact that in other areas, dogs were welcome at meetings to warm the feet of their masters and were kept in line by dog whippers and pelters, who threw out unruly curs. The owners of the dogs found guilty of being "destructive public nuisances" were required to hang them and pay double the cost of the livestock they killed, often a steep fine. Commonly, a pine sapling was bent to the ground and secured with a rope, while another rope was tied to the top of the tree and knotted around the dog's neck. When the rope holding the tree was cut, the noose either broke the dog's neck or strangled the animal—gruesome, but people were often treated even less well.[16]

But the usefulness of dogs always outweighed their crimes. In March 1644, John Winthrop wrote of one daring rescue in his journal, a case where death by drowning—a common fate for the colonists, who were often on or near the water, fishing or traveling—was denied. Walking from Sabbath services in Cambridge to their home near Medford in the pouring rain, Winthrop said, a man named Dalkin and his wife came upon a ford they had to cross. The tide had not yet run out and the water was high, but Dalkin decided to test its depth and, after a struggle, made it across. Once on the far bank, he told his wife that the water was too deep for her, the current too strong, and she should wait for the tide to fall. Soaked and impatient, she ignored him, only to be swept off her feet and down-river with the current. Dalkin dared not plunge in after her for fear he, too, would be dragged under, so he cried out for help. Hearing his cry, the couple's dog bolted from their house and, "seeing something in the water, swam to her, and she caught hold on the dog's tail, so he drew her to shore and saved her life." Any animal that could do that, even once, was guaranteed an honored place in the house, if not at the table.[17]

British Colonial War Dogs—Sometimes

The Pequot War was a crucial event in the first decade of the Massachusetts Bay Colony, because it removed a powerful competitor, opened Connecticut to additional settlement, and placed control of wampum production in the hands of the colonists and their pliable Indian allies. Composed of white and purple beads made from whelk and quahog shells, wampum, or wampumpeag, had become by 1630 the medium of exchange for trade with Indians throughout New England. The Pequot, Mohegan, Narragansett, and local Long Island villages controlled its manufacture and traded it to the English primarily for guns, which made them a threat to the colonists' rising hegemony. The powerful Pequots of Connecticut were the most antagonistic tribe toward the colonists. Following the smallpox epidemic of 1633–34, which killed half their people, the Pequots occasionally killed dishonest fur traders, and they rejected a treaty with the Massachusetts Bay Colony that ultimately would have dispossessed them.[18]

The colonists launched a preemptive strike against the Pequots in 1636, after hearing from the Mohegan sachem, or chief, Uncas, that they planned to attack. The colonists went on the offensive, sacking and burning Pequot villages and cornfields, and leaving fourteen of their people and countless dogs dead. The Pequots twice retaliated against settlers living at a fort near Saybrook, at the mouth of the Connecticut River, under Captain Lion Gardener. The settlers had three mastiffs for protection and for scouting the countryside for Pequots as they traveled the two miles to their fields. The first attack came when the settlers, inexplicably leaving their dogs in the fort, went to bring in their hay before the Indians could torch it. Pequot warriors killed three and captured the brother of one settler, "the minister of Cambridge." Pequot women flayed him alive with clamshells before the men roasted him.[19]

Having learned their lesson, Gardener and a small group of men then went with the dogs to burn brush in a field a half mile from the fort—to remove cover for attacking Indians. The flames rousted

Pequot warriors lying in wait, who shot arrows at the colonists and then charged. Two settlers ran straight for the fort; four were killed; and Gardener and three others were wounded while defending themselves "with our naked swords" as they retreated.[20]

In retaliation, the colonial militia, with 109 men under Captains John Mason and John Underhill, massacred 400 to 800 Pequots—mostly women, children, and old people—at a large village near Mystic on May 26, 1637, while the colonists' Mohegan allies, under their sachem, Uncas, looked on. The battle started at dawn after an Indian dog sounded an alarm, followed by a lookout's cry, and it ended quickly and brutally. By Mason's boastful account, the militiamen torched wigwams and butchered the villagers with their swords as they fled in panic. Only fourteen survived; half were captured and the other seven escaped. The English casualties were two dead and twenty wounded, Mason reported. Reinforcements soon arrived, and despite internal dissension, Mason and Underhill continued to hunt down Pequots through May and June. They defeated most of the surviving members of the tribe under Sassacus, sachem of the Pequot, near what is now New Haven, and ultimately sent 180 captives into slavery among their Indian allies. The war effectively ended in 1638 with a treaty, really a total Pequot surrender, after the Mohawks, among whom Sassacus had sought refuge, killed the sachem and delivered his severed head on a pole to the English colonists.[21]

Two decades later, smallpox struck again, wiping out 90 percent of the Quinnipiac Indians near New Haven. Confined to a small, diseased reservation, the survivors requested new land, and the colonial government granted it, on the condition that they slaughter their dogs, believed to be responsible for killing livestock. The Quinnipiac refused, so they received no land. By then, Connecticut, like Virginia, had outlawed trading or selling English dogs to the Indians, placing them in the same category as guns and ammunition. Colonial leaders had also brought mastiffs from Long Island to hunt non-Christian Indians.

DOGS WERE MORE AGGRESSIVELY EMPLOYED—although on nothing approaching the Spanish scale—during King Philip's War of 1675–77, which brought an end to the last of the once widespread Wampanoags, already reduced by disease from approximately 12,000 in 1620 to fewer than 2,000 at the time of the war. English colonists, on the other hand, numbered 40,000 to 50,000 and had come to believe that the only acceptable Indian was a Christian Indian—and then just barely. Commercial hunting had nearly ruined the fur trade, the Indians' primary source of income, and they had continued to lose land and freedom to the rapidly proliferating colonists. Many Indians believed they had to drive the English from their land, and they rallied behind the sachem of the Wampanoag—Philip, or Metacomet, who had been humiliated by a series of English demands and actions and was fearful that he would soon be arrested and killed. The conflict soon became a war of attrition, resulting in the loss of some 3,000 Indians and 600 or more English settlers, along with the destruction of entire villages on both sides. Throughout the war Captain Samuel Mosely, a buccaneer from the West Indies, led a troop of volunteers, pirates, and a pack of hounds, apparently including Cuban bloodhounds from the West Indies, which he used for hunting Indians. While the effectiveness of the dogs was not recorded, Mosely and his troop proved efficient Indian killers during the defeat of Metacomet.

With Indians and their French allies attacking along the frontier in 1703, in the opening rounds of what came to be called Queen Anne's War, the Reverend Solomon Stoddard of Northampton proposed using dogs to trail Indians. Massachusetts approved the purchase in 1706, and Connecticut followed suit in October 1708, when the assembly appropriated fifty pounds "for the buying up and maintaining of Dogs in the northern frontier towns in this colony, to hunt after the Indian enemy." Their rationale, in part, was that Indians were wild, cunning, and predatory, like wolves and bears, and thus had to be hunted like them—with dogs. Dogs were also employed during the war in Vermont and Canada to haul supplies and the wounded in sledges.[22]

Spreading Out

As the English pushed their colonies from Florida to Canada along the Atlantic coast and slowly inland during the seventeenth and first half of the eighteenth centuries, the French drove south and west from Montreal and Quebec. Samuel de Champlain scouted the St. Lawrence River and the lake that bears his name early in the seventeenth century in an effort to determine the prospects for trapping beaver—their fur being in such demand for felt hats that European beavers were vanishing fast—and other game. Other French explorers and trappers followed. Some, like Louis Jolliet and his partner, the Jesuit priest Jacques Marquette, in the early 1670s and La Salle a decade later became famous for their exploits in opening the waters of the Great Lakes, the Ohio River, and the Mississippi River, along with tributaries. *Coureurs des bois*, "runners of the woods," more commonly called voyageurs, conducted this trade, often settling among the Indians, taking wives, and raising families. These French and French-Indian voyageurs were the grunts of the fur trade in Canada and the northern territories of America, trapping, hunting, guiding, and hauling hides from the interior to trading centers on Hudson's Bay and in Montreal, Quebec, and St. Louis, then hauling manufactured goods to the outlying posts. They carried their cargo by long canoes, by barge, and by dogsled, although even by water they traveled with dogs. They lived on salt pork, cornmeal, a ration of whiskey or rum, and what they could hunt.

The first pioneers who moved west already knew or rapidly learned, if they were to survive, that they were entering territory belonging to Indians, whom they could not always expect to be friendly. Well-worn Indian roads and trails that were carved through the landscape and along with rivers and lakes provided avenues for the long hunters and trappers, the advance agents of mercantilism. The Indian custom of burning the forests twice yearly to clear the understory so they could hunt, travel, and farm more easily also made the way less difficult for new settlers, who came not just from England but from other parts of Europe and Africa as well.

Following the long hunters and trappers, they built isolated farmsteads or created small communities, more dependent on one another and the forbearance of their Indian neighbors than on the more established settlements they had left behind. Their lives tended to be hard and violent, racked by fear of human and animal predators, of mortal illness. Often their dogs howled and barked through the night, incessantly warning them of dangers or simply unknown creatures and sounds. The pioneers' entertainments could be equally extreme. People traveled miles to attend frolics featuring riding, shooting, and hunting contests, dancing, eating, drinking, trading goods and dogs—not to mention fighting between men, between dogs, or between dogs and bears, dogs and bulls, dogs and badgers, dogs and whatever—and revival meetings aimed at inspiring sinners to repent. For many farmers and most pioneers, hunting was essential to survival, and dogs were essential to hunting.

In the opening decade of the eighteenth century, Scotch-Irish and German immigrants began joining the English, often as indentured servants, in the push west to the Appalachian Mountains and beyond. In the South, African slaves were brought along, as well. British colonial policy deliberately steered non-English immigrants westward, away from the established settlements, in part so those areas could retain their social and cultural connections to England. But they ran into French and Indian resistance that flared into open war on numerous occasions and made all advances perilous. Those wars culminated in 1754 with the start of the French and Indian War, a border conflict marked by pitched battles and depredations on both sides.

In 1757, Benjamin Franklin argued that Pennsylvania should obtain fifty tough mastiffs and handlers from England for hunting Shawnee and Delaware Indians allied with the French. He directed that the dogs should be kept leashed and thus fresh until the handlers came to an area where Indians might be hiding, where they would be unloosed; Franklin observed that the Spanish had used their war dogs that way to lethal effect during the Conquest. Other Pennsylvania leaders endorsed the idea, but nothing came of it, although less than a decade later, John Penn, lieutenant governor of the Pennsylvania colony, urged to no avail that soldiers who brought big, strong dogs to muster for finding Indians should be awarded an extra three shillings a month in pay.

The defeat of the French and Indian forces in 1758 at Fort Duquesne, near what became Pittsburgh, by 700 colonists under George Washington, and British troops under General John Forbes; the loss of all French forts south of Canada in the next two years; and, finally, the Treaty of Paris in 1763 ended the French and Indian War. Treaties with the Cherokee and other tribes opened the Ohio River valley and the regions west of the Appalachians to settlement. That virtually guaranteed that, as a matter of simple demographics, America would continue to spread west until it reached an insurmountable geographic barrier. In addition to the English, the newcomers to that territory remained predominately Scotch-Irish—so called because they had moved from Scotland to Ulster, Ireland, and then to America—and Germans who came through Philadelphia to western Pennsylvania, or west from Baltimore through the Cumberland Gap. Scotch-Irish were most numerous from western Pennsylvania through Virginia's Shenandoah Valley and into western North Carolina in 1790, while Germans represented nearly half the population of Pennsylvania, with a large concentration in the west and a sizable percentage in western Maryland.

THE PATTERN OF EXPANSION from the late seventeenth through the early nineteenth centuries followed that of the first days of colonization—cooperation with and reliance on the local Indians, followed by extermination of Indians and predators, and heavy reliance on hunting and trapping for food and furs to trade for staples to ease a hardscrabble life.

The most famous of the late–eighteenth century long hunters, Daniel Boone, of English Quaker stock, went on his extended hunts with a horse and dogs and a few companions, if any, as his family moved along the frontier from Pennsylvania to North Carolina to Kentucky and finally Missouri. Although Shawnee Indians had adopted Boone in Kentucky and he was renowned as a woodsman, he never went "native" to the degree of many of his peers, especially some among the French trappers. Other pioneers settled in western New York and the Northwest Territories—wherever there was land and opportunity. Always, those who followed hard on their heels were a few traders to build and staff forts where hides were collected in exchange for manufactured goods, cloth, blankets, beads and other trinkets, pots and pans, tobacco, whiskey, guns, gunpowder, lead, knives, and other weapons. Close behind the trappers and fur company agents were farmers, clearing land for crops and livestock, and troops to reinforce land grabs when necessary.

An unknown number of those who opened the frontier brought their own hounds and stock dogs with the look and qualities they wanted and sought to preserve. Many of these mixed with other local dogs, perhaps even Indian dogs and, in the Ohio River valley and the Louisiana territory, some French and Spanish dogs. The result was the cur, or cur dog, a tough animal weighing thirty pounds or more with a yellow, ginger, merled, or brindled coat, sometimes with glass or pale blue eyes, which became the ubiquitous dog of the pioneer and small farmer. They were mutts with attitude, and particular lines were sometimes established and maintained for many generations. Their descendants are still around, fragmented into various breeds and types—yellow blackmouth curs, leopard curs, and the like. Others figured in the creation of coonhounds and bear hounds. The smaller version is the feist, used now to hunt squirrels, raccoons, and opossums, just as it was used 300 years ago. Curs were the big dogs, the yard dogs, and feists the little dogs, found on farms and country homes throughout the expanding nation, and still found in some rural areas today.

These dogs served their purpose well, as reports in broadsheets and almanacs regularly attested. For instance, in northern New

York one late summer day, a young mother was gathering beans in front of a newly built log house when she turned to fuss at her little dog for its persistent barking and saw that it was holding at bay a cougar sitting on a stump just twenty feet from her baby. The woman hastily scooped up her child and ran into the house to wait for her husband. He soon returned with his big dog and immediately tracked and killed the cougar. He found in its stomach the remains of their brave little dog.[23]

4

Washington, Lafayette, and Jefferson Make Revolution and Hunt
for Dogs. The Sagacious Dog Appears. What's a Man to Do
Without His Hounds and Sheepdogs?

✌

B ACK AT HIS BELOVED MOUNT VERNON in 1783, the victorious George Washington focused on continuing the transformation of his agricultural practices—converting from
tobacco monocropping to a "scientific" program of crop diversifi-
cation and rotation to improve the fertility of his soil and value of
his five farms—begun before he rode off to fight for the colonies'
independence. He also wished to improve his livestock and his pack
of foxhounds, while finding new dogs for running down the wolves
that continued to kill sheep in his part of northern Virginia. He
sometimes went to great lengths to obtain the well-bred animals
he wanted.

After reviewing his kennels and running his dogs one day in the
spring of 1785, Washington dashed off a letter to his friend, surrogate son, and close comrade-in-arms, Marie Joseph Paul Yves Roch
Gilbert du Motier, the Marquis de Lafayette, asking him to send
some French hounds—and some jackasses as well. A dog lover and
hunter in his own right, Lafayette responded in a letter dated May
13, 1785, that French hounds were "not easily got because the King

Makes use of english dogs, as Being more swift than those of Normandy." Left unsaid was that all good nobles—the only French who could ride to hounds—wanted to be like the king. Nonetheless, he had obtained seven hounds—three males and four females—from Comte d'Oilliamson. Lafayette made sure to inform Washington that one of the females "was a favorite of [the count's] lady, who Makes a present of Her to You." The hounds were to come to America under the care of eighteen-year-old John Quincy Adams, when he returned to New York that summer after an extended trip to Europe and stint as his father's private secretary when he was ambassador to the Court of St. James. The young man was bound ultimately for Boston to attend Harvard.[1]

But as summer waned and he continued to hear nothing, Washington worried. On August 22, he wrote to William Grayson, his assistant secretary and aide-de-camp during the Revolution, in typical fashion mixing politics, plans for "internal improvements" to expand the reach of civilization, and concern over his hounds. After a long account of a tour he had made to investigate extending navigation up the Potomac River, he asked whether Grayson had heard young Adams say anything about the hounds the Marquis had "committed to his care." Bluntly outlining his concerns in militaristic terms, Washington wrote: "It would have been civil in the young Gentleman to have dropped me a line respecting the desposial of them, especially as war is declared on the canine species in New-York, and they being strangers, and not having formed alliances for self-defence, but on the contrary, distressed and friendless may have been exposed not only to war, but to pestilence and famine also."[2]

Washington's sources were impeccable—not surprising, given the number of people who paid their respects at Mount Vernon and his extensive correspondence. With a fast-growing population of around 30,000, New York was locked in one of the paroxysms of fear and loathing that had gripped it periodically since the earliest Dutch settlement and that had afflicted many other cities, especially in warm weather. Some dog problems were constant—strays roaming the streets, fighting among themselves, consuming offal from the butcher shops where livestock was slaughtered on the spot, harassing pedestrians and horses, attacking and stampeding flocks and herds as they were driven through narrow streets to market. Small dogs kept by vendors to protect their carts periodically leapt at passersby, and the big, powerful mastiffs or bulldogs that were used to catch and hold beef prior to slaughter—and to battle bears or bulls in gruesome spectacles—generally offended everyone but their owners and bloodthirsty fans. Terriers competed in pits, usually in taverns, to kill the most rats in a short period of time, and they served the same function on farms and plantations. Dogs were also used to power grinders, for making paint, and other machines, including those for spinning cotton, to pump bellows for blacksmiths, and to turn spits and wheels. The pet population was rapidly rising as well, especially among particular breeds like spaniels, pointers, greyhounds, companion dogs of the terrier and small spaniel type, and the Newfoundland, fueled in part by celebrations of the dog's natural sagacity, loyalty, and devotion.

Whatever their origin, many of these urban dogs joined the ranks of free-ranging strays, at least periodically, and in summer they were believed to become mad, rabid, or distempered. Wiser heads suggested, to no avail, that the dogs ran around panting because of the heat. There was no vaccine then for rabies, often called hydrophobia, nor comprehension of what it was, so the solution to any perceived outbreak was to get rid of free-ranging dogs. New York tried every few years to collect the roamers and fine their owners, to little effect. Making official the war that had been under way since summer, the Common Council of New-York City passed an ordinance on October 26, 1785, "for guarding against the mischief which may arise from distempered or Mad Dogs," basically mandating that dogs be chained, leashed, muzzled, or confined or face arrest and death if not bailed out by their owners.[3]

Boston had tried to solve the problem as early as 1728 by banning dogs taller than ten inches. That worked no better than any other prohibition. Little more than a century later, the *Boston Tribune* protested against a man who wanted to employ forty dogs to power a cotton mill, arguing that the dog, being first among all animals in sagacity and fidelity, should not be subjected to such brutal labor. The dog "in moral qualities often surpasses his master," the anonymous correspondent proclaimed, "but the master rewards his excellence with abuse."[4]

John Adams believed that a person who liked dogs was probably honest and faithful in his own right, but eighteen-year-old John Quincy did not completely share his father's opinion on that score. Feeling poorly used because he had agreed to play escort to hounds he disliked, Adams managed to foist them off on Dr. John Cochran upon his arrival in New York. Cochran had served as an army doctor under Washington, eventually reaching the post of chief-physician and surgeon, and had moved to New York after the war. He soon had the hounds on a fast sloop bound for Mount Vernon, where they arrived on August 31, along with a request that Washington help him secure a government post. Responding promptly, Washington offered to pay Cochran for his services but politely explained that he had a policy of not recommending people for specific positions. He had determined not to do so, he said, because he did not want to give the officials involved the opportunity to reject his advice. After becoming president, he took a different tack and in 1790 appointed Cochran commissioner of loans.[5]

Washington wrote to Lafayette the next day, announcing the arrival of the dogs and then talking at length about politics before asking him to pass along a letter of thanks to Comte d'Oilliamson for the "seven very fine hounds." Ever mindful of the ladies, Washington offered special thanks to Madame la Comtesse for her "favorite hound" and promised that she would receive his "particular attention."[6]

After all of that effort, the French hounds proved a disappointment until December, when they began to improve markedly, probably because it took that long to adjust to their new world and because Washington, as was his wont, grew impatient when they did not adapt as rapidly as he expected. He incorporated them into his kennel, which he had founded more than thirty years before. By 1789, when he became president, he still had two of the original French hounds, Vulcan and Venus, which he had loaned to Lord

Calvert in Maryland, along with Ragman and two other English hounds; Dutchess and Doxy, from Philadelphia; and Countess, Jupiter, and Tryal, all descended from the French hounds. He often boasted that his pack ran so tightly bunched, "they could be covered with a blanket."[7]

WASHINGTON LOVED HIS HORSES, some of which he raced, as much as his dogs, and he loved to ride to his hounds, especially in the mornings on a formal hunt or, more frequently, when he set out on a tour of his farms, which covered 8,000 acres, or to visit a neighbor, and at night when predator and prey were on the move. Then, too, he could study stars and weather, to which he paid close attention. Before the war, he had begun the practice he would later resume, of seeking the best dogs from a variety of places and breeding them. Despite a paucity of well-bred dogs in America, relative to Europe and England, curs and various other types of dogs abounded, and it was often difficult to keep those in heat isolated until they could be matched with the desired sire. Washington recorded in his diary on March 26, 1770, that his hound Countess had gotten loose and been "lined" by his water spaniel, which had cost him one pound, sixteen shillings; twice by a small yellow cur; and finally by Ranger, a hound belonging to Bryan Fairfax, a longtime friend and avid foxhunter who owned the neighboring plantation, Belvoir. Washington referred repeatedly in his diaries to the breedings of his dogs. While president, he pointedly reminded his farm manager at Mount Vernon to make certain that his "Tarrier bitch" was mated only with her male counterpart.[8]

It was a common belief at the time, based on the appearance of puppies of different coloration and size, that a litter could have more than one sire. While that can happen, it is a rare event; most of the variation arose because dogs were not being consistently bred to close relatives to create a uniform appearance, as they would come to be just a few decades later. Washington achieved relative uniformity by drowning puppies that did not match his conception of what his hounds should look like.

More important, he attempted to be rigorous and programmatic in breeding not only his dogs but also his cattle, oxen, sheep, jackasses, mules, and horses—as rigorous as he was in seeking to improve his agricultural practices. And, as with the French hounds, he sought the best bloodlines for those animals from Europe, often through Lafayette. He liked to boast that he had the largest sheep with the best wool and mutton around—better even than those of his friend Thomas Jefferson, known for the rigor of his breeding programs. Washington even collected and tried to domesticate deer from various parts of the world, in part by never letting his hounds run them—a practice he thought detrimental, in any event, to their foxhunting. Thus protected, the half-tamed deer became such compulsive raiders of his garden that, while president, he reversed his policy and repeatedly wrote his farm manager with orders to run the miscreants off with hounds. If that failed, he said, he would kill them himself.[9]

WASHINGTON HAD MORE INVOLVED DEALINGS with his extensive group of American friends and allies, like Bryan Fairfax, than with Lafayette. As with Lafayette, these relationships were often political as well as social, and the exchange or loaning of hounds—and hunting—served to solidify them, as did other social and sporting events. At times the transactions also led to confusion and injured feelings. In the summer of 1722, Fairfax sent Washington two hounds, Rouser and Dabster, and then, after watching his own pack tire while running a fox, added a postscript to a letter of July 5: "If it should happen that either of the Hounds sent down lately should not please you I beg to have the first offer of them . . ." He carefully explained that he understood that no two sportsmen viewed a dog the same way and that Washington—known to be hypercritical of his dogs—had over the years received many "superexcellent dogs" that failed to meet his expectations, including some from Fairfax himself, notably Ranger.[10]

Missing the diplomatic subtlety of the request, Washington concluded that his old friend wanted to renege on the gift and took offense. Martha Washington slipped word of the problem to Fairfax through his wife. Fairfax stated clearly in an August 3 letter to Washington that he had simply wanted to make certain that Washington found the hounds satisfactory and would return them if he did not, adding, "I should be sorry that you should have occasion to return 'em." The two men remained friends throughout the War of Independence, notwithstanding that Fairfax was a Loyalist.[11]

Back Track: Revolution

Washington's plans for Mount Vernon were put on hold during his command of the Continental Army, but he never lost his concern for dogs and other animals. Headquartered at Morristown, New Jersey, in February 1777, Washington wrote to the president of the Continental Congress, detailing how his army foraged near enemy lines for food, how he had moved to raise additional troops and establish foundries, and how desperately he needed money. Then he appended a copy of a letter from his third-ranking general, Charles Lee, a captive of the British since December 13, 1776, when he was nabbed while sleeping with a prostitute at a tavern near New York. A man known for never appearing without at least two dogs, Lee was dogless in his New York captivity and wanted Washington to remedy the situation through negotiation with the British. Washington replied on February 16 that while he was sorry that Lee was deprived of the friendship and amusements of his pets, he would do nothing. Lee's dogs were safe in Virginia, Washington said, where they would stay.[12]

In an attempt to curry favor with the British and have them release him or arrange for his dogs, Lee delivered a plan for suppressing the rebellion to General William Howe at the end of March, but it was neither pursued nor mentioned when he was exchanged on May 9. In fact, the plan became public knowledge only well after Lee's death and so did not play a role in the events that ruined him. That it remained unknown kept him from being judged a traitor on the scale of Benedict Arnold.

Lee fetched his dogs and rejoined the Continental Army, performing without difficulty although not with great success, despite his reputation as the best military strategist and warrior among the American commanders. He was also known for his violent temper, his slovenly dress, his vindictiveness, his gluttony for food and drink, and his fondness for prostitutes and profanity. For all that, his men and dogs loved him. But on June 28, 1778, ordered by Washington to attack the rear of Sir Henry Clinton's army as it pulled out of Monmouth Courthouse, New Jersey, bound for New York, Lee instead led an inglorious, chaotic retreat, directly for Washington's main army, camped to his rear. In hot pursuit, Clinton's force nearly overran the surprised and dismayed rebels. With a timely warning from Lafayette, however, Washington's men rallied and, in fierce fighting, battled Clinton's forces to a standstill. Clinton soon decamped.

Brigadier generals Anthony Wayne and Charles Scott promptly accused Lee of retreating without warning in a disorderly fashion and putting the entire army at risk—basically of cowardice, or "want of courage." Lee cried foul and wrote a letter, by turns fawning and condescending, to Washington, claiming the success of the day was due to his "maneuvers" and that Washington himself was "guilty of an act of cruel injustice" for listening to the charges leveled against him by a "wicked or stupid person."[13]

In effect, Lee, not realizing that Wayne and Scott spoke for their commander, challenged Washington's authority and integrity, a bad move, and the general responded that what he said "was dictated by duty and warranted by the occasion." He warned Lee that if he persisted in his complaints, he would be charged with disobedience, cowardice, and insubordination. Lee demanded a court-martial to clear his name—a common occurrence when an officer's judgment was questioned—and Washington obliged. Lee was found guilty of disobeying orders for not attacking Clinton, of misbehavior before the enemy, and of disrespecting the commander in chief in his letters. Suspended from his command for a year, he returned to his Virginia plantation, where he sulked with his dogs while swearing to clear his name. He appealed to the Continental Congress, but it confirmed his conviction. Stunned, Lee pointed to his dog and exclaimed, "Oh! That I was that animal, that I might not call man my brother." The sentiment has often been repeated by other people under a wide range of circumstances; indeed, when caught in the maelstrom of politics, Washington himself might have agreed.[14]

Some historians have argued that Lee's behavior did not warrant so severe a penalty, but their argument is hard to credit. Because of his superior rank, he had assumed command of the American forces at Monmouth Courthouse from Lafayette, already known for his courage and leadership. But upon receiving the orders to plan for attack, Lee had balked, and Washington returned the command to Lafayette. Lee then decided he would lead and did, into desultory retreat. Lafayette's warning helped prevent a total disaster, and the troops under his command acquitted themselves well in the chaos. Lee's dogs may even have fought better than their master, given the chance.

ALTHOUGH ON APRIL 27, 1779, William McClay of Pennsylvania's Supreme Executive Council proposed that big, fierce dogs be turned against England's Indian allies, dogs fought on neither side in the Revolution. Early in the war, Washington ordered his troops to treat animals well and applied his rule even to those of the enemy. On October 6, 1777, the Continental Army was licking its wounds from its defeat at Germantown, compliments of bad luck, Howe, and Hessian mercenaries, yet also congratulating itself for inflicting heavy casualties on the British. After the field had cleared, Howe sent a letter to Washington, protesting that he had violated the rules of war by burning the mills of Loyalists, thus cutting their food production. Washington countered that the British had burned Charles Town, Massachusetts, and committed other atrocities against civilians and that he would stop as soon as they did. A short while later, he sent Howe a little dog and a message, penned by young Alexander Hamilton: "[Washington] does himself the pleasure to return to [Howe] a dog, which accidentally fell into his hands, and by the inscription on the collar, appears to belong to General Howe." There is no record of Howe's response, but it appears that he did not let the dog escape again. Washington himself returned to his own dogs five years later.[15]

Off the Wolves

After the grueling years of war and the satisfaction of victory, foxes and wolves would seem minor annoyances, yet they stood in Washington's way, obstacles to creating a smoothly operating farm where all was in balance. Washington evidently disliked such obstructions, whether harmful to his crops or animals, to transport by land or sea, or to success in battle or politics. A few years after obtaining the French hounds, he attempted to find dogs to help him kill wolves that were threatening his prized sheep.

The problem of sheep-killing canids was as old as European settlement in North America, but it no longer involved the survival of a few colonists and a handful of sheep. Now planters like Washington and Jefferson, who were not devoted solely to monocropping tobacco, rice, indigo, or cotton, and farmers from New England and western nonslave territories, were more intent on improving the quality of their sheep, other livestock, and even their dogs than their forebears had been a century before. Sheep meant wool for homespun clothes, which freed many pioneers from reliance on settlements, as well as a source of revenue, especially if the wool was high quality. Sheep also meant cheese, lamb, and mutton. The emphasis therefore shifted from mere survival to something more sophisticated, to notions of scientific breeding for quantity and quality, both of which required more time and intensive effort on the part of the farmer. As the value of the livestock increased, so did the importance of protecting it from predators.

At Monticello, Jefferson complained regularly about the depredations of wolves and dogs in northern Virginia—dogs alone in southern Virginia—preventing the sheep population from growing and farmers from achieving greater self-sufficiency. The yeoman farmer was the backbone of the republic for Jefferson, and he saw improvement of livestock—and even people—through selective breeding, as well as scientific farming methods involving crop rotation and fertilization, as central to the success of the people and nation. Although Washington and Jefferson sought the assistance of dogs, they found no easy solution and continued to fight the problem for the remainder of their lives, as did many sheepmen before and more after. After extirpation of the wolf from nearly all of the lower forty-eight states, the coyote became the favorite bandit predator of sheep ranchers, and without question, coyotes can and do take sheep. But in many areas the star sheep killer was always the dog, fearing no human or domesticated beast, smart enough to let its wild cousins take the rap.

EVER PRACTICAL, Washington sought to solve the problem of marauding wolves and dogs in several ways. Caught up in the struggle to gain approval of the Constitution, he appealed again in 1787 to his friend Lafayette, himself fully involved in France's revolutionary ferment, for help in finding some "true Irish wolf dogs." These were the same fierce "Irish greyhounds" John Winthrop had imported to the Massachusetts Bay Colony 150 years earlier to kill wolves, the same fell beasts the conquistadors had turned on Native Americans in the Caribbean and Central and South America. Despite his political activities, Lafayette tried, but there were none to be had, Washington lamented in a February 5, 1788, letter to his friend Charles Carter. He had recently accused Carter of releasing for publication comments from a letter Washington wrote him regarding the not yet adopted Constitution—that the new nation faced a choice between adopting an imperfect Constitution or falling into "disunion," and that, once adopted, the Constitution could be "peaceably" amended, but not before. But in this letter he accepted Carter's explanation that he had shared the remarks with only a few people after they pledged to keep them private, and one of them had broken faith. Indeed, Washington seemed more concerned with the apparent breach of trust than with his words being printed. That business aside, he moved on to the equally pressing issue of wolf-killing dogs.[16]

Washington quoted a letter he had just received from Sir Edward Newenham, an Irish Protestant who favored some degree of independence from the English king, explaining that he had just heard from Lafayette of the two men's search for the dogs to hunt down wolves on their lands in France and northern Virginia, respectively. "I have been several years endeavoring to get that breed without success; it is nearly annihilated," he told Washington. "I have heard of a bitch in the north of Ireland, but not of a couple anywhere. I am also told that the Earl of Altamont has a breed that is nearly genuine, if he has I will procure two from him." Newenham said that he could send mastiffs, which he used as guard dogs. They are "very fierce, faithful and long-lived," but they are useless for hunting and killing wolves by "pursuit," the way Virginia plantation owners were accustomed to killing foxes, and thus were of no interest to Washington. After passing the news to Carter, who also wanted the dogs, Washington wrote to Newenham on February 24, telling him not to go to any trouble obtaining the pseudo-wolf dogs because they would be "too dearly bought." The big dogs appear to have died out following extirpation of the wolf from Ireland around 1720, although none of the correspondents were aware of the connection. They were re-created as the Irish wolf-hound late in the nineteenth century.[17]

Washington took a draconian approach toward unwanted dogs. In a December 16, 1792, letter to his farm manager, Anthony Whiting—just months after Jefferson had written to him about sheep-killing wolves and dogs—Washington complained about the constant loss of sheep and other livestock to marauding dogs. He then told Whiting to kill any dog that killed sheep on his plantations and to kill strays that had no apparent purpose or owner. He further declared that, based on his observations of the control slaves exercised over their dogs—the way the dogs obeyed them—they must raise and keep dogs only to steal livestock. He closed with "a positive order, that after saying what dog, or dogs shall remain, if any negro presumes under any pretense whatsoever, to preserve, or bring one into the family, that he shall be severely punished, and the dog hanged." Then he became more adamant, saying, "I would no more allow overseers than I would the Negroes, to keep Dogs." By his count, there should be only one or two dogs in total "among the slaves and overseers."[18]

Years after making his escape in 1838, Frederick Douglass complained bitterly about the dehumanization of slavery and the hypocrisy of the laws surrounding it, including a provision in the Virginia code that mandated thirty lashes for any slave caught hunting on his own with dogs in the forest. That same slave, of course, handled the hounds when his master and his guests hunted for deer in that same forest. That slave could also be run down and torn apart by hounds, like any other prey. Indeed, in 1752, Virginia's Assembly, convinced that it had to protect the budding sheep industry from dogs, passed a law forbidding Negroes from traveling with dogs and specifying that any such dog who killed a sheep could itself be ordered to death by a judge. The law specifically exempted slaves traveling with the hounds, spaniels, pointing dogs, and setters of slave owners, the argument being that those well-bred animals did not kill sheep—wrong, of course. After the Revolution, laws regulating dog owning among slaves were stiffened, as were other laws pertaining to slaves and free blacks. Douglass lodged his complaint when memories of Nat Turner's rebellion were still fresh and anything that hinted at freedom for slaves—including owning a dog—was banned in many states.

Jefferson's Sheepdogs

Thomas Jefferson shared Washington's fondness for horses and dogs but not, apparently, his love of the chase and hunting with hounds. It is hardly surprising, then, that while Washington sought dogs to hunt and kill wolves, Jefferson quested for flock herders and guardians. In 1789, after working early in the summer with Lafayette on material that would be adopted as the Declaration of the Rights of Man and Citizen, he found time to collect several rustic French sheepdogs—*chiens de plaine*—or "shepherd dogs," as he called them. He clearly considered them among his most significant acquisitions during his five years in Europe as minister plenipotentiary, charged with negotiating treaties for the new American government. He was pleased enough with the dogs to breed them and give them to his friends as gifts. In 1791 he even took for himself a couple of puppies from a sheepdog his son-in-law was preparing to present to Washington as a gift.[19]

Legend has it that these dogs were briards, *bergers de Brie*, long-haired sheepdogs, as opposed to the short-haired beauceron, *bergers d'Beauce*, but legend is wrong. Both dogs, as they are known today, are creations of the middle to late nineteenth century, when dog breeding had captured the fancy of many wealthy people—not just nobles, but merchants and emerging industrialists—in Europe, England, and America. The briard made its appearance in Paris in 1809 and took its "modern" form around 1888 through crosses with the barbet, an all-purpose dog considered the forebear of the poodle, and the beauceron. The beauceron was so named around 1863. Both French breeds trace their origins to the *chiens de plaine*, of the Paris basin, a medium-sized, active, alert sheepdog, indifferent to human attention and rustic in appearance, that always bred to type. Georges-Louis Leclerc, Comte de Buffon, France's foremost naturalist, described the *chien de plaine* in his encyclopedic *Histoire naturelle, générale et particuliere*, as the ur-dog from which the nineteen other types of dog, including the mastiff, greyhound, and "great hound mongrel," were descended. Jefferson corresponded with Buffon, stayed at his house, and even wrote his *Notes on the State of Virginia* in response to Buffon's theory that North American animals were degenerate versions of their European cousins.

Jefferson continued to seek more authentic French sheepdogs in the first decades of the nineteenth century, although he knew that the world of dogs, like that of men, was changing. Like Washington, in his letters he mixed his quest for dogs with comments on politics and his own fears and desires. On March 2, 1809, the eve of his retirement to Monticello, with the clouds of war gathering, he wrote to P. S.

DuPont Nemours, preparing to embark for France: "Never did a prisoner, released from his chains, feel such relief as I shall on shaking off the shackles of power." Then the self-proclaimed "hermit of Monticello," who confessed he would have preferred science to politics, added a postscript: "If you return to us, bring a couple of pair of true-bred shepherd's dogs. You will add a valuable possession to a country now beginning to pay attention to the raising of sheep."[20]

In 1813, Lafayette sent him yet more sheepdogs, and Jefferson thanked him on November 30: "The shepherd dogs mentioned in yours of May 20, arrived safely, have been carefully multiplied, and are spreading in this and neighboring states where the increase of our sheep is greatly attended to." With the spread of merino sheep, farmers were producing enough wool to clothe "all our inhabitants," he boasted, and there was a spinning machine in every house.[21]

The merino arrived from Spain only after a struggle. In the seventeenth and eighteenth centuries, England attempted to ban sheep imports to its American colonies in an effort to force the settlers to purchase English wool. The ban failed, as smugglers evaded it, and at the time of independence, there were around 100,000 sheep in the United States. But new bloodlines were needed, which arrived in 1808 in the form of Spain's famous wool producer, and the rush was on to improve the American wool industry.

A few of the big, fierce Spanish dogs that guarded flocks in the Southwest came into the country with merinos, as did various crosses with them, but the big dogs never gained much of a foothold, despite the occasional appearance in agricultural journals of articles extolling their superior virtues. The tradition in America was primarily English and northern European, and that meant active herding dogs. From colonial times into the nineteenth century, drovers driving their mixed herds of livestock and hogs to markets in big cities like Charleston, New York, Baltimore, Philadelphia, and, later, Cincinnati used one dog to nip at the heels of bulls, "fat cows," calves, and hogs, often hard to manage because of their temperament, and a more gentle dog for sheep. By most accounts these dogs were the same basic animals, divided into drover's dogs, sheepdogs or shepherd's dogs, and butcher's dogs according to their disposition and training. Edward N. Wentworth, in his comprehensive history of sheep husbandry, *America's Sheep Trails*, describes them as "rough-coated dogs of rather general breeding," strongly built, intelligent, and black and white, blue or gray, white, fawn, brindled, or solid white in coat color. A bobtailed sheepdog from England could also be found in the colonies, although it was much different from the Old English sheepdog of modern times. A wolfish Hungarian sheepdog, the size of a Newfoundland, appeared along with dogs from Germany, usually brought by immigrants from their homeland because they desired to work livestock in ways they knew. But in typical fashion, the dogs often mixed, because of a shortage of similar dogs, and the successful crosses were put to work because those people familiar with sheepdogs knew each one was worth three to six men. Where labor was in short supply, the dogs were indispensable.[22]

Up to the spread of the railways in the nineteenth century, dogs and laborers—slaves in the South, apprenticed children and indentured servants in the North—were used to drive livestock into the cities, where it was sold at market to individual butchers, who killed and butchered it at their shops. In the seventeenth and early eighteenth centuries, these drives involved scores to hundreds of animals; by the late eighteenth century, the numbers could reach 1,000 or more in some areas. It was dirty, dangerous, arduous work, especially if the animals had to be bedded at night and guarded against rustlers, predators, and stampedes. Tough, independent, but biddable and savvy dogs were essential to maintaining control over the animals, maneuvering them into the corrals, retrieving strays, and holding them together in the face of natural disasters and urban obstacles, including stampeding horses and packs of street dogs.

The slaughter of bulls was a public spectacle in colonial cities, just as it was in England. Butchers collared and tied up the bulls and then turned loose one or more dogs to attack them. Ideally, one particularly bold animal would seize the bull by its nose and hold it or bring it to its knees to be killed. Snapping, snarling dogs, bulls bellowing in rage and panic, screaming people placing bets, spraying blood—all were part of the "sport," repeated when a captive bear was to be had as well. Butchers drained blood into the streets and threw unusable portions and offal into it—everyone threw their waste onto the streets—where dogs ate their fill.

Slave-owning Hunters

At the time of its independence, America was a fast-growing, complex, contradictory new world of class, caste, and racial divides, with cities like Philadelphia, Boston, Baltimore, New York, and Charleston connected to the international triangle trades in slaves, raw materials, and agricultural and industrial products linking Africa, the Americas, and Europe. Its economic and intellectual elite seized upon new ideas and made them their own. In many ways besides politics, Washington and Jefferson were in the vanguard of their time, although they were quintessentially of their time regarding slavery. They were among the first Americans, certainly among Southerners, to embrace new agricultural ideas involving plowing, crop rotation, and rejection of monocropping of tobaccos—pressed for funds, Jefferson returned to the practice toward the end of his life—and to breed for appearance and "improvement" of livestock. Each in his own way celebrated self-sufficiency, although Jefferson was better known for his reliance on the yeoman farmer and adherence to the cause of liberty and revolution. Washington, on the other hand, had an anticonsumer streak—he wrote from Philadelphia while president: "The practice of running to stores & co., for everything that is wanting or thought to be wanting, is the most ruinous custom that can be adopted and has proven the destruction of many a man before he was aware of the pernicious consequences."[23]

Yet for all their idealism, Washington and Jefferson and their colleagues from Maryland, Virginia, and the other Southern colonies, who helped create the United States, were among the richest men and largest slaveholders in the country. While they often condemned the institution of human bondage, they did not stop relying on slaves for labor and wealth. Washington himself was one of the largest slaveholders in Virginia, although he did free the slaves of Mount Vernon upon his death—something Jefferson, who had

taken his young slave Sally Hemings as a lover and fathered children by her, slave children, would not do. The society they inhabited and their own lives were built on slavery. By some estimates, 50
percent of all immigrants to the United States during the eighteenth
century were Africans, brought to these shores involuntarily and
sold as chattel. By the end of the eighteenth century, Maryland and
Virginia housed half of the 750,000 slaves in the country, and most
of the rest were found on the rich coastal plantations of the Caroli-
nas and Georgia. Virginia alone was home to 292,627 slaves in
1790—the year of the first official census—representing 41 percent
of its population. Yet only 34,026 Virginians, 7.6 percent, owned
slaves, and the number of those with more than ten slaves—taken
by many contemporary historians as the minimum for a "plantation"—was smaller, and shrank as the number of slaves increased.

In other states, many families did have one or more slaves,
which served to spread involvement in the cruel institution more
fully. Slaves' value went up markedly after their importation was
banned in 1808 and planters opening western Georgia, Alabama,
middle Tennessee, Louisiana, Mississippi, Florida, and east Texas to
cotton demanded more and more slaves. But the fact remains that
the vast majority of Southern whites did not own slaves. Most
Southern whites were squatters and hardscrabble farmers, drovers,
teamsters, and Crackers—the poor whites of the piney woods, eking
out a living however they could; or petty merchants, tradesmen, or
layabouts in small, stunted towns; or illiterate hunters and trappers.
Even in South Carolina, where, by the late eighteenth century, slaves
represented nearly a majority of the population—a status they
reached by 1840—and ownership of them was widespread, most of
the whites with slaves had fewer than five. People with more than
ten slaves were a small minority and those planters with more than
twenty a thin slice of society.

IN ESSENCE, slaves freed plantation owners and their families from
hard labor and allowed those who chose it to develop and pursue a
life that, to their minds, represented that of gentlemen or -women:

intellectual, paternal, politically involved, chivalrous, mannerly, patrician, demanding, autocratic, enlightened, skilled in the manly or womanly arts, and terrified that the slaves would launch a bloody rebellion. Washington's love of foxhunting on horseback with full-throated hounds was well known to his contemporaries and became so fixed in popular lore that he is often credited as the father not only of his country but also of American foxhunting. Of course, he was neither; the first pack of hounds dedicated to running foxes was reportedly brought to the young colony of Maryland by Reverend Robert Brooke in 1650, when he settled with his family in the area where the Potomac River flows into the Chesapeake Bay. The sport spread throughout the eighteenth century as a means of predator control and as a social event, but just as Washington's ability to walk away from power, and his integrity, pragmatism, and organizational skill helped create and establish on firm footing the young United States, so did his fame and reputation increase the popularity of foxhunting. Like Washington, other planters regularly ran their dogs alone or in the company of friends—visiting between plantations was common—and hosted organized hunts. These could be long affairs, especially for the relatively small number of large slaveholders, beginning with breakfast and ending with a champagne lunch, with wives and young ladies serving as enthusiastic spectators—and sometimes participants.

Although Washington preferred fox hunts and protected his deer from dogs and hunters—he protested angrily when a neighbor shot one—until they became garden-destroying pests; many Southern planters, following the sport of kings, ran deer with hounds, as well as bear, panthers, and bobcats, and even feral cattle. Like other organized hunts, these were social and cultural events that helped solidify alliances and common prejudices and beliefs. Hunts also served as venues for political campaigning and deal making. On other occasions, hunts presented an opportunity for men and women to meet and flirt or slip away for assignations. In most cases involving planters, slaves handled dogs throughout the hunt to drive the game or redirect the animals or even to assist in the kill when necessary. They also cared for people and horses and dressed the prey, supporting events intended to show the skill and courage of their participants—the white ones.

Early-nineteenth-century publications, like the *American Turf Register and Sporting Magazine* and *Spirit of the Times and Life in New York*, reported on fox hunts, generally from the South or Middle Atlantic states, where the sport was most popular, only slightly less regularly than they covered horse racing and fishing, two other major recreations. Often the accounts carried a moral lesson, proving that hunting was not mere sport or frivolity, and that hounds had the capacity for intelligence, sagacity, tenacity, morality, and even parental affection.

Yet most of the hunters at the end of the eighteenth century cared little for uniform packs or rigorous breeding, just as they cared little for agronomy or anything that cut into their cash crop, or any whiff of social reform. They would spend money for a pair of top hounds, but then complete the pack with dogs of "every possible variety and attitude." There were males, generally referred to as dogs, and females, called sluts or bitches. There were laggards, speed merchants, and "unintellectual and ill-natured" hounds always intent on the kill. There were dogs who gave full cry and those who had less mouth, dogs with great noses and dogs who apparently could barely smell game. On deer and bear hunts—used to obtain food and hides in many regions, especially those that were newly or sparsely settled—people included terriers and mastiffs to harass or fight with the bear. Cuban bloodhounds and greyhounds, the traditional slave- and Indian-hunting dogs, often appeared in the mix, but most of the dogs were curs, often worth a dozen well-bred hounds, when it came to work.[24]

An Odd Tandem: The Rise of Breedism and the Sagacious Dog

In their quest for top-quality dogs, Washington, Jefferson, and Lafayette were also involved in a movement to improve the animals through controlled, selective breeding that saw the differentiation of broad types of dogs into separate breeds based on size, coat color, and behavioral characteristics—retrieving, pointing, and the like. As the nineteenth century progressed, breeding and possession of those dogs, no less than of well-bred horses, cattle, goats, sheep, asses, mules, pigs, and fowl, became marks of accomplishment and wealth. Arguments regularly flared over which of the breeds was the most intelligent, sagacious, and talented, with more sane voices arguing that some of those refined creatures were actually losing their ability to work—an argument that reverberates more forcefully today.

The Cambridge physician Johannes Caius had first attempted a classification of English dogs in 1576 at the behest of the Swedish naturalist Conrad Gessner. *A Treatise on Englishe Dogges* sorted breeds by function, identifying the Bludhunde and Harrier for smelling; the Gasehunde for quick spying; the Grehunde for swiftness and quick spying; the Leuimer, a cross between the Harrier and Grehunde, for its nose and agility; the Tumbler, a sly dog that bunched game and grabbed its prey by the nose; the Theevishe Dogge, a poacher's cur; the Terrare, or terrier; two spaniels; a water spaniel, or retriever; the Shepherdes Dogge; and various mastiffs, among others. Just over a century later, Richard Blome published *The Gentleman's Recreation*, which added beagles, lurchers, and a few other dogs to Caius's list. The process of classifying dogs had begun—albeit primarily by function—and would accelerate in the next century with the rising interest in natural history and the notion that through reason a person could systematically make society, livestock, government, his farm, his life, and his dogs better.

The publication in 1735 of Carolus Linnaeus's binomial classification system for species, which included man as a mammal, had the effect of encouraging the burgeoning number of "naturalists" to focus on individual and group characteristics of animals and to see them as not so different from humans. Buffon's *Histoire naturelle*, which began to appear a decade later, explicitly challenged Linnaeus's notion of fixed species, arguing instead for one species emerging from one or more others, often through interbreeding, or nutritional or environmental causes. Buffon understood that organisms evolve or, to his mind, devolve or degenerate, in an organic way, but he could not quite make the leap to a full theory of evolution. Still, the work of these and other thinkers fed a boom in the pursuit of natural history, with many educated men—as well as newly rich merchants and industrialists trying to flex their financial muscle and their global power—wanting to study plants, animals, insects, rocks, and geography, especially in exotic, uncharted territory. Amateur naturalists began to deem the slightest variation in appearance or behavior in a group of animals or plants significant and declare it a new species. Following Buffon, Erasmus Darwin, grandfather of Charles, started thinking seriously about the origins of life, a study his grandson would pursue with great success. The philosopher Jeremy Bentham set forth a view of animals as moral beings capable of suffering. Naturalists like America's own William Bartram also believed that nearly all animals possessed feeling, emotion, and intellect, a view Charles Darwin articulated more fully.

It is axiomatic that, on the whole, dogs have been poorly served by humans, treated with such brutality, abuse, and contempt that even slaves and tortured Indians have found it degrading to be called a dog. According to their detractors, dogs are vile, foul, garbage- and excrement-eating creatures, indiscriminate fornicators, slavish beyond all reason and pride, disease-carrying killers. Kick them, the saying goes, and they beg for more. Their loyalty and devotion were seen as a character flaw or, sometimes, a tragedy. Without doubt, most dogs, like humans, have lived hard lives for millennia, but there were always many people who recognized their value and treated them with respect—indeed, like the disgraced Charles Lee, preferred their company to that of their fellow men. The number of those people is not easy to quantify at any time, much less during periods in which dogs operated in the background or became canine hamsters in order to power the machines of their masters, but there are accounts of dogs being mourned, celebrated, and protected dating to the beginning of recorded history. Among men and women of all backgrounds were those who recognized that mistreatment of the dog was abuse of its loyalty, a manifestation of the cruelty and evil of men.

Of course, larger questions revolve around what constitutes abuse at any period in history, in different cultures. Those definitions change over time and geography. For now, the point is that during the eighteenth century, a shift occurred in people's perception of dogs and other animals and of human relationships to them, the ramifications of which are being felt to this day. These changes derived from broader shifts in society during the Enlightenment—the expansion of the mercantile class and then the rise of industry, agricultural reform and the growing emphasis on selective breeding to improve animals, and the rise of natural history, fueled in part by exposure to new and exotic lands. In America the simultaneous and contradictory expansion of plantation slavery and political freedom and equality—not to mention attempts to arrest that expansion—contributed to and reflected the socio-economic, cultural, political, and intellectual crosscurrents sweeping the age.

Michel de Montaigne, whose essays were known to nearly all educated men, praised the talents and devotion of dogs and argued for the similarities of men and animals in the sixteenth century, and that view gained wider currency and strength throughout the seventeenth and eighteenth centuries, coincident in the latter with demands for greater individual liberty. Because of their utility, domestic animals were considered superior to wild animals until the diametrically opposite view began to emerge with the rise of Romanticism in the late eighteenth and early nineteenth centuries, with its celebration of the inherent virtue and goodness of a Nature beyond human control.

But even with change, the dog retained its place as humans' first animal. By the end of the eighteenth century the "sagacious," loyal, adoring, faithful dog was becoming a fixture in popular articles; together with the horse, the dog was deemed far more reliable and devoted than servants or slaves. But unlike the horse, the dog made the transition into the bourgeois home. This transition was shaped by the same intellectual, social, and economic forces that were reshaping society itself, and it was not always easy.

The Key of Frederick Town, Maryland, published a typically anonymous story entitled "The Faithful Dog" on February 17,

1798, about an army officer who, while hunting with his gun and dog, had wandered far from the post. Leaping from ambush, an Indian shot and wounded him, then knocked him on the head with his tomahawk and scalped him, leaving him for dead. The officer's dog, Tray, licked his wounds with "inexpressible tenderness" and applied all his sagacity to reviving his master and treating him, without success. Tray then ran to the nearby river and tried to persuade a couple of fishermen through his "natural language" to follow him. Suspecting the dog was a decoy, they refused, and Tray flew off again to tend his master before returning to the river and this time convincing the men that he might have hit upon some valuable game. Following the dog, they found the wounded officer, and he ultimately recovered, ever grateful to Tray for saving his life.[25]

Although 95 percent of the American population was rural, the cities were expanding fast through immigration and the growth of trade and industry, especially with the advent of the steam engine. Philadelphia stood first into the early decades of the nineteenth century, until upstart New York passed it in 1830 and never fell back. Dogs and horses moved into the cities along with the people who relied on them for transportation, companionship, protection, and labor. But the increase in animals in the cities exacerbated the kinds of health and safety problems that led to the war against dogs in New York decried by Washington. The constant fear of rabies spurred New York to pass an ordinance in 1801 forbidding dogs from running at large between July 15 and November 1. Owners of loose dogs were subject to a $5 fine, the dog to execution. In 1803 the fine was increased to $25, and half that could be paid to anyone who informed on a dog. But as always, the laws proved largely unenforceable for lack of cooperation, if not active resistance.[26]

About the same time, urbanites also started denouncing bullbaiting as cruel and inhumane. For decades, proponents of the practice put them off, claiming not only that the torture improved the flavor of the meat but also that opponents were out to destroy "rural sports"—the same argument used today by proponents of foxhunting. In Britain, bullbaiting was banned in 1835, and dogfighting, which could be conducted in more secluded venues, immediately replaced it as a favored blood sport. American states and cities followed suit more slowly, with New York City outlawing bullbaiting and dogfighting in 1867, although both legally continued elsewhere for decades to come. A subculture of illegal dogfighting continues to flourish.

Dog ownership cut across class—and even racial, where not illegal—lines, and many wealthy owners of purebred dogs understood that any campaign against dogs recognized no distinctions between their "superior," well-bred dogs and the curs of the poor. Rather, the divide then and now was between those who feared and disliked, even loathed, dogs, and those who welcomed and loved them. That said, the owners of well-bred dogs generally considered their dogs smarter, better behaved, and worthy of different treatment from the common roaming cur or rough working dog, just as they themselves were superior to the owners of those animals. It was an easy step from there, if one possessed a modicum of charity, to wanting to improve the lot of dogs, children, slaves, and women— the downtrodden in general.

Hard-pressed were the short-legged turnspits running in shifts on their millwheels, the dogs dragging carts of milk, rags, and offal dredged from the gutters, and any other working dogs. Generally, when they faltered, they died. Scientists regularly dissected dogs and other small animals alive, without a thought to their suffering, and so, too, did Jefferson, with such frequency that in 1800 the Federalists accused him of "having turned Monticello into 'Dog's Misery.'" It was as much a political attack as it was a protest against animal suffering, of course, but it also reflected the forces already swirling around dogs and humans, reshaping their relationship. Dogs and humans had already been together for tens of thousands of years and colonized the world, but the next 200 years were to bring greater changes in their circumstances than any they had yet experienced, as industrialization, global communication, and trade remade the world.[27]

5

Crossing the Great Divide: Travels with Dog

⌀

INDEPENDENCE SECURED, Jefferson dreamed the rest of the continent. He approached George Rogers Clark, the Kentuckian who had secured the Northwest Territory during the Revolutionary War and who was also a contributor to Jefferson's natural history collection—he had promised to hunt for a mammoth fossil—about taking an expedition across the Mississippi to the West Coast. Jefferson knew the Spanish were trading from New Mexico up the Mississippi and its major tributaries, including the Missouri, north into the Plains. More disturbing, he had heard rumors that the British were ready to invest money in exploring from the Mississippi to California, he told Clark in a letter of December 4, 1783, and he feared they were intent on colonization. Would Clark, he asked, be willing to lead an American expedition if Jefferson and his friends could raise the necessary funds?[1]

Clark declined and later recommended his younger brother William, a skilled backwoodsman and negotiator with Indians in his own right. Jefferson went to Europe in 1784, where as minister plenipotentiary he negotiated treaties, helped the Revolution in

France, hunted for gadgets and sheepdogs, and pursued more physical pleasures. But upon his return, he continued to push for an expedition that would catalog the geography and natural resources of the continent. The traders and long hunters were not prone to collecting botanical or animal samples or describing and mapping where they had been—why give away your secrets to the competition?—so Jefferson and his colleagues knew they had to find a man of some knowledge, objectivity, and curiosity. They needed maps and honest assessments.

At the time, the individual most capable of such an effort intellectually, if not physically or psychologically, was William Bartram, who had traveled thousands of miles with his father, John, and on his own through the South and Florida in the 1760s and 1770s, documenting plants and animals. Named Puc Puggy, or Flower Hunter, by the Seminole Indians, he was deemed America's only living zoologist of international stature in 1794, three years after publication of *Travels through North and South Carolina, Georgia, East & West Florida, the Cherokee Country, the Extensive Territories of the Muscogules, or Creek Confederacy, and the Country of the Chactaws: Containing an Account of the Soil and Natural Productions of those regions, together with observations on the manners of the Indians*. Generally called *Travels*, it is an exuberant account of his solo four-year journey, 1773 to 1777, that reaches a crescendo when he hits the St. Johns River in Florida and encounters twenty-five- to thirty-pound largemouth bass; ten- to twelve-foot rattlesnakes, thick as tree limbs; vast, spreading live oaks, up to eighteen feet in girth; fifty-foot-tall cypresses, twelve feet in diameter; and alligators that gathered in such great numbers and were so ferocious that they dammed the river and threatened to consume him and his boat. His descriptions of Florida's pellucid springs rushing forth from underground caverns inspired the English Romantic poets Samuel Taylor Coleridge and William Wordsworth, as well as generations of naturalists, including Henry David Thoreau.

Bartram did not travel with dogs, but he described the Indian dogs he encountered as similar to wolves and also recognized among the Indians common curs, adopted from Europeans. In middle

Florida, Bartram encountered a black dog "which seemed to differ in no respect from the wolf of Florida, except his being able to bark as the common dog," who spent his life guarding and herding the horses of his Seminole owner. Raised with the horses from birth, the dog would leave his herd only in the evening to get food from his master. On watch, he would move quickly, Bartram says, to head off and bring back to the herd any horse that wandered off.[2]

Brilliant though he was, Bartram was more widely known in Europe than in his homeland, where his fame and influence did not reach beyond a tight circle of intelligentsia. Among the subscribers to the first—and for 138 years only—American edition of *Travels* were George Washington, John Adams, and Thomas Jefferson. Many of Bartram's admirers traveled to his botanical garden at Kingsessing, Pennsylvania, founded by his father on the banks of the Schuylkill River, to seek his advice.

Samuel Hearne and the Coppermine River

A year after Bartram's masterpiece appeared, there came from England Samuel Hearne's posthumously published account of an incredible journey with Indian guides and their families from Fort Prince of Wales, where the Churchill River entered Hudson's Bay, that ultimately covered some 3,500 miles in nineteen months. A young ensign with the Hudson's Bay Company, Hearne was instructed to search for rich copper mines reported to exist on an unexplored river in north-central Canada, somewhere above Lake Athabasca. He was also to follow that river, which he called the Coppermine, to the Arctic Ocean, then called the Northern Ocean, or Polar Sea. If along the way he proved the existence of the fabled Northwest Passage that for more than a century had eluded mariners seeking to sail through or above North America from Europe to Asia, thereby avoiding the perils of the two southern capes, so much the better. Having organized the expedition to counter long-standing criticism that it had done too little to explore northern Canada and exploit its potential, the Hudson's Bay Company also ordered Hearne to map and claim all territory he traversed.

Hearne set out in November 1769 with two white companions and a group of Indians who more or less lived around the company's Fort Prince of Wales, now Churchill, Manitoba. He aborted the trip almost as soon as he began it, after the Indian guides stole the food and supplies. He started again in February 1770, this time the only white man with three "northern Indians" and two "southern Indians." They added more northern Indians, but once provisions ran low, the northerners stuck together, cutting out Hearne and his southern Indian companions. After numerous difficulties, Hearne reached 63°10' north and 10°40' west—closer to the Arctic Circle than any white man had traveled by land in North America. But after taking his reading, he accidentally broke his quadrant and decided to head back to Fort Prince of Wales for a new one. Along the way he suffered more deprivation because of desertion by the Indians, and in one instance actually had a young man steal his gun. The Indian returned it because he lacked ammunition, but the event stuck with Hearne as he labored toward the fort, picking up as companions a growing number of Indians with furs to trade. Finally he met Matonabbee, a "famous" and "responsible" leader who had been raised at the fort and agreed to escort Hearne there. As they neared the fort one evening in November 1770, Hearne's dog, "a valuable brute, was frozen to death; so that his sledge, I was obliged to haul." Hearne found that pulling a load without a dog was exhausting, and he then understood why the Indians relied on them.[3]

On December 7, 1770, with Matonabbee as his guide, Hearne began his third trip in just over a year, and this time he made it up the Coppermine River to the Arctic Ocean. In nineteen months, he traveled 3,500 miles, most of it on foot. The Indians generally refused to travel without their families, Hearne wrote in his *Journey from Prince of Wales's Fort in Hudson's Bay to the Northern Ocean*, but for the final push they left behind their "women, children, dogs, heavy baggage, and other incumbrances" so they could conduct a lightning raid on a group of Inuit living on the Coppermine River and press quickly onward. It was bloody business, and Hearne liked it no better than the Indians' habit of killing excessive numbers of deer and letting the surplus feed other predators and scavengers. But he could not dissuade them from the practice, and the Hudson's Bay Company itself was built on overkilling.

Hearne was the first white man to see much of the country he crossed, and his observations of the lives and habits of the Chipewyan Indians, whom he calls northern Indians, and the Cree, or southern Indians, including the place of dogs in their cultures, have proved invaluable. So, too, have his straightforward descriptions of the land and its plants and animals. Henry David Thoreau, that voracious consumer of natural history books by travelers, among others, knew and celebrated his work.

Although the results of his trip were widely known, his manuscript collected dust at Fort Prince of Wales. Hearne became factor at the fort in 1776, but even then he apparently made no effort to publish his journal. After France entered the War of Independence, General Jean-François la Pérouse took the fort and sent Hearne back to England with his manuscript, having gotten a promise from Hearne that he would have it printed. But the traveler had waited too long. Official geographers, who had never seen Canada, challenged his accomplishments, and his manuscript remained unpublished until after his death in 1793. The book failed to correct the record; in 1818, Admiralty Secretary Sir John Barrow denounced Hearne in his definitive history of polar exploration.

In 1819, Barrow sent a thirty-one-man expedition under John Franklin to travel by land from Hudson's Bay to the Coppermine River, paralleling Captain William Parry's sea search for the Northwest Passage. To the chagrin of Barrow and many other experts, Franklin's expedition confirmed that Hearne had, indeed, reached the Arctic Ocean at the mouth of the Coppermine. But Franklin himself proved a hapless Arctic traveler, not least because he used no dogs. Ignoring the advice of his Indian guides to cache food for winter and wait out the cold months in warm quarters, he pressed on, outstripping his food supplies. The expedition splintered, and some men turned to cannibalism in a desperate effort to survive, while Franklin led a small party in search of relief. Fully a third of his men died, but Franklin was accorded a hero's welcome in England and promoted to captain. His book, unlike Hearne's *Journey*, became a best-seller.

Alexander Mackenzie Hits the Pacific, the Second Time Out

Exploration of the continent continued through the 1780s, as fur traders vied for new markets. Peter Pond, a Connecticut-born adventurer and fur trader who had charted the area surrounding Lake Athabasca, presented his map to the Continental Congress, with a proposal that it fund his search for the Northwest Passage. The Congress rejected Pond's plan. A temperamental, bombastic man, he became a partner in the North West Company, based in Montreal, and in 1787 took on as his protégé Alexander Mackenzie, a young Scotsman sent to Canada from New York by his loyalist parents during the Revolution. The following year, the company, in a rare act, expelled Pond from the backcountry for excessive violence, including two murders he had either committed or commissioned— the evidence is unclear.

In 1789, looking for a way to the Pacific, Mackenzie discovered the river that now bears his name and followed it north to the Arctic Ocean with twelve companions, including four voyageurs, plus the wives of two; an Indian chief with his two wives and two followers; and a German fur trader. The explorers paralleled to the west Hearne's trek up the Coppermine River and, in so doing, further confirmed the absence of a Northwest Passage in that part of Canada. Mackenzie also built Fort Chipewyan on Lake Athabasca in order to open more of the interior to the fur trade for the North West Company. Successful though his exploration was soon considered, Mackenzie had obviously missed the Pacific by a considerable distance, so he decided to try again—after learning some navigation in London.

Returning to Canada from London, Mackenzie traveled from

Montreal to Fort Chipewyan, headed west from there in late summer 1792, and wintered at Fort Park, at the confluence of the Peace
and Smoky rivers. His expedition included Alexander Mackay,
Joseph Landry, five French-Canadian voyageurs, and two Indian
hunters and interpreters in a large canoe, towing supplies behind in
a smaller craft. He also had an unnamed, undescribed dog, mentioned only when it got into difficulty or did something strange or
heroic. On May 9, the group left their fort, bound for the ocean.
Hunters and scouts walked the shore while the voyageurs drove the
boats with the current. On May 19, as the party approached the
Peace River Canyon, now just west of the Alberta–British Columbia border, Mackenzie and Mackay spotted a herd of bison with
calves but held their fire for fear of alerting unknown Indians to
their presence. "We, however, sent our dog after the herd," Mackenzie reported in his journal, "and a calf was soon secured by him."[4]

Unable to safely pass the rapids running through the canyon,
which terrified some of the most experienced voyageurs into pleading unsuccessfully with Mackenzie to turn back, the group took to
land for a long portage that shredded the soles of their moccasins
after only a few hours of walking. Parched and exhausted, they
completed the portage and, nearing the Rocky Mountains, encountered tens of thousands of beavers that had cleared acres of poplars,
jamming and damming the river so thoroughly that the men had to
stop regularly to reseal their battered canoes. Finally Mackenzie
sent Mackay and one of the Indians to seek a "broad river" running
out of the mountains to the sea. They reported a river filled with
dangerous deadfalls, telling Mackenzie that "the country through
which they passed was morass, and almost impenetrable wood." At
one point, the dog, who had accompanied them, fell into the river
and was swept by the fast current under one of the deadfalls. He
was rescued, Mackay told Mackenzie, "with very great difficulty."[5]

A month after the dog killed the bison calf, the expedition
passed over the Rockies and entered what Mackenzie believed was
the "great river" to the Pacific, but he was too optimistic. The river
was Herrick Creek, a tributary of a tributary of what is now called

the Fraser River, which does drain into the Pacific. Progressing by water, they shot at two deer, wounded one, and sent the Indians ashore to track it. The dog followed but proved he was better at attacking game than waiting patiently for someone else to bring it down, when he scared off yet a third deer as the Indians prepared to shoot it.

On June 25 the party took off overland for the ocean. The Indian guides were fed up and in full revolt, and everyone and the dog were in agony from the ceaseless attacks of sand flies. It was an arduous hike and a hungry one, the local Indians having hunted and trapped out most of the game to trade to the Russian merchants who regularly coasted the shore from their outposts in Alaska. Most of the Indians lived on salmon and other fish they caught in weirs built into earthen dams across the rivers and streams. When the curious Mackenzie attempted to view the constructions, however, the Indians held him at bay, apparently fearing that if he gained knowledge of their technology, he would ruin the fishing—and them.

At the Great Village of the Bella Coola Indians, on the eponymous river, the travelers again took to the water and by July 19 were within sight of the Pacific. But Mackenzie's joy was much diminished, for at the Great Village "we had lost our dog, a circumstance of no small regret to me." He finally left a modest calling card three days later in a rock: "Alexander Mackenzie, from Canada, by land, the twenty-second of July, one thousand seven hundred and ninety-three."[6]

Mackenzie and his men tarried long enough to examine the seal traps of the natives, then returned to the Great Village of the Bella Coola, where, after welcoming ceremonies, Mackenzie was told that his dog "had been howling about the village ever since we left it, and that they had reason to believe he left the woods at night to eat the fish he could find about the houses." Mackenzie promptly sent off his second in command, Mackay, and one of the voyageurs to find the dog, but they failed.[7]

Leaving the village, the travelers followed a well-worn—several-thousand-year-old—Indian trail into the mountains, toward home.

Along the way, "we all felt the sensation of having found a lost friend at the sight of our dog, but he appeared, in a great degree, to have lost his former sagacity. He ran in a wild way backwards and forwards, and though he kept our road, I could not induce him to acknowledge his master." The mere use of the word *sagacity* indicates that this was a European dog, perhaps brought by Mackenzie from England. "The poor animal," Mackenzie writes, "was reduced almost to a skeleton, and we occasionally dropped something to support him, and by degrees he recovered his former sagacity." Later, he joined the ten men, for none were lost on this excursion, in consuming an entire elk in one sitting—voyageurs were known, like the Indians, for their enormous capacity for food, but then they were burning thousands of calories daily. Although nameless, the dog clearly was a full member of the expedition. Whether that was unusual is difficult to say. Hearne had a dog, but it was not in the same class as Mackenzie's. Indeed, from this time, the dog became a standard member of many expeditions and journeys in America, often in self-conscious imitation of previous treks. Frequently the intrepid traveler picked up the dog along the way, almost as part of the expedition's supplies.[8]

From the time they left Fort Fork until their return to Fort Chipewyan, Mackenzie and his men averaged twenty-five miles a day walking and thirty-six miles a day by water. They crossed the Rockies and reached the Pacific in two months. Traveling under the auspices of the North West Company, Mackenzie and his companions became the first white men on record to cross North America from coast to coast by land. At the time, the North West Company traded more furs through Quebec and Montreal than the Hudson's Bay Company handled, and that discrepancy increased into the nineteenth century. In 1798 alone, the year before Mackenzie quit the North West Company, trappers and Indians brought in 200,000 pelts, more than half of them beaver. That was five times the haul of Hudson's Bay. The two companies finally merged in 1821—the height of the Rocky Mountain fur trade—as the Hudson's Bay Company, which then had a virtual lock on the Canadian fur trade.

Lewis and Clark with Seaman and the Corps of Discovery

The year of Mackenzie's journey, Jefferson, while secretary of state, pursued his own dreams of exploration, persuading the American Philosophical Society to send the French naturalist André Michaux along the Mississippi, but the scientist proved a spy for France against Spain, and the expedition collapsed. Jefferson took no further action until Mackenzie's ghostwritten account of his voyages to the Arctic and Pacific oceans appeared—first in England, in 1801, and then in the United States, in 1802. Jefferson read *Voyages* and worried all the more, for Mackenzie proposed that British fur traders establish a fort with overland links to Montreal at the mouth of the Columbia River.

Alarmed by the possibility of a British advance, Jefferson twice asked Bartram to serve as chief scientist on major explorations of the Red River and the American West, but Puc Puggy declined because of his age and bad health. He was over sixty and often had eye problems, perhaps from syphilis, and other ailments. In 1802, Jefferson chose his personal secretary, Meriwether Lewis, to lead a Corps of Discovery, and completion of the Louisiana Purchase from France the following year gave more impetus to an expedition beyond the Mississippi and lower Missouri to the Pacific, country largely unknown to the whites. Voyageurs trapping and trading up the Missouri brought their pelts to the Spanish-controlled Missouri Fur Company, run out of St. Louis by the Scotsman James Mackay. Other residents in the vicinity of St. Louis were settlers from Tennessee and Kentucky, including Daniel Boone and his family, who had received a Spanish land grant. By all accounts they were a motley crew, willing to bet all they had on a horse race or rifle shot.

Despite those scattered outposts, crossing the continent to the Pacific to gather specific knowledge and attempt to secure the allegiance of the Indians represented a bold adventure. On his own initiative, Lewis approached William Clark, his former commander in the battle for the Northwest Territory, and offered him the co-command at equal rank, but at the last minute the Department of War refused to make the appointment. While Lewis recognized Clark as captain—as has history—officially the redheaded co-commander was commissioned a second lieutenant, an insult he never forgot nor forgave. Indeed, at the expedition's end, he mailed the commission back to the War Department.

From all indications, Lewis and Clark were a well-matched team of opposites: the seemingly manic-depressive, or perhaps only depressive, Lewis, mercurial, devoted to his dog and task and notions of discipline; and the pragmatic and oddly romantic, slaveholding Clark, protector of Sacagawea from her cowardly, lazy, abusive husband, Toussaint Charbonneau. Clark adopted and educated their son, Jean Baptiste, born during the Corps's winter at Fort Mandan, an act of philanthropy and friendship sometimes read as evidence, along with his treatment of her, of an affair with the young woman. The assertion is probably untrue. The Indians generally viewed Clark as a mighty medicine man because he could heal many of their maladies from the Corps's meager medical kit, and respected him throughout his life as an honest broker.

The high point of Lewis's life, on the other hand, was the journey; he was lost back in society. After botching a stint as governor of the Louisiana Territory and failing to get his journals together for publication—the journal of Patrick Gass, a carpenter who joined the expedition at the beginning of 1804, was actually published first, in 1807—Lewis committed suicide at Grinder's Stand, a cramped log inn on the Natchez Trace, on the night of October 10, 1809, three years after the end of their adventure. Rumors and whispers say he was murdered, but they appear to be founded only in a desire to deprive the man of his mental illness.[9]

The journals provide a fascinating view of the journey, with Clark copying Lewis or vice versa, usually verbatim but occasionally altered, like a slightly out-of-phase mirror, especially in the sequences about dining on dog. Apparently alone of all the party, Clark hated eating dog, was revolted by even the thought, while the rest, including Lewis, considered dog more nutritious than any meat but bison. Clark wrote alone for months; Lewis sometimes did most of the original writing. Their spelling, especially Clark's, is idiosyncratic even for the time, and their entries are usually dry and businesslike, mere records of events. But the facts in those records are far better than any speculation would have been, providing the nit and grit, the insects and petty grievances, the constant quest for food, the struggles during their wet winter on the coast, and occasional glimpses of tedium, anger, joy, relief, or sheer wonderment mixed with awe, as when they encountered grizzly bears.

In the years between the journals' first appearance in print and the beginning of the expedition's bicentennial in 2003, and especially during the past decade, Lewis and Clark's exploration has been dissected and bisected, their trail mapped, their "discoveries" and descriptions of flora and fauna confirmed, their role in opening the lucrative and ruinous Rocky Mountain fur trade and inspiring the legendary mountain men analyzed, forgotten, and resurrected. The men were renowned, their accomplishments little appreciated. The expedition became mythic, a model for others to follow, including Bible-toting Jedediah Strong Smith, the greatest of the mountain men, who loved exploring more than trapping beaver and so mapped much of the West, including California. Lewis's dog, Seaman, the energetic Newfoundland who traveled with them every step of the way, has also been celebrated in children's books and on film. (Until the historian Donald Jackson corrected a transcription error in 1987—easy to make, given the poor penmanship of both Lewis and Clark—the dog was often called Scannon.) The same is not true of the anonymous Indian dogs, who kept the Corps alive and healthy for months on end.

Lewis said that he bought Seaman for twenty dollars, outside Pittsburgh, while on his way to meet Clark in late August or early September 1803, to accompany him on his long, uncertain journey because he considered him a trainable hunter, sagacious companion, and courageous guard. Seaman's age, like his appearance, was unrecorded, but his behavior and stamina indicate he was no puppy. Most people paint him black, but he could as easily have been black and white with a rough coat.

Seaman first appears in the journals on September 11, 1803, when Lewis, traveling the Ohio River, observes a large number of squirrels swimming the river from west to east. "I made my dog take as many each day as I had occasion for," he writes, "they were fat and I thought them when fried a pleasant food—many of these squirrels were black, they swim very light in the water and make pretty good speed—my dog was of the newfoundland breed very active strong and docile, he would take the squirrel in the water kill them and swimming bring them back in his mouth to the boat." The hunt continued daily until Lewis picked up Clark at Clarksville, Indian Territory, on September 15.[10]

Off they went to meet their men, arriving on November 16 at a camp of Delaware and Shawnee Indians near the confluence of the Ohio and Mississippi rivers. Lewis records that "one of the Shawwnees a respectable looking Indian offered me three beveskins for my dog with which he appeared much pleased . . ." Lewis refused the offer, noting that he had chosen the dog as his companion and had already paid hard cash for him.[11]

During that first winter in Camp Dubois, near St. Louis, they gathered intelligence of the Missouri and prepared for their expedition, collecting the men for their Corps of Discovery and the *engagés*, the keelboat men who would literally haul them and their supplies up the Missouri as high as the Mandan village in what is now North Dakota. That village marked the beginning of terra incognita for America and thus was where the expedition's real work began. Still, the trip there was no fun. The Missouri was filled with snags, sandbars, and sawyers—trees sunk on end and waving in the current that could rip the bottom out of boats that ventured over them. Mosquitoes, ticks, dysentery, and boils plagued the men. Meanwhile, the hunters stalked the shore, shooting deer in what is now Missouri, and bison and elk once the ecosystem changed to prairie above what became Leavenworth, Kansas.

On July 15, 1804, Clark went ashore to look for a village of Missouri Indians with 300 warriors, 500 children, and 300 pack dogs— no word on the women—that French explorer and fur trader Etienne Veniard de Bourgmont had stumbled upon in 1724, but it

had vanished, the victim of war or disease. Earlier that day, the boat
had gotten snarled in driftwood, forcing an early stop for dinner—
the midday meal—at a beaver lodge. Seaman seized the opportunity
to invade the lodge and drive the beaver out, a feat given the
beaver's ability to inflict considerable damage on any dog that en-
ters its element, as Seaman later discovered.

Hunting ashore on July 18, 1804—neither Clark nor Lewis enjoyed spending time on the slow-moving keelboat when there was so
much to see and do ashore—Clark saw a starving dog near present-
day Penn, Nebraska, and, assuming that he had been abandoned by
hunters, "gave him some meat, he would not come near."[12]

They were perpetually rescuing dogs early on and observing
their uses: for example, Clark records on August 24, 1804, that the
Sioux "follow the buffalow, & kill them on foot, they pack their
Dogs, which carry their Bedn." The next day, eight miles north of
the Vermillion River in South Dakota, Seaman overheated during a
hike across open prairie to investigate a spirit mound, where evil little people were said to ambush approaching Indians. The double-
coated hunter was clearly no match for the brutal heat of the Plains
in August; indeed, the men barely were. The party had also entered
Sioux country, and dog, raw and cooked, was on the menu whenever they met a new band. They attended a feast among the somewhat threatening Teton Sioux on September 26 and were served,
Clark writes, "the most delicate parts of the dog," which were raw.
He ate "little of dog."[13]

The Corps continued its long haul upstream, finally reaching
the territory of the Mandans in late October. The Mandans were
the "white" or "Celtic" Indians, believed to be descended from a
colony established around 1170 by Madog, son of the Prince of
Wales. The colony failed, but according to a legend popular well
into the twentieth century, the survivors became the Mandans of
the upper Missouri. Legend aside, the Mandans were American Indians, as far as anyone can tell, their reportedly light skin, hair, and
eyes, their civility and openness to white visitors, their supposed
Celtic locutions, their elaborate and painful rituals, the variety of
dogs they maintained, including some European breeds, notwith-

standing. When Lewis and Clark arrived, they were a people decimated, like their cousins the Hidatsas—called at the time Minitarees
or Gros Ventres—by smallpox brought by fur traders in the 1780s
and by the expanding Sioux. Moving west across the Missouri, the
Sioux were transforming themselves from woodlands Indians into
High Plains bison hunters and horsemen, among the largest, most
powerful, and most feared of the nineteenth-century tribes.

The Corps settled that winter in Fort Mandan, met Charbonneau and Sacagawea, the young Lemhi Shoshone slave Charbonneau had purchased to be his wife, and soon added them and her
newly born son to the party. The Mandan and Hidatsa chiefs periodically brought dogs for their visitors to eat—all but Clark—while
the women gave most of the enlisted men syphilis. It was a cold,
long winter, but by April 7, 1805, the river was clear enough of ice
for Lewis to send the keelboat back to St. Louis. Clark started upriver with the smaller boats, the pirogues, while Lewis walked
along the shore. The entire party numbered thirty-six, including
Clark's slave York, Charbonneau, Sacagawea, their child, and the
engagés and enlisted men.

BUT THEY WERE NOT WALKING into completely unknown country. British agents from the North West Company were already
trading whiskey to the Assiniboin and Cree for pemmican and bison grease, to fuel their voyageurs, and for wolf pelts. And, of
course, the Indians were around, if not immediately apparent.

On April 14, an Indian dog left behind by its people approached
the camp and followed the men until May 2, when, above the confluence of the Yellowstone and Missouri rivers, one of them shot it
for repeatedly stealing food—there is no indication that they ate the
dog. In between, on April 22, Lewis was out walking with Seaman
when a buffalo calf "attached itself to me and continued to follow
close at my heels until I embarked and left. It appeared alarmed at
my dog, which was probably the cause of it's so readily attaching itself to me." That grants considerable consciousness and thoughtful-

ness to the bison, since there is no reason a bison would expect that a two-legged creature—or any creature—would succor it, but it makes more sense than most other explanations. That same day, Clark watched wolves cut a calf out of a herd of bison and kill it while the others continued on their course after realizing they had no way to save it.[14]

SEAMAN APPEARED frequently in the journals that spring as a hunter or a fugitive. Lewis again signaled his dog's importance in his entry of April 25: "my dog had been absent during the last night, and I was fearfull that we had lost him altogether, however, much to my satisfaction he joined us at 8 O'clock this morning." The dog had probably run off in search of game or a dog in heat while Lewis and Clark were pursuing their continuous hunt to keep the ravenous Corps in meat. On May 5, Seaman took matters into his own teeth, so to speak, when he caught a "goat"—a pronghorn— "which," Lewis boasts, "he overtook by superior fleetness," adding, to be fair, "the goat it must be understood was with young and ex- treemly poor." That qualifier did not stop Clark from calling the conquest "a fair race" in his own entry for that day.[15]

Clark also recorded, as did Lewis, that he and George Drouil- lard, known throughout the journals as Drewyer, one of the best hunters in the Corps, had killed a grizzly bear that same day, a first for the party. Drouillard was half French and half Shoshone and so served as an interpreter in the often laborious process of translating from English to French and then into an Indian dialect and back again. That kill inspired many members of the Corps to seek their own grizzly, Lewis reports, while others wanted nothing to do with the big creatures that could rip the face off a man in an instant. Lewis took pleasure in hunting, no matter the game: "now the only amusement for Capt. C. and myself to kill as much meat as the party can consume . . ."[16]

Two weeks later, amusement turned to near tragedy. A hunter wounded a beaver, which most of the men considered good food, especially the tail, as well as valuable for its fur, and Seaman, as was his custom, dived into the water for the kill. This time the beaver struck back, biting Seaman through his hind leg. With difficulty, Lewis stanched the blood flow, although he feared that the bite had severed an artery and that, despite his efforts, the wound would prove fatal. More dispassionate, Clark says, "Capt. Lewis's dog was badly bitten by a wounded beaver and was near bleeding to death." There is not talk of an artery, which they would have had no capacity to repair. Seaman recovered.[17]

May 25 found Clark staring into the distance at the Rocky Mountains, a sighting he half doubted until the next morning, when he saw them more clearly. That afternoon, Lewis saw them as well. They then had a real sense of progress, which was nearly obliterated two nights later when a bison bull crossed the river and panicked upon finding himself in one of their pirogues rather than on firm ground. The bull bolted up the bank and was, as Lewis told it the next day, a mere eighteen inches from trampling the heads of some of the sleeping men before the sentinel could turn him. To the sentinel's dismay, the rampaging bison then charged across the camp, nearly crushing more men before taking direct aim at the tepee where Lewis, Clark, Sacagawea, Charbonneau, and Drouillard slept. This time Seaman stood his ground, barking, and forced the bull to turn slightly to the right, so that it missed the tepee and cleared the camp. By then the men were awake and ready for battle, but there was scant damage. Only York's rifle and a blunderbuss in the pirogue were broken.

Pushing through the Missouri Breaks toward the Great Falls of the river, the group found the wolves ubiquitous in their studious attendance on the buffalo and so fearless that Clark walked up and killed one with a spear he carried. Game was abundant: Clark identified one site as "a buffalo jump," where Indians drove bison into a depression and then slaughtered them. Below the Great Falls, Lewis observed scores of drowned bison upon which wolves and grizzly bears feasted. He speculated that on the steep trails down to the river, leading animals in the herd either lost their footing and fell or were pushed into the water by bison following them. Swept under by the swift current and battered against rocks, they drowned.

The abundance of game drove Seaman to distraction, especially before and during the portage around the falls. On June 19, he sounded so alarmed just after dark that Lewis ordered one of the sergeants to check for Indians or grizzlies—referred to as white bears for their light coloration—but the scout soon reported that another buffalo bull had been swept past the camp while trying to cross the river. During the portage nine days later, a grizzly stole thirty pounds of "buffalo suet," which was used for making pemmican, from a rack about thirty yards from camp. "My dog seems to be in a constant state of alarm with these bears and keeps barking all night," Lewis writes on June 27. The next night, portage complete, he complains that the bears are so numerous and aggressive that he dares not send any man out alone, for fear he will be mauled. But Seaman's nightly patrols seem to keep the bears out of camp.[18]

Seaman constantly proved his mettle and suffered with the men during this stage of the expedition. On July 15, near what is now called the Smith River, Lewis reports that Seaman pursued a deer Drouillard had shot into the river, where it had fled. He "caught it drowned it and brought it to the shore at our camp." When the Corps encountered a flock of geese on the Missouri less than a week later, Seaman caught several, "as he frequently dose," Lewis says with apparent pride. But a few days later, near the three forks of the Missouri, they encountered vast stretches of "needle and thread grass" with barbed seeds that "penetrate our mockersons and leather leging's and give us great pain until they are removed. my poor dog suffers with them excessively, he is constantly biting and scratching himself as if in a rack of pain." Prickly pears, mosquitoes, and biting gnats added to the misery of people and beast.[19]

They crossed the Continental Divide on August 13, 1805, at Lemhi Pass, looking all the while for Sacagawea's relatives. On first encounter, the Shoshone dogs proved less shy than their owners, and Lewis cleverly thought he would attach some beads to their necks to show that he and his people were friendly. The dogs would have none of that. But Sacagawea soon recognized her relatives, and a deer from Drouillard also helped turn fear into curiosity. "Every article about us appeared to excite astonishment in their minds," Lewis writes, "the appearance of the men, their arms, the canoes, our manner of working them, the black man york and the sagacity of my dog were equally objects of admiration." Finally, they were able to trade with the Shoshone for horses.[20]

The Corps crossed the Bitterroot Mountains at Lolo Pass in late September and early October, following the Clearwater River toward the Snake River, and ultimately the Columbia to the Pacific. But once they were across the mountains, the hunting turned bad, and they were forced to eat fish and roots, supplemented occasionally with horse meat. The diet caused the hardworking men to lose muscle mass. On October 10, Clark traded for more fish and dogs from the Nez Percé, who were not dog eaters, and then expounded on the situation and his own difficulties in his entries for October 13 and 14: "our diet extremely bad haveing nothing but roots and dried fish to eate, all of the party have greatly the advantage of me, in as much as they relish the flesh of the dogs. Several of which we purchased of the natives for to add to our store of fish and roots &c. &c." Soon the Nez Percé were bringing them dogs for trade. After leaving Nez Percé country, they bought forty dogs from the Yakima on October 18, and Clark himself had little choice but to partake, since the river was filled with dead and dying fish he feared to eat. None of the men seemed to understand that the salmon died after spawning, but they realized their flesh was no good. Then, too, the Indians were reluctant to sell the dried fish they had stockpiled for the winter, so the Corps followed their taste buds. Even when game began to increase after they left the high country, they continued to eat dog.[21]

THE MERE PRESENCE of Sacagawea and her baby assured the Indians below the Columbia River Gorge that the large band of armed white men, with their black mystery man, was no war party, since

Indians left their women and children at home when they went marauding. Early November found the Corps nearing the mouth of the Columbia River, buying dogs, and observing the habits of a people who lived by the water. On November 7, Clark joyously announced that they were within view of the ocean, but they were merely observing a rough patch of the extensive Columbia estuary they still had to cross, and it was a morale-battering, canoe-bashing journey—as wet and miserable as any they had yet made. Finally, they looked upon the Pacific on November 15, a significant event for the transcontinental travelers, but they were not the first men of European descent to reach the mouth of the Columbia—of African descent, perhaps.

Following traders who had visited the coast since the 1770s, George Vancouver had sailed up the Columbia to its confluence with the Willamette River in 1792, and other traders had been back since, training the Indians in barter, much to Lewis and Clark's dismay, because they demanded higher prices than the captains were accustomed to paying. Those traders also brought smallpox, which appeared to the captains to have ravaged tribes up to the Willamette Valley in the 1770s and again around 1800. Some tribes were decimated; the survivors abandoned their villages.

By a democratic vote of all adult human members, including York and Sacagawea, the Corps decided to winter just inland from the coast and so built what they named Fort Clatsop, after the local people. It was a damp, flea-ridden place they came to hate. In fact, the fleas they encountered all along the Columbia, especially in seasonally abandoned homes, drove Clark to distraction. The damp weather depressed them all, as meat spoiled and clothes rotted, and the men—except the captains, who appear to have abstained from sex, except perhaps Clark once—suffered from venereal disease they caught from the local women, if they did not have it already.

On December 10, Clark shot two brants and a duck and watched in wonder as several Clatsop "plunged into the water like Spaniards Dogs [spaniels] after those fowls . . ." They were a people who spent their lives on or in the water. But fowl weren't sufficient food, so the Corps hunted winter-scrawny elk, scavenged the remains of a beached whale along the coast, and traded for dogs at very high prices. They also consumed vast quantities of *wappetoe*, the root of the arrowhead fern, which they baked. Lewis discussed their diet in his entry of January 3, 1806: "Our party from necessaty having been obliged to subsist some length of time on dogs have now become extreemly fond of their flesh; it is worthy of remark that while we lived principally on the flesh of this animal we were much more healthy strong and more fleshy than we had been since we left buffaloe country. For my own part I have become so perfectly reconciled to the dog that I think it an agreeable food and would prefer it vastly to lean Venison or Elk."[22]

Clark repeats the entry verbatim until the end, which he amends: "as for my own part I have not become reconsiled to the taste of this animal as yet."[23]

The Indian dogs of the Clatsop and Chinook people on the south side of the Columbia were, according to Lewis, as small as or smaller than the common cur and particolored in some mix of black, white, brown, and brindle. They had long heads, pointed noses, small pricked ears, and short, smooth hair. He says on February 16, 1806: "the natives do not eat them nor appear to make any other use of them but in hunting the Elk . . ." The people of the tribes, who numbered about 100, must have had considerably more dogs, given that they were supplying them regularly to the Corps.[24]

Finally, on March 11, needlefish started running up the Columbia, bringing with them the promise of a healthier, more varied diet—enough that the captains began to make plans to head home. They left Fort Clatsop on March 23, glad to be under way and acutely aware that they were running short on tobacco and other trade goods. Heading for the Columbia Gorge, they began to stockpile dogs, planning to use them, smoked elk and deer, and *wappetoe*, as well as the horses they intended to reclaim from the Nez Percé, to carry them over the Lolo Pass and back into bison country. They did so in part because they knew they were running ahead of the salmon due on May 2, and the people had little of their dried salmon and berry cakes left from the winter.

On April 11, they were among the Wah-clel-lars at the portage around the Columbia Gorge. Lewis considered the tribe "the greatest thieves and scoundrels we have met with"—the people harassed the Corps at every turn. Finally three men stole Seaman on the evening of April 10. Mindful of their charge to bring the Indians into alliance with the United States and aware of their precarious position deep in Indian territory, outnumbered, in terrain they did not know, the captains and their men had generally avoided confrontations with their hosts, but this time a member of the party was involved, and Lewis reacted without hesitation. When he heard of the dognapping from another Indian, Lewis "sent three men in pursuit of the thieves with orders if they made the least resistance or difficulty in surrending the dog to fire on them . . ." Fortunately for all, when the Indians caught sight of their pursuers, they abandoned Seaman and fled. But Lewis remained disgusted, because an ax was also missing, and earlier in the day several Indians had tried to steal back a dog they had sold to John Shields—stopping only when he pulled his knife—until the chagrined chief apologized for his people and presented a tomahawk pipe as a peace offering.[25]

On April 13, still trying to complete the portage, Lewis repeated his paean to fresh dog meat. This time Clark, most likely because of exhaustion, copied Lewis's entry without his usual amendment, but four days later he was back to eating anything but dog. Most of the Indians among whom they traveled also refused to eat dog, some finding it abhorrent. Only once did the culture clash break into the open, and Lewis again dealt with it firmly and nearly with violence—behavior dramatically opposite that of Clark, who was healing various ailments with lineaments and "eye water" and setting broken bones. On May 5, he even received "a very elegant grey mare in exchange for a phial of eye-water . . ."[26]

In camp that same day, near the confluence of the Clearwater and Snake rivers, Lewis was eating a dog when a Nez Percé approached and threw "a poor half starved puppy nearly into my plait by way of derision of our eating dogs and laughed very heartily at his own impertinence." Incensed, Lewis picked up the puppy and "threw it with great violence at him and struck him in the breast and face." He then threatened the man with his tomahawk, and he "withdrew apparently much mortified and I continued to repast *on dog* without further molestation."[27]

The hunters and Seaman began shooting deer again on May 8. Drouillard and Pierre Cruzatte, a nearsighted, one-eyed French–Omaha Indian boatman and skilled hunter, each killed a deer. John Collins, a trapper and hunter, wounded one, and Seaman hauled it down not far from camp. A couple of weeks later, Seaman and two mounted Nez Percé helped bring down another wounded deer that had sought refuge in the river.

Finally, in mid-June, the snow melted enough for the Corps to recross the Bitterroots at Lolo Pass. They split apart on July 3 near present-day Missoula, with Lewis leading three men—the brothers Joseph and Reubin Field and the invaluable Drouillard—and Seaman north, and Clark taking the main party to explore the Yellowstone. They planned to meet at the confluence of the Yellowstone and Missouri rivers. Shortly after the split, Lewis named a creek for Seaman—it was common to name geographical features after members of the Corps. On July 7, Seaman was again fretful in camp, perhaps at the sudden surfeit of game. Fretfulness turned to distress a week later as the party prepared to explore the Marias River. Under constant bombardment from mosquitoes, Seaman howled in anguish while the men hid under their bedrolls.

That is effectively the last word in the journals on Seaman. On July 17, eight Piegans tried to steal the group's guns and horses but failed when Lewis shot one in the stomach and Reubin Field stabbed another in the heart. The survivors fled back to their village; Lewis and his men sprinted for safety. Disaster nearly struck Lewis on August 11, when Cruzatte mistook him for an elk and shot him; the bullet passed through his thigh and plowed across his right buttock. Fortunately, Lewis's group rejoined Clark and the larger party the next day, and Lewis recovered. On August 15 the captains discharged John Colter so he could return to the mountains to trap beaver; he became one of the greatest Rocky Mountain fur traders. Charbonneau, Sacagawea, and their child remained at the Mandan village.

CROSSING THE GREAT DIVIDE 121

Leaving the Mandan village, bound for home, the Corps encountered the Cheyenne, said by Clark to have 350 to 400 men in 130 to 150 lodges, with many horses and dogs, which carried most of their light baggage. The Cheyenne, he learned, were at war with the expansionist Sioux.

On September 6, Clark purchased to split among the men "the first Spiritious licquor which had been tasted by any of them since the 4 of July 1805." Repeatedly as they drew close to home, they mistook the barking of coyotes and even the animals themselves for what Clark called "our Common Small Cur dogs." They found the heat oppressive. On September 17 they met a trader heading north who told Clark that nearly everyone but Jefferson had given them up for lost, perhaps enslaved by the Spanish, who had sent four expeditions out from New Spain (Mexico) to intercept them. The Spaniards, of course, wanted to protect their lucrative trade routes from Santa Fe up the spine of the Rockies. All the intercepts failed, in no small measure because the Indians would not help the Spaniards. The long-absent men found no game near white settlements or Indian encampments but plenty of whiskey and tobacco; nonetheless, they had enough food to avoid eating dog. Finally, on September 27, 1806, they reached St. Louis.[28]

Seaman's loss surely would have been recorded and lamented, so it appears he made it back as well and probably stayed with Lewis. What happened after that, no one knows. He apparently was not present when Lewis killed himself on the Natchez Trace.

By then, too, the Newfoundland dog had established itself in America and England as a strong, bold, courageous hunter, guardian, and companion, a black or black-and-white dog with a wavy coat. In 1803, the year Lewis and Clark set forth on their great adventure, a Newfoundland born in England came into the possession of George Gordon, Lord Byron, the archetypal Romantic swashbuckling poet, who named him Boatswain. Byron eulogized his beloved Boatswain in verse carved on a memorial built to him at Newstead Abbey in 1808, after he died of rabies. The poem reads, in part:

But the poor dog, in life the firmest friend,
The first to welcome, foremost to defend,
Whose honest heart is still his master's own,
Who labors, fights, lives, breathes for him alone,
Unhonour'd falls, unnoticed all his worth,
Denied in heaven the soul he held on earth.
While man, vain insect! hopes to be forgiven,
And claims himself a soul, exclusive heaven.

6

Moving On: Coast to Coast and In Between

⚬

THERE WERE OTHER WAYS to get West from East than walking or riding overland, and although they might have been faster, they were not always easier. Travelers by sea around South America or by way of a portage across the Isthmus of Panama, or across the Pacific from Asia, risked shipwreck, scurvy, and tropical disease, not to mention piracy, but none of that deterred them. A continent beckoned in the opening decades of the nineteenth century, and people came by foot, horseback, wagon, and boat—keelboats, barges, sailing ships, and increasingly, as the century's second decade wore on, steamboats, which cut travel times along the Mississippi by two thirds and greatly speeded the trip up the Missouri to the interior. They came to trade, trap, hunt, explore, and record what they saw. They came to make a fortune if they could; they came for land and its bounty; they came to escape their past and remake themselves in a new image; they came to be free; and they came because they were not free.

As the young nation grew, so, too, did the number and skill of the wandering naturalists, artists, diarists, observers—all attempting in some way to understand the nation and its wild and exotic lands, its flora and fauna. Some of them, like Lewis and Clark and Zebulon Pike, were sponsored by the government, but many traveled on their own initiative and at their own expense. The artists George Catlin and John James Audubon paid for their travels with their work. Catlin traveled thousands of miles to capture the images and customs of Native Americans. His contemporary, Audubon, covered much of the same terrain, painting birds and mammals, always with a dog for company. The geologist Henry Rowe Schoolcraft explored the Ozarks, married an Ojibwa woman, and then settled into life as an Indian agent on the upper Great Lakes. A steady stream of Europeans included adventurers, hunters, naturalists, journalists, and intellectuals fascinated with all things American, including the experiment in democracy. For the richer or better-connected naturalists, North America was but one stop on extended journeys through the New World, Africa, Oceania, and the polar regions—any exotic, unmapped, by Western standards, part of the globe. If they did not actually travel with dogs themselves, although many did, these travelers encountered them wherever they went, often in great numbers, as everything from free-ranging pariahs scavenging what they could to pampered lapdogs, hunting hounds, all-purpose farmhands, beasts of burden, fighters, trackers, and mascots.

Livestock-guarding dogs—raised, in the Spanish tradition, nearly from birth with the animals they tended—continued to fascinate every naturalist who encountered them. In 1826, French explorer Alcide Dessalines d'Orbigny described in his *Voyage dans l'Amerique Meridionale*, his encounters in Uruguay with *perro ovejero*, the "sheep-guarding" dog. Suckled on ewe's milk, this dog tended his flock, leaving it only to get food at night or to hunt jaguar and partridge with his human master. His master's response whenever he did something wrong was to beat him with sticks or slash him with a knife. Voyaging on the *Beagle* in 1831, collecting material for what would become his theory of evolution, Darwin watched the cross-bred sheepdogs of Argentina perform like those d'Orbigny, whose work he knew, had observed in Uruguay. A dog lover, Darwin considered the behavior of *perros ovejero* in protecting their charges from predators, and even other dogs, additional confirmation of their intelligence and consciousness. Following northern European and English customs, most farmers in the United States had more active herding and hunting dogs, but people who observed Spanish-style dogs guarding sheep in the American Southwest generally shared Darwin's view. Other travelers understood little of what they saw and thus left tantalizing hints that I have tried to flesh out.

Roaming the countryside in the early 1830s, studying the penal system—their official task—and, more important for history, democracy in action, Alexis de Tocqueville and Gustave de Beaumont occasionally encountered the big, loyal dogs who were essential to many farms. A pair of donkey-sized mastiffs greeted—perhaps "frightened" is more accurate—the French travelers one evening when they sought shelter in a cabin in the backwoods of Tennessee. In the vicinity of Lake Erie, two large, "half wild," prick-eared dogs charged from a house to protect children frightened at Tocqueville's approach, then returned at a signal from their master.[1]

Tocqueville had no further comment on America's farm dogs, but tales of their sagacity and utility were staples in the popular press. Typically, the *American Turf Register and Sporting Times* reprinted in June 1831 an anonymous report from the *Poughkeep-sie Intelligencer* recounting how, during a brutal snowstorm the year before, a farmer's chickens had gone missing. As the worried, housebound family sat before the fire discussing what might have happened, the "house dog" came in with what "appeared" to be a dead chicken. Deliberately making his way to the fireplace—aware that the risk of beating increased with every step—he placed the hen on the warm hearth and dashed back out. He returned again and again until he had brought all the birds into the house, where they revived. The grateful family had by then observed that the chickens had crowded together in the yard against the cold and begun to freeze when the dog rescued them.[2]

Believing that the people best suited to run the state were men of property and culture, Tocqueville could not fathom the value to society of unschooled backwoodsmen and their dogs. He gave them scant attention—or worse, filtering all he saw through his class bias and relying only on prejudiced informants, he missed their stories completely. Tocqueville had heard reports of the election to Congress from western Tennessee of Davy Crockett and, without meeting him, described him contemptuously in his book *Democracy in America* as a homeless, illiterate hunter. He was, Tocqueville said, an example of all that was wrong with American politics after Andrew Jackson had forced extension of the franchise to virtually all white males, not just those who owned a prescribed amount of property. Like a true frontiersman, Jackson himself had settled in the Tennessee backcountry with his rifle, a pair of horses, and a pack of dogs and then scratched, clawed, fought, dueled, and gambled himself to wealth and power.

Tocqueville did not know that through an advantageous second marriage, Crockett possessed sufficient money and property to vote and run for office before Jackson's democratic reform. The rest of what Tocqueville had heard was not much closer to the mark; he even misunderstood the importance of hunting to frontier farmers. The semiliterate Crockett launched a relatively brief but intense political career in the 1820s and early 1830s, based largely on his concern over the fate of small farmers and his accounts of his bear-hunting exploits with his dogs. In so doing, he became one of the most famous, and infamous—depending on the prevailing political and cultural winds—of the backwoodsmen. As a youth, Crockett worshiped Daniel Boone, and on several occasions, first as a young homesteader and then as an older yeoman farmer looking to recover from financial setbacks and move into the planter class, he lived by hunting. His greatest exploits occurred between 1822 and 1826, his first years in west Tennessee, newly opened to white settlement, when he became perhaps the greatest hunter of black bears on record.

Smaller and less fierce than its cousin the grizzly, the black bear, *Ursus americanus*, was nonetheless formidable prey for hunters with a single-shot, muzzle-loading rifle. Fast, powerful, and intelligent, it could maim and kill dogs and men, so the hunter who could consistently bring home fresh bear was considered among the elite. Crockett claimed to have killed 105 bears in the winter of 1825–26 alone, including one that, wounded, had fallen from a tree, battered his dogs, and then sought refuge in a four-foot-deep crevice. After a long struggle, Crockett succeeded in creeping up on the bear from behind and stabbing it in the heart with his knife while his dogs held it at bay. In addition to hunting bears, he and his dogs hunted raccoons, wolves, panthers, and deer.[3]

Crockett's hunting tales and his defense of small farmers helped win him election to Congress in 1827, as a Jacksonian Democrat devoted to extending the franchise to all white males rather than only to property owners. He was reelected in 1829 but lost two years later after a public break with Jackson. In 1833 he returned to Congress and entered the period of his greatest fame after publication of his autobiography the following year. Ghostwritten by Kentucky congressman Thomas Chilton and self-consciously modeled on the autobiographies of Daniel Boone and Benjamin Franklin, Crockett's adventure-laced narrative drew heavily on his hunting and militia experiences and caused an immediate sensation. Promoted by the Whigs, who wanted a backwoodsman to challenge Jackson—if only to mock him—Crockett became a national celebrity—and, at times, a deluded self-parody, imagining himself a contender for the presidency against Jackson's handpicked successor, Martin Van Buren. Politically, Crockett had betrayed his roots, but his notoriety spread. In 1834 John Gadsby Chapman prepared to paint his portrait in his typical hunting garb and asked him to pose with Chapman's own pedigreed spaniels. Refusing the spaniels, Crockett pulled three curs off the streets of Washington, saying they more closely resembled his own bear dogs.[4]

Crockett's break with Jackson once again cost him reelection, this time to the House of Representatives in 1835, and his Whig sponsors deserted him. Bitter, in debt, he packed off in search of cheap land in Texas, to establish the cotton plantation he had long dreamed of, and met a martyr's death at the Alamo. History has remembered him alternately as a fallen hero—as he is portrayed in films, television programs, and plays—a drunken coward who hid as the Alamo fell and was captured and executed on the orders of Santa Anna; and a bombastic mountebank, star of hundreds of crude racist almanacs published in the decades after his death. For much of the nineteenth century, he was also memorialized as a great hunter and was one half of the Boone and Crockett Club, founded by Theodore Roosevelt in 1887 to keep track of big-game records, promulgate a hunter's code of ethics, and bring together hunters and conservationists.

Crockett was a market and subsistence hunter, and his dogs common curs—backwoods and low class compared with the gentlemen sport hunters and their "pure blood" dogs. Sport hunting started to become more widespread at the end of the eighteenth century, with the appearance from England of a more refined shotgun, or fowling piece, ideally suited for killing at close range with large slugs and also for killing birds with scatter shot. The gun encouraged development of pointers and retrievers, dogs that would hit their peak of popularity when market and sport hunting for birds did, in the second half of the nineteenth century. In addition to his hounds and terriers, Washington had at least one pair of pointers, although they clearly were more oddities than workers. As befitted a sportsman, he also had a water spaniel, sometimes called an Irish retriever. The year after his death, "foreign ships" dropped on the Maryland shores of the Chesapeake Bay a rough-coated animal that looked like an otter hound and came to be called the Chesapeake duck dog, or Chesapeake Bay retriever, renowned for its ability not only to haul waterfowl tirelessly out of the cold, choppy bay, but also to protect a wagon full of those birds on the way to market.[5]

WHAT TOCQUEVILLE MISSED ABOUT DOGS and hunters, Alexander Philip Maximilian, Prince of Wied, naturalist and sport hunter, saw and understood clearly. A major general in the Prussian army at the age of twenty-one, present for Napoleon's defeat at Leipzig in 1813 and Paris the following March, Maximilian took off in 1815 for Brazil and a new career in natural history. He traveled in the Arctic as well before visiting the United States in 1832–34 with the young Swiss landscape painter Charles Karl Bodmer and his Jäger, or hunter, Driedoppel, to find "uncivilized" America—that is, to sail up the Missouri to the Yellowstone and then head deep into the Rockies, if he could, like the great explorers Lewis and Clark. But to get there he had to pass through the growing regions of western Pennsylvania, Kentucky, Indiana, and Ohio, meeting along the way German-American farmers who always traveled with their big hunting dogs and long rifles in case they encountered game. "They have powerful *dogs*, resembling our German bloodhounds, brown or black, with red marks; or striped like the wolf, and sometimes, but seldom, their ears are cropped," Maximilian wrote in *Travels in the Interior of North America*. "These dogs are used in chasing the bear or the stag." Yet, he noted, much of the large game in the East was already severely depleted from overhunting, and the native people nearly gone.[6]

Maximilian spent his first winter in America at New Harmony, Indiana, with Thomas Say, great-nephew of William Bartram and one of the country's most renowned naturalists in his own right. On a duck-hunting excursion with Say, who died of typhoid fever the following year, Maximilian bemoaned the absence of European retrievers for fishing their fallen prey out of the Fox River before it drifted away. The two men also blasted large numbers of Carolina parakeets out of the sky. In their actions, Maximilian and Say were men of their day, capable of decrying the rapid loss of buffalo and mournfully predicting their extinction while thinking nothing of slaughtering birds for sport—to measure their shooting skill.

Audubon and Plato Dog Birds

Among the Americans on the move at that time, exploring the country on their own, was a thirty-six-year-old failed businessman from Haiti by way of Kentucky and debtors' prison, John James Audubon, who traveled down the Mississippi to New Orleans in

1820 pursuing his dream of painting birds and other wildlife. Little more than a decade later, he had begun producing *The Birds of America* and made a quick and exhausting trip to paint birds in Labrador, where he appears to have obtained a Newfoundland, perhaps inspired by Lewis's dog and the breed's renowned retrieving ability.

To recover from his Labrador excursion—the long days allowed him to overwork—Audubon set out for the St. Johns River in northeast Florida, and from there he traveled south to the Florida Keys with his sons, his assistants, his collaborator, and his Newfoundland, Plato, his most frequent companion and helper. Audubon hated the sand flies and mosquitoes, the heat and muck, and he criticized Bartram for having set off a land boom in Florida with his lyrical descriptions of the springs, lush foliage, and exotic wildlife, but he loved those things himself, especially the birds. He killed and painted birds along the St. Johns, down the coast, and through the Keys. Near St. Augustine, Plato hauled in countless cayenne terns Audubon and his companions shot from small boats, including one wounded bird that latched on to his nose as he swam through the surf. On another hunt, Plato retrieved fourteen anhingas in one day, carrying them gently in his mouth, then depositing them and himself next to Audubon. Audubon called him "a well-trained and most sagacious animal," observing in his discourse on the great white heron how, coming upon a rookery, he summoned Plato and ordered him to approach the birds. As the dog crept near, one heron took offense and, jetting his head forward on his long neck, as if snagging a fish, whacked Plato on the nose with his bill. Rather than retaliate, Plato "brought" the bird alive—whether by herding or carrying is unclear—to Audubon, who captured it.[7]

In 1833 Audubon returned to Labrador and visited Newfoundland aboard the schooner *Ripley* with his sons and a group of naturalists, including one W.I., who recorded the event for *The New-England Magazine*. Audubon liked the land no better the second time than the first, complaining about the summer cold, the long hours of daylight and work, and the behavior of eggers, men who stole eggs from the rookeries. Plato must surely have traveled along, although he is unmentioned. While Audubon shot and drew birds, W.I. looked at dogs, reporting that the Eskimo dogs, left to fend for themselves in summer, often went fishing with some success, although in general their lives were harder than those of their masters. He also gave voice to Audubon's and many other people's attitudes toward wildlife at that time, writing of two "new" species of hawk: "The world will see them as they were seen in Labrador, perched on a dead branch, and apparently conversing in their own way, little aware of the good fortune that awaited them, of dying in the cause of science, and securing posthumous fame." In Newfoundland, the party obtained seven of the sagacious local dogs, "one of which . . . dived five fathoms, and brought up a seal that had been shot, larger than herself."[8]

Audubon planned to return to Florida and the Keys in the late 1830s, but the guerrilla war between the Seminole Indians and various Florida militia and regular troops of the U.S. Army intervened. This Second Seminole War was actually a continuation of a struggle between the Seminoles, the runaway black slaves living among them, and white Americans for control of Florida, begun when Spain wrested the peninsula from Britain through the Treaty of Paris in 1783. The second war was launched in large measure to recapture slaves fleeing to safety in Florida and to open new plantation land. It produced for the Seminoles the war leader Osceola, captured under a flag of truce in 1837 and shipped to St. Augustine, then Fort Moultrie, South Carolina, where he died of malaria. The Seminoles kept fighting, however, and in 1839 the Florida Territorial Council purchased from Cuba thirty-three slave-hunting bloodhounds—at an outrageous $151.72 each—and four handlers for use against the Indians. Florida's leaders liked the notion that Cuban bloodhounds had ended Jamaica's Maroon Rebellion and enjoyed the backing of the secretary of war and other army officials. But when they offered the hounds to General Zachary Taylor, commanding the U.S. Army's futile but costly efforts to track down Seminoles hiding in South Florida's wetlands, he unenthusiastically agreed to take two on a trial basis. The hounds helped "find" two Indians—a dismal showing—and Taylor refused to have anything more to do with them. Florida's leaders then billed Taylor and the army nearly $2,500 for the hounds, but he refused to pay, saying they were trained to track slaves and couldn't follow the scent of Indians.[9]

Abolitionists were outraged over the entire program, claiming that the dogs were really brought into Florida to hunt runaway slaves, known to hide among the Seminoles. There was some truth to the argument, since Florida and its Indians represented the possibility of freedom for those slaves who could reach them. Protests from those appalled at the use of dogs against people of any color flowed regularly into the House of Representatives and Senate. Resolutions demanding an explanation from the secretary of war were introduced and laid aside. The most colorful of these came on March 9, 1840, from the former president and then representative John Quincy Adams, who as a young man had abandoned Washington's hounds in New York. His voice dripping with sarcasm and anger, he demanded that the secretary of war report to the House on "the national, political, and martial history of the bloodhound, showing the peculiar fitness of that class of warriors to be associates of the gallant army of the United States, specifying the nice discrimination of his scent between the blood of the freeman and of the slave; between the blood of the armed warrior and that of women and children; between the blood of the black, white, and colored men; between the blood of the savage Seminole and that of the Anglo-Saxon pious Christian." He wanted to know the number of bloodhounds and "their conductors" bought from Cuba and whether they would be brought to Maine in anticipation of a possible boundary dispute—or simply to serve as an example to potential enemies of the United States of weapons the army might deploy against them. Finally, he asked whether it would be necessary to grant pensions to the bloodhounds and their heirs.[10]

Adams, it appears, chose to ignore or forget the history of his own Massachusetts, but the protests had their effect. The dogs were returned to the territorial government, which doubtless sold them to slave hunters, and official U.S. military experimentation with dogs effectively ended until World War II. The Seminole Wars themselves finally subsided in 1855, with the last 300 to 400 Indians ensconced in the vastness of the Everglades and the Big Cypress Swamp of South Florida—land no white man wanted at the time—and another 3,824 Indians and blacks on a reservation in Arkansas Territory.[11]

The winter of 1838–39 marked the apogee of a program of Indian removal begun under Jefferson and prosecuted with all due prejudice under Andrew Jackson and Martin Van Buren. The desire was to force all Indians in the East to move west of the Mississippi River, thereby opening their ancestral homes to white settlement. The Seminole Wars cleared nearly all of Florida's arable land; the removal of the Cherokee in 1838–39 along what became known as the Trail of Tears did the same for western Georgia and parts of Alabama and Tennessee. Fully a quarter of the tribe, some 4,000 people, died of hunger, exhaustion, exposure, and disease during that forced march to Indian Territory, now Oklahoma. The dogs fared little better.

WITHOUT QUESTION, Audubon loved to hunt as well as paint, but there are indications that as he aged and saw in his travels the depredations of market hunters, like the eggers of Labrador, he lost some of his taste for blasting away at animals and began to mourn the loss of wild places. That is the lament of Daniel Boone and other avid hunters who discover too late that their excessive killing has helped create a world they no longer recognize and do not admire. Nor was Audubon alone in mourning what America was losing on a daily basis.

Catlin, Maximilian, and the Upper Missouri

The same year Audubon coasted the Florida Keys painting birds, the young lawyer-turned-painter George Catlin decided to throw over his comfortable life, the wishes of his family, and the company of his wife to retrace the trajectory of Lewis and Clark—and then visit as many other tribes as he could—in an effort to capture the customs, cultures, appearance, and way of life of the Indians the captains had encountered before they fell prey to smallpox, alcohol, religion, war, and the rest of the "sterner stuff of civilization." That he sailed from St. Louis up the Missouri on one of the first voyages of the steamer *Yellow Stone*, which made in two months a trip that took eight by keelboat, illustrates how the flood tides of history he sought to arrest were already sweeping away native cultures. Upon seeing the smoke-and-flame-belching steamboat and hearing its whistle blast and cannon boom its arrival for the first time, some Indians, Catlin said, threw themselves to the ground, while others "shot their horses and dogs, and sacrificed them to appease the great spirit, whom they conceived was offended . . ."[12]

At Fort Yellowstone, near the confluence of that river with the Missouri, he found Madeira and port for dinner every evening and a collection of hunters for the American Fur Company, about 100 of their Indian "wives" and children—when these men returned to the settlements, and many did over the years, they usually abandoned their Indian families—and at least that many dogs and puppies. Outside and along the river were the tepees and camps of Indians who came and went according to what they had to trade— mostly buffalo hides and tongues, a delicacy from St. Louis east, and pemmican for cloth, beads, guns and ammunition, and whiskey, although it was technically illegal to supply alcohol to the Indians. In his letters home, which serve as a gloss for his paintings, Catlin described the thousands of dogs—largely white, prick-eared animals, like the wolves of the upper Missouri—and their central role in Indian life.

The Indians often considered this odd painter some kind of medicine man or magician—and not always a benign one—because of his ability to portray them. More than a few, especially among the women and medicine men, distrusted him, fearing he was in the business of capturing souls. He usually had enough protectors in the villages he visited to remain safe, or at least to allow him to retreat intact when circumstances grew unpleasant, and so compiled a remarkable record of life among the forty-eight tribes he visited. But he also became a wanted man among the Blackfeet, Mandans, and Sioux because people he painted sometimes died unexpectedly.

His portrait of the Mandan girl Mink was considered so realistic that when he attempted to carry it away, he was accused of stealing her life. Catlin left the painting with the tribe, but Mink died nonetheless, and the painter and his work were blamed. The deaths of at least four warriors painted by Catlin were also attributed to his foul "medicine."

In words, not paint, he described how, after a buffalo hunt by Hidatsa warriors, women and children raced to skin, butcher, and carry the meat to the village, while following them were "at least one thousand semi-loup dogs, and whelps, whose keen appetites and sagacity had brought them out, to claim their shares of this abundant and sumptuous supply." Later, riding into a Comanche village on the southern Plains, he observed that the white cavalry-men with him "create a sort of chill in the blood of children and dogs, when we make our appearance." Among the Comanche, as among other Plains Indians, women, dogs, and horses did all the hauling when the village moved, and there were often as many or more dogs than people.[13]

Catlin planned to visit the Seminoles in 1837, but the war thwarted his effort as surely as it did Audubon's, and he decided instead to visit the captive Seminoles at Fort Moultrie, South Carolina. Early in 1838, he interviewed and painted Osceola, who died of malaria scarcely a month after Catlin captured his spirit.

MAXIMILIAN, BODMER, AND DREIDOPPEL failed to reach the Rockies because of illness and trouble between the white trappers and the Blackfeet, who blocked access to the mountains from the Missouri River. The Germans wintered in 1833–34 at Fort Clark, near the Mandan village, which allowed them to observe, like Catlin, how integrally related dogs and people were among the tribes lying along the Missouri. Whenever tribes with large numbers of dogs and horses approached one of the fur company forts to trade, as they perpetually did, Maximilian said, the prairie was a swirl of color and motion, with the women driving the dogs and packhorses, and the warriors galloping back and forth in a constant display of horsemanship and bravado. Maximilian also observed differences between the tribes' dogs, noting that the Mandans had fewer dogs than the Assiniboin, Crow, and Blackfeet. Although as poorly treated as all other Indian dogs, the Mandan animals, he said, "are rarely of the true wolf colour, but generally black, or white, or else spotted with black and white . . . We likewise found, among these animals, a brown race, descended from European pointers, hence the genuine bark of the dog is more frequently heard here . . ." Maximilian even learned to eat and enjoy the taste of dog, despite his initial aversion.[14]

Maximilian, like Catlin, observed dogs joining wolves in scavenging buffalo kills, and he even more clearly understood how the tribes had been dragged into a market economy by the traders and how, as a result, they were destroying the very resources, the buffalo and other game, on which they relied for life. Noting the often wasteful slaughter along the Missouri, which left all commercially useless parts of the animals to the wolves, dogs, and other scavengers, he predicted the demise of the enterprise within a few years. He had no way of foreseeing the smallpox that came upriver on the steamboat *St. Peter's* to Fort Union in 1837 and decimated the Hidatsa, Mandans, Assiniboins, Arikara, Crow, and Blackfeet, among other tribes, for a total of some 20,000 people killed. John Jacob Astor had sold the American Fur Company and its forts in 1834 to Pratt, Choteau and Company, and it was Pratt's supply ship that bore the pathogen upriver. Maximilian was long gone, but he heard of the epidemic by letter and reported that the survivors "are as submissive as the poor dogs which look in vain in the prairie for the footsteps of their masters."[15]

California Dreamin'

As Maximilian was finishing his tour of the American interior, young Richard Henry Dana, Jr., on leave from Harvard College because of eye problems, set sail aboard the brig *Pilgrim*, an American merchantman, for California by way of Cape Horn. He was gone for two years, returning in September 1836 to Boston and Harvard, to become a lawyer and a champion of maritime reform—ending the brutal treatment of seamen—and of fugitive slaves. But he is remembered most as the author of one the great books in American literature, *Two Years Before the Mast*, an account of his voyage. Initially written to give voice to the anonymous sailors in the forecastle, the book was an immediate success in England and America, a corking good sea adventure written by a man with an eye for detail and a social conscience. It also provides a close look at coastal California on the cusp of major social and political change. Dana and the *Pilgrim* arrived just as Mexico was secularizing the Catholic missions, fewer than fifteen years before California became a part of the United States and the discovery of gold set off a rush for riches that would forever transform it. Wealthy Mexicans of Spanish descent had gained control of the missions, which, along with the privately owned ranchos, were the center of life, making much of their money trading cattle hides, horns, and tallow to scores of ships, like the *Pilgrim*, that plied the coast, stopping at the inconsequential villages of Monterey; Santa Barbara; Yerba Buena, now San Francisco; San Pedro, which served Pueblo de los Angeles and provided more hides than any other, though it was also considered the ugliest place on the coast; and San Diego, site of the hide houses, where small ships would bring their cargo to feed larger vessels.

The ranchers kept scores of dogs to manage their cattle and eat offal after the slaughter. Packs of dogs also trailed behind the slow-moving, two-wheeled, oxen-drawn carretas, the wagon of choice throughout Mexico, which hauled hides for pickup on the coast or carried supplies and people under the guidance of Indian or Mexican peasants. The missions in California and New Mexico were also home to great numbers of dogs, often more than people. They were divided into those who, like the sheepdogs in New Mexico, actually performed a task, and the vast majority who lay about, occasionally chasing game, warding off approaching strangers, and scavenging waste. When the layabouts became too obnoxious or too pestiferous because of their fighting, they were rounded up and killed—the chief form of population control available at the time.[16]

Because he had taught himself Spanish, Dana managed to transfer from the *Pilgrim* to one of the San Diego hide houses, where he worked among an international cast, including Kamakas-Sandwich (Hawaiian) Islanders. Dogs, he said, were "an important part of our settlement. Some of the first vessels brought dogs out with them, who, for convenience were left ashore, and then multiplied, until they came to be a great people." There were forty to fifty dogs of nearly every breed living by their own devices on the beach, keeping unwanted visitors, especially Indians, from the hide houses. The workers kept that population fairly constant by drowning another forty to fifty dogs a year. "The father of the colony, old Sachem, so called from the ship in which he was brought out, died while I was there," Dana wrote, "full of years, and was honorably buried."[17]

Working sunup to nearly sundown, with an hour break at midday, the hide-house crews cleaned and prepared for shipping 125 hides a day. On Mondays and Thursdays, they scoured the brush for firewood, "followed by the whole colony of dogs, which were always ready for the bush, and were half mad whenever they saw our preparations." The dogs regularly flushed birds, snakes, rabbits, and foxes. They also generally chased and killed coyotes in "squads," because a coyote could beat every dog but one in single combat. That champion was "a fine, tall fellow, and united strength and agility better than any dog that I have ever seen," Dana said. A mastiff-greyhound mix from Hawaii, called Welly because of his perceived resemblance to the Duke of Wellington, this "favorite bully of the beach" had killed two coyotes by himself.[18]

Dana adopted a brown puppy with four white paws from this pack of pariahs, separating him from his mates at an early age and raising him to bond with him. He named the pup Bravo and trained him to human ways, aware all the while that he would have to abandon him and his Kamakas friends when his ship returned. In September 1835 he went back to sea aboard the *Alert*, under the sadistic and only marginally competent Captain Francis A. Thompson from the *Pilgrim*, who had swapped commands when the larger ship arrived in California. An uncharitable cheat and liar, Thompson died of fever some years later in Sumatra, apparently contracted while he was held captive briefly in a native village he later blew up for revenge. Returning on October 15 with a load of hides, Dana learned to his distress that Bravo had taken sick the day after he left and died.

Soon he was off again on the *Alert* to finish collecting the 40,000 hides they needed before leaving the coast, bound for Yerba Buena, where he learned of Santa Anna's plans to invade Texas and teach the rebellious Americans, who called themselves War Dogs, a lesson. Of course, on his way to defeat by Sam Houston at San Jacinto, Santa Anna besieged a small mission in San Antonio de Béxar and massacred its garrison of 148 War Dogs, including Crockett, William Travis, and Jim Bowie. Whether Crockett had any of his favorite bear hounds traveling with him is unknown, as is the number of dogs in the Alamo and their fate, although one might assume they escaped. Dana's San Diego beach pariahs were not so lucky.

Before heading home in 1836, Dana and his fellow sailors heard rumors of gold, but the focus at the time was on cattle hides, and although the ship brought some gold back to Boston, no one pursued the rumors or the gold. In fact, general knowledge of California was so poor that when the gold was "discovered" in 1848, Dana's memoir was nearly the only book available in English that told anything about the place. Dana himself returned to California in 1859 to revisit the places he had been and assess the changes. He found that in San Diego "the past was real. The present, all about me, was unreal, unnatural, repellent." The Kamakas are gone, he said, along with the ships and hide houses that supported them. "Even the animals are gone," he lamented, "the colony of dogs, the broods of poultry, the useful horses; but the coyotes still bark in the woods, for they belong not to man, and are not touched by his changes." Sailing for the Sandwich Islands to look for his old friends, his first ship, the clipper *Mastiff*, burned at sea and was abandoned after the crew was rescued by a British bark. There was something unlucky about Dana and dogs.[19]

Wagon Trains

Ships dominated the West coast trade, but once overland routes were opened, they gained in importance, especially for moving people. Traders had been coming overland from Independence, Missouri, across what became the Oregon Trail, since the 1820s, crossing the South Pass through the Rockies. Found by Robert Stuart in 1812, the pass was forgotten, then "opened" by the intrepid Jedediah Strong Smith. Joe Walker and Captain Benjamin de Bonneville blazed the California cutoff from the trail in 1832, a year after Comanches killed Smith while he tried to dig water out of the seasonally dry Cimarron River bed after he became lost on his way with a wagon train of traders to Santa Fe across the Cimarron Desert in southern Kansas.

The crossing Smith attempted without a guide—because Rocky Mountain fur traders and trappers believed no natural obstacle could defeat them—was born in suffering in 1822. Seeking a shortcut to the Santa Fe trail he had pioneered a year earlier, William Becknell turned south of present-day Dodge City, Kansas, crossed the Arkansas River, and led a group of men, mule-drawn wagons, and dogs into the dry, featureless fifty-mile stretch of sand hills separating the Arkansas from the Cimmaron River. But like many a wagon train after them, they ran out of water. In desperation, the men slit the throats of their dogs and drank their blood, which upset their stomachs and made them feel more thirsty. They scattered, chasing mirages, and were saved only after several of them discovered a bison corpse with a water-filled stomach. Assuming it had recently been drinking, they backtracked the bison to the Cimarron River.

Existing records suggest that dogs usually accompanied—and sometimes ruined—these wagon trains. At night the oxen and mule teams were brought inside the circle of the wagons for protection from Indians and to keep them from wandering off. The barking and howling of camp dogs, troubled by something on the prairie or simply fighting among themselves, sometimes caused the teams to break through the wagons and stampede across the prairie. Dogs also stole food and killed livestock. Their bad behavior was generally tolerated because of their obvious value as companions, guards, hunters, and sometimes herders, but some promoters of Western migration encouraged emigrants to leave their dogs behind.

In 1842, on one of the first wagon trains of emigrants bound for Oregon out of Independence, Missouri, headed by Elijah White, a missionary and recently appointed Indian agent for Oregon, open warfare nearly broke out over dogs. With 160 people, 80 of them armed men, the group considered itself well suited to meet all challenges and set off on May 16 for "the long desired El Dorado of the West." But within days, disputes between the members threatened to tear the group apart, and the wagon train stopped to establish a governing board and laws. Factionalism was common on wagon trains, composed as they were of disparate families and individuals bound only by a common ambition—not shared with equal intensity—to go West. In this case the group, with only men voting, as was customary, succeeded in passing just one law, over strong opposition— a mandate that all dogs with the wagon train be killed forthwith. Proponents argued that the dogs wouldn't be able to travel the entire 2,000 miles—a bogus assertion—and that their barking and howling would attract Indians, all of whom were considered threats. The dogs' owners countered that dogs were more likely to guard against Indians than summon them. Despite that, the keepers of order immediately killed several dogs, leading the opposition, especially the owners of the "most valuable mastiffs," to declare they would shoot anyone who killed their dogs. The threats forced a new meeting, in which "the dog decree was abrogated," said Lansford W. Hastings, a member of the party and later its leader, who reported on these events in his 1845 book, *The Emigrants Guide to Oregon and California.* Hastings was silent on whether Elijah White was behind the dog killing, as some have charged, but he described how the party subsequently split and regrouped at various times along its path.[20]

A YEAR AFTER White's wagon train made it to Oregon, the missionaries Marcus and Narcissa Whitman brought 1,000 emigrants across the Oregon Trail, marking the beginning of a flood of wagons and people that exceeded 500,000 before the transcontinental railroad opened in 1869. The pilgrims left their dead, their possessions, their livestock, their dreams, and often themselves strewn along the wagon tracks carved into earth. At their extreme, they achieved a level of depravity matching that of the first Jamestown colonists, and the man partly responsible for that was Hastings. In his *Emigrants Guide* and in person, he promoted a shorter route that crossed the Wasatch Mountains and cut south of the Great Salt Lake, across the desert to the Humboldt River, and offered himself as a guide, although he had never gone that way himself.

In April 1846 the families of James F. Reed and George and Jacob Donner left Springfield, Illinois, bound for Independence and then the long trek to California. As was customary, they joined a larger train that grew and shrank along the way. Finally, in July, Reed and George Donner opted to take the Hastings Cutoff. Following directions from Hastings, who was traveling the route ahead of them with other wagon trains for the first time, the Donner Party, as it became known to history, arrived in Truckee Meadows, now Reno, Nevada, in October with eighty-seven men, women, and children, twenty wagons, livestock, and dogs. An early snowstorm prevented most of the party from crossing the Sierra Nevada, so they established a camp at Truckee Meadows, where, before long, they had consumed all their livestock. They then ate their horses and dogs before turning to mice. A few, including Reed, who had been banished from the wagon train for killing a fellow traveler, made it to Sutter's Fort, at the confluence of the American and Sacramento rivers, where Sacramento now stands. Another small group, sent to seek help, successfully crossed the Sierras on snowshoes, only to founder. A few of them survived by eating their dead companions before they were rescued. The Mexican War prevented rescue parties from being launched for Truckee Meadows for months, and when they finally arrived, they discovered that the survivors had also been cannibalizing the dead. Perhaps not surprisingly, women and children survived better than men, with two thirds of the former living through the ordeal and two thirds of the men being among the forty-one dead.

Gold Fever

News of the Donner Party's depredations spread around the world, and in an America obsessed with its Manifest Destiny, the story became a cautionary tale against taking untested cutoffs on unknown roads. It did little to slow the tide of emigrants; indeed, just two years later, caution itself was thrown to the wind. A laborer, James Marshall, discovered gold at a sawmill on the 47,000-acre ranch of John Augustus Sutter, the owner of Sutter's Fort and one of the wealthiest men in California. A year later, in 1849, 100,000 people feverish for gold crossed the Oregon Trail for Sutter's ranch and environs, with more arriving by boat in San Francisco, the renamed Yerba Buena. Effectively dispossessed by miners, his cattle and sheep stolen and killed, his workers obsessively panning for gold, Sutter himself soon went bankrupt, but the country he had first entered in 1838, after a stint as a Santa Fe and Oregon trader, became known for its fabulous wealth, its cosmopolitanism, and its shattered fortunes and dreams. The Gold Rush of 1849 became the prototype for a wave of boom-and-bust gold and silver finds that rolled across the West and finally played itself out in Alaska and Canada's Northwest Territory as the nineteenth century gave way to the twentieth.

People with their dogs came from all over the world to the gold fields, with many of them taking boats to Panama, to cross the isthmus, a perilous place where travelers could be robbed or, more likely, succumb to malaria or yellow fever. Chinese who worked in the city and the gold mines sailed directly from Asia, often as indentured servants, like their seventeenth- and eighteenth-century European counterparts. San Francisco itself was a boomtown made of wood—which, in the first years after the start of the Gold Rush, seemed to be always on fire and overrun with rats. Rats were so numerous—as they were in many cities—that residents paid top dollar for terriers or other proved rat killers, and the dogs regularly drew a crowd when loosed on their prey in city streets. They would also race the clock in barroom competitions designed to see how many rats they could kill in a set period of time. When not ratting, the dogs—in San Francisco, as in other cities—were often considered unwanted pests.

Mining towns were men's creations, built on avarice and dreams of wealth, grandeur, power, and freedom, where vigilante justice ruled and women were rare and always in high demand. Some dressed as men and mined, drove wagons, or ran businesses, while others worked the brothels and saloons, the gambling houses and opium dens. San Francisco grew beyond that early boomtown phase; many of the smaller mining towns did not, becoming ghost towns after they had been picked clean.

In mining country, dogs served foremost as companions to miners; as beasts of burden in the high country, hauling sledges or carts; as fighters for sport against other dogs, badgers, and bears; as herders; and as hunters. According to perhaps apocryphal reports, a failed young miner, Henry L. Hooker, used all his remaining money to buy turkeys in Placerville in 1858 and haul them to his cabin on the Fraser River. Once he had bred a sizable flock, he used his dogs to herd them, with some difficulty, to Carson City, Nevada, a thriving mining town, where he sold them for $500 each. Hooker later became a cattle baron in Arizona. Other prospectors went into the backcountry and faded into oblivion or, if lucky, left their name on a part of the landscape, their accomplishments in local lore. During his first summer in Yosemite, John Muir learned of an ever hopeful miner, David Brown, who lived in what came to be called Brown's Flat, between the North Fork of the Merced River and Bull Rush Creek, with his curdog, Sandy. While Brown failed to find his fortune in the mountain streams, he and Sandy became accomplished bear hunters, always making their kill and never getting injured themselves. Sandy tracked the bears and distracted wounded ones when necessary, while Brown killed and skinned them. They shared the meat.[21]

IN 1850, Frank Marryat, a young British adventurer and travel writer, crossed the Isthmus of Panama and landed in San Francisco with his servant, Barnes, a poacher turned keeper of his father's estate, and three bloodhounds, mostly, it appears, to hunt, have a good time, and maybe dabble in gold mining. After building a redwood cabin in Napa, Marryat and Barnes joined several friends in a grizzly bear hunt with the owner of a "little high-couraged dog." The dog ran forward and boldly distracted the bear by attacking it from behind. But when the bear turned, the dog lost its courage and sprinted back to his owner, the bear in pursuit. Attempting his own hasty retreat, the owner fell down, and the bear, despite being shot three times by Marryat, ripped off half the man's face and tore out an eye before escaping. The man survived, barely, but grizzlies ultimately lost far more battles with men with guns and dogs than they won and were eventually extirpated from California.[22]

After two of his bloodhounds died, Marryat acquired three Australian kangaroo dogs, created by crossing a bulldog with a bull mastiff and then breeding that animal to a greyhound, and kept two, Tiger and Bevis. Large, fast, powerful, and lethal, they were his constant companions for the second of his two years in California, regularly running down hares and coyotes. Marryat sold Bevis and Tiger before returning to England in 1852, believing they would be better cared for by someone who bought them rather than received them as a gift. "A good horse or dog is a treasure in California," he proclaimed, as he planned his return even before his departure for England and marriage. But yellow fever contracted on his return through Panama killed him in 1855, while soon thereafter his new wife died of malaria and dengue fever caught on the same trip.[23]

Marryat had also observed the popularity of bear and badger baiting in the rough-and-tumble mining camps but dismissed it as unsporting and uninteresting because of what he believed was a natural inclination of the bears, badgers, and dogs to ignore one another and not engage in unnecessary combat. But Marryat must not have watched closely, because even by the standards of the day, the events were sordid affairs. Hunters captured, rather than killed, grizzlies and black bears and hauled them into San Francisco, Sacramento, or any number of mining camps for battle with dogs. Refusing to fight was not an option. J. Ross Brown described a badger fight in *Harper's New Monthly Magazine* in 1865. Tied up in a ring, the badger was left to fight for its life against a series of dogs, each sent into the ring accompanied by a number of bets. In this case a large yellow cur attacked first, but the badger seized his lower lip, and the dog, after breaking free, fled in agony to the "jeers of the crowd." Next came a black wolf dog hybrid that refused to fight. Finally, after the wolf dog's owner forced him forward, the badger grabbed and nearly tore off his hind leg. The third dog was a bull terrier, the prized fighting dog of the period, who went to work "with a will—straight, quick, fierce, like a well-trained bruiser who meant blood." The badger grabbed the dog's lower jaw and didn't release it until the nearly dead bruiser was dragged away. Violating all the rules they had established, the miners then turned six dogs loose on the badger who held them at bay for an hour. Finally, three men leapt into the ring and bludgeoned the badger to death with clubs, while it fought back. By that point, Brown had turned away, finding "that there was something about the whole business very much like murder."[24]

Brutality was a way of life at the mines, where the vigilante justice of Judge Lynch was the law, and fights with fists, guns, knives, or whatever other object was handy were the favored means of settling arguments. Combat between dogs was more common than badger and bear baiting and often more bloody, because the dogs would generally fight vigorously and high-stakes gambling meant that their lives and those of their masters could be at stake if they lost. With luck, a fighting dog that lost survived and was adopted by a more compassionate owner, but luck was no more abundant for most dogs than for prospectors. Many of those who lost in the pit were killed or deemed worthless fighters or cowards and left to die from their wounds. Those who won were celebrated, which, of course, meant that everyone with a rough cur or bull terrier or crossbred hound wanted to challenge them, and inevitably one of the upstarts would one day win, just as inevitably one day a miner's dog or the miner himself would find a fist-sized nugget, and the promise of the mother lode would reinspire everyone.

Bummer to Lazarus

As in every city, free-ranging dogs were regularly condemned and hunted in California, accused of harassing horses, attacking women and children, fighting with each other, barking and howling. In some cities they outnumbered people—Los Angeles had 1,600 people and 3,000 dogs in 1847. Residents poisoned them; municipal officials paid bounties for them dead or alive; and many were killed, skinned, and turned into kid gloves.

Despite the odds, some streetwalking dogs achieved renown far above their station by dint of personality and accomplishment and came to embody the essence of dog—for their human supporters. Perhaps the most celebrated of these in the West were Bummer and Lazarus, two bar-begging street curs in San Francisco in the early 1860s who just happened to establish their headquarters outside the saloon of Frederick Martin, a drinking establishment for San Francisco newsmen and artists. Bummer, a black-and-white Newfoundland mix with an overshot lower jaw, showed up in 1860, claiming a territory formerly held by Bruno, who had been poisoned, and quickly established himself as a superb ratter. A year later, he saved a smooth-coated cur from a larger dog, who had already come close to biting off his leg and was angling for the kill. Bummer brought food to the cur, subsequently dubbed Lazarus for his recovery from death, and tended him till his wound healed. After that the two were nearly inseparable—especially when they engaged in prodigious feats of rat killing. In one orgy, they joined club-wielding men in destroying 400 rats, with Bummer and Lazarus accounting for eighty-five in twenty minutes.[25]

Reporting on their exploits for the *Daily Alta California*, *Daily Morning Call*, *Daily Evening Bulletin*, and *Californian*, local newsmen turned them into a canine morality play, symbols of human virtue and deceit. Bummer was the well-bred gentleman who had fallen in life through his own "indiscretions" but who nonetheless maintained his dignity. Lazarus was a cur of uncertain origin, shifty, feckless, ultimately watching out only for himself. When Bummer was shot in the leg, within months of his rescue of the lowly cur, Lazarus abandoned him, "trotting off to hunt up more profitable acquaintances." Bummer, said the *Daily Alta California* in reporting the abandonment on April 12, 1861, was left to experience "the sting of ingratitude. That is, he may be supposed to experience it, for there is no question as to the chivalrous care which he took of his companion when their conditions were reversed. He might console himself, however, with the reflection that such instances are not confined to the canine race."[26]

Once Bummer recovered, Lazarus returned, and the two became fixtures in their neighborhood and famous around town. On June 14, 1862, Lazarus was busted in violation of the unspoken law protecting him and Bummer from arrest, and his supporters bailed him out. On June 17, they filed a petition with the city supervisors praising Lazarus's ratting skills and Bummer's "fidelity, gratitude and unflinching courage" and asking that they be declared city property so they could "wander unmolested in pursuit of their daily food." The proposition passed, and a week later, as if to prove their worth, the two stopped a runaway horse. In October 1862 they were featured in a revue, "Life in San Francisco." But they also ransacked stores when the merchants inadvertently locked them in, and Bummer was a street fighter of the first rank—Lazarus agitated from a safe distance—and a sheep killer. The pair charmed their numerous fans until, on the morning of October 3, 1863, Lazarus died of poison, believed given to him on doctored meat by a man who had accused the dog of biting his son. "Lazarus is dead," lamented the *Daily Evening Bulletin*. "He began to swell up in the course of the night, and passed gently away before the hour that Bummer has generally given him a rat for his morning meal." The obituary went on to praise the dogs' virtues and recount their exploits. Later that month, Lazarus was stuffed.[27]

The following year, Mark Twain, working for the *Daily Morn-*

ing Call, reported that Bummer, after avoiding other dogs for nearly a year, had allowed a black puppy into his life. "Whether that puppy really feels an unselfish affection for Bummer, or whether he is activated by unworthy motives, and goes with him merely to ring in on the eating houses through his popularity at such establishments, or whether he is one of those fawning sycophants that fasten upon the world's heroes in order that they may be glorified by the reflected light of greatness, we can not yet determine," Twain wrote. But, he added, the puppy was doing well to date.[28]

The puppy's subsequent fate went unremarked, and news of Bummer grew scarce until early November 1865, when the *Daily Morning Call* reported that after being kicked down a flight of stairs by a drunk, he had died of age and injuries. The obituaries and eulogies poured in for days. On November 11, *The Californian* weighed in with a reprint of Mark Twain's obituary from the *Virginia City Enterprise*: "The old vagrant 'Bummer' is really dead at last; and although he was always more respected than his obsequious vassal, the dog 'Lazarus,' his exit has not made half as much stir in the newspaper world as signalized the departure of the latter." Twain suspected that Bummer's natural death was the reason, saying, "he died full of years, and honor, and disease, and fleas. *He* was permitted to die a natural death, as I have said, but poor Lazarus 'died with his boots on'—which is to say he lost his life through violence . . ." Bummer, Twain maintained, had outlived his glory years.[29]

Bummer, too, was stuffed and displayed for years with his friend Lazarus, but in time they were lost, and they exist now only as paragons of devotion, friendship, and loyalty, as creatures whose virtues outweighed their faults.

7

Polar Opposites: North–South, City–Country, Rich–Poor,
Black–White, Purebred–Cur, and the War Between the States

∽

T HE WAY WILL GLASS REMEMBERED it, his uncle Anderson
Fields had a bad master in Alabama in the years before
Emancipation, so Fields ran away whenever he could—just
took off. His master always set the hounds on him. After the dogs
treed him, the master or overseer ordered him down, stripped and
whipped him, and sometimes allowed the dogs to bite him, as a reward for their efforts. Glass said that Fields decided one day that
he'd had enough, so when one of the dogs bit him, he grabbed it and
bit off its foot—to the dismay of his master, who couldn't fathom
that a slave would bite a dog back. Anderson Fields apparently survived the subsequent beating and dogging, but some slaves were not
so fortunate.[1]

Uncle Hilliard Johnson, one of seventy-five slaves on another
Alabama plantation, recalled that his owner, Nep Johnson, had
"nigger dogs," trained to pursue runaways, but that some of the
slaves knew how to escape by "hoodooing," or casting a spell over
the dogs. He did not recall the incantation, but once uttered, it rendered the runaway invisible to the dogs, who would then literally

bark up the wrong tree. Even the best hunting hounds have been known to do that occasionally, so it is difficult to say that hoodooing was responsible when a slave escaped. But hoodoo at least gave the hope and confidence believers needed to try for freedom.[2]

Traveling through east Texas in the early 1850s, Frederick Law Olmsted, then a farmer and correspondent for the *New York Daily Times*, as well as an ardent opponent of slavery, encountered a slave hunter pursuing a man who had slashed with a knife his owner, a judge, and his son, then fled. Caught once, he escaped again, this time from an armed posse that promptly gave chase, guns ablazin'. Soon, the slave hunter said, his dog, leading the chase, closed on their quarry. "If he'd grip'd him," the man told Olmsted, "we should have got him, but he had a dog himself, and just as my dog got within about a yard of him, his dog turned and fit [*sic*] my dog, and he hurt him so bad we couldn't get him to run him again."[3]

Such battles and victories, like successful flights to freedom, localized uprisings, and even legal challenges in some areas by slaves trying to win freedom from bad owners, while significant enough to keep the South in constant fear of a full-fledged slave revolt, were insufficient to break the slave system. The number of slaves involved in direct action was probably a minority, although the figure is notoriously hard to gauge because slave owners desired to suppress news of unrest and successful flight in order not to encourage other slaves or provide fodder to abolitionists. But when a revolt did occur, it struck terror throughout the slave South that resonated for years, none more than Nat Turner's "insurrection," as it was known, on August 21 and 22, 1831, in Southampton, Virginia. Turner and his collaborators killed fifty-five people before, fearing hot pursuit, they split up, with Turner literally going to ground in a dugout for six weeks. Ironically, a slave's dog, illegally owned, as were all, discovered his hideout one day while he was away and stole some of his meat. The next day, the dog returned with two slaves who were hunting with it, according to Turner's confession, and, discovering him, began barking. Turner begged the hunters not to reveal his hideout, but they did. Although he had sought cover elsewhere, as a precaution, he was soon captured, along with his fellow rebels, tried, convicted on the basis of his own confession, and hanged. Resistance more commonly took the form of slow work and subversion—both of which regularly drew the lash on many plantations and even in cities, from owners with only a few slaves. But fugitives were a significant enough problem that a Louisiana physician, Samuel A. Cartwright, declared in 1854 that they suffered from "drapetomania," a mental illness manifest in an uncontrollable desire to run away—to be free. To prevent the disease from taking hold, he recommended that surly slaves be whipped.[4]

Slavery was inherently cruel, founded as it was on the notion that a person could be owned, bought, sold, bred like livestock, and treated however the owner pleased. Families were regularly ripped apart, their members sold to different owners in other states or territories. On many plantations and farms, especially in the cotton and sugar lands of west Georgia, Alabama, Mississippi, Louisiana, east Texas, and middle Florida, where slaves often outnumbered whites and profits could be high, beatings and whippings were commonplace, administered at the whim of the master, mistress, overseer, or any other white in authority. Slaves throughout the "upper" South trembled at the prospect of being sold "downriver" to the cotton states precisely because they feared the harsh, brutal conditions there and the breakup of their families. Other punishments included cutting slaves with knives; branding them; keeping them in irons, stocks, or plowshares; starvation; exposure; and rape. Forced sex on a black woman—slave or free—was never called rape by white authorities, of course, but even consensual sex involving a black man and white woman was. Not infrequently, punishment resulted in disfigurement or death. On many occasions, dogs were encouraged to attack and bite slaves—sometimes with the slave in the middle of a circle of chained dogs, who were then allowed to lunge, bite, and rend flesh before being reeled back, to prolong the victim's suffering. Physical violence in the form of duels, knife fights, and no-holds-barred brawls was a widely accepted form of social intercourse at the time, especially for resolving questions of honor; children and animals were regularly subject to abuse and had no rights. Women had precious few, for that matter. Oxen and mules were routinely beaten with whips often purely to please the teamster. But even by those standards, the treatment of slaves on many plantations was appalling.

Along the east Texas coastal plain, Olmsted encountered "a gang of negroes, three men, two women, and two boys, under guard of a white man and a very large yellow mastiff." Bound from New Orleans to an east Texas plantation, the slaves had no extra clothing to protect them against the cold and, like beasts of burden, were forced to carry their household goods. Such slave trains, combined with the smuggling of slaves from Africa or South America, fed the demand for labor. Perhaps up to a million were smuggled into the country between 1809 and the eve of the Civil War, 1861, with that many again purchased or moved from the Old South.[5]

In the age of freedom, liberty, and equality ushered in by the Revolution, the ownership of another human demanded considerable rationalization, so Jefferson's suggestion that the Negro race might be inferior by birth—genes were unknown at the time—became "scientific fact" in the middle decades of the nineteenth century. Bolstered by a whole series of brain and body measurements and other evidence, "scientific racism" confirmed the inferiority, indeed the subhuman character, of Negroes and Indians. Race was the line of divide, and the slave owners went to great lengths, after the legal importation of slaves was abolished, to justify an unjustifiable system in the face of rising opposition. Black Africans were, by their being, deemed inferior in intellect and morality to white, no matter the socioeconomic station of the whites, and that judgment of racial inferiority became a justification for whatever slave owners wanted to do with their chattel, as well as for discrimination against free blacks in nonslave parts of the Union. It was a common belief, even among many white abolitionists, like Harriet Beecher Stowe, that blacks were better adapted to working in the heat and sun than whites, an argument that faltered when applied to extremely pale-skinned mulattoes, the result of forced and voluntary miscegenation. Indeed, although Jefferson had once believed that miscegenation "improved" the Negro race, by the 1820s or 1830s the mere presence of black blood—the percentages were carefully calibrated by studying genealogy—in the American South became enough to classify a person as black.

Under such circumstances, it is little wonder that slaves were hunted like animals and treated like recalcitrant livestock when captured, nor is it surprising that a culture as fond of hunting dogs as the South would freely employ dogs to track missing slaves. In fact, the practice was widespread, well known through reports of fugitive slaves and whites familiar with the institution of slavery, and widely condemned long before Stowe made Simon Legree and his dogs, "raised to track niggers," universal villains with the publication of *Uncle Tom's Cabin* in 1852. At the end of that year, Olmsted started his thirteen-month journey through virtually the entire slave South, with the exception of middle Florida, for his health and for the *New York Daily Times*, writing under the nom de plume Yoeman. He later expanded his reports and journals into a trilogy of books that provides a remarkable look at slavery at the beginning of its final decade. For more than half of that trip—through west Texas and then back to Richmond—his main companion was a bull terrier named Judy, "made of muscle, compactly put together behind a pair of frightful jaws" and possessed of "a general aspect which struck awe into small Mexicans and negroes wherever she appeared." Judy kept guard over the saddle, supplies, and camp and also loved to attack the hogs that were abundant and pestiferous in much of east Texas. She was much coveted by various slave owners Olmsted encountered along his path, many of whom sought to borrow her for breeding.[6]

Wherever he went, Olmsted encountered "nigger dogs," or "negro dogs," trained specifically for hunting runaway slaves. He first encountered the dogs near the Great Dismal Swamp along the border of Virginia and North Carolina, extending from near the coast inland, a favorite hiding place for fugitive slaves. Any breed would do, he found: bloodhounds, foxhounds, bulldogs, curs, and crosses between Scotch staghounds and foxhounds. Although some of these dogs may have been used to hunt a variety of game in addition to slaves, most were specialists, trained from puppyhood only to chase blacks. As puppies, according to Olmsted's informants, they were allowed to see a black person only when being trained to catch him. Then a slave was made to run from them and the dogs to pursue him until he climbed a tree. They were then rewarded with meat. After learning to chase a running slave, they were taught to follow a person's trail and finally to associate scent from a shoe or piece of clothing with a particular individual—only blacks were used in the training because the owners thought the dogs would learn to follow the odor of a black. Slave hunters regularly advertised their services in local newspapers while boasting of their dogs' prowess, or offered dogs for sale for prices ranging up to three hundred dollars or more for a well-trained, proven pack leader. In Alabama, the owner of an enormous plantation, with 135 slaves and a large pack of dogs, told Olmsted that some people took "just as much delight" in running slaves with hounds as in hunting foxes.[7]

Passing through Mississippi, Olmsted met a farmer who told him that Spanish or Cuban bloodhounds were often crossed with common hounds or curs to create "negro dogs" and that slave hunters in that area also trained their horses to the task. As a rule, the farmer told him, the dogs were allowed to chew on their quarry only if he fought back, whereupon they inflicted considerable damage—to the point of death. In Tennessee, to Olmsted's displeasure, a white man even tried to use Judy to frighten a group of black children, telling them she was a "nigger dog" that could "snap a nigger's leg off" if they didn't behave.[8]

Olmsted, of course, saw and recorded dogs in most of their uses during his long circumnavigation, and his own choice of a bull terrier—a purebred "gentleman's dog"—revealed something about his own biases that became more apparent a few years later when he designed Central Park and embarked on his true calling as a landscape architect, creator of parks and suburbs. While he was traveling through Kentucky by stagecoach on his way to Texas, a fellow passenger, observing a chained black bear cub on the roadside, launched into a story about bear—pronounced "baar"—baiting. It seems that this passenger had a sorry, worthless cur who one day took a look at a roadside bear and discovered his life's calling. He attacked the bear with ferocity and, while losing his tail, became champion of the pack because of his courage and viciousness. After that, people would come from twenty or more miles around to watch the dog tangle with a bear, and "the most respectable, sober old members of the church, became so excited as to hoot and howl like mad men almost jumping over the fight."[9]

Cattle Hunters

Continuing the well-established Southern traditions, dogs in the period before the Civil War played a vital role not just in maintaining slavery but also in putting meat on the table—for free people and for slaves. Generally, the South was in as much of a time warp when it came to breeding and using hunting dogs as it was in holding slaves, in social customs, and in economic development. Most Southern states had tightened legal restrictions on slave ownership of dogs by the 1830s, but slaves continued to run and hunt dogs, usually at the sufferance of their masters. While wealthy Southerners celebrated their purebred animals, most other people—slave and free—relied on their curs.

Charles Hallock captured some of the contradictions surrounding slaves and dogs, slaves and freemen, and race and class in describing for *Harper's New Monthly Magazine* a hunt for cattle that had gone feral on a dilapidated plantation on Green Island off the coast of Georgia in the mid-nineteenth century. When the owners abandoned the property years earlier, they left a large family of slaves as caretakers, their sole responsibility periodically helping the white owners hunt the feral Devon cattle and pigs. Otherwise, those animals were theirs for the taking, and they were effectively free to live as they pleased.

The white hunters brought their horses and a mixed pack of bulldogs, hounds, and mastiffs by boat and supplemented them with curs belonging to the slaves, Hallock said. Under the leadership of the slave Sambo and his cur Sanch, the slaves—mounted and on foot—and dogs drove twenty cattle from the dense scrub into an open field where the mounted white hunters, each armed with two revolvers, a knife, and a rifle, charged into the herd and started shooting. Bellowing, barking, and shouting, cattle, dogs, and people clashed and collided amid the smoke of gunpowder and flying sand. When a bull gored his horse and threatened the plantation owner—given the ubiquitous honorific of the antebellum South, "Colonel"—Sanch grabbed its nose and held it while two bull terriers grabbed either ear, and other dogs attacked its legs, flanks, and tail. Not trusting the dogs, the dismounted Colonel ran for a cluster of palmettos, where he hid, while Sambo, the best rider of the lot, closed on the bull and finally killed it. Four other animals were corralled, and the rest escaped to be hunted another day. The best hunters clearly resided on the island, yet the beef belonged to the Colonel and his guests.[10]

ON THE VAST PALMETTO PRAIRIES flanking the Kissimmee River in central Florida, Cracker cowmen made their living not by killing feral cattle but by rousting them out of the scrub and cypress swamps with the help of tough, half-wild curs—often leopard curs, so named for their distinctive markings.* Descended from cattle brought to Florida in the sixteenth century by the Spanish, Cracker cattle, as they came to be known, reverted to the wild and adapted to their hot, humid, parasite-riddled environment with poor forage by becoming smaller and disease-resistant. In the nineteenth century most weighed in at 400 to 500 pounds and were considerably shorter than Texas longhorns and other common cattle. Catch dogs, like Sanch, grabbed cattle by the nose and held them until a hand could rope or brand them, and the best among them, although weighing only sixty to eighty pounds, could seize a moving cow by the side of its head and, with proper leverage, toss it to the ground, much the way a rodeo cowboy throws a steer, or grab the animal's nose and force it to the ground.

*Now derogatory, "Cracker" technically referred to the poor Anglo-Americans of the piney woods and swamps of the South. The word is variously believed to be derived from "cracked corn"—grits—the staple, with fat back, of their diet, or the sound of their livestock whips. Descendants of British Loyalists who had fled to Florida during the Revolutionary War were also called Crackers.

After the roundup, a handful of men and twenty dogs regularly moved hundreds of head of wild cattle across land filled with panthers, wolves, alligators, snakes, and natural hazards—not to mention mosquitoes and flies that swarmed so thickly they could suffocate cattle and horses—to ports on the Gulf of Mexico for shipment to Cuba. The Seminole Indians had first started herding these small Spanish cattle across the open prairie of palmetto and pine, which they burned yearly from mid-February to the end of March to kill saplings and encourage the growth of grass.

After the Seminoles were driven off in the 1840s, Crackers moved in, the land being too marginal for the plantation slavery that flourished in north and middle Florida. By the late 1850s, the cowmen's trade with Cuba had become so lucrative that gold doubloons were the currency of exchange throughout the region. During the Civil War, with the Confederacy in desperate need of a secure food supply, Florida cattle were shipped north while the Cracker cowmen were exempted from the draft, but that did not free them from fighting. Just as it had once served as a haven for Indians fleeing persecution and runaway slaves, so Florida became a refuge for Confederate draft dodgers and deserters. Their poaching, as well as raids by Union sympathizers and troops, became so frequent that cowmen formed their own irregular Cracker Cavalry. They probably rode with dogs, although there are currently no known accounts of the curs seeing action. After the war, Cuba quickly regained its position as the chief buyer of Florida scrub cattle and remained so, except for the disruption of the Spanish-American War, until the 1920s.

Visiting the palmetto prairie in 1895 for *Harper's New Monthly Magazine*, Frederic Remington illustrated and also described the work of Cracker cowmen, which continued much as it had for forty years, albeit without enthusiasm, since he considered them far less romantic than his beloved vaqueros of the West. The Cracker cowmen always ate fresh beef, hog, or deer, Remington acknowledged, which they killed on the range with the help of their dogs, and were generally well paid. But mostly he complained: "The heat, the poor grass, their brutality, and the pest of the flies kill their ponies, and, as a rule they lack dash and are indifferent riders, but they are picturesque in their unkempt, almost unearthly wildness. A strange effect is added by their use of large, fierce cur-dogs, one of which accompanies each cattle-hunter, and is taught to pursue cattle, and to even take them by the nose, which is another instance of their brutality."

Remington wrote at a time when attitudes about the treatment of dogs were changing, and when lingering resentment over the Civil War and Reconstruction were fueling dismissal of white Southern males in general. In fact, commenting on the few blacks on the palmetto prairie, he says ironically that the Cracker cowboys are "not but recently reconstructed." He was right, in part, but he did not calculate that the area had not been plantation country and thus always had few blacks. Indeed, it had few people of any color.[11]

The open range is history now, as nearly are Florida Cracker cattle. Blooded cattle are raised on improved, fenced pasture and often herded by all-terrain vehicle or pickup truck. But the old ways have not vanished entirely. It remains possible in the late spring, just before the rainy season begins, on the palmetto prairie and the ranches south of Lake Okeechobee, to find men who work their cattle with cur dogs, preferred because of their resistance to heat and their habit of rousting and bunching their prey, and some of those dogs are as ferocious as their forebears.

Marching As to War

Because of the writings of Stowe, Olmsted, and abolitionists and former slaves like Frederick Douglass, the notoriety of "nigger dogs" was such that the Union troops cutting a swath through Georgia to the sea under William Tecumseh Sherman slaughtered every hound in their path, often with their bayonets, knives, and swords to save ammunition. They also burned mills, granaries, and crops in their campaign, which allowed Southerners to blame them for mass starvation and death in the infamous Andersonville prison camp, where 13,000 of 45,000 Union prisoners of war died between

December 1863 and April 1865. The Confederacy also blamed Lincoln and Grant for refusing to engage in prisoner exchanges; of course, both sides knew that such exchanges would help the South, which was running low on fighting men, more than the North.

Captain Henry Wirz, the commandant of Andersonville, who was ultimately tried and convicted of war crimes, added a chapter to the history of these dog packs by using them to track and maul escapees, often so severely that they died. In his 1879 narrative of his time in the camp, John McElroy described the packs as led by two bloodhounds, commonly believed "debased descendants" of the Cuban dogs brought to Florida during the Second Seminole War. The remainder of the twenty-five to fifty dogs in each pack were curs. "They are like wolves," McElroy wrote, "sneaking and cowardly when alone, fierce and bold when in packs." Their handlers rode mules and controlled them with cow horns and whips.[12]

As a rule, though, dogs played little role in the Civil War. They were mascots to soldiers and officers, to be sure, and may have served occasionally to carry messages, but not in any official or organized way. They could also be a hazard, as David Dodge reported in an article for *The Atlantic Monthly* in October 1891, recalling his youth during the Civil War in central North Carolina. Many small farmers, with few or no slaves, in the central and western parts of the state hid out in the woods during the war to avoid serving the Confederacy, he said, and they were generally ignored until 1863, when, with losses mounting, the army wanted everyone. Then regulators and the home guard began to hunt them down, sometimes with hounds. The deserters and draft dodgers used the hiding places of runaway slaves, which, in central North Carolina, because it lacked mountains and swamps, literally meant going to ground— hiding in caves and dugouts whenever the patrols were riding. Often they built multiple caves that could hold as many as four or five men at a time, and moved from one to the other, while the women developed elaborate codes, commonly based on hog calls, for communicating with them. "Indeed the deserter had three staunch friends," Dodge says, "his wife, his negroes,—for, as I have said, some of them owned slaves,—and his dog." But the dog, so useful in warning of danger, could also jeopardize his owner, no less than the slave dog that betrayed Nat Turner, by following or tracking him to his hideout or raising a ruckus when he came home at night, thus alerting any nearby home guard.[13]

Miserable Mongrel Curs: Racism Goes to the Dogs

The antebellum South was backward, an economically stunted land, a class and caste society, divided among whites between landowners and piney-woods Crackers, and between white and black, freeman and slave. To sustain their wealth, plantation owners needed fresh land for cotton production and expanding markets for their slaves, so they sought to require that newly opened western territories allow slavery. Because of their wealth and the structure of the republic, they controlled national politics for years, and despite rising opposition, they managed to add Texas to the Union as a slave state and to force the Missouri Compromise and the Compromise of 1850 as ways to maintain a political balance. The endless compromises faltered with passage of the Kansas-Nebraska Act of 1854, widely seen as having hastened the nation along the path to Civil War by encouraging bloody warfare between Free Soilers and proponents of slavery.

The historian Frederick Jackson Turner, who wrote so eloquently of the importance of the frontier in American life and thought, believed that ultimately slavery would be a blip on the course of American history, largely because it erected nothing of note. But slavery helped force open the frontier, and, more important, it created a legacy of racial discrimination and prejudice that continues to shape politics. Suffice it to say before leaving the difficult, bloody subject that dogs, despite the uses to which they have been put and the opinion of uninformed people on all sides, are color-blind and apolitical—with one exception. They do not like to be caged, confined, leashed, kept from running and being dogs. But in the middle decades of the nineteenth century, the drive to do just that took a new, harsher turn, not only in San Francisco but in other cities and in many states as well.

The campaigns coincided with a rise in raising pedigreed sheep for wool, increasing urbanization and industrialization, and the growing popularity of purebred—often called pure blood—dogs as companions and representatives and, indeed, creations of the burgeoning mercantile, industrial, and professional classes, also known as the bourgeoisie. In short, they were becoming pets. In theory, such dogs became the perfect servants of the people who created them, who bred them to conform to standards of blood, and thus class, purity and ascribed to them innate qualities and virtues that set them apart from common curs, no matter their talent. Indeed, every attempt was made to strip the cur of its dignity and sagacity, because of its low breeding, just as blacks were denied full humanity, and other ethnic groups, including poor European and Irish immigrants, were deemed morally and intellectually deficient.

In July 1850 the *American Agriculturalist*, dispenser of all manner of practical advice, told its readers that if they truly wanted to rid themselves of rats—a major problem on farms and in cities—they should "kill off some of their miserable mongrel curs" and get a wire-haired or "rough-coated" terrier, the best ratter around. It was an absurd claim, of course, as countless of those miserable curs would continue to show for years to come, but the magazine's advice ultimately had less to do with the talents of dogs than with people's expectations and the ability in some cases to concentrate particular hunting traits, like pointing, through breeding and training. The degree to which those traits can be concentrated is unknown, but clearly what mattered, in addition to talent, were size and shape and certain levels of alertness and boldness. People bred for those traits, as well as for physical characteristics, like coat length and color. The result in hand, they made up histories and attributes and then sought to prove they were right.

Dog breeders in the 1820s understood full well that the pointer they hunted over was the result of crossbreeding a foxhound and a Spanish pointer, and they also knew that training from an early age was essential to any dog's performance. A foxhound can be trained

to stop and point a wounded deer, to work close to its handler, and
to hunt silently, wrote "C" in the December 1829 issue of *American
Turf Register and Sporting Magazine*, and a pointer can just as easily learn to run game over a long distance. But for every wise hand
like "C," there were a growing number of bourgeois hunters who
wanted a dog that reflected their own status. To do that, it had to be
well bred.[14]

"Miserable mongrel" by the mid-nineteenth century had become a frequent modifier to "cur," to underscore the animal's low-
bred origins. They were the unkempt dogs of the urban and rural
poor and of laborers, unfit for proper canine or human society, and
although some dog lovers might actually own one, they commonly
reserved their highest praise for the pure blood. In 1857, *Putnam's
Monthly Magazine of America*, which Olmsted briefly edited after
his tour of the South, carried a lengthy discussion of the virtues of
dogs, questioning whether they possessed souls, why they were at
once loved and despised, and concluding that there was no reason
to deny the immortality of dogs. The anonymous author praised his
own dog, Snap, a mongrel foundling: "He is not a handsome dog,
and he is not intelligent, and he is, so far as I know, entirely useless—
not good for a thing—but he loves me and I love him, and he growls
for me, and I growl for him, and wherever I go he goes, and I am
never desolate or forsaken." Yet he believed that instinct and learning were passed down only through the best dogs—the well-bred
animals, like pointers, and the intense sheepdog, as long as it met
certain expectations. At the end of his piece, reflecting the rising
preference for purebred dogs, the *Putnam's* commentator requested
that any reader with a good dog—an English, Scottish, or Skye terrier, all of them popular ratters and gentlemen's companions in the
city and house—and looking for a good master for him contact *Putnam's*. Of such contradictions was the world made.[15]

THE WAR AGAINST CURS carried into sheep husbandry, with a
number of rural counties, like cities, attempting to count, license, and
control dogs. The curs were ruthless sheep killers, it was charged,

responsible for ruining the New England sheep industry—true only if overgrazing and the opening of new land in the West were ignored. Jefferson had championed the rustic French sheepdogs, but they apparently never caught on, perhaps because, like French immigrants, they were relatively rare. By the 1840s the Scotch colley, or collie, was becoming more common, and it soon established itself as the herding dog of choice for promoters of sheep husbandry. For guarding sheep from predators, including "worthless curs," they preferred the large Spanish dogs, but they understood that the tradition of shepherding from which those dogs came was not their own.

Henry Stephens Randall, a Jefferson biographer and author of the 1858 treatise *The Practical Shepherd*, a best-seller that went through scores of editions, especially with revival of the wool market during the Civil War, praised both types of sheepdogs—as long as they were well bred. "They are the true dog of Nature, the stock and model of the whole species," Randall wrote, citing Buffon and Darwin. Much as he approved the pure-blood Spanish sheepdog, Randall maligned its Mexican cousin, calling it a cur, a cross of every dog around, "miserable, snarling, cowardly," charges based more on its lack of blood purity than its performance. The Argentine sheepdog Darwin had praised so highly in *The Voyage of the Beagle* was, after all, a cur, but Randall overlooked that.[16]

The Scotch colley, on the other hand, was active, intelligent, sagacious—unequaled, Randall believed, as long as the task was to manage and herd, not defend, the flock. The good colley, he proclaimed, was worth five shepherds, an essential worker on any large sheep ranch. The sheepdog's innate purity was also manifest in its ability to keep its "type" even without selective breeding. But, he added ominously, sometimes a colley learned to kill sheep and thereby became their worst enemy. Reflecting the racist spirit of the times, he added, "I think the mongrel Colley learns to kill sheep as readily as a cur; but whether this is true of the pure blood dog, I am not prepared to say." Writing some three decades later in *The Century*, Thomas H. Terrry echoed Randall's bias, complaining that most American farmers failed to understand fully the colley's wisdom and abilities and so used "worthless, sheep-worrying curs" on their farms. By then, the colley had become a fashionable, pampered pet among urban dog owners and split into working and show dogs, from which companion dogs were also drawn.[17]

The chief objection was to miscegenation, mongrelization, and toward people and dogs, with few exceptions, who were not Northern European—Anglo-Germanic, basically—and who were poor. In the cities, the war against cur dogs focused most of its attention at those of the poor—often at the poor themselves. Perhaps nowhere were the conflicts between social classes and ethnic groups over nearly everything, including dogs and their treatment, more apparent than in New York. By 1850, it was far and away the largest, most robust city in the nation, drawing tens of thousands of immigrants a year, mostly Irish and German. Between 1850 and 1870, the population leapt from 515,547 to 942,292, despite the Civil War, and then exploded to 3,437,202 in 1900, with immigrants from all over Europe and America. The number and types of dogs increased dramatically as well. Although maligned because they were poor or, in the case of those arriving after the failed uprising of 1848, socialist, the German immigrants were always described as cleaner and more industrious than their Irish Catholic neighbors, as if for them poverty were merely a temporary inconvenience as opposed to a heritable condition. To most of America's economic and political leaders, "socialists," like labor organizers, were rabble-rousing apostates, but they were not necessarily viewed as inferior, the way the Irish, blacks, Chinese, and other ethnic groups were.

In a real sense, what saved New York from becoming an uninviting sinkhole for poor immigrants was Central Park, created by Frederick Law Olmsted and Calvert Vaux between 1857 and 1864. The two also designed Prospect Park in Brooklyn. Andrew Jackson Downing, Vaux's first partner in landscape design and a friend of Olmsted's, had conceived of Central Park as a place to bring together all New Yorkers, including the shantytown dwellers, in a bucolic setting. He believed such a unifying experience would forestall the sorts of socialist rebellion that wracked Europe in 1848. Olmsted, who was also superintendent of Central Park, agreed, but his sense of the rustic did not extend to free-running dogs. He believed that dogs should go through the park leashed and muzzled, because that was how well-bred dogs were properly kept in the city—not a universally accepted position then or now.

By the time construction of Central Park gathered steam, New York was awash in dogs, and demand was so high that breeders began mass-producing puppies in New Jersey and bringing them across the Hudson for sale on Broadway and other thoroughfares. Indeed, Newfoundlands were so popular in 1855 that sixty socially prominent passengers sailing on the steamer *John Adger* from New York to St. Johns, Newfoundland, to witness completion of the Submarine Telegraph Cable linking Europe and America took on a large pack of dogs and puppies before leaving. The trip—with Samuel F. B. Morse, inventor of the telegraph, and Peter Cooper, president of the Telegraph Company, aboard—failed in its primary mission because bad weather forced the captain of the cable-laying ship, the *Sarah L. Bryant*, to ditch forty miles of cable in deep ocean. Meanwhile, the *John Adger* became a floating kennel, with dogs barking, yipping, fighting, and howling in unison with the hymns sung during religious services. The humans argued perpetually over whose dog was the most pure "Newfoundland dog," and most of them, speculated *Harper's New Monthly Magazine*, were probably sold in the booming New York market for pets. Like other trappings of wealth—the proper address and the latest styles, for example—the well-bred pet conferred status on its owners in a society.[18]

The Esquimaux (Eskimo) dog, or spitz, as it was known, was also relatively abundant on the streets, especially the white one, reflecting popular interest in Arctic exploration, particularly in the fate of the British explorer Sir John Franklin. In 1845, Franklin, fifty-nine years old and veteran of a failed expedition twenty years earlier that had seen his men resort to cannibalism to survive, set out on two ships, with 134 men, a dog, and a monkey, to find the Northwest Passage. They vanished, setting off repeated international searches to determine what had happened to them and inspiring a generation of explorers to attempt to reach the North Pole. Those early efforts usually failed, as many succumbed to scurvy, starvation, exposure, and their own stubborn ignorance, but they also brought the Inuit and their dogs to public attention, once it became clear that without dogs and Inuit clothes, an explorer could not hope to survive, much less triumph, in the Arctic. The eighteenth-century traveler Samuel Hearne had learned that the hard way, but his lesson was ignored by "civilized" men who considered using dogs as beasts of burden ignoble and low-class. Reinforcing their bias, the Royal Society for the Prevention of Cruelty to Animals successfully lobbied in 1845 for a ban on the use of dogs in transportation in England. The ban also reinforced a strong bias among British Arctic explorers against employing dogs, although the more successful among them overcame their inhibitions.

Dogs for Arctic Exploration—Grabbing the Obvious by the Tail

The man most responsible for revealing the value of sled dogs was Elisha Kent Kane, leader of an 1853 expedition financed primarily by Henry Grinnell, a wealthy New York City shipping merchant, to search for the lost John Franklin, find the Northwest Passage, and reach the North Pole, if possible. Kane took with him a "noble team of Newfoundland dogs" and then added fifty Inuit dogs, "the majority of whom might rather be characterized as 'ravening wolves.'" But of necessity, he soon learned to appreciate "their power and speed, their patient, enduring fortitude, their sagacity in tracking these icy morasses, among which they had been born and bred."[19]

Kane sailed with his seventeen-member crew and two interpreters to an anchorage on the northwest coast of Greenland, which he called Rensselaer Bay, where he allowed his brig, *Advance*, to become icebound for the winter. It was a desolate part of Greenland, windswept, devoid of game, and by late in the first winter all but two of the men had scurvy, supplies were running low, and forty-five dogs had died, including all but one of the Newfoundlands. Most of them perished from an ailment common to confined huskies on polar explorations—its symptoms including frothing at the mouth, convulsions, and sudden death—which Kane called Arctic cholera and the Inuit called *piblotko*. By midsummer 1854, it was clear that the ice was not going to break up, and the brig was trapped for at least another winter. But Kane obstinately refused to leave on foot and foolishly spent time and energy on futile explorations rather than on laying in food for the winter. Without timely help from the Inuit, who occasionally supplied dogs, fresh meat, and aid in hunting—because of the useful American guns—the explorers could not have endured the brutally cold winter of 1854–55. Only five dogs survived it, including Whitey, the last Newfoundland. Kane himself remained relatively healthy by eating rats, which his crew refused, and an occasional puppy. He also learned to dress like the Inuit and use dogs, as they did, to haul and to hunt caribou, seals, walrus, and polar bears.

On May 17, 1855, Kane finally decided to abandon ship. While the least sick men dragged lifeboats across 200 miles of ice to open water, Kane ferried the most ill men and food with his team of four, and sometimes only two, dogs. They reached the water on July 16 and set sail with all but two men—a crewman who had died while crossing the ice, and one of the interpreters, who had stayed among the local Inuit. Kane gave all but two of his remaining dogs to the Inuit, keeping Whitey and Toohla, a husky, with an eye to eating them if necessary. But the men were able to subsist on birds and a seal until a Danish merchant ship rescued them on August 4, and the dogs were spared. A hero in a heroic age and a best-selling author, Kane died fewer than two years later in Havana of rheumatic fever.

Urban Canines

Whether mongrel curs or inbred pure-bloods, dogs were crowded into cities with their people in midcentury, and attitudes toward their welfare and treatment were changing. The New York Society for the Prevention of Cruelty to Animals was founded in New York in 1866, sixty years after its British predecessor; two years later came the Massachusetts SPCA, and the American Humane

Association followed in 1877. All opposed abusive treatment of animals, including dogfights and the use of dogs as beasts of burden, and combined their support for animals with campaigns to protect women and children.

An outspoken advocate for the humane treatment of animals, Darwin, already renowned for his theory of evolution, advanced a comprehensive view of animal intelligence and emotion in his 1871 treatise, *The Descent of Man, and Selection in Relation to Sex*, using his beloved dogs as the prime example. They inherit the capacity for terror, suspicion, fear, deceit, timidity, bad and good temperament, rage, and vengefulness, he said, and possess the powers of reason, imagination, love, jealousy, and pride. They believe in the supernatural and are also religious in a way, substituting the master for God. Not possessed of human language and learning, they nonetheless communicate through their barks, chortles, growls, bays, yodels, and howls. Dogs, and other animals, possess a sense of beauty, or aesthetic appreciation, although it is mostly confined to sexual attraction. Their moral sensibility is manifest in their knowledge of right and wrong and their assistance to their family, pack, or herd. Indeed, they are also altruistic, Darwin argued. "It must be called sympathy," he said, "that leads a courageous dog to fly at any one who strikes his master, as he certainly will." Darwin admitted that animals may lack self-consciousness, the ability to reflect on the meaning of life and death and their place in the cosmos. "But," he slyly asked, "how can we feel sure that an old dog with an excellent memory and some power of imagination, as shown by his dreams, never reflects on his past pleasures or pains in the chase?"[20]

Darwin also proposed, most clearly in 1868 in *The Variation of Animals and Plants under Domestication*, that various types of dogs were derived from different wild stock—European and North American wolves, coyotes, and jackals—and then selectively bred into a plethora of shapes and sizes. Sometimes dogs from different wild stock were hybridized to create new breeds; often, he warned, existing breeds could become so inbred that they would lose their physical and intellectual vitality, through what is now known as inbreeding depression. But few breeders of pure-blood dogs heeded his advice; as the century drew to a close, complaints about deterioration of purebred dogs increased. In most cases, though, dogs were more biddable than their wild forebears, Darwin said, more intelligent, and better able to serve their masters than human servants. Indeed, they were the perfect servants to humans, responding with love even to those who abused them.[21]

CONSTRUCTION OF CENTRAL PARK and the upscale development it inspired destroyed many shantytowns, including a number on the land dedicated to the park itself. Chief among them was Seneca Village, founded in 1825, the oldest settlement of free blacks in the city. By 1855, the eve of its destruction, it included among its 264 residents blacks, Germans, and Irish. They were dispossessed, and the park became a haven for the wealthy, who ringed it with brownstones. The park did occasionally give working-class and poor New Yorkers who could get there a chance to study "the habits of one of the most pastoral as well as sagacious of the canine family—the colley, or Scotch sheep-dog," as it drove cattle and sheep to one of the city's many slaughterhouses, wrote Charles Dawson Shanly in the May 1872 issue of the *Atlantic Monthly*. He cautioned that the drovers did not always have "genuine colleys," but that when they did, anyone willing to get up before dawn could watch the dogs herd the flock through intersections already crowded with people and carriages. The dogs, he gushed, would even dash across the backs of sheep to retrieve a runaway.[22]

In the 1870s the Newfoundland was still among the most popular dogs sold by the street merchants, despite an overall increase in the number and variety of purebred animals. English breeders were busily turning the black-and-white, active Newfoundland into a predominantly black, large dog and making its short-haired cousin the Labrador retriever. Coach dogs—dalmations—were frequently seen attached by a chain to the axletree of a wagon and running in harmony with the horses. The best and boldest of the dogs ran unchained in that position with the horses, after they were trained. Firefighters adopted street dogs as mascots who guarded the open firehouse from thieves when the men answered a call, or ran with the fire wagons and horses, often in front to help clear the road. The dogs were a fixture at the houses long before dalmatians became known as "fire-engine dogs" and long before the internal combustion engine and concerns about lawsuits rendered them obsolete. Gentlemen paraded with their Russian wolfhounds and their favorite pointers and setters—some of which they also kenneled outside the city. Ladies had their pugs and King Charles spaniels, while everyone had terriers, especially the bakers, who kept them in their carts to ward off thieving humans and dogs. In the city's French quarter, Shanly reported, were "little curly poodle-dogs." German tradesmen and "beer-house keepers of the sporting kind" took the ferries to the New Jersey meadowlands in the morning with their "fowling pieces slung at their backs and attended by sundry dogs," largely mixed breeds, to assist in their bird hunting.[23]

Market hunting, especially for waterfowl, had become a lucrative enterprise on the East Coast, where demand for fresh game was high. With refrigerated railroad cars still more than a decade away, it remained difficult, despite improved roads, trains, and steamboats, to ship fresh meat and produce quickly enough to distant markets to prevent spoilage. Food had to come from local farms, forests, and the rich waters of the Long Island Sound and Chesapeake Bay. There it was common for hunters to fill their wagons with waterfowl and other game and then haul it to market, their tough Chesapeake duck dogs guarding from thieves the birds they had pulled from the water. Sport hunters usually considered these men low-class louts, and many were, but the sportsmen killed equally large numbers of animals, albeit for fun, not profit.

Shanly reserved his most pointed comments for dogs of the poorest people, meaning German and Irish immigrants, and, ironically, those of the richest New Yorkers. His remarks echoed those of observers a decade earlier while anticipating those two decades later. "The most thoroughly Bohemian of dogs are the nondescript ones maintained by the rag-pickers and cinder-sifters, who occupy feculent cellars in the vilest and most repellent byways of New York," he said. Many also lived in a shantytown on the west side—

between Sixty-fifth and Ninety-fifth streets, the park and Eighth Avenue—or in shanties on the boulders where Fifth Avenue met the park. "Lean, sneaking curs of no particular breed are to be seen foraging about everywhere in that vicinity," he said, as well as mongrelized Newfoundlands, hounds, and pointers. They pulled carts and guarded homes, and they got thrown in the pound or shot, especially when the weather warmed and fear of hydrophobia, or rabies, raced through the city.[24]

In fact, the shantytowns had gardens, birds, goats, cats, and other creatures; day laborers as well as rag-pickers and cinder-sifters. On the corner of Eighth Avenue and Seventy-second Street, according to H. C. Bunner, writing in October 1880 for *Scribner's Monthly*, was the "Swell" Saloon, kept by "an intelligent, bristly old German, with 'exile of 48' written all over his socialist face . . . A mighty mastiff, chained up in one corner, growls at us suddenly and unsettles our nerves." But when Bunner suggested that the ugly mastiff should be killed, the German replied that only a friendless misanthrope would want to kill such a beast. Bunner was no less a man of that sort than Shanly. "The dog in Shantytown is everything that is vile, degraded and low in canine nature," he said. "In him survives the native savagery of the wolf, blent with an abnormal cunning learnt from his association with men. He draws the rag-picker's little cart, not by way of making himself useful, not as the friend and helper of man, but simply to delude you into believing in his docility and sweetness of disposition. Then he bites you . . ." It is unclear whether dog or saloon survived the demise of that west-side shantytown, as the wealthy of New York continued to build on both sides of the park and reach to the rivers.[25]

Everywhere, dogs reflected the split in society between high and low, white and black, Anglo-American and nearly everyone else. Bullbaiting had been banned in 1867 at the city's slaughterhouses and butcher shops, but the practice, along with bearbaiting, continued underground for a number of years, with the same large, rank dogs involved. Dogfights and rat-killing contests, requiring smaller venues and dogs, were increasingly popular, including among gentlemen eager to gamble on their champions. The first "recorded" dog show took place in Mineola, New York, in 1874, the same year that the first official field trial for pointers was held in Tennessee. But owners and breeders of pure-blood dogs had begun holding bench shows, where they displayed and compared the relative merits of their specimens, during the 1860s. Sportsmen organized the Westminster Kennel Club, to improve the pointer, and made its first show in 1877 especially noteworthy by including nonsporting dogs—pets.

The pointer had become the dog du jour among sportsmen and, with the setter, was deemed the equal of the Scotch colley in sagacity, its superior in its ability to serve man. "No dog possesses greater intelligence or more excellent disposition than those used by sportsmen," wrote William M. Tileston in the April 1877 issue of *Scribner's Monthly*, "and where careful education has developed them to a high degree, they are fitted in every respect to be the trusted and beloved companion of man." Flop ears became a measure of the dog's level of trainability, its evolution into a suitable, obedient servant and member of the household, even if its ears were then cropped—a practice many people considered cruel—to give it a more intimidating demeanor.[26]

Shanly was more unforgiving of the nonworking pure-blood dogs of the rich. "With regard to dogs moving in the fashionable society of New York, little, if anything, need be said. Like their masters and mistresses, they have become so artificial in their lives and manners as to have but little either of canine sagacity or eccentricity to recommend them to notice." Shanly's disapproval notwithstanding, the rising middle class considered these inbred creatures, mutants though some were, emblematic of their own good taste. They themselves might not possess pure bloodlines, but their dogs did, and that breeding made them more "aristocratic." It had become commonplace to see these and other dogs with meerschaum pipes in their mouths, wearing bowlers, bonnets, ribbons, and ties, signs of their acceptance into the home. But just as the wealthy waged war against the poor, seeking to limit their dogs' freedom, so the poor struck back—dognapping purebred dogs and turning them in to the pound on the East River for fifty cents apiece, knowing they would probably be redeemed, dognapped, and sold again; or catching them, tying tin cans to their tails, and sending them running through the streets, chased by curs. The humiliation, many dog owners believed, could ruin their well-bred but sensitive pets, causing them to degenerate and begin to mix with the very low-bred curs who abused them. So, too, was a person, especially a woman, who drew too close to the lower classes—or had sex with or married such a person—demeaned.[27]

Shanly reported that of the forty to fifty animals in the East River pound at any one time—hardly a large proportion of the New York canine population—most were "curs of evil associations and low degree." Unredeemed dogs were periodically put in a large tank into which water from the river was allowed to flow while a lid was lowered over it, pressing the dogs underwater. They were drowned en masse, howling, barking, and screaming in protest.[28]

In the warm summer months, unmuzzled and free-running dogs could be shot on sight by police, acting on the assumption that warm weather brought hydrophobia and any panting dog could be afflicted.

8

Fights Indians; Runs with Dogs: The Domestication of
the West Through Extermination

⌘

O N A THREE-WEEK HUNT in 1874 with a fellow U.S. Army
officer and three Englishmen, including William Blake-
more, a financier, collector, explorer, and hunter—in
short, a typical mid–nineteenth century gentleman—southeast of
Fort Dodge, Kansas, on a tributary of the Cimarron River, Lieutenant Colonel Richard Irving Dodge killed, among other animals,
127 bison, 2 red deer, 11 antelope, 154 turkeys, 5 geese, 223 teal, 45
mallards, 49 shovel-bills, 57 wigeons, 6 cranes, 187 quail, 32 grouse,
84 field plovers, 33 yellowlegs, 12 jack snipes, 1 pigeon (passenger
pigeons were virtually extinct), 9 hawks, 3 owls, 8 butter ducks, 3
sheldrakes, 17 herons, 143 meadowlarks, doves, robins, and assorted other songbirds, 1 bluebird for his sweetheart's hat, 2 badgers, 7 raccoons, and 11 rattlesnakes. Together, the five sportsmen
killed some 1,262 animals, averaging 63 a day—12 to 13 per man.
Typical sportsmen of their day, they blasted everything in sight
with shotguns, rifles, and pistols, and, of course, they had along a
brace of the requisite pointers. "A well trained dog is most invaluable to the sportsman, for whatever his skill as a marksman or

trailer, he will lose more or less game unless he has the assistance of man's best friend," wrote Dodge in his 1876 hit, *The Plains of North America and Their Inhabitants.*[1]

Dodge's hunting dog of choice in most instances was the pointer because of its speed, strength, endurance, and biddability. A trained dog, Dodge believed, was thoroughly under his command, staying at heel until sent forward to find the trail of a wounded animal. "He should be taught, when he has found, or pulled down the wounded game, to bark loudly and continuously until his master comes to him," he said. He found pointers particularly useful for tracking wounded red deer and "black-tail" deer, rejecting setters because with their long coats they could not stand the heat and dryness of the Plains, greyhounds and bloodhounds because they were stupid, and curs and foxhounds because they were difficult to train. Even his beloved pointer, like a dimwitted but enthusiastic junior officer, was not always totally under control. Dodge complained that "a very fleet, powerful and favorite pointer of mine, once caught and killed an unwounded antelope" and afterward, convinced of his prowess, chased every antelope he encountered despite "repeated and severe thrashing." The noble hunting dog, after all, was expected to starve in a room full of fresh-killed game rather than violate its master's wishes and eat food intended for humans.[2]

The decades following the Civil War marked the dawn of mass tourism; people were carried by the rapidly expanding system of railroads and steamboats that reached into many previously remote areas. Perched on the decks of steamers, sportsmen shot anything that dared to move on land or in the water, especially in Florida, with its alligators and brightly plumed birds, whose feathers adorned the hats of fashionable ladies. Trains on sections of the Union Pacific Railroad, and adjunct lines, frequently stopped to allow passengers to obliterate herds of bison congregating near the track. Indeed, the Great Plains were a favorite destination because of the abundance and diversity of their wildlife and their stark beauty. Important travelers—and there were many with money, political connections, aristocratic titles, and combinations thereof—received military escorts so they could run down bison on horseback using fleet staghounds or greyhounds; send the dogs in pursuit of wolves, cougars, wildcats, grizzlies, black bears, antelope, deer, a subspecies of Rocky Mountain bighorn sheep, and elk, an animal that could kill a careless dog in the flash of a hoof; and loose them on rabbits and smaller game for the adrenalin rush of the chase. With pointers and shotguns, they hunted birds and tracked larger game. They often had their trophies stuffed and mounted, and many of them carefully recorded each kill, like birders keeping their lists of sightings. They also collected eggs, nests, and live specimens for their natural history cabinets. In areas where they were welcome—although sometimes welcome on the hunt, they were more commonly excluded—the hunters' wives and children did the same. The business of the world may not have been conducted on the hunt, but it was a shared experience that helped sustain the personal relationships of power and privilege. For boys, an extended hunt for a bear or other large game often helped mark their coming of age. It is important to note, too, that much as the hunters "loved" or admired their dogs, they left their management to servants and orderlies. If the dogs got in trouble during a hunt—if a bear turned and attacked, for example, or they found themselves trapped in a den, face-to-face with a cornered panther and no room to maneuver—it was the handler's job to bail them out, not the owner's. That the handlers were black or Mexican or poor white underscores the race and class divide—and absurdity—inherent in the frequent boast of owners that the dog was more devoted to them than any human, even the human who cared for them.

Despite their massive body counts, these sportsmen seldom if ever thought of themselves as wasteful or profligate; rather, they believed they were carrying on in the true tradition of European nobility, proving their manly prowess, their courage and skill as marksmen and horsemen. Dodge thought he was helping to preserve the game birds he slaughtered by destroying the animals, like wildcats, that fed on them or their eggs. Yet he also proclaimed, "Civilization ruined the game, the Indian, crushing the romance, the poetry, the very life and soul of the 'plains,' leaving only the bare and monotonous carcass." Dodge was uniquely placed to make such a lament.[3]

Arriving in the West fresh from West Point in 1849 and working his way through the ranks there for forty-two years, except during a stint east for the Civil War, Dodge served or saw action in Indian Territory, Kansas, Colorado, Wyoming, and Dakota Territory, protecting traders and mail carriers on the Santa Fe Trail, settlers, especially those arriving after the Homestead Act of 1862, and workers on the railroads, including the Union Pacific. He helped found Dodge City, Kansas, in 1872. The city was named for the fort, which was named for its founder, General Grenville Dodge, no relation to Richard Irving Dodge. In 1875, just months before taking a leave to peddle his book, Richard Irving Dodge escorted the geologist Water J. Penney on his five-month mission to investigate a recent report by Lieutenant Colonel George Armstrong Custer of the Seventh Cavalry that the Black Hills were awash with gold. After his black servant was gunned down in the notoriously lawless Dodge City in 1883, during the infamous "Saloon Wars," Dodge helped force reform through the creation of the Peace Commission, which included former lawmen Wyatt Earp, lately a participant in the gunfight at the O.K. Corral, and Bat Masterson. By then the Santa Fe Trail was history, supplanted by the railroad, and Dodge City was nearing the end of its heyday as the railway terminus for cattle drives along the Chisholm and Western trails that saw some 5 to 10 million cattle entering town between 1875 and 1885. Dodge fought and negotiated with Indians, bargained with settlers, and knew most of the often shabby forts and towns of the Plains. Soldiers, he writes, were proverbially fond of dogs and, as a result, most forts resembled breeding kennels featuring countless dogs of seemingly limitless variety. The majority were curs, lacking the snap and obedience Dodge demanded of his favored pointers. Generally, the dogs of both officers and men traveled with the troops when they went on patrol or to war.

The changes wrought on the Great Plains during the nineteenth century are almost incomprehensible, largely because no one living today has seen even a fraction of such abundance. Prior to Lewis and Clark's exploration, 27 to 30 million bison grazed the Plains in vast herds, providing food as well as hides for clothing and shelter to 500,000 to 1 million Indians, from Canada into Texas. By the end of the century, fewer than 1,000 bison remained, with the largest American "herd," comprised of twenty-five animals, in Yellowstone National Park, protected from poachers by the U.S. Army, an ironic shift from the days when army commanders encouraged the slaughter of the big grazers as a way to break the Indians' resistance. Established in 1872, at the height of the slaughter, the park became a refuge for other species as well, but it is fundamentally a mountain, not a Plains, environment and is thus not optimal for bison. At least 1.5 million buffalo hides were shipped by rail from Dodge City alone between 1872 and 1876. Market hunters killed the bulk of those, taking the hides and tongues and generally leaving the rest to scavengers. If they deemed the hide unsatisfactory, they would leave it as well. Bones were ultimately collected and pulverized into fertilizer. Indians took perhaps a quarter of the total bison for traditional use and for sale. Sportsmen killed the rest. The land became putrid with the stench of rotting bison, Dodge said, and water holes were fouled. During the same period, the passenger pigeon and the Carolina parakeet were gunned to extinction.[4]

Market hunting for bison began with the fur trade and relied on the Plains Indians. It accelerated with the arrival, beginning in the 1840s, of white hunters and their superior weapons. But bison also appear to have suffered from a devastating drought, with a powerful, if unconscious, assist from army and emigrant caravans, according to a study reported in 2002 by Connie Woodhouse, a meteorologist, and her colleagues. Lasting from 1845 to 1856, that drought was as severe as the one that caused the Dust Bowl of the 1930s, destroying vegetation and drying the soil to dust that sailed away on the prevailing winds. During that time, the constant parade of army troopers and emigrants, looking for forage and wood, denuded the lush river valleys that for thousands of years had harbored bison and other animals during dry periods. Indians engaged in market hunting also made greater use of those valleys for grazing their growing horse herds, and killed other animals seeking refuge there. With their refugia gone, bison were stuck on the increasingly dry, barren Plains, where they perished from thirst and starvation or were struck down by bullets. Antelope, elk, and deer suffered only slightly less. When the drought broke, cattle and sheep supplanted them all, while the campaign of extermination against wolves, grizzlies, and Indians continued.[5]

Running with Custer

Dodge appears to have been a solid career officer—efficient, involved, organized, and more capable of diplomacy than of combat, not unlike many of his contemporaries in the western officer corps—judging from constant complaints lodged against them for lack of aggression in pursuing and killing Indians. He was the polar opposite of one contemporary, however—the impulsive, brash, thoughtless, self-indulgent George Armstrong Custer. Custer seems to have gotten stuck on the manic side of manic-depression, constantly driving himself, his animals, and everyone around him past the breaking point. He carelessly misjudged and charged his enemy one time too many, and it cost him his life overlooking the Little Bighorn River in Montana—not to mention the lives of 209 men in his command, including his brothers and brother-in-law.

Early in his career, at the height of the Civil War, Custer's life appeared charmed, and his recklessness for the Union won him renown. At Gettysburg, he broke through the cavalry of the dashing, mythic Confederate horseman James Ewell Brown "Jeb" Stuart. Finishing the job in the Shenandoah Valley, he rode in advance of a headlong cavalry assault that killed Stuart and overwhelmed his troop. He also proved himself more ruthless and cunning than another legendary Confederate cavalryman—the South was deemed superior in horsemanship—John S. Mosby, leader of the marauding Rangers. At Appomattox Courthouse, Custer received Robert E. Lee's white flag of surrender. He was a hero, the favorite field officer of Union cavalry commander Phil Sheridan, who after the Civil

War became the scourge of Indians. Custer was a top-notch horse-man who, during a stint in Kentucky with the Seventh Cavalry some years later, advised his officers to buy thoroughbred culls—animals whose only fault was that they were deemed too slow for racing. He was also a lover of hounds. Ordered west in 1866, in command of the Seventh, he traveled with his customary pack of greyhounds, staghounds, and foxhounds—sometimes numbering forty dogs. It is said he dearly loved his wife, Elizabeth, known as Libbie—and said by none more loudly than she—but it appears that nothing came between him and his hounds, neither his multiple concubines nor his long-suffering, adoring wife.

He had run hounds as a child but received his first pack in adulthood as a gift from a Texas rancher following the Civil War. After that, he had at least two dogs with him whenever he was in the field. The dogs always came to lie beside Custer when he napped on the trail, Libbie Custer wrote in *Boots and Saddles*, her memoir of life with her husband after his "heroic" death at Little Bighorn. "I've seen them stretched at his back and curled around his head, while the nose and paws of one rested on his breast," she said. The staghound Blucher, a favorite named for a favorite who died at the Washita massacre, would leap to join Custer on his saddle, while the epileptic old hound Rover would leave the kennel and scratch at the Custers' door whenever he felt a seizure coming on. Inside, he would lie next to Custer, knowing his master would comfort him, Libbie reported. She always called Custer "the general," his last field rank in the Civil War, although at the time he was a lieutenant colonel.[6]

Custer's own 1874 memoir, *My Life on the Plains*, while judged a self-serving prevarication in many regards, appears to describe accurately, if unconsciously, how his behavior with his hounds mirrored his style of command. First published in twenty installments in the popular magazine *Galaxy* between 1872 and 1874, it detailed his adventures on the trail of fearsome Indians and wild game. Custer recounted how he took two "English greyhounds" with him on his first Indian campaign, in the spring of 1866, a drive organized by Major General Winfield Scott Hancock to punish the

Sioux and Cheyenne for raiding mail stations. His guides were a group of Delaware Indians and "plainsmen," one of them Wild Bill Hickok, a fearless blond dandy with two ivory-handled pistols—not unlike Custer himself. Eager to test the speed of his greyhounds against antelope, the fleetest animals on the Plains, Custer rose at four one morning when his troops were pursuing a group of Indians, and took off hunting. Drawing near some antelope grazing about two miles from camp, he loosed the greyhounds, and off they charged, Custer in hot pursuit, astride the horse he had ridden in the closing days of the Civil War. It was a "rashly imprudent" move, he said, but that never stopped him. Finally, seeing that his dogs weren't close to the antelope, he called them off, blaming their failure on lack of exercise. His sole companion, the troop's chief bugler, had already returned to camp, and Custer understood full well that he was in hostile territory, his whereabouts unknown. It was past time to return, but on his way back to his troops, he spotted a buffalo "nearly a mile distant" and could not restrain himself.[7]

Using a ravine as cover, he tried to sneak up on the bison bull, but it discovered him and took off, with Custer forcing his tired horse into a gallop. "I only know that even the greyhounds were left behind," Custer said of that wild chase. He repeatedly gave up clear shots to prolong the race, despite his awareness that his horse was near its limit. Riding without reins, he was finally about to pull the trigger when the buffalo wheeled to confront his tormentor. The horse veered away, and a startled Custer, grabbing for the reins with his pistol hand in an effort to keep his saddle, accidentally pulled the trigger, shooting his horse through the brain. Recovering from a sudden headfirst dismount, he realized that he was thoroughly lost. After his greyhounds arrived, Custer, a revolver in each hand, followed their "gaze" toward what he assumed to be his camp. Seeing horsemen approach, he hid in a ravine until he determined they were his men, and thus was saved from his own folly. The troop had left Fort Riley, Kansas, and traveled west about 120 miles across the prairie without preventing the destruction of a single mail station or capturing one Indian. But their horses were so malnourished, exhausted, and abused that they were dying when they arrived at Fort Hays, Kansas. In short, it was a typical Custer excursion.

During a sixty-five-mile forced march in July 1867, up the North Republican River to the Platte River, Custer, by his own admission, inflicted untold suffering on man and beast: the horses and draft animals were given no water, and even "many of the dogs accompanying the command died from thirst and exhaustion." Along the Platte, forty men deserted one night. When another thirteen sneaked off the next day at noon, Custer ordered them hunted down: Seven escaped on horseback; six afoot were caught in a shootout that left three wounded and one dead. After the Seventh Cavalry arrived in Fort Wallace, in far western Kansas, Custer decided to take one hundred of the best remaining men and horses on a rapid 150-mile trip to Fort Hays for much-needed supplies. But on July 25 he abruptly abandoned his troop to travel by train to Fort Riley to see Libbie. She called it the mad romantic dash of someone deeply in love, but other observers believed it due to a letter Custer had received warning him that Libbie was smitten with a junior officer at the fort. Custer himself was a renowned fornicator, but he could not tolerate being a cuckold. Incorrigible romantic or jealous philanderer, he was arrested, court-martialed for desertion, convicted, and suspended from his command for one year, pay forfeited.[8]

That slap on the wrist was made lighter when General Phil—"The only good Indian is a dead Indian"—Sheridan took over the Indian wars and brought his favorite cavalry commander back before the year was out. This time Custer proceeded with two favored Scottish staghounds, Blucher and Maida. They were stronger hunters than the greyhounds, he said, Blucher having run down and killed a wolf by himself, a difficult feat for any dog. While on patrol through the snowbound Wichita Mountains in the late fall of 1868, Custer spied a herd of bison not far from his advancing force and spurred his horse and dogs forward. He wanted to test Blucher and Maida's courage, he said, so he cut a young buffalo from the herd and gave chase. The dogs were so close that he could not shoot, and he watched as the bison, bogged down in the snow, turned to face his pursuers. Blucher grabbed his throat and Maida his shoulders. The

bison tossed Blucher into the snow and would have crushed him
had Maida not hung on. Fearing the bison would best them, Custer
leaped from his horse and with his knife cut the bison's hamstrings,
causing it to fall. Then he shot it.

Not long thereafter, the troop approached a camp of Cheyenne
on the Washita River. It was a peaceful group under Black Kettle,
but to Custer all Indians were combatants and fair game. According
to some accounts, that night he ordered his troopers to kill their
dogs so their barking would not reveal the presence of the troops to
the Indians, but the evidence for that is scarce. Certainly, he did not
include his own dogs in the order. They were present at the next
morning's assault, which came four years after the massacre at Sand
Creek, Colorado, that killed 180 of Black Kettle's followers. In
Custer's surprise attack at Washita, 103 died officially—11 warriors
and 92 women, children, and old people, including Black Kettle
himself—but the number may have been greater. Custer then ordered his men to collect and slaughter 800 Indian ponies and burn
the village and all its goods. During that bloodbath, surviving Indians from adjoining villages made off with the troopers' coats, laid
aside for combat. Blucher gave chase and was killed by an arrow,
according to Custer.

Custer was again a hero, having scored a "great victory" in the
war to clear southern Kansas of Indians. That he had luckily avoided
charging headfirst into the main village of 6,000 or so Cheyennes,
Arapahos, Kiowas, and Comanches, camped, like Black Kettle, in
the Washita valley for the winter, mattered little to those, including
Sheridan, who wanted dead Indians. Nor was it troublesome to any
white soldiers or politicians that Black Kettle, the aging top chief of
the Cheyenne, had just two days earlier pledged to an Indian agent
that he was friendly, and the day before was planning to send emis-
saries, with a message of peace, to Sheridan himself. More problematic, though, was the fact that in his haste, Custer not only had
failed to discover the larger encampment but also had abandoned a
subordinate, Major Joel H. Elliott, and a detachment of eighteen
men without determining their fate. Feeling under pressure from a
gathering group of warriors, he abruptly left the field. Returning

days later with Sheridan, to gloat over his victory and bask in his commander's praise, Custer learned that Elliott and his men had pursued escapees from Custer's assault into the teeth of warriors charging upstream to join the battle. The larynx of each American soldier was cut out. But Custer was more upset when he discovered the corpse of Blucher, and he was more interested in the behavior of the troopers who captured surviving Cheyenne puppies and raised them as their pets, even though to Custer's mind they were definitely not well bred.

Custer's personal spoil of war was Monahsetah, a nineteen-year-old Cheyenne girl, seven months pregnant, the daughter of Little Rock, a chief. Traveling south to meet more Cheyenne in January 1869, he took her as an interpreter and concubine. This time he left the Indian camp without a fight, after negotiations and a threat to kill three hostages brought the release of two captive white women and a pledge that the Cheyenne would return to the reservation. Medicine Arrow, a leader among the Cheyenne and powerful medicine man, warned Custer during that visit that if he ever betrayed the promise of peace he had just made while smoking with the Cheyenne, he would die. After their return to Fort Hays in February and the delivery of her baby, Monahsetah lived as Custer's mistress and apparently became pregnant with his child. But shortly before Libbie's arrival for the summer, he sent her to live among other Washita refugees encamped near the fort and finally to the reservation. He never saw her again; the child may have lived only in legend.

Late that summer, an officer shot and killed Maida during a bison hunt staged for a group of influential visitors who had traveled by railroad to see the hero of the Civil War and the battle of Washita and, if lucky, ride to hounds with him. Leading the pack, Maida leapt and seized a bison by the throat. Several overeager army officers then opened fire, despite the presence of the dog, and one of the bullets hit Maida in the head, killing her instantly. Custer eulogized her in the November 1869 issue of *Turf, Field and Farm* in a poem it would have been best not to print.

The next year, Custer was foxhunting and buying thoroughbred culls and unhappily chasing the Ku Klux Klan and moonshiners in Kentucky. Apparently his hounds were as bored as he and Libbie, for whenever orderlies took them for walks, they attacked the Elizabethtown dogs and cats, killing more than a few. In January 1872, Custer joined Sheridan in escorting Grand Duke Alexis of Russia on a hunting excursion to the west that employed Buffalo Bill Cody as a guide and 1,000 Sioux as stage props. Hunting along the Platte River, that massive party was able to kill only 300 bison, but they supplemented them with other game, Sioux women, pageantry, and enough extravagant tales from Cody and Custer to satisfy any royal blood. Indeed, Alexis visited the Custers in Kentucky and had them accompany him to New Orleans for his twenty-first-birthday celebration, before he departed for Russia.

Later in 1872, Custer and the Seventh Cavalry were ordered to Dakota Territory to protect workers on the Northern Pacific Railroad, especially from Sioux and Cheyenne upset at continuing incursions into their territory. For much of the time, Custer was on holiday, riding off with Libbie to follow the hounds. In 1873 he escorted a party of railroad surveyors up the Yellowstone. He was also hunting and counted among his prey his first grizzly bear, the mark, he said, of a great hunter. He boasted of the kill in a letter to Libbie at Fort Abraham Lincoln, near Bismarck, told of learning taxidermy from the expedition's scientists, and apprised her of the performance of his staghounds—Tuck, Cardigan, and the second Blucher. Tuck, he reported in a letter of July 23, 1873, had become his favorite, for her devotion to him and the hunt. He described how she had used her speed to pull down a full-grown bull antelope she had chased for a mile, outstripping the other dogs. At night, she would lay her head on his knee and then slowly climb into his lap, where she would sleep soundly.

The following summer Custer led a geological expedition into the Black Hills, known to the Sioux as Paha Sapa—a game-rich area sacred to the Indians—to investigate rumors of gold. When he confirmed that the streams there ran with gold, the rush was on, despite an initial government decision to keep the miners out. The following year, Dodge led the expedition to negotiate the miners' removal, which ended up with his superior, General George Crook, ordering them to leave but tacitly leading them to understand that he would do nothing if they stayed. In the summer of 1876 the army sent three commands to herd free-ranging Sioux and Cheyenne back onto the reservation in the Dakota Badlands and to build a road into the Black Hills to secure a supply line for the miners. Custer and the Seventh Cavalry rode point for General Alfred Terry's force as it moved up the Yellowstone River from Fort Lincoln to the Little Bighorn. Custer had with him his beloved Tuck, who, he told Libbie in a letter of June 12, one of his last, "regularly comes when I am writing, and lays her head on the desk, rooting up my hand with her long nose until I consent to stop and notice her. She and Swift, Lady and Kaiser sleep in my tent." Given his habit of riding at the front of his troops with his hounds, even when in hostile territory, it is possible that they were with him at Little Bighorn on June 25, 1876, but whether they were captured, killed, or had been left earlier with the supply train and thus survived is unknown.[9]

Libbie Custer was silent on the point. She mentioned only that her favorite staghound—her own most cherished dog was her little spaniel, Ginnie—was the cream-colored Cardigan, who was with Custer on the Yellowstone expedition and would, when Libbie was present, always try to engineer his big frame into her lap. His valor impressed her, as did his suffering: reintroduced to the kennel once after a long absence, he was set upon by the pack and so badly injured that it took months for him to heal. As she prepared to leave Fort Lincoln following the massacre, she asked that Cardigan be sent to a clergyman friend of Custer in Minneapolis. After the dog finally died, the preacher had him stuffed and presented to "one of the public buildings in Minneapolis," she reported, calling it a "worthy tribute, not only because of the testimony it gives to the friendship of the people for his master, but because he was the bravest and most faithful of animals." She issued an appeal in Chicago in early August for an individual or group to take the pack, but there is no apparent record of their fate. Still, more than a decade later, Theodore Roosevelt hunted on the Plains with descendants of Custer's hounds, so they did not simply vanish.[10]

Following the counterattack at Little Bighorn that wiped out five of the Seventh Cavalry's nine companies, Cheyenne women who had seen Custer in 1869 and knew of Medicine Arrow's curse prevented the mutilation of his corpse, to honor Monahsetah. Instead, they pierced his eardrums with awls so that he might hear in the spirit world, something he seemed incapable of in life. Custer, who at one time or another betrayed nearly everyone who trusted him, made one rash, headlong charge too many, and this time some of his own subordinates failed to ride to his rescue. Yet like the brave, hapless defenders of the Alamo forty years earlier, Custer in defeat became a greater hero than he had ever been in life, celebrated for his courage, his risk taking, his flashy style, and his mad dashes across the Plains after his hounds. Libbie contributed to the deification, to be sure, but it worked because Custer embodied many of the qualities that Americans at the time admired. They wanted Indian lands so they could fulfill their destiny, and they wanted the Indians gone—confined on reservations or dead. They also—at least the men—loved hunting.

Upon spotting the advance of a combined force under generals Alfred Terry and John Gibbon, the victorious Sioux and Cheyenne packed their travois and left Little Bighorn the next day in a long, noisy trail of horses, dogs, and people. Sitting Bull, Crazy Horse, Gall, and their allies and tribesmen had achieved an impressive, if pyrrhic, victory. Crazy Horse and many of the other victors were run to ground by relentless U.S. Army pursuit and confined to a reservation within a year. Indian guards killed Crazy Horse on September 5, 1877. Sitting Bull led his people into Canada and remained a free man until hunger and the deprivations of exile forced them to return to the United States and surrender on July 19, 1881.

Trading on his notoriety, Sitting Bull toured with Buffalo Bill's Wild West Show in 1885—to applause and derision. Disgusted with white society, he left the show after fewer than six months, well short of the time he would have become a self-parody, and returned

to the reservation, his reputation as a great spiritual leader and warrior intact. His name continued to rouse fear in the West until the
early hours of December 15, 1890, when Indian guards killed him
while arresting him on orders from the federal authorities, including the army commander for the upper Missouri, General Nelson A.
Miles, nicknamed Bear Coat for the distinctive coat he wore, from a
grizzly he had killed. They wanted to keep Sitting Bull from becoming involved in the Ghost Dance, a religious revival founded by
the Paiute holy man Wovoka, which promised a return of the buffalo, fallen ancestors, and the way of life that had existed before the
arrival of white people—God would remove the interlopers. The
army next moved against the Ghost Dance, and on December 28,
1890, the reconstituted Seventh Cavalry, renewing the tradition of
Washita and avenging Little Bighorn, opened fire and killed 300 unarmed Sioux men, women, and children in the "battle" of Wounded
Knee, considered the last major engagement of the Indian wars.

Hunting Geronimo

Perhaps nowhere was the effect of war on people and dogs more
apparent than in the Southwest, among the Apache and Navajo. By
the mid-nineteenth century, the Navajo were relatively prosperous,
with peach orchards, gardens, sheep, goats, horses, and mules,
which they replenished through theft—of course, the thieving went
both ways, but the Americans counted only when the Indians did
it. The Navajo also used descendants of the large Spanish mastiff as
guardians of their flocks, or raised their own dogs from infancy
with the sheep and goats, following the common Spanish practice.
The Churro sheep of the Southwest, descended from the ancient
Iberian Churra breed brought by the Spanish to the New World in
the sixteenth century, were herded to California through the 1850s
to feed gold rush settlers. They also formed the bulk of Navajo
flocks; their wool was employed for weaving, their meat prized for
its flavor. After a Confederate invasion of New Mexico, defeated by
Union sympathizers and troops under the former mountain-man-

turned-Taos-rancher Kit Carson, attention turned to the Navajo. Like the Apache, they were accused of stealing livestock and committing atrocities against American settlers, including a growing number of prospectors. More to the point, gold was discovered in Arizona, and people were on the move to the Southwest, chasing fulfillment of the dream that first brought the Spanish to the region in the sixteenth century.

In 1862, General James Carleton arrived from California with a mandate to move the Mescalero Apache out of the Rio Grande Valley and the Navajo from their homes in northwestern New Mexico and northeastern Arizona, to Bosque Redondo, a dry, desolate nothing on the Pecos River in eastern New Mexico. With Colonel Kit Carson again taking the lead, the army first forcibly moved several hundred Mescalero, then waged a scorched-earth campaign against the Navajo, destroying their maize, their orchards, horses, mules, sheep, goats, and dogs by the thousands. In 1864, Carson and his troops, under orders from Carleton, forced 8,000 Navajo to walk 300 miles to Bosque Redondo with their remaining livestock and dogs. Most of the Mescalero had escaped by then and returned to their ancestral home around White Mountain, Arizona. But the Navajo were held captive in grinding poverty—their crops failing, their livestock dying—until 1868, when they were allowed to return home and resume their pastoral life. Today the Navajo-Churro sheep are recognized as a rare and endangered breed uniquely adapted to their arid environment, but they are threatened by the failure of young Navajo to pursue the sheepherding life of their grandmothers on severely degraded pastures, despite the popularity of traditional Navajo weavings. The guard dogs now are small and agile, many of them looking like the old Indian dog, but whether they will survive the decline in herding and the onslaught of Anglo-American collectors intent on owning an "authentic" Indian dog is unclear.

Numbering perhaps 6,000—far fewer than the Navajo—the Apache waged guerrilla war against the Spanish for 250 years before the Americans assumed the Spanish role in the mid-nineteenth century. The Apache, too, herded sheep, and the description by a traveler in the early 1870s probably fits the Navajo and mestizo as well as the Apache herder. "Each flock was accompanied by one or more herdsmen," wrote Samuel Woodworth Cozzens in *The Marvelous Country, or Three years in Arizona and New Mexico*, "wild, gaunt, half-naked creatures, whose clothing consisted of a sheepskin tied about their loins, and whose only weapon of defence was a 'sling . . . '" Their dogs were nearly as intelligent as they, Cozzens said, describing how he had seen one shepherd "with a single word send his dog among a flock of several thousand in pursuit of some sheep that had chanced to stray from a neighboring flock, and invariably the quick-witted animal would single out the intruder in an almost incredibly short time."[11]

Apache dogs in general would answer a warrior's yell with a cacophony of howls that made it sound as if they numbered in the thousands, said Cozzens, not realizing that in the past the dogs had reached that number. But a decade of intermittent war and close to full-time raiding on both sides of the U.S.–Mexican border had reduced the numbers of people and dogs. Families were torn apart, as were larger bands; children were raised in silence; dogs were often killed, abandoned, or kept only in small numbers, lest their barking and howling alert pursuing soldiers. The Apache believed that the distinctive copper spots above their dogs' eyes represented the sunset and their white paws were the morning light, meaning they would protect their people day and night as long as they lived. Killing them represented a significant sacrifice.

In 1876, the year Custer fell at Little Bighorn and Cozzens published his book, a band of Nednhi Apache of the Sierra Madre under Juh and Noglee, with the forty-seven-year-old Bedonkohe medicine man Goyahtlay, or Geronimo, renowned for knowing what was happening elsewhere, was "asked" by the new Indian agent, John P. Clum, to report to the barren San Carlos Reservation, their government-approved home in central Arizona. Mexicans had murdered Geronimo's mother, wife, and children in 1849, and the Americans had continued capturing people under flags of truce and then killing or exiling them, so he wanted nothing to do with the proposal; nor did the chiefs Juh and Noglee. That night, they cut the throats of their dogs, abandoned their old people—desperate acts both—and headed for the mountains in southwestern New Mexico. But the gambit failed, and they were forced to move to San Carlos. In September 1880, Juh fled the reservation with a group of Chiricahua Apaches under Nachez, a son of Cochise. Closely pursued by the troops of General Orlando Wilcox, they slit the throats of their light-colored horses and their dogs, so their howling would not betray their departure, and slipped into Mexico, where they resumed their marauding.

Between 1876 and 1886, bands of Apache, usually numbering several hundred or fewer, under their older leaders Juh, Victorio, Nana, Nachez, Geronimo, and others, struggled to preserve some semblance of dignity, freedom, and their free-ranging way of life in the rugged mountains of New Mexico, Arizona, and northern Mexico. Geronimo became the most visible and despised war leader of the Chiricahua Apaches during that decade, when the brutality and torture practiced on both sides exceeded any that had come before, as did the demonization of the Apache. White settlers became so fearful that they began to accuse Geronimo and his small band of Chiricahua and other Apaches of every theft of livestock and murder, though many of them were perpetrated by other Apaches, Comanches, or renegade vaqueros. Geronimo and his warriors were accused of wanton killing, rape, mutilation, scalping, and burying naked captives up to their necks near anthills, so the ants would eat the skin off their faces.

In 1886, his name synonymous with butchery on both sides of the border, Geronimo was tracked down for the last time in Mexico and persuaded to trust his fate to the notorious Indian fighter Bear Coat Miles. Miles had made his reputation hounding Chief Joseph and the Nez Percé with such tenacity that they had to surrender or die of exhaustion and hunger, and tracking down Sitting Bull and his Sioux following Little Bighorn, and he was ambitious for higher command. He had been ordered to Arizona specifically to run Geronimo and other Apache warriors to ground.

Bear Coat Miles did save Geronimo from hanging, a fate demanded by Americans, including President Grover Cleveland, frightened out of their wits by tales of his depredations. Miles ordered him sent with his small band from Fort Bowie—the bulk of Chiricahua and other Apaches were shipped from Fort Apache at Holbrook, Arizona—into exile in Florida, the men to Fort Pickens in Pensacola, the women and children to the sixteenth-century Fort Marion in St. Augustine. They were separated for more than a year before being reunited. Both forts were hot, dank, mosquito-infested places antipodal to the arid mountains the tribe had called home for more than a thousand years.

Several months after Geronimo's surrender, Mangas, son of the great chief Mangas Coloradas—sometimes spelled "Mangus"—and the last free Chiricahua followed suit and were soon sent into exile from Fort Apache. Anglo-American soldiers and civilians there and in Holbrook considered the thousands of dogs of the 382 Indians major pests. The dogs regularly invaded the telegraph office and other buildings, stole food, and marauded around town. In the fort, they disrupted the evening dress parade with their play and noise. Disgruntled soldiers and citizens finally adopted the tactic of tying tin cans on their tails, so they would know of their approach. Judging from the New York model, the cans were also intended to embarrass the dogs enough to make them behave. The dogs were distressed, as were the people, both sides knowing they were to be split apart forever, and nothing could be done.

The late Ed Dorn, in his epic comic-book poem *Recollections of Gran Apacheria*, vividly captured the grief of the Chiricahua Apache dogs when their people were loaded into a train bound for exile and death.

> *As the train moves off at the first turn of the wheel*
> *With its cargo of florida bound exiles*
> *Most all of whom had been put bodily*
> *Into the coaches, their 3,000 dogs,*
> *Who had followed them like a grand party*
> *To the railhead at Holbrook*
> > *Began to cry*
> *When they saw the smoking creature resonate*

With their masters,
And as the máquina acquired speed they howled and
*   moaned*
A frightening noise from their great mass
And some of them followed the cars
For forty miles
Before they fell away in exhaustion[12]

A hint of what happened next comes from Charles Fletcher Lummis, an editor for the *Los Angeles Daily Times*, covering the hunt for Geronimo in 1885–86, which had become a national obsession. Lummis described the departure of Geronimo's wife, children, and others from Fort Bowie on April 7, 1886, the eve of General James Crook's transfer of power to Bear Coat Miles. Geronimo was still free, but his dependents were being sent to Fort Apache. After arriving with their horses and dozens of dogs, they were unceremoniously placed in the train cars, the doors locked. The dogs yelped and howled their distress and chased the train as it chugged out of the station, with one keeping pace for some twenty miles. White settlers milling around to witness the departure used the dogs for target practice, killing nearly all of them. They then corralled and auctioned off the horses, knowing the Indians would never reclaim them.

Hundreds of the exiled Apaches died in forts Marion and Pickens of tuberculosis and other diseases, an ironic fate given that thousands of wealthy white Americans were traveling, many of them with dogs, to luxury hotels in St. Augustine and down the Florida coast seeking a cure for the same deadly disease and to escape the foul air of their cities. Apache children were taken from their parents and shipped to Indian schools in Carlisle, Pennsylvania, where many of them also perished from diseases to which they had never been exposed. Geronimo himself lived until 1909, as a prisoner of war, becoming something of a sideshow freak—the savage defanged and put on display like a grizzly bear or other frightening beast. His American jailers never allowed him to return to Arizona.

Walking Shadow

Covering Geronimo's capture and exile represented a return for Lummis to the region that had captivated him just a year earlier. In 1884, three years after leaving Harvard, where one of his friends was Theodore Roosevelt, Lummis decided to walk from Cincinnati to Los Angeles to take a job with the *Daily Times* (now the *Times*). He was "vagabondizing," he boasted in *A Tramp Across the Continent*, his 1892 account of that adventure, a feat that might have gotten him thrown into a Southern work camp for vagrancy but in the more open and Wild West was just another eccentricity—albeit a dangerous one. In 143 days, he traveled 3,057 miles, the "longest walk for pure pleasure that is on record," he said, with the immodesty and hyperbole that marked his style. For approximately half that distance he traveled with a young greyhound, Shadow, he adopted from some hapless Italian miners in Pueblo, Colorado. They had inherited the puppy from a miner who, before he died, had starved and beaten him during his first four months. "How little I dreamed then what that careless mercy meant—of the pleasure, the privations, and the deadly dangers we were to go through together, this slender black dog and I; or of the awful experience that was to mark our parting, and leave with me some of the brightest and some of the saddest memories of a crowded life," Lummis wrote of Shadow, who despite his horrible beginning was "a fine specimen of his blood."[13]

Lummis's walk nearly ended soon after it began, when, in Indiana, a "huge and savage dog" leapt at him from a farmyard and just missed ripping out his throat—that being the job of farm dogs in isolated regions. Renewing its attack, the dog seized the stick Lummis brandished in his left hand and held fast, while Lummis with his right hand stuck the eight-inch blade of his hunting knife into the dog's throat, killing it instantly. From there, Lummis made his way through Missouri, where he met Frank James, of the notorious James-Younger gang. He crossed Kansas the long way and found the buffalo nearly gone, victims of "the pot-hunter, the hide-hunter, and, worst of all, the soulless fellow who killed for the mere savagery of killing." The cowboy dandies in their "beaded dog-skin coats" depressed him, as did the food. After narrowly escaping a convict laborer seeking to club him with a sledgehammer and steal his .44 caliber pistol, he rescued Shadow and headed for the Sangre de Cristo Mountains and Santa Fe. It was, he says, a "civilization that was new to me—that of the swarthy Mexicans and their quaint adobe houses, with regiments of mongrel curs and flocks of silken-haired Angorra goats." To his credit, he recognized his bias and overcame it, while falling in love with the land and its people. On a later, four-year sojourn in Isleta Pueblo, south of Albuquerque, because of paralysis in his left arm, probably from a stroke, he penned the phrase See America First and promoted the region not just for its history but also for its healthy climate and magical chiles. He also became a staunch defender of Indian rights, frequently lobbying his friend Roosevelt and anyone else who would listen about the horrors of an educational system that ripped Indian children from their homes and cultures and sent them off to be raised in distant states and to learn "white" ways.[14]

In Santa Fe, Shadow delighted in the fresh rabbits and other game hanging in the market and in the sights and smells of a place that even then was intent on promoting itself as the "oldest" city in North America, with the "oldest" house—good for entertaining tourists but not true (St. Augustine, Florida, wins). Leaving the city, Shadow took off after a pair of coyotes, only to beat a hasty retreat to Lummis when they suddenly turned on him—two coyotes being more than a match for the larger greyhound. Lummis explored the largely abandoned gold and copper mines in Golden, south of Santa Fe, with Shadow his reluctant underground companion. But the dog could not follow him down a thirty-foot rope into one of the mines and so "sat at the very brink of the shaft and howled at the top of his voice till I came up again." Crossing the Sandia Mountains, the two vagabonds were caught in a late afternoon snowstorm that added rapidly to the two feet of snow already on the ground. After several hours, the puppy gave out and Lummis carried him draped over his backpack until, stumbling, he fell on top of Shadow and, exhausted, lay facedown in the snow. Finally, fearing nightfall and death, he struggled to his feet with the greyhound and staggered into the first house he reached. Lummis and Shadow recovered, within days, and Lummis had developed a lifelong love for New Mexican chiles—the addictive peppers that form the basis of the local cuisine.[15]

Man and dog crossed New Mexico, passing Acoma Pueblo, which Lummis, with only some hyperbole, called the most wonderful aboriginal city on earth, and then through the otherworldly Navajo country of Monument Valley and Valley of the Gods. At the Fort Defiance trading post, they encountered a gunfighter Lummis quickly dismissed as a coward, "living in constant terror of Navajos and tramps, which he endeavored to conceal by murderous talk and braggadocio." He admired the "inbred but tireless and beautiful ponies" of the Navajo, as well as the people's blankets, cattle, sheep and goats, and silver jewelry. But in that beautiful country, Lummis fell twenty-five feet from a sandstone rock face he was attempting to climb, for the challenge of it—Shadow whining below in protest—and fractured his left arm. He came to consciousness with Shadow licking his face and "whining plaintively." Lummis managed to set and splint the arm himself and then to walk, despite the pain and cold, the remaining 700 miles to Los Angeles. Compounding his distress, he was a natural lefty and had to teach himself to do everything with his "wrong" hand.[16]

He succeeded admirably, killing a buck with Shadow's help, and descending into the Grand Canyon to sleep by the banks of the Colorado River. Yet tough as he was, Lummis could not bear the filth and fleas of the railroad station houses where they occasionally stopped for shelter, and in the end, he barely survived Shadow. In the desert near Yucca, Arizona, Shadow ran away and then attacked Lummis when he tried to lead his oddly behaving companion by a leash: "As I strode carelessly along, there came a snarl so unearthly, so savage, so unlike any other sound I ever heard that it froze my blood; and there within six inches of my throat was a wide, frothy mouth with sunlit fangs more fearful than a rattlesnake. *Shadow was mad!*" Lummis kicked him down an embankment, but Shadow rose and attacked again. Lummis kicked him down the embankment again and freed his gun just before Shadow attacked a third time. The bullet grazed the dog's skull and struck his flank. Yelping, he ran into the desert.[17]

Lummis shrank from the thought that his friend would die painfully alone. "A great wave of love swept through me," he wrote, "and drained my horror. I had tried to kill him to save myself, now I must kill him to save him from the most inconceivable of agonies." Dropping on one knee, he fired his pistol and hit the dog running 150 yards away, killing him instantly. Lummis dug a shallow desert grave: "There I left Shadow to his last sleep, and went alone down the bitter desert."[18]

The Grizzly Hounds

The American hero Bear Coat Miles became chief of staff of the army and returned in 1893 to the rugged Mogollon Mountains on the New Mexico–Arizona border, where a young Englishman, Montague Stevens, had carved out a ranch in the early 1880s. With him rode his son, several aides, and the artist Frederic Remington, writing and illustrating for *Harper's New Monthly Magazine*. An avid sportsman, Stevens had hunted throughout Wyoming in 1880, on one of those big-game expeditions that were so popular among wealthy Europeans and Americans. After graduating from Cambridge University in 1881, he returned to Wyoming with eight friends and hired his guide from the previous year, James H. Cook, a cowboy, Indian scout in the aftermath of Little Bighorn, and amateur paleontologist. Cook had negotiated permission with the Sioux chief Red Cloud for Yale University paleontologist Othniel C. Marsh to hunt for dinosaurs in the Badlands in 1870, a time when the Sioux distrusted anyone digging on their land. According to legend, Cook correctly told Red Cloud that Marsh was hunting bones, not gold, but more important, he also conveyed Marsh's promise to intercede with the president on behalf of the Sioux.

British and American investors were mad for Western cattle

ranches in the early 1880s, investing tens of millions of dollars to fuel a boom in local economies, and Stevens, already in love with the adventure of the West, became his family's agent. In 1882 he took on Cook and other investors in the purchase of a ranch in the Mogollons that at its height had 60,000 head of cattle. Theodore Roosevelt, a young, wealthy New Yorker, joined the investment fad a year later when he bought two ranches in western North Dakota, after hunting the area with friends and their dogs. Stevens eventually bought out his partners and had ranches spread over 2,400 square miles on both sides of the New Mexico–Arizona border. During the Apache guerrilla war, Stevens befriended the military commanders and allowed their troops to bivouac on his ranches; he also frequently rode with the patrols. In that way, he developed a friendship with Miles, based in part on their mutual passion for reckless hunting. Stevens's obsession cost him his left arm a few years later when he accidentally blew it off with a shotgun while hunting geese on horseback in California.

Rather than quit, he turned his attention to grizzly bears, and within a few years had established a reputation as a bear hunter that extended far beyond the arid mountains of the Southwest. Stevens wrote in his remarkable memoir, *Meet Mr. Grizzly*, that he obsessed over grizzlies because he decided that killing them from horseback using a pack of trained dogs represented the epitome of hunting, of the chase. He pursued them with such passion and skill that by the turn of the century he had played a major role in their extirpation from the Southwest. What made his feat all the more remarkable was that he used only food rewards to train his dogs. That method is considered revolutionary today; on the late-nineteenth-century frontier, it was believed insane, but it worked beautifully.

In preparation for Miles's long-planned arrival in 1893, Stevens scouted for and found fresh grizzly tracks leading from a dead cow near one of his Mogollon ranches. After establishing a hunting camp near the carcass, he rode out to meet the general and his party. Stevens's pack had a "great variety of dogs," Remington wrote in the July 1895 *Harper's*—bloodhounds, staghounds, fox terriers, a big yellow mastiff, and "one or two dogs which would not classify in a bench show." The next morning the pack hit the trail running, literally leading the hunters up hill and down dale at a gallop. Remington and an aide, Colonel Michler, soon dropped behind. Stevens, Miles, and the rest of the lead group eventually lost the dogs and returned to camp, only to find the grizzly's hide waiting for them. The bear had come to bay near three of Stevens's cowboys, who lassoed its arms and legs, then stretched it out, while one killed it with a pocketknife. "Michler and I rode into camp, thinking on the savagery of man," Remington said. "One never heard of a bear which traveled all the way from New Mexico to Chicago to kill a man, and yet a man will go three thousand miles to kill a bear not for love, or fear, or hate, or meat; for what then?"[19]

When Miles first appeared, Stevens had just begun to hunt with dogs, so his pack was ill-formed, but he soon realized that a big bear could lead dogs and riders on a hard chase of thirty or more miles, then turn and lay waste to the pack and be gone before the hunters even arrived. To solve that problem, he began building a pack of specialists—hounds that ran in front, trailing hounds that stayed between riders and lead dogs, slower dogs to bring the riders up to the pack if they got lost in rough terrain, and baying dogs and fighters, to distract the bear so Stevens could kill it with a pistol. His first leader was Old Drive, a black-and-tan hound he had obtained from an abusive, transplanted Southerner. Stevens also added a wolfhound, Czar, lent to him by Miles, who had received the dog as a gift from the czar of Russia; and a Great Dane, Princess, a prize-winning show dog from Massachusetts who, because of an unfortunate habit of knocking down anyone who hugged her owner, had been exiled to the country as a "fighting dog." Finding that Princess had no taste for rumbling with grizzlies, Stevens used her to train other dogs and to keep track of the hounds while staying close to him. A deliberate crossbreeding of Czar and Princess produced dogs that, as they matured, attacked anything in sight; indeed, Stevens found them so predatory that he gave them to a neighboring hunter of coyotes and wolves.[20]

In 1896, twenty years after the Battle of Little Bighorn, Miles appeared again at Stevens's ranch to renew his hunt for a grizzly, this time with an escort from the reconstituted Seventh Cavalry. Again, he came up empty-handed, while Stevens himself killed one bear after a daylong chase with Old Drive, and one of his hired hands killed another that was being driven to the general. Shortly after that hunt, a black bear killed Old Drive, and Stevens began training a bloodhound, Sleuth, as his leader—the dog also pointed and herded sheep. Behind the brilliant Sleuth, the pack included a bobtailed, blue-eyed English sheepdog, a fox terrier, several pit bulls, Princess, and crosses between the sheepdog and bloodhounds. With them, Stevens enjoyed success seemingly every time out.

His reputation grew, and as the century ended, he prepared to invite Theodore Roosevelt to hunt grizzlies with him. Remington had introduced him to Roosevelt in New York in November 1896, when Roosevelt was a young, ambitious politician and already an accomplished writer, rancher, and hunter. Remington had illustrated Roosevelt's book *Ranch Life and the Hunting Trail*, and Roosevelt, having heard all about the mountain hunts, was eager for the chase. But he was also skeptical about the ability of hounds to hunt grizzlies and wanted a guarantee that he would bag one, and Stevens admitted he could not give it. While continuing to hunt black bears and other animals behind or over dogs, Roosevelt found other diversions, adding to his list of accomplishments, to name but a few: warrior/hero, governor of New York, and vice president of the United States. The same war in Cuba that exhilarated Roosevelt, whose Rough Riders occasionally employed dogs while on patrol, depressed his friend Remington, whose feelings toward even the slaughter of animals, which he reported on regularly, had always been ambivalent. His attitude is encapsulated in the famous but apparently apocryphal exchange of telegrams with William Randolph Hearst, who had hired him as a "war artist" to accompany correspondent Richard Harding Davis. Upon receiving Remington's message that the conflict was dull and disgusting, Hearst ordered him to stay, saying, "You furnish the pictures. I'll furnish the war."

Meanwhile, Stevens built his Sleuth-led pack and finally felt confident enough to guarantee the newly elected vice president his grizzly bear. It would have been quite a hunt. As a cocreator of the

Boone and Crockett Club, Roosevelt was the world's best-known sportsman and adventurer. He had probably hunted every type of game North America offered, and had run hounds on the Dakota Plains—a staghound after wounded deer; a mixed pack with a Scottish deerhound, a greyhound, a lurcher, and a crossbred hound after coyotes and foxes. But game had become scarce there by the late 1880s, and by the time he first met Stevens, Roosevelt had shifted his interests to mountain hunting "because of the nerve, daring, and physical hardihood implied in its successful pursuit." But before Stevens could finally issue his invitation, disaster struck—and it was not McKinley's assassination and Roosevelt's elevation to the presidency.[21]

While hunting, Stevens routinely let his dogs feed on cattle carcasses and other carrion, which abounded. As he searched for a grizzly likely to please Roosevelt, he left his dogs in camp, near a spring where a freshly killed steer lay. Unknown to him, another rancher had shot the steer and laced its carcass with strychnine in order to kill coyotes, wolves, and bears. Instead, it sent Stevens's dogs into convulsions and death before his horrified eyes. Having played a significant role in killing off all the grizzlies along the New Mexico–Arizona border, Stevens became an ardent conservationist, but his conversion failed to stem the tide of destruction that had nearly extirpated grizzlies from the lower forty-eight states. Although he continued to keep dogs as pets, Stevens never created another hunting pack—he had lost the heart.

9

Don't Fence Me In:
Seeking New Frontiers When the Old One Closes

∽

I T IS OFTEN SAID of the present moment that time moves more quickly and change occurs more rapidly than at any period in the world's history. The hyperbole behind that statement becomes clear when one considers that in the forty years following the start of the Civil War, an entire socioeconomic system was overthrown as millions of slaves were suddenly awarded their freedom; bison and several other species were extirpated from the Great Plains and replaced by cattle, sheep, and horses; western Indians were obliterated or confined to reservations in greatly reduced numbers; the age of the cowboy and long cattle drives out of Texas blossomed and died; expanding railroad and steamboat lines transformed travel, "shrinking" the world for growing numbers of people; prairies were plowed and fenced, forests clear-cut, waterways drained or dammed. Those years brought disastrous freezes and droughts; range wars between cattlemen, sheepmen, and farmers; more gold and silver discoveries; the rise and spread of the telegraph; the invention of refrigerated railcars and lush Pullman cars, of electricity, the telephone, and radio; the growth of the Standard

Oil Company and other monopolies and attempts to control them; deployment around the nation of horse-drawn fire wagons; labor unions, strikes, riots, and killings; and an expansion of wealth and privilege such as the world had seldom seen. Those years marked the final flowering and end of the period of the frontier in American history, the historian Frederick Jackson Turner declared in Chicago in 1893, the year Bear Coat Miles went grizzly hunting with Montague Stevens.

IN FORCING EUROPEAN SETTLERS to adjust to new circumstances, the frontier had shaped American culture and consciousness for more than two hundred years, Turner said in "The Significance of the Frontier in American History," an address delivered to a meeting of the American Historical Association at the site of an international exposition marking the 400th anniversary of Columbus's voyage. The frontier meant "perennial rebirth," the opportunity for the individual to pick up and go into the wilderness to create a new life. Moving inland from its first toehold on the Atlantic Coast—in the mid-1800s, it also began a movement from the Pacific inland—the frontier followed river valleys to natural "fall lines," Turner said: the Alleghenies, the Mississippi and Missouri, the Great Plains and Desert, and the Rocky Mountains. The pattern was always the same, as the pioneers—the fur traders, long hunters, and subsistence herders—pressed into Indian country, followed by the farmers or sometimes miners, and then the entrepreneurs. Ultimately, those who followed the trappers and traders seized and secured the land through war with the Indians. When Turner presented his thesis, the grand historical process had just been played out on the canvas of the Great Plains, and consolidation had become the order of the day: filling in the remaining blank areas on the map, including the polar regions; solidifying "civilization's" hold on the land by taming the wild man and wild dog within; holding on to some pristine landscapes and relict animal populations so they could be used and hunted another day; recording pedigrees and creating standards of beauty and performance to measure an animal's worth, measuring, for that matter, human worth through performance; and establishing rules of the hunt and of sport and of behavior in a world suddenly limited.[1]

In the West, the filling in meant replacing bison and antelope with cattle and sheep, planting ranchers and farmers where nomadic tribes had once roamed. The transformation was sometimes violent in its own right, and in many ways continues to this day, as people fight over proper uses of the land and water. Although the first open-range cattle drives of "mavericks," feral longhorns from Texas, had begun in 1846, they basically ran their course between 1866 and 1890, the years of the Plains Indian wars, with the heyday of the long cattle drives from Texas to the Kansas railheads along the Chisholm and Western Trails occurring from roughly 1875 to 1885. Then expansion of railroads, desire of ranchers to improve their stock through breeding and their pasture by planting grass to replace what remained of the overgrazed prairie vegetation, led to the widespread fencing of rangeland. Farmers fenced, as well, in an effort to keep livestock from their crops.

Cowmen used dogs on their ranches both to help round up cattle and to manage other livestock, especially sheep, if they raised both, but dogs apparently did not help drive the cattle along the Western trails, as they did in Florida and the Gulf Coastal region, and as they had done through the mid-nineteenth century in the East. Indeed, some cowboys appear to have considered dogs liabilities on the long drives because they could spook and stampede a herd, especially if the cattle were unaccustomed to them. Irate that cowboys had cut their fences and let cattle trample and eat their crops, farmers occasionally loosed their own dogs to stampede a herd, but the tactic was counterproductive: The cowboys usually shot the dogs—and not infrequently the farmers. If dogs accompanied the drive, and they doubtless did, since it would have been impossible to keep them away, they remained largely invisible. While it lasted, the cattle drive was the cowboys' show, and the vaqueros cut a trail of legend across the West that still looms large in American culture, often larger than that of the more complex and interesting long hunter.

WHEN IT CAME TO SHEEP, the dog took center stage, and sheep, though maligned then and now as smelly, stupid despoilers of land and water, were crucial to the development of the West. "The drama of the West belongs to the trapper, soldier, miner and cowboy," said the historian Edward N. Wentworth, "but its economic success was made certain by the great sheep trails." When, following the Civil War, cattle were driven north out of Texas by the vaqueros, who took the Spanish ranch system with them, sheep were "trailed" east first from California into Arizona and New Mexico mining towns, and then into Idaho and Montana. After the defeat of the Sioux and Nez Percé, the sheep trails began to run east out of Oregon and northeast from New Mexico, into all the Plains and mountain territories. In 1870 an estimated 5 million cattle grazed on the seventeen Western states: Texas, Oklahoma, Kansas, Nebraska, North and South Dakota, Montana, Idaho, Wyoming, Colorado, New Mexico, Arizona, Nevada, Utah, California, Oregon, and Washington. By 1885, the number had reached 35 to 40 million, only to crash over the next five years of drought and bitterly cold winters to around 27 million. Those cattle shared the Western rangelands, often uneasily, for few ranchers raised both species, with an estimated 53 million sheep, largely Merinos. Sheep munched their way over slopes stripped of their pines to feed steam engines, frame mine shafts, build houses and towns, and fuel fires, effectively pastoralizing the landscape while aiding the destruction of the ecosystem. At their peak in 1910, as many as 70 million sheep and 57 million cattle may have grazed the West, at least double the number of wild grazers.[2]

Flock masters drove up to 25,000 sheep at a time on a six-month or longer journey that could cover 1,000 miles, with the flock divided into bands of 4,000 to 6,000 animals under the care of a herder and his dogs. Although many of those sheepdogs were mixed

John Woodhouse Audubon painted the now extinct Hare Indian dog and the Esquimaux dogs of Canada for *The Viviparous Quadrupeds of North America*, written by his father, John James Audubon, and John Bachman.

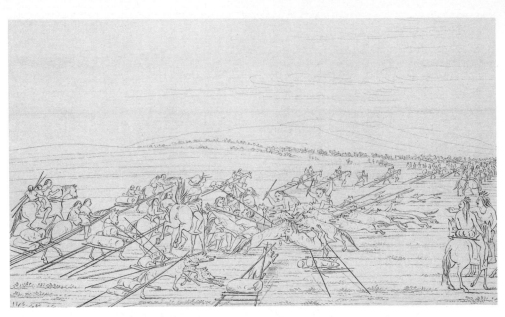

George Catlin captured the chaos of a dog fight that broke out
as Comanche Indians moved across the Plains.

The dashing young Union cavalry officer Lieutenant George Armstrong Custer with
his "Newfoundland dog," during the Civil War's Peninsula Campaign, Virginia,
May–August 1862. Years later, he died after a reckless assault on
a Sioux village on the banks of the Little Bighorn River.

According to the inscription on the back of this graphite-and-paper drawing, Union troops, under orders from their commander, General William Tecumseh Sherman, killed bloodhounds, the hated slave-hunting dogs of the South, and all other dogs they encountered on their march through Georgia to the sea, in 1864.

The all-purpose farm dog, or cur, was a fixture in rural America for several centuries. This "typical" Aroostook County dog was photographed by John Collier on the Gagnon Farm in Fort Kent, Maine, in 1942. A century earlier, Edward Hicks had included a boy and his cur (*right*) in his painting *The Grave of William Penn*.

The sagacious sheepdog and wizened shepherd with their flock are romanticized in *Resignation* (*above*), a lithograph by Dominique C. Fabronius, published in New York in 1859, from an original by English artist Richard Westall. For *Harper's New Monthly Magazine*, August 1895, Frederic Remington turned a more critical eye on the tough leopard cur (*left*), the essential herding and hunting dog of Florida's Cracker cowboys.

The pug, commanded to "speak" for a treat in this 1890 Armstrong & Co. chromolithograph, *Speak for It*, was a popular pet of wealthy city dwellers in the late nineteenth century.

A woman with her gun and hunting dogs looks for game in the piney woods near Tallahassee, Florida, in the 1880s, proving that women, too, put meat on the table.

Sport hunting was the rage among gentlemen in the 1890s. Here, bird hunters and their dogs stalk quail in Lake County, Florida.

African-American handlers, like these two men at Live Oak Plantation in Leon County, Florida, around 1907, frequently managed the dogs for wealthy whites. In this part of the country, they still do.

Dogs bring a grizzly bear to bay, and cowboys, seeking sport, lasso and kill it
at the end of a hunt in the mountains of western New Mexico that involved the rancher
Montague Stevens, who owned and trained the pack; General Nelson A. "Bear Coat" Miles;
and the artist Frederic Remington, among others. Remington sketched and reported on
the hunt for *Harper's New Monthly Magazine*, July 1895.

An Alaska prospector at
the beginning of the twentieth
century packs his dog for a summer
of searching for gold. Dogs carried
goods and people year-round in the
Arctic until the advent of small
planes and snowmobiles.

A heavily loaded train of dog sleds on Richard Byrd's 1928–30 expedition to Antarctica, when he flew over the South Pole. Dogs were essential to polar exploration through the first half of the twentieth century.

The caption by Technical Sergeant J. Sarno on this photograph, dated November/December 1943, reads: "U.S. Marine 'Raiders' and their dogs, which are used for scouting and running messages, starting off for the jungle front lines on Bougainville." The 1st Marine dog platoon was deployed for the first time in the battle for this island.

breeds, by the late-nineteenth century most were derived from black-and-white border collies from Scotland, or an Australian strain of the same dog, said Wentworth in his comprehensive *America's Sheep Trails*. Some local bloodlines became famous, like the McNab dog of Northern California, and the sheepmen began matching them in herding trials as early as 1876, although the events did not gain wider popularity until the 1920s. Predominantly Anglo-American, the ranch owners imported dogs from England and Scotland for their Basque, Portuguese, French, Scotch, Irish, English, and—less popular, but not less numerous—Mexican and Chinese herders.

Usually a solitary figure who lived months at a time with only his sheep and dogs as company, the shepherd in America was maligned, marginalized, and abused. Chinese shepherds, not uncommon between 1870 and 1890, were considered the lowest of the lowly and were frequently attacked and beaten. Americans were considered hapless herders, primarily because they could not tolerate the isolation and poor conditions. Wentworth observed that on cattle drives, cowboys faced challenges from floods, stampedes, rustlers, and Indians, whereas flock masters had to contend with all those plus toxic grasses and plants, wolves, bobcats, coyotes, eagles, alkali, and sage in the dry country they crossed moving from the West Coast. As the nineteenth century advanced, they also had to deal with hostile ranchers and homesteaders, who objected to sheep crossing their land, claiming that they ate everything down to the roots and so befouled water holes that cattle would not use them.

The dogs sometimes performed heroically. Having driven his band of 6,000 sheep—the leaders in a flock numbering 25,000—through the baking-hot Nevada desert for eight days without water, Darwin B. Lyon stopped in despair, wondering how he was going to avoid death, Wentworth recounted in one of his numerous scholarly papers on the sheep industry. Lyon and his dog had been without water for twenty-four hours themselves, and his horse and herders had simply quit that morning, passively waiting for a miracle or death. After much effort, Lyon persuaded one of his men to

take all the dogs and press ahead in a last effort to locate water.
Only Lyon's dog returned to camp that night, but he had clearly
drunk his fill, so Lyon determined to drive his 6,000 thirst-crazed
sheep forward under the dog's guidance. When they finally reached
a stream the next dawn, the sheep refused to drink and repeatedly
tried to flee the water. But each time, the dog drove them back and
finally succeeded in holding them at the water's edge until they began to drink. His short-haired black-and-tan sheepdog, Lyon told
Wentworth, had been imported from Scotland by Leland Stanford,
founder of the Central Pacific Railroad and Stanford University,
and the dog's progeny became popular in southwest Wyoming, the
flock's destination. It was Stanford who, in 1872, commissioned the
photographer Eadweard Muybridge to make the first photographic
studies of horses galloping. Those led in turn to his revolutionary
studies of dogs and other animals in motion, which number among
the great photographic accomplishments at a time when many photographers featured dogs in various states of domestic bliss, or
dressed in hats, with pipes and other human accessories.[3]

ON OCCASION, even the dogs had difficulty with notoriously re-
fractory and stupid sheep. John Muir recounts in his diary of his
first summer in Yosemite in 1869 how three men and two dogs, one
sheepdog and one Saint Bernard, devoted the better part of a day
trying to force 2,500 sheep to cross Yosemite Creek. The dogs spent
most of their time collecting animals trying to break from the back
of the flock. Finally, after the men quit to contemplate their dwin-
dling options, the sheep stampeded into the creek, and only the
quick reaction of the flock master saved some of those in the middle from being drowned by those charging in behind them. The
Saint Bernard, Carlo, was good at hunting stray sheep but worthless at guarding them from bears—although he was present as
Muir's companion, not as a working dog—and the first shepherd,
an American, was fired before the summer was out for letting his
Jack, "a common-looking cur of no particular breed," dog the
sheep too frequently.[4]

Sheepdogs were known to disappear periodically, often either to chase dogs in heat or to turn their talents to killing rather than herding sheep—a thin line separating the two behaviors. Wentworth told of a sheep-killing Iowa cattle dog of his acquaintance "who escaped detection for two to three years because he plunged into the stock watering tank on his own premises after each foray and washed off his victim's blood." Killing livestock remains a capital offense, but the tendency has always been to find ways to control dogs while relentlessly persecuting wild canids—and often falsely attributing to them the bulk of the killing, invariably carried out by dogs. Nonetheless, states consistently passed laws requiring confinement of dogs at night, licensing, and other steps to cut down on the losses and end a source of friction on the range. Of course, miscreants could always be shot on sight.[5]

Wherever they crossed paths or tried to occupy the same valleys or grasslands, sheep and cattle ranchers fought each other, battled with farmers, and sometimes took on miners. Barbed wire, invented by Joseph Falwell Glidden in 1874 to keep the family dogs out of his wife's garden, proved the perfect material for carving the open range into private domains, and by the early 1880s ranchers and farmers were stringing it across miles of territory. Because they had to move their flocks between pastures and water holes, the sheepmen objected—actually, anyone who found himself on the wrong side of a fence blocking access to public land or water complained—and cut fences. These territorial disputes often erupted into range wars, or sheep wars, marked primarily by senseless atrocities. Cattlemen and their cowboys generally inflicted the most damage, driving out "sodbusters," slaughtering thousands of sheep at a time and killing the shepherds and dogs as well.

The conflicts almost literally burned themselves out in Wyoming early in the twentieth century, when 53,000 sheep, scores of men, and countless dogs were shot, clubbed to death, blown up, beaten, stampeded over cliffs, and incinerated. As the Wyoming sheep war reached its peak, the carnage became so horrific that it helped hasten the demise of the open range. On August 24, 1905, along the banks of Shell Creek in the Big Horn Mountains, ten masked cowboys invaded the sheep camp of Louis Gantz and shot, clubbed to death, or dynamited some 4,000 sheep. They also killed his two horses and burned his wagons and supplies. "Most brutal of all," said Wentworth, "the sheep dogs were tied to the wheels of the flaming wagons and scorched to death." The final, and one of the most brutal, assaults occurred on April 2, 1909, near Tensleep, where Tensleep Creek, running fast and clear out of the Big Horns, meets the Norwood River. A sheep rancher, Joe Allemand, was camped there with his nephew, three hired hands, several dogs, and 5,000 sheep, when seven masked cowboys torched the camp and killed Allemand, his nephew, one of the shepherds, several dogs, and all the sheep. Allemand was found dead with a puppy curled up asleep on his chest and another sleeping snugly against his side, their mother having been killed during the raid. The cowboys consciously spared only a shepherd, Pete; a boy named Bounce Helmer; and Helmer's dog, Smoke, whom he risked his life to save. With their help, the cowboys were arrested and ultimately convicted, and the people of Wyoming, shocked by the senseless brutality of the crime, finally brought an end to the mayhem. In 1953, Helmer was still herding with a trio of mongrel border collies.[6]

The Cathedral of the Wild

Today the fight is more about how to protect what remains, to restore lost habitats, to bring back to the Plains and mountains, at least in some areas, the full range of flora and fauna that existed there before the great onslaught. But even this fight is not new. It was joined as soon as it became clear that the destruction of Indians, bison, antelope, and elk and their replacement with farms, cattle, and sheep were bringing not just "civilization" but also large-scale changes to an entire ecosystem, although neither that word nor the full ability to analyze what was at stake existed at the time. Indeed, market and sport hunting and collecting were taking their toll on wildlife around the country. Hunters routinely wiped out rookeries containing tens of thousands of wading birds in Florida to obtain plumes to adorn the hats of fashionable ladies, leaving the rest of the birds to carrion eaters. Large-scale logging, mining, canal digging, and agricultural development were altering whole landscapes.

A number of states had already attempted to protect deer, often from being hunted with dogs, in part because many people had come to see the practice as inhumane—a pre-*Bambi* argument, as it were. In his 1878 book on the Adirondacks, *In the Wilderness*, Charles Dudley Warner, coauthor with Mark Twain of *The Gilded Age* and one of the foremost essayists of the period, graphically described a dog separating a doe from her fawn and driving her into a lake where hunters in a boat overhauled her when she was exhausted and panic-stricken and slit her throat, leaving the fawn orphaned. Such antihunting books and articles roused public sentiment against certain practices, but on the whole, efforts to conserve species, especially those that humans liked to hunt or fish for sport or subsistence, intensified in direct proportion to their decline. The federal government made its first attempt to protect wildlife nationally with enactment in 1900 of the Lacey Act, named for Iowa representative John Lacey, to protect waterfowl and other migratory birds. Other legislation followed, although much of it remained poorly enforced for years.[7]

Efforts to preserve landscapes began in 1864, when President Abraham Lincoln granted the Mariposa Big Tree Grove of giant sequoias and Yosemite Valley to California to be held as a public trust. Having moved to California in 1863 after leaving his work on Central Park and then his post as U.S. sanitary commission chairman to become manager of the Mariposa Mining Estate of John C. Fremont, Frederick Law Olmsted served briefly as one of the new preserve's first commissioners. He developed a plan for protection of Yosemite and the sequoias that called for keeping the area as pristine as possible for the aesthetic illumination of people who could appreciate raw nature. His fellow commissioners shelved the report as too radical, and it vanished from view for years. Still, the Yosemite grant is widely credited with paving the way for creation in 1872 of Yellowstone National Park, the first in the nation.

Unquestionably, at least among a sizable number of people in

America, attitudes toward Nature, often called the Wild, and man's place in it had changed dramatically. The Romantic movement in the arts presented Nature as the pure state of being, in direct opposition to the Judeo-Christian view that wild Nature was a fallen, violent version of the Garden of Eden and its pastoral harmony. Bartram, Catlin, Audubon, and other travelers in America—not to forget Rousseau and the English and European Romantics— influenced later generations of America's leading creative intellectuals and artists, among them the Transcendentalists Henry David Thoreau and Ralph Waldo Emerson and the historian Francis Parkman, who sought fundamental truths in Nature. The breathtaking physical beauty of America fed directly in to an aesthetic of the Sublime—the notion that a landscape, mountain, waterfall, valley, glacier, canyon, or other monumental feature, or a storm or sunset, could be at once overpoweringly awe-inspiring, beautiful, terrible, transcendent in its emotional effect, perfect in its essence.

Discoveries in natural history and geology were daily revealing natural processes that shaped the world along with its plants and animals, including humans. Darwin's theory of evolution had clearly tied man to natural, not divine, creation, and further inspired scientists seeking evidence of those connections in the living world and among the fossil remains of the past. In 1864 George Perkins Marsh published *Man and Nature*, documenting the destructive effects of man's agricultural and forestry practices and forcefully presenting the argument that natural resources had to be managed for the benefit of all and for the future. Marsh also observed that native foragers, like bison, were always less destructive of their native grasslands than were the domestic animals that came later.

Even more than its aesthetic and scientific value, the West was precious precisely because it was Wild, as Thoreau said, and it was the future. Far from being something to be conquered and transformed, Nature, wilderness, the virgin forest, wildness itself underlay and sustained civilization. Theodore Roosevelt adopted the philosophy of Nature and the wilderness as the seat of manliness and virtue and made it a guiding principle of his life and presidency.

Coming from the hyperbolic tradition of Bartram, from the perspective not of a hunter, like Roosevelt, but of an aesthete, an observer, an artist, and a scientist, John Muir did the same. The two men not only helped found but also were avatars of the two dominant strains in the American conservation movement. Both men took dogs with them, as did many of their friends and colleagues, because in addition to being good hunters—if one were hunting—dogs were great companions on a walk.

There was so much to do in those early days that the contradictions inherent in an alliance between sport-hunting conservationists and usually nonhunting, sometimes vegetarian wanderers were not as apparent as they are today, when the two groups are often split. Roosevelt in particular and hunters in general did come under attack in the late 1890s from the recently formed New England Anti-Vivisection Society, which opposed the torture of animals in the name of sport or science. But early conservationists, like Muir and Roosevelt, also shared certain basic attitudes: that being in the wilderness was inherently healthy because it forced a man—it was generally a man's world—to be tough, courageous, and strong; that wilderness and Nature were essential antidotes to urbanization, which was making men soft; and that refinement and education, an aesthetic and scientific sensibility, were necessary if a person was really to appreciate the glory of Nature. By their nature, "savages" and uneducated rubes could not experience nor understand fully the country they called home, and because of that the government was justified in acting in the name of the people, of future generations, to protect vast sections of land and preserve wildlife.

The hunters Theodore Roosevelt and George Bird Grinnell, editor of *Forest and Stream*, founded the Boone and Crockett Club in 1887 in reaction to the senseless slaughter going on around them. In addition to recording trophy animals and promulgating a code of ethics, they helped preserve chunks of wild nature where wealthy young men, growing soft in the city, could be made tough and hard through the hunt. Grinnell had served as a naturalist on Custer's Yellowstone Expedition of 1870, searched for fossils in the Badlands, and hunted animals in many places. An ornithologist, he also founded the first bird preservation society in 1886, naming it for John James Audubon. Unable to keep up with rising membership, he disbanded his Audubon Society two years later, but the idea for such an organization had been planted. Grinnell worked diligently to record the languages and cultures of Plains Indians tribes and to improve their living conditions, and also pushed for the establishment of Glacier National Park in 1910.

Roosevelt owed a heavy debt for the evolution in his own thinking on the value of wilderness to the Transcendentalists, the nature writer and Walt Whitman biographer John Burroughs, and John Muir. Ralph Waldo Emerson's friends had not permitted the aging philosopher to go camping with Muir on his sole visit to Yosemite in 1871, an event Muir recalled in his 1901 book, *Our National Parks*, his paean to his beloved Yosemite and his call to protect such places, and in a letter to Roosevelt. A popular writer, artist, outdoor adventurer, and botanist, Muir had led the successful battle to have Yosemite named a national park in 1900, worked to preserve other lands and to end destructive agricultural and logging practices, and founded the Sierra Club in 1902. In short, he was perhaps the most widely known champion of wild places in the world. Roosevelt conveyed to the then-famous conservationist that he would be glad, although years after the fact, to take Emerson's place, and in 1903, Muir and the president traveled for three days and two nights through the valley.

Recalling the excursion in an appreciation of Muir for *Outlook* magazine in 1915, Roosevelt, ever the hunter, observed that Muir cared nothing for the wildlife that delighted him but was a man fixated on large, grand landscapes and trees. The comment may have been a bit extreme regarding Muir, but it captured the divide between the two camps of conservationists, which the two men, and like-minded men and women, bridged in the coming years to put in place the structure of public lands and conservation strategies that for years made America a model for the rest of the world, albeit one with its own flaws and blind spots. Roosevelt, "the conservation president," oversaw the creation of 150 national forests, 51 bird reservations—they became the national wildlife refuge system—5 national game preserves, and 5 national parks, encompassing 230 million acres, more than a third of the 600 million acres of public lands in 2003. He also established the National Park Service and the National Forest Service and signed into law the Monuments and Antiquities Act.[8]

IN THE TRADITION of Bartram and Audubon, Muir had thrown over his old life to pursue his passion following an accident that nearly blinded him in his right eye. He was twenty-eight, working in a factory in Indianapolis, frustrated and bored, much the way Bartram had been a century earlier, and he determined to change. After his vision returned in 1867, he started walking through the war-ravaged, "reconstructing" South, hitting the Gulf of Mexico at Cedar Key, Florida, taking a boat from there to Havana, and then sailing to New York. The schooner's captain, Muir said, had as a mascot a large Newfoundland dog who amused himself by catching and devouring, before the crew could get them, flying fish that landed onboard. From New York, Muir sailed to San Francisco, intent—having seen the "hot gardens of the sun" in Florida—on the mountains, the Sierra Nevada, where he found his life's passion. After a summer following sheep and exploring with Carlo, a borrowed Saint Bernard, Muir lived in Yosemite for several years, wandering, guiding, observing firsthand the damage grazing sheep and cattle wrought. Then, in 1880, he married the daughter of a wealthy fruit farmer, who brought him financial security.

An avowed dog lover, Muir shared with Darwin, Jack London, and many of their contemporaries a belief that dogs were sentient beings, with many of the same emotions as humans but also with strong connections to their wild origins. More important for the time, Muir celebrated the dog as a companion, not an aid to hunting or a beast of burden but a unique individual who, in fact, could teach humans something about themselves and the value of simply

experiencing Nature in all its glory and fury. He did so most famously in "An Adventure with a Dog and a Glacier," which first
appeared in *Century* magazine in 1897, and has been reprinted
many times since as "Stickeen." It was an immediate hit at a time
when the noble-dog story was becoming a distinct and popular
subgenre, fueled in part by a desire to celebrate the inherent worth
of the dog as companion.

Having discovered Glacier Bay, Alaska, in 1879, Muir returned,
following his marriage the next year, to explore its "ice mountains"
more closely, with an Indian canoe crew, his friend Samuel H. Young,
a Presbyterian missionary at Fort Wrangell, Alaska, and Young's
"little black dog," Stickeen. Muir initially suggested that Young leave
Stickeen behind because he deemed the "short-legged and bunch-
bodied" long-haired dog of mixed parentage, with little copper buttons over his eyes, "small, dull and worthless." But the reverend
assured him that Stickeen "was a perfect wonder of a dog," a strong
swimmer, impervious to hunger and cold, and, to the Indians for
whom he was named, "a mysterious fountain of wisdom." Muir relented and soon found himself fascinated by a dog who appeared
good for nothing, who neither obeyed orders nor assisted the Indian crew on their hunts nor showed affection for anyone, but who
nonetheless followed the non-hunting Muir on his explorations
whenever possible, without "complaint as if, like a philosopher, he
had learned that without hard work and suffering there could be no
pleasure worth having." Stickeen was a "true child of the wilderness," Muir said, with eyes that were simultaneously ancient, young,
and wild.[9]

After landing at Taylor Bay, Muir determined to hike in the
morning across a glacier that now bears his name and set out, despite a howling storm, hoping to give Stickeen the slip because he
did not want responsibility for him under dangerous conditions.
But the little dog found him out and would not be deterred from
following. Muir finally slipped Stickeen a piece of bread, his only
food, and they set off, crossing seven miles of ice in three hours despite a continuing if diminished storm. Stickeen flew easily over
crevasses that gave Muir pause until, racing a near whiteout back to

camp, they came to a fifty-foot-wide, 1,000-foot-deep crevasse that could be crossed only by way of a knife-edged ice bridge, eight to ten feet below the glacier's surface. Turning back with night approaching was not an option, Muir said, nor was staying put in the storm, the wind howling, temperature plummeting, and snow swirling so densely that he could see little. He cut narrow steps down the vertical wall with his ice ax and then carved a six-by-eight-inch platform from which he could straddle the sliver of ice that spanned the chasm diagonally for a total distance of seventy feet. Smoothing the sharp edge of the ice before him, he slid across, the blizzard buffeting him. Reaching the far wall, he carved a set of narrow steps and finger holds to the top. "Never before had I been so long under deadly strain," Muir said of his crossing.

In a sign of his sagacity, Muir said, Stickeen had sized up the danger at once and begun running up and down, looking for a different crossing, but there was none. He returned to howl and whine in protest and despair, screaming all the louder when Muir reached the other side. In his hopes and fears, his understanding of all that was happening, Stickeen was "perfectly human," Muir said. Muir shouted encouragement, but Stickeen's "natural composure and courage had vanished utterly in a tumultuous storm of fear." After trying several strategies, Muir approached the edge of the crevasse and firmly told Stickeen, as if he were a ten-year-old boy, that he had to leave but would return in the morning to save him. In the meantime, he cautioned Stickeen to avoid the woods on the other side of the glacier, where wolves would surely kill him. Heeding the lecture, Muir said, Stickeen screwed up his courage and inched his way down the ice face to the small staging area. Gingerly he stepped on the narrow ice bridge and, bracing himself against the buffeting wind, crossed it only to freeze when he reached the narrow, carved deck on the far side. Stickeen hesitated, measured the steps, and then sprang up the wall and immediately launched himself into a manic celebration. Muir tried to catch him, to congratulate him, "but he would not be caught. Never before or since have I seen anything like so passionate a revulsion from the depths of despair to exultant, triumphant, uncontrollable joy."

From that time, Muir said, "Stickeen was a changed dog," staying close by him, eating only when Muir fed him, going where he went, laying his head on Muir's leg in the evening and looking into his eyes "as if to say, 'Wasn't that an awful time we had together on the glacier?'" The shared experience of danger had bonded and altered them, Muir said, making Stickeen less wild, more whole, more complete, more domestic, and giving him a "deeper sympathy" for his fellow mortals. The wild, Muir effectively argued, using Stickeen as his surrogate human, can transform a person as surely as any rite of passage, or religious experience, and thus is essential to civilization. Moreover, a person can have such an experience in Nature at any moment with the least likely of companions, without the blood lust and excitement of the hunt. Yet in a dreadful, ironic twist, not long after Muir left Alaska, Stickeen was stolen by a tourist at Fort Wrangell and never seen again, confirming, although Muir did not say it directly, that the same civilization he celebrated is corrupt and in need of constant renewal.

Dogs of the North

The immortal dog, the wolf dog, the wild dog made domestic and the domestic dog turned wild, the heroic dog, the faithful dog, the dog betrayed by man and the dog redeemed by man—all came to the fore in the waning decades of the nineteenth century and blew right into the twentieth, with nary a pause for the economic distress of the 1880s. Those themes were most clearly played out in the far North and the Antarctic, where the dog pack under the domain of its forceful leader held sway. Exemplifying the principles of social Darwinism, observers reported that a leader emerged through conflict and held his position because he was inherently the strongest, the boldest, the best, and, knowing his place, he ran the team at the behest of his human master. Under the best of circumstances, the master himself was fair and noble, but as all good Victorians, including the American variants, knew, civilization was hard won and maintained only through sacrifice and discipline. Most dogs had to serve hard masters, just as most civilized men and women found themselves confronted at every turn by barbarians of one sort or another.

"A good dog is so much a nobler beast than an indifferent man that one sometimes gladly exchanges the society of one for that of the other," said the British soldier and adventurer William Francis Butler, in *The Wild Northland*, the best-selling account of his 1872 journey from Canada's Fort Chipewyan to the Pacific by dogsled. For pleasure, Butler was paralleling the route Alexander Mackenzie had traced to the Pacific by canoe and on foot 100 years earlier. Until he retired him from sled hauling before crossing the Rockies, Butler's leader was Cerf-vola, a one-hundred-pound Inuit husky who had accompanied him on an extended survey of Canada's Northwest Territory several years earlier. After reaching the Pacific coast, Butler gave his team dogs to the Hudson's Bay Company and traveled overland through the United States to Boston with Cerf-vola, who, he said, feared the ubiquitous brass bands but loved butcher shops. Before leaving Boston for England, Butler presented his beloved Cerf-vola to an acquaintance, declaring in typical fashion for the age that a man must lay aside his emotions for the sterner stuff of civilization.[10]

No one more clearly delineated the dog's role as a bridge between the wild and civilized, and the vagaries of man in dealing with his best friend, than the poet laureate of the Klondike, Jack London. He made the dog the hero as well as the vehicle for exploring the tug between individual needs and social responsibility, between self-sacrificing love and self-preservation, between forced servitude and willing help in *The Call of the Wild*, *White Fang*, and a fistful of stories that, in terms of dogs, are remarkable for their accuracy. But the half-wild husky also took center stage in the great decades-long race for the poles that captivated the public, pulling to glory—and sometimes death—men crazed with the idea of being first to reach a geometric point, a blank space on the map.

THE GOLD RUSHES that rolled across Alaska and Canada's Yukon Territory from Juneau in 1880, the year of Muir's adventure with

Stickeen, to Iditarod in 1908, transformed the region and its dogs. For sixteen years after Juneau, prospectors found gold deposits in Fortymile, Circle, and other scattered sites along the Yukon River and its tributaries before finally striking it rich near the confluence of the Yukon and Klondike rivers, at a place called Dawson City. The great Klondike Gold Rush, as legendary as the California rush of '49, was on, with tens of thousands of fortune seekers, largely men, sailing out of Seattle to Skagway, a gritty little coastal village north of Juneau. If they made it out of Skagway without being robbed or killed, they traversed several rugged mountain passes to the Yukon and then traveled another 500 miles by small boat, or by foot and dogsled, to Dawson City. After 1897, the North West Mounted Police, who patrolled their vast territory by dogsled during the winter, began requiring that each person carry at least three quarters of a ton of food, enough for a year. How many met the minimum is unclear. Certainly, many brought far too much of the wrong gear and then hitched their overloaded sleds or toboggans or carts to anything that moved—themselves and their mates, horses, mules, oxen, dogs, wolves, goats, even turkeys. In the first frantic year, more than 3,000 of those animals perished crossing White Pass through the coastal ridge out of Skagway. Thousands more dropped on twenty-six-mile Chilkoot Pass. Prospectors quit in droves, but more than 30,000 had made it to Dawson by the time the boom busted in 1904, not counting those who left town on the 1,000-mile trek across Alaska to Nome, where gold was discovered in 1899. More than 40,000 people poured into that Seward Peninsula boomtown and left nearly as quickly when the gold played out.

Because they are carnivores, dogs were the best working animals in that land of long winters, when forage was at a premium, and with fortune hunters pouring in all over the territory, the demand for dogs skyrocketed. Boatloads came from the States with every sort of dog imaginable, except the Lilliputians—setters, curs, collies, Saint Bernards, Newfoundlands, Airedales, bull terriers and pit bulls, hounds, retrievers, spaniels, pointers, German shepherds, mastiffs—many of them stolen. With prices in Skagway or along the trail reaching $1,000, a good dog could be bought and sold several times. Dogs that could not pull sleds might survive if they were outstanding fighters or hunters, but on the whole, if a dog could not pull, it was deemed worthless. The most desirable of all were big, strong, stoical Inuit huskies or Athabascan dogs with thick double coats and tough feet. The Athabascan lived along the inland rivers, while the Inuit hugged the coast.

In *The Call of the Wild*, the 140-pound, four-year-old Scotch shepherd dog and Saint Bernard mix, Buck, the favorite dog of his wealthy owner, a judge, enjoyed a special status as neither a kennel dog nor a house dog. He moved freely between the indoors and outdoors, between the roles of companion and hunter, until one night in 1897 the gardener's helper betrayed him for $100. Stolen, he was shipped from his Santa Clara estate to San Francisco, then to Seattle, where he was sold for $300, and finally to the Northwest Territory. Along the way, he was savagely beaten, taught to pull an overloaded sled, abused, forced to fight other dogs for his survival, and compelled to learn, London said, the "law of club and fang." His senses became keener; he began to howl. He fought and killed, was sold again to witless American prospectors who drove their dogs to death. Rescued from a near-fatal beating by the noble John Thornton, after he refused to pull any longer for the American tenderfeet, Buck was brought back to human society through gentle treatment. He saved Thornton's life twice and pulled a 1,000-pound load by himself to win a large bet, a grubstake. Buck performed that supercanine task after Thornton asked him to do it "for love" of him—precisely the emotion believed to motivate the best dogs in human society.[11]

But Buck continued to be drawn to the wild spirit that had awakened in him. While Thornton and his partners panned for gold, Buck hunted. "His cunning was wolf cunning, and wild cunning; his intelligence, shepherd intelligence and St. Bernard intelligence," London said, ascribing to him the qualities of the most popular dogs of the period, "and all this, plus an experience gained in the fiercest of schools, made him as formidable a creature as any that roamed the wild." He was strong, purposeful, reactive, and he was just returning from a four-day moose hunt when marauding Indians invaded Thornton's camp and killed Thornton. Surprising the celebrating Indians, Buck exacted a terrible vengeance, mourned Thornton, and then, his only remaining tie to civilization severed, fought his way into leadership of a wolf pack and ran with them into legend. Yet each year he visited the site of Thornton's murder and howled in memory of him. London's other classic dog book, *White Fang*, reversed the story line, of course, with the true, wild-born wolf dog White Fang, after abuse and betrayal at the hands of humans, becoming not just a companion to a kind man but a hero as well. For London, a person's character was revealed in the way he treated a dog, but the dog was also a sentient being balanced sometimes precariously between the Wild and Civilization, torn between those who embodied love and kindness and those who lived by brutality and betrayal.[12]

Indeed, life ranged from hard to brutal for most dogs of the Arctic gold rush. They hauled everything from mail to gold and people on sleds, toboggans, carts, and even railroad cars. The mail dogs made circuits in relays of thousands of miles across sparsely populated Alaska. It took a stupid man to kill an animal essential to his survival, but intelligence has never been highly valued among the bulk of humanity, and too often the dogs were driven until they could go no farther, and then they were killed or abandoned. Their corpses filled the rivers and ravines near the mining towns. Although some people treated their dogs with kindness and respect, most "dog punchers" instilled discipline with whips and clubs—differing primarily in their level of violence and their ability to keep their dogs healthy. In instant gold rush towns, "dog jams" turned immediately into fights, with thirty or more dogs aiming to maim or kill one another until the punchers came to break them apart by force. Not infrequently, the enraged dogs then turned on their drivers. In some communities, dogs outnumbered people. Everywhere their voices filled the air; their excrement paved the streets. No one knows how many thousands of dogs were brought into Alaska during the decade of highest demand, but some of those who survived interbred with native Athabascan and Inuit dogs and thus contributed to the root stock of the Alaskan husky of today. Rarely, if ever—one hates to say never—did the newcomers join the wolves.

As the gold rushes played out in 1908, organized sled dog racing began in Nome and rapidly grew in popularity all over the state, with most races covering twenty to sixty miles. A team of huskies from the Chukchi Peninsula won the 1909 All Alaska Sweepstakes, and the fast little Siberian dogs, as they were soon known, became the dog du jour among many white racers. The native racers, and some local Anglos, maintained their own stock, crossed, according to legend, with wolves or even hard-running European dogs. Airplanes were soon employed in hauling cargo in some parts of Alaska, and a railroad connected Anchorage to Fairbanks, but big, strong, hard-pulling dogs were still needed for hauling freight and other heavy loads, and dog punchers selected for them whenever possible. They remained in demand until snowmobiles came into widespread use in the 1960s, when dogs began to be employed primarily for racing, which required smaller, lighter, faster animals. The old type began to grow rare in Alaska, the purebred malamute being but an inbred dog-show variant of the original dog that helped keep the Inuit alive from Alaska to Greenland for thousands of years, and that pulled explorers to both poles.

Polar Dogs

Recognizing that the person who wanted to live and accomplish anything in the far North had to adapt to the Inuit way of life, Elisha Kent Kane "pioneered" the use of dogs for Arctic exploration during his aborted search for John Franklin's lost expedition between 1853 and 1855. The custom prior to that had been to turn crewmen into beasts of burden, hauling heavy sledges filled with food and gear, and some British adventurers continued to travel that way for years to come, partly because of their aversion to using dogs as draft animals. The obsession with Franklin's fate waned somewhat after evidence found in 1857 by yet another expedition confirmed that he had perished with all his crew and ships in one of the great expeditionary disasters on record. But the lure of the Arctic was not so easily stilled.

During the 1860s, Charles Francis Hall made several extended trips to the Arctic to seek more definitive answers about Franklin, and in the process became expert on Inuit culture, including dog-sledding. In 1870 he persuaded Congress to fund his attempt to reach the North Pole, and he set out on the appropriately named *Polaris* the following year, picking up Inuit dogs and drivers in Greenland before pressing on to 82° north, a record that still left him about 550 miles short of his goal. Despite that achievement, a miserable crew put into harbor in October, to weather the northern winter. Hall was feuding with the ship's captain, a heavy drinker, with the doctor/scientist, and with the assistant scientist over nearly every matter. After securing the ship, Hall went on a two-week scouting expedition to find a route north to the polar ice cap. Returning in early November, he requested coffee, drank it, took sick, and died shortly thereafter, accusing the doctor, Emil Bessels, of poisoning him.

Perhaps he did; fingernail and hair samples taken from Hall's body in 1968 by Chauncey C. Loomis showed elevated arsenic levels, although the poison could have been used in treatment as well as murder. The *Polaris* stayed through the following summer, and in the fall of 1872 was slammed into ice by a gale and damaged. The Inuits and some crew members abandoned ship for an ice floe, but rather than retrieve them once the ship was out of danger, the captain left them adrift. They managed to survive, floating on ice for six months until a sealing vessel from Newfoundland rescued them. Meanwhile, after scuttling the *Polaris*, the captain, doctor, and remaining crew worked their way back to New York in 1873. Despite the testimony of the ice floe survivors that Hall believed he had been poisoned, a court of inquiry ruled his death had come from natural causes.

By then a deadly Euro-American race had been joined, not just

for the Northwest Passage but also for the poles, with major newspapers, geographical societies, wealthy patrons, and governments
sponsoring the assaults, for the publicity and glory. A number of
them were spectacular failures, like that of Lieutenant Adolphus
Greely, the narrow-minded commander of a U.S. government–
financed expedition in the early 1880s. After spending the long,
dark winter getting established in his base camp, Fort Conger on
Ellesmere Island, Greely sent two of his subordinates with a dog
team they overworked and underfed to set a new record for northern latitude, 82°23', in May 1882. The twenty-five men then conducted further explorations while waiting more than a year for a
supply and relief ship that never arrived. As the time passed, Greely
faced increasing resentment from his men and near mutiny from his
second in command, Frederick Kislingbury, and the expedition's
doctor, Octave Pavy. Finally, in August 1883, Greely and his men
took their remaining forty days of rations and abandoned the camp
in their lifeboats. Unwilling to take their huskies but unable to shoot
them, the explorers abandoned them, hoping they would learn to
hunt before they starved. That was as far as their compassion went,
for they let drown one of the dogs, Flipper, who swam after them for
miles in the icy Arctic waters until he exhausted himself.[13]

The ordeal that followed probably cannot be attributed to
karmic justice for dog abuse, since Greely survived, but dense ice
forced the fleeing men ashore at Pim Island near Ellesmere's Cape
Sabine, and over the ensuing winter, eighteen men, including Kislingbury and Pavy, died of starvation, with one more dying after their
rescue in June 1884. Charges of cannibalism were never proved, and
Greely went on to a distinguished military career and prominence as
the first president of the Explorers Club in New York, of which President Theodore Roosevelt was a cofounder. After Greely's tragic
farce, the government stopped funding the quest for the Pole.

FOR THE NEXT TWENTY-FIVE YEARS, despite multiple attempts by
other explorers, the race for the North Pole settled into a contest
between the American Robert E. Peary, a Navy engineer, and the

Norwegians Fridtjof Nansen and Roald Amundsen, who became a player after traversing the mystical Northwest Passage in 1905. All used dogs: the Norwegians sometimes drew theirs from Russia; the Americans occasionally took animals from Newfoundland; and all relied heavily on Greenland Inuit huskies, averaging 80 to 100 pounds for males, somewhat less for females. "They are sturdy, magnificent animals," said Peary of the Greenland dogs in his account of his conquest of the Pole. "There may be larger dogs than these, there may be handsomer dogs; but I doubt it. Other dogs may work as well or travel as fast or as far when fully fed; but there is no dog in the world that can work so long in the lowest temperatures on practically nothing to eat." Yet the Inuit regularly broke the meat-shearing carnassial teeth on their dogs, to keep them from chewing through their tethers, and their lives were, as a rule, unremittingly hard and short—but then so were the lives of the Inuit. Nansen and Amundsen worked their dogs hard and then killed them one or two at a time on the return journey to feed themselves and their remaining dogs, effectively carrying their food on the paw, and cutting down on what they had to pack or cache. Peary carried twice the number of dogs he felt he would need from Greenland's west coast, taking in their Inuit owners and their owners' families. He used the men, along with his crew and his black assistant, Matthew Henson, to lay down caches of food and fuel at set intervals for use as resupply depots. Routinely, teams of eight to twelve dogs would haul loads of 1,000 to 1,200 pounds, sometimes for hundreds of miles.[14]

More fully than Kane, whose adventures had inspired him as a child, Robert Peary understood that the Inuit, precisely because they were native to the region, were the best people to staff a polar expedition, and that the wise explorer would adopt and adapt their ways, which included hunting for provisions, wearing clothes similar to theirs, and appreciating their culture. The prudent explorer also—and here his words resonated with dog lovers throughout America—celebrated the "Eskimo dogs, which furnished the traction power for our sledges, and so enabled us to carry our supplies where no other power on earth could have moved them with the requisite speed and certainty."[15]

When the sleds were empty, the Inuit hunted, using guns and knives they received in payment for their labor, for Nanuq, the polar bear, musk oxen, walrus, and seal. Often Peary, Henson, or the crewmen joined the hunt, which could stretch for miles across rough country. Whenever a bear was spotted, the dogs quickened their pace until, drawing near, the sled drivers, as they had for centuries, began loosing one or two at a time so they could quickly bring the bear to bay. But now the hunters shot the bear, a less dangerous business than attempting to drive a spear into its heart, although not without peril to humans and dogs. The Inuit also loosed their dogs to charge musk oxen, which in defense bunched up in a circle, facing outward, like cattle. The dogs circled and harassed the herd until the lead bull charged them. The hunter shot it, then took out each new challenger in turn. Dogs also pulled freshly harpooned walrus and seal out of the water.

When dog food was scarce, as it was in December 1908, Peary would kill the weakest dogs to feed to their mates or their owners, although it appears that Peary himself did not eat dog. He always calculated that 60 percent of the dogs would die from injury, illness, or *piblokto*, the mysterious malady that afflicted huskies and Inuits. "It is absolutely impossible to figure on the Eskimo dog's uncertain tenure of life," Peary said. "The creature will endure the severest hardship; they will travel and draw heavy loads on practically nothing to eat; they will live for days exposed to the wildest arctic blizzard; and then, sometimes in good weather, after an ordinary meal of apparently the best food, they will lie down and die."[16]

PEARY BEGAN EXPLORING Greenland as a launching pad for the Pole in 1886. Two years later, Nansen became the first man on record to cross the island's ice cap, and the race for the grand prize was joined. Taking off with one companion and twenty-eight dogs from *Fram*, the ship he had designed to drift with the Arctic ice pack, Nansen came within fewer than four degrees of the North Pole, about 270 miles, in 1895. On the way back, Nansen and his companion, Frederick Hjalman Johansen, took turns slicing the throats of each other's favorite dogs until all twenty-eight had been killed and eaten. In 1899, Peary suffered such severe frostbite that eight of his toes had to be amputated, but he remained in the Arctic close to three more years despite being nearly crippled. The dogs saved him then and in 1906, he always said, with their hunting skill, power, and stamina. In 1901, the British explorer Robert Falcon Scott hauled Russian dogs to Antarctica for an attempt on the South Pole, but he failed to reach his mark, partly, it is said, because he would not beat the dogs with whips and clubs. Just two years later, Amundsen locked his ship *Gjøa* in ice northwest of Hudson Bay, at King William Island, and began a two-year journey, literally drifting with the ice, through the Northwest Passage, seizing the prize that had cost so many lives.

In 1908, Peary, fifty-three, took his own custom-built, ice-hardy steamer, *Roosevelt*, named for his friend and patron, out of New York for what he knew would be his last polar expedition. He had the backing of his Peary Arctic Club, whose sponsors included some of the wealthiest men in New York, of the National Geographic Society, and of *The New York Times*, in exchange for an exclusive report. The *New York Herald* was backing the rival expedition of the upstart physician-adventurer Frederick Cook, already in the Arctic with 150 dogs, although his precise location was unknown when Peary sailed. Peary had already accused Cook, the physician on his 1891 expedition and his predecessor as president of the Explorers Club, of stealing his techniques for travel and survival in the Arctic.

Peary put into winter quarters on Ellesmere Island in the fall of 1908 with 246 Inuit huskies, his 22-man crew, including Henson, his 50 Inuit assistants, and their wives and children. On March 1, 1909, he left land to set up his depots on the frozen Arctic Ocean— crossed with pressure ridges where ice had heaved up, crevasses, and unexpected leads of open water—with Henson, 7 Anglo-

American crewmen, 17 Inuit, 133 dogs, and 19 sleds of his own design. He varied the size of the team according to the sled's load.

At the end of March, Peary, supply depots laid, vaulted free of his seven crewmen and took off for the Pole with Henson, four Inuit—Egingwah, Seegloo, Ootah, and Doqueah—five sleds, each carrying about 400 pounds, and the forty strongest dogs left in the pack. They were, he says, "powerful males, hard as iron," without any fat, and they pulled the group the final 140 miles to the North Pole in twenty-seven days. They reached the Pole on April 6, 1909, stayed there thirty hours making observations, and returned in sixteen days, losing ten dogs along the way. Peary later protested that he dropped his white colleagues because he needed to travel fast, and Henson was nearly as skillful driving a dog team as the Inuit. But the feeling remains that after so many years of frustration, he wanted no one to share his glory, and he knew that neither a black man nor any number of Inuit would be considered "explorers." When the time came to reap his rewards, they would be invisible; indeed, no Inuit names even appear on the commemorative marker they themselves helped build at land's end, Cape Columbia, although it does include the names of the American expedition members. Henson, Peary wrote in his account of the expedition, showed great skill and ability when working with him, but because of his "racial inheritance" lacked the "daring and initiative" of the white group leaders. Peary professed to admire the Inuits' "primitive communism," which he feared conversion to Christianity would ruin, but considered them an "inferior race." They had respected and depended on him for twenty-five years, receiving guns, ammunition, tools, hatchets, knives, boats, and tents for their labor, but after his success he never saw them again, including the son he allegedly sired during his 1906 expedition. Peary's views were not unique for the time—in many ways he was more enlightened—but they came back to haunt him.[17]

Exhausted, depressed at having achieved his goal and at losing a man in an accident, perhaps seeking maximum drama, Peary tarried before leaving for home and did not announce his accomplishment to the world until September 5, 1909. The problem was that Cook had resurfaced a few days earlier with his own announcement that he had reached the North Pole, with two Inuits, two sleds, and twenty-six dogs, on April 21, 1908, a year before Peary. He actually had mushed into a Danish settlement on Greenland after appropriating a dog team Peary had left at the village of Etah in case of emergency. The Danes had promptly recognized his claim, despite his comments that the Pole was on terra firma, and a nearly complete lack of reliable records. Ultimately, his Inuit guides testified that they had never left sight of land to venture onto the polar ice, and Cook was dismissed as a fraud at the close of 1909. But, fought out in the *Times* and the *Herald*, the battle left Peary sullied, accused of "arrogance" and "ungentlemanly behavior."

Leading the assault on Cook's credibility, Peary left himself open to criticism, not least that he, too, lacked reliable "white" witnesses and because many people believed erroneously that he could not have traveled as fast as he claimed he did, especially on the return over broken sea ice notorious for its treachery. His own readings that certified his position were said to be too perfect, his diary too clean. Nonetheless, with the backing of the *Times*, Roosevelt, and the important geographical societies, he began in 1910 to receive the recognition that he felt was his due. In 1911 he received the National Geographic Society's highest honor and, with his white crew, special congressional recognition, as well as promotion to rear admiral. Henson was awarded the geographic society's prize only posthumously, in 2000; Congress recognized his contribution in 1944. It is now considered almost certain that Peary, Henson, and the Inuit missed the Pole, although it is unclear whether Peary was aware of his failure and chose to fudge the facts.

AMUNDSEN WAS PREPARING to float Nansen's *Fram* over the North Pole when he heard news of Peary's accomplishment. Abruptly, he changed course for the South Pole, knowing that Scott was already on his way to Antarctica. Despite the fact that Ernest

Shackleton had taken Manchurian ponies that proved worthless and died on his aborted 1908 attempt at the Pole, Scott, refusing to use dogs, repeated the experiment in 1910, with the same result. He also carried motorized sledges, which failed, leaving him to drag his own sleds to the South Pole, while Amundsen, after laying out his depots, set out with four men driving four fourteen-dog teams. An indifferent musher, he skied to the South Pole, reaching it on December 15, 1911, after averaging forty miles a day. On the return journey, Amundsen and his men killed and ate all the dogs. But the trip was so well executed that all five men reportedly gained weight. The hapless, heroic Scott and his four companions reached the Pole a month later, after walking 150 miles, only to die of starvation and exposure on the way back.

Just three years later, Shackleton, seeking to become the first man to cross Antarctica, nearly met a similar fate after his ship, *Endurance*, became icebound in January 1915. He had on board 28 men and 69 dogs, heading for the Weddell Sea, while a companion boat, *Aurora*, with 20 men and 30 dogs, headed for the Ross Sea. That crew was to lay down supply depots that Shackleton would use on the last half of his crossing. But the ice that held *Endurance* crushed it in October 1915, and the men, unable to reach shore and running low on provisions, finally had to kill all but two teams of their dogs in January 1916. During that year the dogs, purchased with money collected by British schoolchildren, had proved tremendous morale boosters and sources of entertainment, Shackleton said in his report on the expedition. By his account and the evidence of Frank Hurley's photographs, the dogs were big crossbred huskies meant to pull heavy loads, whom the men came to view as pets as much as beasts of burden. On April 2, Shackleton ordered the last two dog teams killed and, with supplies low, eaten. A few days later, using the ship's lifeboats, the men finally escaped the Weddell Sea ice and reached Elephant Island, from which Shackleton and five companions made a desperate 800-mile voyage to South George Island and assistance. In August 1916 he pulled his remaining crewmen from Elephant Island, but in the meantime, the crew of *Aurora*, unaware of Shackleton's failure, had proceeded with their work, a futile endeavor that cost the lives of three men and all the dogs. Conducted in the middle of World War I, Shackleton's expedition marked the end of what is generally called the Heroic Age of polar exploration. There was more to come, but the focus shifted to science and new means of reaching the old goal—a geometric point imposed on the world.[18]

10

Civilizing the Dog but Forgetting the Man:
Obedience in a World Gone Mad

❧

WILDERNESS MIGHT BE USEFUL for strengthening a man's character, might even help civilize him and his dog, but conventional wisdom in the late nineteenth and early twentieth centuries held that nature was best when serving human needs. Social Darwinism dictated that the strong not only survived but conquered and flourished, and while those on top did not stoop from exercising their power, they also promoted adherence to rules and proper behavior in social exchanges and in sports. Gentlemen were expected to fight to win, within the rules, just as they were to follow the proper rules of the hunt. Of course, when battling socialists, populists, labor unions, foreign revolutionaries, or anyone else challenging their power and position, the rules became secondary to victory. In a society where all men were created equal, class became the great source of inequality, but hierarchy was acceptable, so attempts to break down the barriers of class—not to mention caste—challenged not just God and country but natural law as well. The only way to rise above your condition, if you were poor, was through your own labor, discipline, initiative, and genius;

collective action was debased pack or herd behavior. Everything and everyone was to serve the cause of progress, dogs included.

"The dog is everywhere what society makes him," observed Charles Dudley Warner in his Editor's Study column for *Harper's New Monthly Magazine* in January 1896, and, in turn, a "civilization" is defined by the kind of dog it breeds. Thus in America the dog was "often tamed and registered, sometimes collared, occasionally muzzled, and now and then pounded. But as a general thing the dog is too free and has not learned his place." It was time, Warner concluded, for Americans to complete the process of transforming their animals into well-bred, obedient, pliant creatures that performed on command and lived only to please their masters. He believed that humans were raised above all other creatures by virtue of their ability to reason, even if they did not always use it, and so they had to direct the dog, who, for all his virtues, was not capable of rational thought, just as they had to tame their own animal impulses and nature. So the dog, half wild by instinct, should be tamed by breeding and beaten into shape, if necessary, to teach it to live in human society, especially in the city. Dogs who could not or would not learn should be killed.[1]

Not coincidentally, demands for licensing and kenneling dogs not actively employed at a task grew along with the drive to clean up sickly, filthy, polluted cities by establishing proper sewage systems, building secure and clean water reservoirs, paving streets, and banning, in some cities, the burning of soft coal. There were also louder cries for government and individuals to crack down on crime, much of it associated with public drunkenness. Beyond those issues, in a rapidly industrializing and urbanizing America that nonetheless remained deeply rural, people were pulling and pushing the dog in multiple directions. A variety of dogs was wanted for different types of hunting, still hugely popular; for racing on tracks; for herding livestock; for guarding homes, farms, and factories; for performing in traveling circuses; and, in the cities, for displaying status and competing in shows, as well as for companionship. At veterinary schools and in medical school vivisection laboratories, dogs and other animals were literally pulled apart—flayed, sliced, and diced alive in the name of science and humanity. The irony—call it paradox—was then, as it had been and would be, that the people demanding strict obedience and proper behavior of their pets were themselves hardly "civilized," as their perpetual wars proved.

Warner proclaimed the American dog "too free," when, in fact, it arguably was not free enough. The tension between those views, between different visions of the place of dogs in human society, remains with us. In many ways, it follows a fault line between those who consider the dog a working animal, meant to serve humans, whether as a hunter, herder, guard, or beast of burden, those who consider the dog an accoutrement, a symbol of status and accomplishment, and those who consider the dog a companion, a partner in life, different but significant. That is a bit of an oversimplification. Indeed, humans began creating the dog in their own image at an early point in their relationship, but by the late nineteenth century they were doing so more thoroughly than ever before, just as they were attempting to redefine themselves—self-consciously, haltingly, and not always successfully. Keeping pets was not new; it had simply expanded with "science" and industrialization, which then, as now, both concentrated and spread vast wealth, so that more people were able to exercise their power to reshape the world and its creatures, and the dog, with its rapid reproductive rates, its plasticity and availability, was an ideal subject.

BY THE MID-1880s, the scramble for prestigious, expensive dogs had become a scandal, a manifestation of crass, tasteless consumption—"luxurious self-gratification," Gaston Fay called it in *The Century* of May 1885, a year after the founding of the American Kennel Club to promote purebred dogs. "The best products of the kennels of Europe and quaint sorts from the far East are eagerly sought for by our people, without regard to cost," he said. Indeed, American dog fanciers bid prices on Saint Bernards and collies up to £1,000, about $5,000, and kept them high. Terriers and toy dogs cost £200 to £300 pounds, or $1,000 to $1,500—not unlike today's prices. Dogs of the wealthy were displayed at bench shows and often bejeweled, bedecked, and presented at "canine receptions at which cards, flowers, and elaborate refreshments are as much *de rigueur* as their own social reunions." The family's chef prepared the dog's food, of course. While asserting that in many cases the dog's looks were being "modified" for the "caprice of the moment," Fay also argued that some breeders were producing "animals of extraordinary beauty and value." But other commentators demurred.[2]

British dog expert and historian Hugh Dalziel unloaded a broadside in the March 1886 *Harper's New Monthly Magazine* against dog-show participants whose sole purpose was "to secure themselves a fame or notoriety through their dogs that they appear instinctively to know it would be hopeless for them to seek in channels opened up by their merits." Dalziel was by training and inclination a champion of purebred dogs and people working to "reconstruct" breeds, like the Irish wolfhound, Tibetan mastiff, English mastiff, and Saint Bernard, or those seeking to refine old types, like sheepdogs. But the social-climbing show people should vanish, he said, because they neither loved nor understood their dogs. He also excoriated "self-styled dog lovers" who failed to teach their dogs to behave around strangers, arguing that they were responsible for making people dislike and fear dogs. He listed an owner's duties to his dog: to take care of its "physical wants," like feeding, exercise, and ending its life at the appropriate time; to attend to the "training of orderly habits and to the higher education of the dog"; and "to save the dog, from the suffering of disease as far as our powers permit." Finally, he recommended feeding them table scraps and giving them abundant exercise, preferably ten miles a day with a horse and rider.[3]

Reconstruction of ancient breeds fed on the same atmosphere that spawned the Arts and Crafts movement that swept much of Europe and the United States. In the face of the socioeconomic disruptions of industrialization and the destruction of individual craftsmanship inherent in mass production, reformers sought to resuscitate local artisanal traditions. They found local craftsmen and paid them to make objects—furniture, pots, jewelry—that resembled idealized past forms. In reconstructing types of dogs, breeders took a similar approach, combing through old paintings and written descriptions, then scouring the countryside to find animals that most resembled their conception of what had existed. They bred litter after litter, first trying to match that look, then taking the dogs that came closest and breeding them to fix those characteristics. They were helped in their efforts by the fact that females come into estrus twice a year, and by the already well-known "founder effect," whereby the same favored sire could be mated over and over again until breeders had produced the dog they wanted. Breeders involved in the reconstructions would then compose histories, bestowing on their creations long and heroic lineages reaching into the depths of time. They also attributed to them enhanced or specialized dog powers that were unique to their breed, usually exaggerations of normal behavior.

Generally, breeders selected small numbers of different types of indigenous dogs—sheepdogs, for example—with the traits they wanted, crossed them to create a dog that matched their physical ideal, and sought to perfect them through intensive inbreeding, use of a favored male or two, and culling. The original stock, the rustic dogs, worked beautifully, which was why they were sought out and were already celebrated for their sagacity and ability in Europe, as in England and America. But they were variable in looks and size, and so those that did not fit the program became expendable, denounced as degenerate versions of the pure form. Among the most famous products of this procedure were the Belgian shepherd, the German shepherd—called briefly after World War I the Alsatian wolf-dog—and the show collie. European breeders also created new breeds of gundogs and protection dogs, like the German shorthaired pointer and the Doberman pinscher. Many found their way to America.

The "refined" and "created" breeds were deemed more trainable and intelligent, not to mention more handsome, more civilized, and more valuable than their lowborn forebears. Although that belief in the superior intellect and biddability of the purebred dog has long since become received wisdom, it has never been proved true. Most evidence appears to refute it and, in fact, points to a central paradox in the dog world: despite measurable differences in talents, behavior, and certain inclinations between breeds—reliance of greyhounds on sight more than smell, for example—there are greater differences in talent, behavior, and temperament between individual dogs, even those within a given breed. In other words, dogs will be dogs. But humans will also be humans, and so, in keeping with their nature, they will continue to believe, for example, that all retrievers are programmed from conception to swim and retrieve or that pointers are preprogrammed to seek and point birds. Belief in the superiority of the pure-blood dog and of scientific breeding were of a piece with the justifications of class, racism, and eugenics. Convinced that humans, like dogs and livestock, could be improved through selective breeding, even many progressive Americans sought ways to encourage "superior" people to reproduce and to stop those deemed "inferior" from doing so.

Keeping the purity of the "race," or breed, was as important as breeding a handsome or mutant dog, perhaps more so because miscegenation was perceived to corrupt behavior, as well as blood, now called genes. Inbreeding was the order of the day for breeders attempting to maintain blood purity and fix physical characteristics they desired. They might outcross to other strains or to other types of dogs in their initial experiments or to achieve a specific effect, as when greyhound breeders in England crossed bulldogs into their lines to improve their dogs' courage and endurance. But after that infusion, they would turn back to the family, despite continued warnings from scientists, and the evidence before their own eyes that the practice of inbreeding, while creating "perfect" dogs, also produced freaks with defects, like blindness in the popular pug and structural weakness in the hips of large dogs, now called hip dysplasia. Much of the breeding produced midgets, giants, dwarves,

brachycephalic dogs, and freakish combinations thereof, with particular coat colors, floppy ears, and other characteristics, and the
"fancy," as it was known, wanted such mutants.

Perhaps even more than livestock, dogs were a prime vehicle for
expressing human ideas of perfectibility through selective breeding
and blood purity. Through selective breeding, humans could play
God, and they became more convinced than ever of the superiority of their creations, of purebred animals in general. According to
breeders and hunters, the excellent retriever—the Chesapeake Bay
dog or the Labrador dog, a newcomer to the ranks—would always
return first with the wounded duck and then go fetch the dead one,
and it would never kill the wounded bird. Of course, *never* is not a
good word to use with dogs. Darwin himself observed that when
confronted with two wounded ducks, the smart dog would kill one
and leave it until he had retrieved the wounded one, although many
harsh taskmasters disputed that, arguing that it was not acceptable
to kill either.

FOR ALL THE ATTENTION they received in national magazines that
catered to the wealthy, purebred dogs remained a small minority in
dogdom, just as their upper-middle-class, rich, and professional
owners did among the general populace. The social philosopher
and economist Thorstein Veblen—who, in his 1899 book, *The Theory of the Leisure Class*, coined the phrase "conspicuous consumption" to describe the practices of wealthy Americans—argued that
they valued the dog in general because it could slavishly anticipate
its masters' moods. Veblen said nothing about working dogs, although he intimated that they were at least marginally acceptable
because they actually performed useful tasks, and he granted that
even the purebred hunting dogs of the wealthy could be of some
slight practical value because they reminded their owners of the
chase, the chief occupation of predatory man in ancient times. In
general, though, he was no fan of dogs, deeming them filthy, expensive to keep, and too quick to leap to their masters' defense. More
important, he called the purebred monstrosities, the deformed crea-

tures prized by dog fanciers, "items of conspicuous consumption," whose only "utility" was that they were expensive to breed and maintain. Their costliness made them more valuable socially—as a measure of their owners' wealth—and that, in turn, made them more admirable and beautiful to their owners, although to Veblen and most objective observers they were ugly. In 1908 the first Model T cost $825, while the most desirable purebred dogs routinely started at $1,000 and ran to $5,000. The price of a new Model T fell in years to come; dogs remained steady or rose in value.

In his analysis of the power of greed and the desire for material goods, and on the way America can persuade its poor people not to rebel but to embrace their envy of the wealthy and pursue conspicuous consumption as the highest calling of life, Veblen has proved more accurate than Marx. But his criticism had no greater effect on the production of mutant dogs than similar comments had fifteen or twenty-five years earlier, or would have forty or a hundred years later. Social-climbing dowagers continued to parade around with their yappy, pampered sleeve dogs, hosting teas and even elaborate canine weddings, a rage imported from Paris, as the toy dogs, bred, like a pug, to have a flatter face and more forward-looking eyes, became the little boys and girls of the house.[4]

It has become commonplace among some evolutionary biologists to describe dogs as neotenic, or "juvenilized," wolves—that is, animals that continue to resemble young wolves when they become adults. As evidence, they cite the morphological changes that separate dogs from wolves—dogs overall are more slightly built than wolves of equivalent size, with less powerful jaws, curved tails, a more domed head, smaller feet and teeth, and less dense bones. Dogs are also said to resemble juvenile wolves behaviorally, because they play a great deal. Although the biological processes underlying domestication are still unclear, over thousands of years humans in some parts of the world have consciously and unconsciously, as Darwin observed, selectively bred dogs for a longer socialization period than wolves and for great attentiveness to humans, among other traits. But the push to breed dogs that looked more "docile," even servile and doll-like, dates from the middle of the nineteenth century and the rise of the cult of the purebred dog as a devoted, loving servant, a member of the household. The more refined or juvenile look, especially of the eyes, ears, and head, distinguished these dogs from the wolflike dingo, rustic sheepdog, and other "primitive" dogs. For that reason it is, perhaps, better to speak of some breeds as neotenic dogs.

Old Dogs; New Tricks

While fanciers were trying to make the dog more humanlike or exotic through breeding, the dogs themselves, often aided by their more practical-minded human companions, proved their adaptability by sliding into new, distinctly urban niches. Along with cats and even monkeys, dogs were well ensconced in firehouses around the country by the end of the nineteenth century, and although some were the popular coach dog of the wealthy, the dalmatian, many were mongrels or other breeds. Engine Company No. 45 in New York City had a Saint Bernard who cleared the street in front of the firehouse so the horse-drawn truck could exit and then, because the firemen never closed the door when they answered an alarm, kept thieves from robbing the place. A "scandal" erupted when a wealthy New Yorker and dalmation breeder gave one of his dogs to Engine Company No. 39 on East Sixty-seventh Street. The dog, Mr. Oakie, replaced Pinkie, a mutt, who died "sliding down the pole in the engine house in response to an alarm," according to Alfred M. Downer, secretary of the New York Fire Department. "One Saturday afternoon Mr. Oakie took it into his head to disappear, then the papers told how he had foresaken Third Avenue for [more fashionable] Fifth Avenue, but this was a cruel libel," Downer wrote in his 1907 homage, *Firefighters and Their Pets*, without giving a date for the event. Downer's favorite was a dalmation mix, Jack, whose best friend was Billy, a fire horse with the hook and ladder company on West Twentieth Street. Jack rode on Billy's back until the alarm rang, and then he leapt down and ran next to the right lead horse, barking for people and other animals to clear the way. He followed men into the fire and stayed with them until they came out, and when Billy was injured, Jack nursed him.[5]

With the advent of motorized fire trucks in the 1930s, dogs like Jack gradually vanished from the firehouses, their services no longer needed. But by then dalmatians were firmly fixed in the public imagination not only as firehouse dogs but also as coach dogs— flashy, fast, sleek, and fearless around horses. They were called hippophiliacs—horse lovers—because of the way they seemed naturally to run with the horses. At the end of the 1930s, two Harvard biochemists, Clyde E. Keeler and Harry C. Trimble, began poring over the records of a large kennel that had bred and trained dalmatian coach dogs during the first quarter of the twentieth century, a period that had seen their peak of popularity and their decline after the motorcar supplanted the horse-drawn carriage. Writing in the February 1940 issue of the *Journal of Heredity*, the scientists dismissed the notion that dalmatians inherited a love of horses, showing instead that the dogs were trained at six months of age to run with horses by being yoked to an experienced dog. After that, they were untethered and allowed to find their own favored position in relation to the horses and carriage. Breeding two "good" dogs who liked to run near the horses—optimally between the front axle of the coach and the horse's rear leg—tended to produce puppies with the same inclination, while breeding "good" and "bad" dogs produced laggards, and two "bad" dogs produced shy, fearful animals. The scientists concluded that "hippophilia" resulted from a complex interplay of "inherited tendencies capable of training" and the dog's level of fear. Their findings reconfirmed what close observers of dogs had said for decades: if you don't train the dog, it won't work or behave, no matter how good its breeding.[6]

Increasingly in the 1880s and 1890s, dogs and other animals also fed the lust for goods, appearing in advertising in a variety of poses or dressed in human garb. In 1900 the Gramophone Company, founded three years earlier by the machine's inventor, Emile Berliner, licensed a painting by British artist Francis Barraud of his dog,

Nipper, looking at and listening to a recording of his master's voice on an Edison cylinder. The Royal Academy had rejected for its summer exhibition of 1899 Barraud's painting of the terrier mix he had inherited from his brother, but after he changed the Edison cylinder in the original to a gramophone, the image became one of the most enduring and widely recognized symbols in advertising for RCA Victor. Nearly as famous was Tige, Buster Brown's little cartoon mutt, who in 1904 went to work for the Brown Shoe Company. By this time, the dog was woven into the fabric of life as a pet, of whom little more was expected than companionship, unqualified adoration, and sometimes protection of home and children.

As if to show its adaptability, the dog embraced the horseless buggy nearly as quickly as people, staking its claim through an indifferently bred bulldog to playing copilot or "riding shotgun," preferably with its head in the onrushing air. In 1903, Horatio Nelson Jackson and Sewall Crocker drove a Winton, a chain-driven, open-air horseless buggy, from San Francisco to New York in just over two months. Accompanying them most of the way was Bud, a bulldog Jackson bought for $15 in Idaho—a bargain price—who proved that the dog intended to take a backseat to no creature. It was another five years before Henry Ford made the car affordable to a large number of Americans, effectively kick-starting a passionate affair between people and machine that has transformed the landscape and society. The changes have not always benefited the dog, who too frequently has become confined to suburban backyards or city apartments, with few places to run, but in general, it seems, he was not about to miss the ride. It beat running under the axles of a horse-drawn wagon, after all.

INTO THE EARLY TWENTIETH CENTURY, the Chesapeake Bay dog was celebrated for its work ethic as a guard and retriever and its devotion as a pet, despite complaints from some dog show fanatics that the people around the Chesapeake Bay had not maintained its "purity." Theodore Roosevelt praised the Chesapeake Bay dog— they were not then called retrievers—that his children had while he was president in his immodest 1913 memoir, *Theodore Roosevelt: An Autobiography*. Sailor Boy was top dog in a house full of dogs, possessed of a "masterful temper and a strong sense of both dignity and duty." He broke up fights between the other dogs and never fought himself, unless combat was unavoidable, "but he was a murderous animal when he did fight." He also loved the water, and fireworks of all sorts. If the dog sounds like a surrogate for Roosevelt and his doctrine of speaking softly and carrying a big, imperialist, monopoly-busting stick, he was, and, all the better, he was an American breed, not an European import. He was also clearly a pet, not a working dog who camped out at night in the house.[7]

Of course, Roosevelt romanticized Sailor Boy and dogs in general, forgetting Pete—variously identified as a bulldog or a bull terrier—who terrorized the White House between 1905 and 1908. He caused an international incident in 1905 when he treed the French ambassador, Jules Jusserand, who had come to play tennis with the president. Many contemporary accounts claim that Pete chewed a hole in the ambassador's pants at a reception, but that was not so. He tore the pants and flesh of a naval clerk, John T. Thomas, on May 11, 1907, just ten days after his return from an eighteen-month exile after the Jusserand affair. At the time, Pete had been assigned to help the police patrol the White House grounds at night—specifically, it was said, to hold at bay the reporters who staked the place out, observing and questioning visitors.[8]

Carving the Dog for Science

No matter the purity of its blood or wealth of its owner, it was widely accepted that the dog was meant to serve humans in any way humans chose; thus, the opposite image of the primped and preened dog was the shaved dog stretched out on an operating table in a medical school laboratory, its guts exposed while it howled or, if lucky, passed out and died. Vivisection, the dissection of living animals and people without anesthetic, dates back more than two millennia but was in abeyance in Europe for much of the Middle Ages. It was resurrected by the eighteenth century—Jefferson operated on dogs at Monticello—and became established as an academic discipline at Harvard's medical school in 1871. Soon laboratories were cropping up at medical schools around the country, all demanding a steady supply of animals that were obtained from local pounds and dog thieves. They were also using insane and "retarded" people, including children, paupers, and criminals, for experimentation, but in smaller numbers and greater secrecy. Doctors and scientists argued that the dog, along with many other animals, was useful in helping them better understand the functioning of the human body so that they could develop treatments for common diseases.

The more "humane" vivisectionists debarked the dogs before the procedure to silence their cries of agony, but the prevailing view at the time was that only humans experienced pain and so the cries of the animals were little more than reflexive noises. In 1883, opponents of live-animal dissection formed the American Anti-Vivisection Society in Philadelphia, followed twelve years later by the New England Anti-Vivisection Society, both of which helped spearhead demands for legislative action, with New York and other cities not far behind. The most compelling and simple argument against vivisection was a question: How can someone bring such anguish to another sentient creature, especially one that serves him so well?

The antihunting, antivivisectionist Mark Twain posed the question in his 1903 story "A Dog's Tale," through his narrator, a Saint Bernard and collie mix. The dog saved her owners' baby from a fire in the nursery and was rewarded by the uncomprehending master of the house—a university president and scientist—who thought she was trying to harm the child, with a kick that shattered her foreleg. She limped into hiding, returning only when she heard the pleas of the family members who belatedly recognized the father's mistake. Later, he rewarded her by blinding and killing her puppy in an "experiment," while his wife and children were away. Keeping

watch over the grave—he at least buried the puppy in the garden—
without eating, she died of a broken heart. Men who committed
such atrocities to gain a shred of knowledge, not the dogs, according to Twain, were the unfeeling, ignorant, insensate brutes. Presenting a strong case for animal rights, other antivivisectionists
argued fervently that no man had the moral right to operate on a
dog without its permission. While much of the public tended to
agree with that assessment through the eve of America's entry into
World War I, opponents failed to ban vivisection.

Their repeated efforts faltered in large measure because vivisection's defenders successfully argued that it did help save lives. In
1894, researchers using guinea pigs and rabbits developed an antitoxin for diphtheria, a bacterial infection that at the time could produce a 40 percent mortality rate during its periodic epidemics. Their
success became the primary support for an argument, articulated by
Harvard's president, Charles Eliot, that the life of even one child
was worth more than the lives of thousands of animals dying in laboratories. Indeed, vivisectionists claimed during World War I that
their experiments taught them how to treat head and chest wounds,
suture blood vessels, diagnose and cure pneumonia, treat gangrene
and other infections, and establish safe protocols for surgery—all of
which saved lives. In Russia, Ivan Pavlov's work with dogs in the
last decade of the nineteenth century, which began with examina-
tions of the digestive tract, led to numerous discoveries about the
brain and central nervous system, and most particularly about con-
ditioned reflexes. Whether some of those discoveries could have been
made without vivisection is a question that cannot be answered, but
it is hard to imagine a society that accepted the brutalization of dogs
with clubs and whips in the name of discipline and training ever
would have supported a ban on the use of dogs for the benefit of
humans, however cruel the procedures involved.

A more significant advance from the standpoint of dogs and
people came in 1884 and 1885 when French chemist Louis Pasteur
developed, using laboratory rabbits, and successfully tested on a
human, a vaccine against rabies. Although it took decades longer to
develop a safe vaccine to use on animals, especially dogs and cats,

Pasteur's work also advanced understanding of rabies, so that it was no longer seen as "hydrophobia," a disease caused by hot weather. Even so, dogs remained the primary reservoir for rabies in the United States until the 1960s, when mandatory rabies vaccination became widespread, according to the federal Centers for Disease Control.

Training the Mutt and the Purebred

Despite the growth in ownership of purebred dogs, the majority of dogs being sacrificed in the laboratory and doing the hard work on farms, in hunting packs (except for the stylized fox hunts of the wealthy), in the fighting pits, in cities and in the Arctic, in advertising and entertainment, were frequently of the rustic type or mongrel curs. Technically, all could be considered different from one another based on their looks, size, and behavior, but they all shared impure lineages, in that other types of dogs were often mixed in by design or accident, or simply because they lacked pedigrees documenting the purity of their bloodlines. The keepers of purebred dogs generally devalued the efforts of those mongrels, while occasionally accepting certain geographically distinct types because of their unique abilities or rarity: the Inuit dog, because of its pulling power and usefulness to white explorers; some rustic sheepdogs, like the Scotch collie, if they could be shown to be from established, "ancient" lineages in specific areas; and exotic types, like the chow, said to be an ancient hunting and herding dog from China. But the acceptance was always qualified and inevitably breeders would begin "refining" and "improving" the breed. When writers like Muir, London, and Twain praised the crossbred dog or, worse, the dog of uncertain parentage, they were subverting the emphasis on bloodlines as the proof of worthiness, intelligence, and talent—in humans and dogs.

The emphasis on the virtues and special traits of purebred dogs over mixed breeds strengthened through the first decades of the twentieth century and slowed the deployment of dogs in new ways in the United States. The brutal training methods employed by many dog owners, regardless of the dog's lineage, also served to limit its usefulness. Most advice to "gentlemen" was that they reward their pointer's good behavior with a pat and kind word, and correct the bad with a whip and boot heel, presumably a kinder, gentler version of the club and dogwhip favored by many dog punchers. Punishment of dogs, no less than people, was the order of the day in many quarters, although some trainers recommended other approaches, which still seem radical even if well established among people who understand dogs. S. P. Hammond, a writer for *Forest and Stream*, advocated in his columns and 1885 book, *Practical Training*, the use of meat and praise, not punishment, and Montague Stevens trained his New Mexico grizzly bear dogs using pieces of bread as a reward. Other people trained their dogs, as people still do, by talking to them and showing them what they wanted done. But training remained an individual, generally punitive endeavor in the United States for decades to come; arguably, despite great progress in developing and using more reward-based methods, it remains so—or people simply do not train their dogs at all. Although there are no statistics, as Warner and other writers regularly observed, untrained and poorly trained dogs accounted for most of the complaints lodged against dogs and their owners and inspired much of the opposition to their presence in cities. Dogs of the working class and poor continued to be condemned most loudly for their lack of training, their impure bloodlines, and their roaming ways.

Trainers like Hammond and Stevens employed methods that at the turn of the century received scientific support and, a century later, have finally begun to move into the mainstream of dog training—such is the grip of custom. By studying how long it took cats and dogs to find their way out of an experimental maze and then how long it took them to learn the route, Edward Thorndike developed a theory of learning based on stimulus and response. Basically, he demonstrated that a desired effect or result to an action or decision reinforced learning, while an unpleasant one made it more difficult and did not, in fact, lead to correction of mistakes. Thus, a dog or cat who escaped a maze learned the route more quickly than one who was frustrated; more to the point, a dog rewarded for an act learned more quickly than a dog clubbed for the wrong act. Thorndike also showed that practice reinforced learning, while a lack of practice allowed it to slip away—"Practice makes perfect." Thorndike's work, together with Pavlov's training of a dog to salivate at the sound of a bell by teaching it to associate food with the sound, paved the way for John B. Watson to establish the behaviorist school of psychology in the second decade of the twentieth century. Always controversial, behaviorism nonetheless opened the door to the whole new world of behavior modification and training of everything from rats to humans, dogs, and dolphins.

Police Dogs

Many of the breakthroughs in training occurred in other parts of England and Europe. In 1886 in Hildesheim, Germany—the year of Geronimo's surrender and deportation from Arizona with his fellow Apaches—police used trained Great Danes to keep public order during the expulsion of Roma (gypsies) and Jews who years before had fled a Russian pogrom. The experiment was successful, but it was apparently not systematically repeated until 1899, when the burghers of Ghent, Belgium, established the first police canine training school in the world, using their own Belgian shepherd, recently established as a breed. Thus began an experiment in employing dogs to herd and manage people that has grown over the years, albeit in fits and starts, into an international industry constantly finding new uses for the dog's innate talents. The Germans, Austrians, French, and Italians soon followed their Belgian counterparts, using breeds of indigenous dogs that were big and imposing. The mere appearance of a policeman walking a beat with his intimidating, attack-trained dog proved a deterrent to crime, most people being much less willing to confront such an animal than a person, even if that person was armed.

Although not counted as police canines in official histories, descendants of the feared slave-hunting dogs were still at work in the South, tracking suspects and fugitives. Thousands of the suspects tracked and arrested well into the 1940s—many of them black—never came to trial. Their guilt having been established by angry white men, often belonging to the Ku Klux Klan, they were lynched for crimes of rape, murder, and mayhem, more imagined than real. Hounds were also deployed as trackers and intimidators of convicts attempting to flee the South's brutal convict camps, erected to bring black people back into peonage. In the late 1870s, free from the oversight of Reconstruction, Southern states passed vagrancy laws permitting people to be arrested and locked up for debt, for not carrying enough money or proper identification, for walking off a job in protest or in search of another job, or simply for moving from one town to another. Initially passed off as a reform by cash-poor states unable to maintain prisons, the system became an enterprise of forced servitude, with convicts "leased" as laborers in crude camps in the piney woods that produced naval stores—turpentine and rosin—through a process destructive to humans and trees; or forced to build railroads, dig canals, log cypress trees out of swamps, and construct roads. For years, 95 percent of these "criminals" were black. By the 1890s, in Florida, where the camps were so notorious they earned the state the nickname American Siberia, about one third of the convicts were white. They could be Crackers convicted of murder or some equally heinous crime, or young white men jumping freight trains. They were thrown in with black prisoners whose only crimes usually were to be black, poor, and unlucky, especially the women, who were at the mercy of guards, trustees, and male prisoners.

Camp captains and guards exercised total control. They punished any behavior they considered offensive by floggings; by consigning prisoners to a cramped, lightless, ventless "sweatbox"; by suspending them by their wrists or thumbs and coating their faces and torsos with molasses that attracted ants and biting flies; or by forcing water through a tube into their stomachs. The guards also ran down escapees with dogs—in Florida, foxhounds were preferred for their speed and agility—so despised that prisoners often tried to kill them and the guards by lacing their food with powdered glass, according to a former guard, John C. Powell, who first exposed the brutality in an 1891 book, *The American Siberia, or Fourteen Years Experience in a Southern Convict Camp.*

Florida's hellish system was finally abolished in 1923 after an investigation into the death of Martin Tabert. A young white North Dakotan exploring the South, Tabert was arrested for hopping a freight train in Leon County in December 1921 and, after failing to pay his twenty-five-dollar fine, sentenced to ninety days in jail. Money arrived from his parents two days after his conviction, but by then the sheriff had leased Tabert to a Putnam Lumber Company camp in a cypress swamp in Dixie County. Like the thirty whites and sixty blacks in the camp, he was held in virtual peonage until, on the eve of his release, the overseer and "whipping boss," Walter D. Higginbotham, believing he was malingering, flogged him to death, delivering 107 lashes and then battering him about the head with the butt of his whip. His parents were told he died of pneumonia, complicated by malaria, but shortly thereafter a newly released convict who had witnessed the torture told his story. His parents and the state of North Dakota demanded an investigation, which Florida finally undertook a year later. The Leon County sheriff confessed to colluding with railroad detectives to collect train hoppers and to accepting twenty dollars for each person he turned over to the camp, plus three dollars for transporting them from Tallahassee to Dixie County. He was fired. Indicted for second-degree murder, Higginbotham was ultimately acquitted, but Florida's convict-lease system was history. Alabama abolished its system in 1928, making it the last Southern state to do so.

IN 1907, POLICE BEGAN PATROLLING with trained, imported Belgian shepherds and reconstructed Irish wolfhounds in South Orange, New Jersey, and New York City. In New York, the initial patrols were made in the Parkville tenements around Twentieth Street, and the dogs, trained as they were to grab anyone they encountered by the leg and throw him to the ground, proved effective in calming the streets. In 1915, Baltimore began using Airedales imported from England, where the Barnsley Railway Police had first imported trained Airedales from Belgium in 1908 for controlling drunken sailors. Baltimore suspended its program in 1917 because officials complained that the dogs had made no arrests, failing to note that no robberies had occurred where the dogs patrolled, said Samuel G. Chapman in *Police Dogs in North America.* Still, programs remained rare and most fell victim to the radio-equipped patrol car by 1954, Chapman noted, with a resurgence beginning two years later when Baltimore reestablished its canine program, now the oldest continuous program in the country.[9]

Dogging in the War to End All Wars

The military in Germany and Russia had opened war dog schools late in the nineteenth century to train messenger dogs and ambulance dogs—also called Red Cross or casualty dogs—but the training schools for police dogs opened a new era of organized, "scientific" dog training in Europe leading to the formation in Germany in 1903 of the DVG, Deutscher Verband der Gebrauschshundsportvereine, devoted to schutzhund, a competition for dogs and trainers involving choreographed obedience, tracking, protection, and attack work. Similar organizations and training schools were established in France, Holland, and other countries, although styles differed. A British army major, Edwin H. Richardson, began training military dogs as a hobby about the same time, because Britain, like America, had no organized program of its own. Progressing quickly, he learned to train ambulance dogs, messenger dogs, human-tracking bloodhounds, sentinel dogs, private watch and guard dogs, and police dogs. Using sugar as a reward, he showed that it was possible to train dogs to detect hashish and cocaine, but no one pursued that at the time. The world was moving inexorably toward war—one day Richardson encountered a German sent to Scotland to buy collies for the German army to train as "sanitary dogs," as Germans referred to ambulance dogs. Richardson was soon advising trainers throughout Europe and North Africa. His credo was simple. He opposed whacking dogs, much less beating them senseless, arguing instead that "the way to teach a young dog is to address yourself to it as one personality to another, to speak to its soul and to credit it with the capacity to understand and to respond."[10]

THE GERMANS had perhaps 30,000 dogs in their military at the start of World War I, a number that by war's end had swelled to an estimated 48,000. They were used for everything from hauling munitions and supplies in inaccessible mountains to carrying messages and sniffing out wounded men on the battlefield, a task at which they excelled. With no canine corps, because of stiff institutional opposition, England and France had to play catch-up. The British military first turned to Richardson, and the French, who became the biggest users of dogs among the Allies, to Sergeant Paul Mègnín, in civilian life an academic who, like Buffon in the eighteenth century, worked with and loved best the French shepherd dogs. The Allies geared up quickly and put into the field an estimated 27,000 dogs, with Richardson employing mostly various crossbred collies—his preference was for farm dogs—Airedales, retrievers, and lurchers (greyhound mixes), while deliberately rejecting hounds, because they followed their noses to the exclusion of all else, and poodles and fox terriers, because they were "too frivolous" to be of use. The German military refused to accept "hunting dogs" of any sort.

Richardson was particularly fond of the messenger dogs, trained to carry dispatches to certain locations, and "liaison" dogs, who raced between two different handlers. Equipped with gas masks, sometimes bearing cages of carrier pigeons, these dogs dodged sniper and machine-gun fire, artillery barrages, and land mines, and picked their way through or leapt over barbed wire and ditches. They were invaluable in keeping open lines of communication in the heat of combat. A story, perhaps apocryphal, holds that a French dog handler, frustrated at watching German messenger dogs speeding up and down the lines, one day loosed one of his liaison dogs who had just come into heat. The next day, the bitch returned with a half dozen German deserters and their messages tagging along behind, tongues dragging. Another French dog, Satan, a black cross between an English greyhound and a working collie, achieved renown when he raced two miles to a small village during the Battle of Verdun, wearing a gas mask and carrying a pair of pigeons and a message to a garrison trapped under heavy fire, according to Ernest Harold Baynes, who covered the war for *Harper's Magazine* and in 1925 published *Animal Heroes of the Great War*. Low on ammunition, exhausted, the soldiers were near surrender when a soldier Baynes identified only as Duval, a top trainer from the French war dog school at Satory, detected a black speck moving quickly toward them. Soon the entire troop was watching Satan fly across the tattered field, only to be felled by a sniper's bullet as he neared safety. But Duval, knowing that Satan loved him above all men, leapt to the top of the trench and, ignoring the bullets flying around him, called his beloved dog. Duval was shot dead, but Satan had heard his voice. Rising to his three good feet, he dashed the remaining distance into the village with both pigeons intact and a message pleading with the garrison to hold out until the next morning. The birds were released with identical messages carrying the coordinates of a German artillery battery on a hill overlooking town. One pigeon was shot down by a German sniper, but the other arrived and the French gunners took out the German threat, freeing the village from the rain of fire until it could be relieved.[11]

Like their German counterparts, the Allied dogs served as more than message bearers and finders of the wounded; they were also prison camp guards, sentries, patrol dogs, occasional combatants with blades strapped to their bodies so they could incapacitate cavalry horses, mail carriers, pack animals used to haul food and ammunition deep into the mountains, and trackers of spies and infiltrators. In addition, said Baynes, they were morale-boosting mascots, along with goats, donkeys, cats, and other animals made homeless in the interminable, civilization-smashing madness. Most of the approximately 75,000 dogs employed on both sides, including a contingent of Alaskan and Canadian huskies used by French forces for hauling munitions and supplies in the Vosges Mountains of Alsace, were mongrels. For war dogs, said Theodore F. Jager in his 1917 book, *Scout, Red Cross and Army Dogs: A Historical Sketch of Dogs in the Great War and a Training Guide for the Rank and File of the United States Army*, "it is character and training that is wanted; nobody has time in days of war to worry about ancestry." Of those who served, an estimated 7,500 died, a fraction of the approximately 8.5 million men killed on both sides, plus 28.7 million wounded or missing, and that does not count civilians. "Most extraordinary risks were taken to rescue those animal pets of the army and navy when they got into trouble," said Baynes, one of America's foremost natural history writers. Yet thousands of dogs were killed at war's end on the ground that they could not be repatriated to human society. (It would take another war before officials could be convinced that war dogs, like soldiers, could return home.)[12]

An enterprising French lieutenant, Rene Haas, who had lived fourteen years in Alaska, brought to the rolling Vosges some 250 sled dogs gathered from Alaska, Canada's Northwest Territory, and Labrador in 1915. Close to half of those dogs, 106, came from the area around Nome, the hotbed of sled-dog racing, most of them from the kennel of Esther Birdsall Darling and "Scotty" Allan, one of the most accomplished racers of the period and winner that April of the All Alaska Sweepstakes, the 412-mile race from Nome to Candle and back. Although they were called malamutes in press accounts, Allan's flop-eared dogs were as much hound as husky— typical products of the crossbreeding that occurred during the gold rush. But they were fast and hardworking and proved invaluable in French efforts to hold the bitterly contested mountains. During one four-day period, working in eleven-dog teams, they hauled 90 tons of ammunition through heavy snow to threatened outposts that horses and mules had been unable to reach in two weeks. When the snow melted, they proved adept at pulling small cars along a two-foot-wide funicular, a small-gauge railroad that ran through the mountains behind the French lines. The French claimed that seven dogs with a driver could do as much work as five horses or mules, and do it more efficiently. Not surprisingly, the dogs were soon eating horse flesh, supplemented with biscuits and rice. Citing a *Times* (London) report, Richardson said that although all the sled dogs performed wonderfully, the Alaskan was best, "'as his courage never fails, and he will work until he drops, though he is perhaps the weakest of them.'" The sled dogs proved so useful that the French awarded each one of the survivors the croix de guerre at the end of the war.[13]

Sometimes the dogs led the way in boldness. At Amiens in 1915, the leader of a regiment of Canadian Scots found a German Alsatian shepherd puppy and adopted him as a mascot, naming him Tommy. Tommy loved to go over the top of the trenches with his men, and he did so recklessly, often leading the charge, according to Baynes. During four years of fighting, he was gassed once, wounded three times, and lost fifteen commanding officers, dead or disabled. At the end of the war, the French awarded the regiment the croix de guerre, and the men hung it on the collar of their adopted shepherd.[14]

While the Alaskan dogs were serving the French, the U.S. Expeditionary Force that went to Europe in 1917 had no official dogs of its own. There was no tradition of using dogs in the military, and the leaders of the War Department did not push Congress for a canine program. The Red Cross and its backers made several attempts to launch casualty dog recruitment and training programs in the United States, but they never got off the ground. The troops were left to use dogs borrowed from the English and French or those they smuggled from home or found in Europe.

Baynes recounted the story of a young marine who on the road in Verdun adopted a setter he named Belle, shared his dinner with her, bathed her, let her accompany him to his listening post, and fashioned a gas mask for her. In the spring, Verdun Belle, as she was known, gave birth to seven puppies just about the time the regiment was ordered to the Marne. After hauling her pups until the weight became too much to bear, somewhere on the road from Verdun to the Marne, he killed four to lessen his burden, and another died before he lost track of Belle in the jumble of troops and refugees in a village near the front. The marine gave the remaining two puppies to an ambulance driver who took them to a field hospital, while Belle attached herself to the first squad of marines that happened by, which, coincidentally, brought her to that same field hospital, where she found her puppies. While she tended them, her marine— wounded, shell-shocked, unconscious—was carried in on a stretcher, and Belle, with the same unerring luck that had brought her to her pups, found him. She went wild, according to Baynes, raising such a ruckus that the hospital staff set up a cot beside him for Belle and her pups, so she could tend them all. Belle became renowned for her devotion.

Staggering through Montmartre, past curfew on Bastille Day, 1918, James Donovan, a signal corps private in the First Infantry Division, kicked a clump of rags on the pavement that promptly yelped. He picked up a little ball of fluff, named him Rags, and then presented his "Parisian gutter pup," as *The New York Times* dubbed the little mutt after his death in 1936, to the military police officers about to arrest him for desertion as the company mascot his captain had sent him to retrieve. Within days, Rags and Donovan were in the second battle of the Marne, keeping lines of communication open between the infantry and artillery. When even the wires for the field telephone went down, Donovan sent the untrained Rags off as a courier, and he took to the task. Cut off with a small group of infantry on the road between Paris and Soissons late that July, Donovan sent Rags back with a plea for artillery cover and rein-forcements. Both arrived, and Rags became a local hero. Like most dogs on the front, Rags became adept at identifying the sound of in-coming artillery rounds and ducking for cover long before the sol-diers heard anything, and so they began to follow his lead. During a brief break from the front, Rags also learned to salute—appar-ently his only stupid dog trick. After his return to combat, Rags had his greatest moment.[15]

In the dense Argonne Forest, late in September 1918, he and Donovan and their troops came under heavy German fire, and Rags was sent back with a cry for help. On the way, an artillery shell exploded nearby, shooting shrapnel into his paw, blinding him in one eye, mangling his ear, and leaving him temporarily dazed and confused, but he completed his trip. In the meantime, Donovan had been wounded and hit with mustard gas before relief could arrive. Soldiers put them both on the same stretcher and then smuggled Rags through field hospitals, aboard a hospital ship back to America, and finally to Fort Sheridan, where gas victims were treated. Rags stayed at the fort, making daily visits to Donovan's room, going there even after he died in the spring of 1919. A wise hand finally let Rags sleep on the empty bed; after a few days he decided Donovan was gone and settled into life as a post dog. In 1920 he adopted the family of a recent transfer, Major Raymond Hardenburg, and traveled from base to base with them, receiving the accolades of a war hero. The New York Anti-Vivisection Society, cashing in on the popularity of heroic dogs, named him to its Legion of Dog Heroes in 1931.

Announcing his death at age twenty in Washington, *The New York Times* identified the undifferentiated mutt as a "Scotch-Irish terrier," it being necessary in that age of eugenics for a mongrel, if he was a hero, to be at least a mix of recognizable breeds. *The Times* did not start the trend, which continues today. Indeed, the paper was more interested in announcing that Rags's remains would return to New York for burial at Fort Hamilton, Brooklyn, where he had lived for many years. A monument was to be built, paid in part by royalties from a popular 1930 book by Jack Rohan, *Rags—The Story of a Dog Who Went to War.* But Rags apparently stayed in Silver Spring, Maryland.[16]

THE MOST DECORATED OF the accidental American war dogs was Stubby, a Boston bull terrier "of uncertain pedigree," belonging to Yale alumnus and army enlistee J. Robert Conroy. No one knows where the young mutt came from, but by some accounts he wandered onto the New Haven field where the Twenty-sixth "Yankee" Division of the 102nd Infantry was training in the spring of 1917, and attached himself to Conroy. More likely, he was Conroy's from the start. With minor difficulty, indicating that the people overseeing the events were more inclined to be lenient than not, Stubby was smuggled to Newport News, Virginia, by train, and thence to France on the SS *Minnesota*. He found himself at the front on February 5, 1918, and proved that he belonged in the trenches with the boys when he captured a German spy during the middle of the night by grabbing his ass. Conroy and his squad taught Stubby to duck from incoming rounds, and he soon persuaded them to trust his ears—and later his nose, as he also alerted the troopers to incoming mustard gas. Stubby himself was wounded during the bloody battle at Seicheprey, involving a German assault, counterattack by the Twenty-sixth Yankee Division, and a brutal German comeback before they retreated with 138 American captives and 634 dead and wounded, including Conroy. Dog and man spent six weeks convalescing in a Paris hospital, where Stubby helped boost the morale of the injured soldiers and, reportedly, saved a girl from being run over in the street. According to a report in *The New York Times*, he became a little gun-shy after his wound, heading for cover whenever the big guns started booming and staying there until they stopped, but he still made it through seventeen battles, including Chemin des Dames, Aisne-Marne, Champagne-Marne, Château-Thierry—where the women made him a chamois vest for holding his growing collection of medals—St. Mihiel, and Meuse-Argonne, where 1,250,00 American troops took 120,000 casualties, including Rags and Donovan, to drive the German forces from the Argonne Forest, nearly tree by tree, and break their will. At Mandres en Bassigny on Christmas Day 1918, Stubby met President Woodrow Wilson. He was a hero, a celebrity, mascot of the American Expeditionary Force, a legendary dog.[17]

Stubby became a world-famous dog in part because he was a good all-American story, unlike the bag of Rags, and the U.S. Marines and American Legion made him an honorary sergeant. After the Armistice and his return to the States, he became even more celebrated, feted at dinners, hauled off to the White House in 1921 to meet President Warren G. Harding after General John J. Pershing awarded him a Gold Medal for heroism, struck by the Humane Education Society, whose members included Mrs. Harding. A quarter of a century earlier, while editing the *Marion* (Ohio) *Star,* Harding had eulogized his own poisoned Boston terrier, arguing that even if he had no soul, he had all the qualities of one—loyalty, faithfulness, modesty, submissiveness, protectiveness, courage, and love—and men would do well to learn by his example. A year later Stubby was the mascot at Georgetown University, nosing a football around the field at halftime, while Conroy attended law school. In 1924 he met Calvin Coolidge, so that he had now met two of the worst presidents in American history. Along the way, some members of the purebred-dog crowd in Boston tried to exclude him from a show, but they were overruled and the judges unanimously awarded the mongrel terrier a gold hero medal. After his death in 1926, Stubby was stuffed and presented to the Smithsonian Institution, there to rest as an authentic canine hero, forgotten until interest revived in war dogs and working dogs in general in the 1990s.

Why one smuggled dog attained the heights of celebrity, while another received but a tantalizing mention only to vanish, nameless, like a ghost or shadow, was often a matter of luck, but in America, it could as easily be due to race. The black soldiers of World War I often trained or were stationed in the South, where they were banned from most public places and many white establishments, where beatings and lynchings were common. At times, black troops, denied justice through the courts and military, sought vengeance on their own, as they did in Houston in 1917, when, after a run of increasingly brutal indignities, they marched on the city and attacked whites. Segregated in their own companies and regiments, commanded by white officers who were not always of the highest quality—in effect treated, as they often complained, worse than dogs—the black soldiers performed with distinction and courage. The French fought in tandem with the 369th Infantry Regiment, the Harlem Hellfighters, counting them among the bravest soldiers in the world and treating them with a respect their American countrymen seldom accorded them. Yet in the opening days of American involvement in

World War I, a little French girl joined forces with the head of the New York License Bureau of the American Society for the Prevention of Cruelty to Animals, where people licensed their dogs, to reunite an African-American soldier, doubtless with the Hellfighters, with the dog he had smuggled to France and lost.

The bureau's longtime director, William H. Groome, told the story to *The New York Times* reporter Herbert B. Mayes in July 1924, in response to a question about lost dogs. In 1917 a French girl found a dog with a New York tag and, after futilely seeking its owner, wrote to the mayor of New York to enlist his help. The mayor, John C. Hylan, sent the letter to Groome, who checked his records and found the dog belonged to a "negro." The soldier's family told Groome where he was stationed, and he sent the information to the little girl. The dog, Groome told Mayes, without mentioning names, was then reunited with its owner.[18]

11

Twenties Roar, Thirties Crash and Rumble: The Nation Falls into
Depression. Dogs Work, Prance, Preen. Race Is the Thing

✍

A T THE HEIGHT OF WORLD WAR I, the Westminster Kennel Club Show in New York attracted 1,636 dogs, according to *The New York Times* on February 17, 1918, ranging
in price from $100 to $20,000 for a pointer, a rarity because he won
both in the show ring and in field trials. Proceeds from dog sales
were earmarked for the Red Cross for use in aiding the war effort, a
controversial and conscious slap at antivivisectionists, who roundly
criticized the Red Cross for supporting medical research with live animals. Wirehaired terriers and Saint Bernards, enjoying a vogue, sold
for $5,000, while chows, popular as car guards and companions—
Queen Victoria had fancied them, among other breeds, and Sigmund
Freud kept them—fetched $2,000. Other popular and costly breeds
were bulldogs, bull terriers, Boston terriers, spaniels, setters, fox
terriers, Pomeranians, and Pekingese. German and Belgian shepherds represented the "war dogs," and wolfhounds from Russia
performed high jumps. Only one Newfoundland was on display,
the darling of the nineteenth century, the dog of Meriwether Lewis,
Byron, and Audubon, having fallen from grace with the fancy.[1]

By comparison, the normal price range for a respectable coon-hound, a dog of poor rural whites and blacks, was $10 to $50 in Ohio, according to the *Cleveland Advocate*, and not much different elsewhere. The *Advocate* raised the issue in marveling in January 1917 at the $100 that William H. Litchferd, owner of the Hotel, in Columbus, "the largest and finest Colored hotel in the country," had paid for Butter, a coonhound from the Tuskegee Institute in Alabama. Black Americans were on the move north from impoverishment, tenancy, and disenfranchisement in the South in the half-century-long flow called the Great Migration—most of these mass movements involved foreign immigrants; this one was domestic—and they wanted their dogs. A passionate raccoon and possum hunter, Litchferd considered Butter, who had treed seventy-two raccoons that season, a bargain. Well bred and brilliant as he might have been, Butter, like most of the working dogs of Americans, was not of a breed recognized by the American Kennel Club, but then gentlemen hunters did not pursue raccoons or possums—fare fit for country folk or, in the case of the raccoon, those who still eked out a living selling furs.[2]

In general, it is fair to say of the years following the Great War that although the majority of Americans still lived on farms or in small towns, the car's replacement of the horse for transport meant that dogs and cats were increasingly the primary connection to the animal world for a growing number of urban Americans, and their stature increased accordingly, as did the pressure placed upon them to conform to human desires. Dog shows were high-society events, and the purebred dog became a more essential fashion accessory for the famous and wealthy than ever before. The divide between "women's pets" and "gentlemen's dogs," apparent since the end of the previous century, had deepened, almost in defiance of rising demands for women's suffrage. Purebred dogs represented perhaps 2 percent of the dogs in America, and the people who could comfortably afford the most expensive among them represented less than 5 percent of the population, but the high-priced dogs and their wealthy keepers had glitz, glitter, scandal, power, and privilege they openly flaunted, even during the Depression, when desirable breeds, like the Great Dane, sold for $12,000. More common breeds cost $100, still a significant amount for many Americans.

Such prices, and the continued production of freakish dogs, confirmed Veblen's bleak theory of the power of greed at a time when communists, socialists, and radical unionists—like the Wobblies, the International Workers of the World, whose advocates included Helen Keller—struggled to bring the working class to life and rebellion; when women, having gained the vote, pushed for more equality; and when black veterans demanded their civil rights and an end to racial persecution. The disparities in wealth deepened. During the 1920s, the income of the wealthiest 1 percent of the population grew from 12 to 19 percent of the nation's total, and the top 5 percent reached a peak share of 34 percent. Annually, 60 percent of Americans earned under $2,000 a year—less than the price of the chow who guarded the rich financier's Town Car. Most Americans got their mongrels or curs or common hounds for free or a few dollars. It is little wonder that many people tended to view the dogs of the fancy, who served no purpose other than to compete in shows and sometimes field trials, as they did the cars and mansions, with a mixture of bemusement, contempt, anger, fascination, envy, and desire.

It was a complicated, tumultuous time. The very attitudes and behaviors that the radicals railed against were embraced by many Americans, who aspired more to goods, money, and private property than to abstract notions of equality, justice, and common ownership. Financial speculation became the order of the day, as those Americans who could afford them bought lots in Florida—many of them submerged—stocks, bonds, and futures, while pursuing sports, gambling, and clothes. A successful person needed to look the part. Indeed, it was the desire to look respectable that had finally brought a halt to the lucrative trade in bird feathers for women's hats that had been outlawed but continued for years with illegal imports from London and Paris to feed the demand of New York society matrons. After prostitutes began wearing the fanciful hats in New York and other cities in 1917, they became unacceptable to proper ladies and the market collapsed.

"Taylorism," the division of labor to speed production as out-lined in Frederick Taylor's 1911 book, *Principles of Scientific Management*, and practiced in Henry Ford's Model T assembly line, which opened in 1913—the first of its kind in the world—reshaped industry, making the mass production of consumer goods a reality. Affordable, reliable, convenient, cars were embraced by many re-formist and populist state governments as a way to break railroad monopolies and clean up the cities, including their air, and by people as a "clean," fast, far-ranging, and reliable alternative to the horse. In 1914 an estimated 1.3 million cars were on the road, and the price of a Model T stood at $99. By 1919, there were 7 million cars, and within a decade that number had soared to 23 million. Dogs hit the road, too.

By 1919, a flood of white Northerners, reversing the migration from the South of African-Americans, had begun pouring into Florida in their cars. They soon congregated along the crushed-shell Florida roads in Tin Can Tourist Camps, so named for the dis-tinctive tanks of extra fuel the travelers strapped to their cars and for their taste for canned, or "tinned," food. Greyhound racing and horse racing were popular attractions at the time, as was speculation in Florida real estate. Wealthy industrialists had winter homes. Middle- and working-class people with a little money to invest in a small fruit farm or business came to stay—in droves. An estimated 2.5 million arrived in 1925 alone, with many of them settling in towns that seemed to spring overnight out of the hammocks, pine flatwoods, and swamps. Outside the burgeoning new communities, government bounty hunters with dogs slaughtered all the deer they could find in an effort to arrest an outbreak of Texas tick fever that had arrived with imported cattle. Across the palmetto prairie, cattle and dogs were dipped in huge vats of arsenic that then sat out in the open, polluting the local groundwater. Tick fever was brought un-der control around 1926, at the same time a hurricane combined with market forces to burst the real estate bubble, in a collapse that contributed to the onset of the Great Depression.

The increase in automobile ownership and the expanding net-work of roads also brought an increase in dog theft and dog—not to mention cat, wildlife, and human—fatalities. Purebred dogs, especially German shepherds, were regularly pulled from the Long Island estates of wealthy New Yorkers and sold in distant cities, while within cities, any dog was fair game for theft and sale to medical centers. The shepherds, popular because of the war, the cinematic adventures of Rin Tin Tin, and their duty on police patrol, could not be trained to avoid dognapping, their owners lamented, as if that were a failure in the dog's intelligence.

In fact, the already exalted reputation of the German shepherd as a police dog and companion was enhanced when it proved adept as a guide dog for the blind. Germans had begun training their shepherd dogs in 1917 to guide soldiers blinded in mustard gas attacks, and the French followed soon thereafter. The German effort appears to have been the first organized guide dog program in modern times, although late in the sixteenth century Montaigne sang the praises of the dogs he encountered in Paris and in French villages, guiding their blind masters through horses, carts, and people, past holes and obstacles. "I have seen them, along the trench of a town, forsake a plain and even path and take a worse, only to keep their masters further from the ditch," he wrote in "Apology for Raimond de Sebonde." The dogs also knew which houses would give them alms and so stopped regularly, like delivery men, making their rounds.[3]

The first of the German-trained dogs, Lux, arrived in the United States in 1925 as a gift from a supporter to Senator Thomas D. Schall of Minnesota. Around the same time, Helen Keller obtained a privately trained dog—one of the first in the country. Dorothy Harrison Eustis established the first American program for guide dogs, the Seeing Eye Foundation, in 1929. Other organizations followed suit, and the deeds of some of the early guide dogs, like Almo, who saved his charge, W. A. Christensen, and Christensen's wife, from a burning motel, became legendary.

Presidential Dogs and Other Notorieties

As their status increased, dogs became good politics. The Republican presidents of the 1920s—Harding, Coolidge, and Hoover—were all dog lovers, and their dogs became newsworthy in their own right. Franklin Roosevelt's Scottie, Fala, nearly achieved cult status. From that time, it has become conventional wisdom that the president should have a dog on display, as a symbol of stability, courage, fidelity, and devotion. Forgotten, of course, were the dog's less acceptable qualities—and Theodore Roosevelt's marauding Pete.

Having won the presidency by a landslide, the isolationist, pro-business Warren G. Harding brought to the White House in March 1921 a rambunctious young Airedale named Laddie Boy, whose first official act was to tree the Wilsons' cat. Tales of Laddie Boy, along with his occasional press interviews and letters to other dogs and people, brought some life and humanity to an administration otherwise noteworthy for its corruption, its support of immigration restrictions, its tax cuts for the rich, its imposition of high protective tariffs, and its veto of a bill providing veterans' benefits. Trained by the African-American White House messenger, Wilson X. Jackson, Laddie Boy held a chair at cabinet meetings, as did Florence Kling Harding, the president's wife. Although there is no evidence that Laddie Boy spoke for the rights of dogs or any other creature, Mrs. Harding did champion women's rights and animal welfare. In August 1921 a supporter presented Harding with an English bulldog, sired by a $4,000 champion stud, but Oh Boy, as he was known, had to pass muster with the imperious Laddie Boy before he could join White House society.

Even Laddie's siblings and offspring joined the ranks of celebrity. In fact, in late July 1921, Albert R. Lowrie, answering charges in court that his Airedale, Dickie Boy, had slaughtered a neighbor's chickens, asked the judge whether he honestly believed a dog who was full brother to the president's own Laddie Boy would stoop so low as to kill some scrawny chickens. The judge agreed that he failed to see how that could happen, and the case was dismissed for lack of evidence. A year later in New York, several boys rescued Laddie's five-month-old son, Happy, from an enraged goat. The puppy had wandered away from his home on Eighth Avenue two weeks earlier to join the ranks of New York's street dogs.[4]

After Harding's death in August 1923, from eating tainted crabs while on a political trip to Alaska and the West coast, Laddie Boy sat for a sculpture, created as a memorial to Harding and paid for by a penny donation from every former and current newspaper delivery boy in the land, including Arthur S. Ochs, publisher of *The New York Times*, himself a former newsboy. Laddie Boy passed the torch to Calvin Coolidge, when he bounded from the White House to meet the car carrying the new president and his wife, Grace, after Mrs. Harding's departure. The Coolidges said that he had given them a sign, and in further recognition of Laddie Boy's stature, they agreed to take a half brother of his as one of three White House dogs. Florence Harding gave Laddie Boy to one of Harding's former Secret Service guards, Clarence Barker, who took him to live in Newton, Massachusetts. There he was busted on November 19, 1923, for trespassing on the lawn of John Weeks, secretary of war under Harding and Coolidge, showing that for some people, hatred of dogs transcends even politics.[5]

WHILE LADDIE BOY'S BROTHER fought charges of chicken slaughter in Denver, one of Harding's major industrial patrons, Daniel G. Reid, battled his former wife over custody of their Pekingese, considered among the most aristocratic of dogs, valued at $1,000 a pound or upwards to $10,000. With W. H. Moore and William B. Leeds, Reid had created one of the first industrial combines in America, by buying and merging during the 1890s some 200 companies devoted to the manufacture of tin plates—sheets for shaping into other products. At its peak, the American Tin Plate Company produced 53 percent of the nation's total. Each of the partners earned the title "tin plate king," and while this was hardly glamorous, the "tin plate trust" was soon producing steel. In 1901 the partners sold out for stock to J. P. Morgan's U.S. Steel Corporation, an even bigger combine. Reid became involved in the Chicago, Rock Island & Pacific Railroad—and was soon accused of diluting its stock and looting the company. He was widely credited with creating the bull market in 1912—the year greyhounds started chasing mechanical rabbits around a track—when he also helped found the Tobacco Products Company to mass-produce cigarettes. Later, Reid started the American Can Company. Known as a financier with the power to move the stock market, in 1899 he had transplanted himself to New York, where he kept a house at 895 Fifth Avenue, Millionaires' Row, with a country estate on the Hudson, an apartment in Paris, his birth home in Richmond, Indiana, and a fortune to go anywhere.[6]

Twice widowed, he married Margaret Carrere, an actress in musical comedies, in 1906 and divorced her in 1920 amid public charges and countercharges of infidelity. He initially sued her for "improper conduct" with a Serbian army officer in 1918 in New York, San Francisco, and the Pullman car between. She countersued, charging him with carrying on affairs with a nurse and with Georgette de la Plante, a modiste, or fashion designer, who made lingerie for Margaret. Reid refused to testify in his case, so it was dropped. Margaret presented evidence that Mme. Georgette, as she was known, had moved into her bedroom for a week in December 1918 and been espied modeling a transparent petticoat, sitting on Reid's lap, and generally acting the mistress for Reid, who called her "baby" and "kitty." Margaret won the divorce, and Reid agreed to give her $200,000 in cash and $30,000 a year. He also allowed her to take $400,000 worth of possessions from the Fifth Avenue house, but he balked when she sought to include in her booty a portrait of King George I and the dog.

Back in court on July 17, 1921, Margaret's attorney proclaimed the Pekingese something of an "institution" around the Fifth Avenue house, adding that had they been fighting over an Irish terrier or a bull terrier, Reid probably would have a point, because those were "gentlemen's dogs," but the Pekingese was "universally regarded as a woman's pet." The judge ordered arbitration, but the case seems to have been settled outside of public view, probably with the dog going to the woman. Mme. Georgette went to court in an attempt to clear her name but ended up exposing herself as a bigamist and perjurer who had accepted jewelry and other gifts from Reid while serving as his mistress. Just two years after the Pekingese row, Reid fell into poor health, suffering from depression, perhaps aggravated by alcoholism, and other ailments that forced him to retire from his business. At his death on January 17, 1925, he left $40 million to his daughter by his first marriage, having already given her the Fifth Avenue house.[7]

Ironically, Reid's physical and mental decline began around the time Laddie Boy approved Coolidge's move to the White House, which ushered in a golden age of American capitalism and speculative frenzy. Coolidge, who had to duck the slime of the Teapot Dome scandal, brought on by Harding's minions, presided over such a massive concentration of business that by the end of his term, 200 corporations controlled just over 50 percent of the nation's wealth. He cut taxes for the rich, signed legislation strictly limiting immigrants from southern and eastern Europe, Japan, and other Asian nations, and did nothing to help small farmers around the country who were already in an economic slump that was forcing many of them—black and white—off the land and into Northern cities. The only thing Coolidge appeared to like more than riding the electric horse he had installed in the White House was walking his dogs—a noble undertaking and not uncommon in an age when people still took long walks. Indeed, Coolidge and his wife were such notorious animal lovers that people from all over the world sent them dogs, including a white collie; cats; and wildlife.

Celebrity Dogs

In 1923, nearing the height of his baseball prowess, Babe Ruth purchased a bull terrier bitch as a badge of his success and entered her, aged nine months, in the puppy competition at the Eastern Dog

Club Show in Boston in late February 1924. She took second prize for bull terrier bitches, and the papers gleefully reported that the Babe had yet another winner in his Cloudland Dot, future queen of one of the most popular breeds in the land, a fitting dog for the slugger who had led the Yankees to their first World Series victory. Known as something of a puppy himself—or at best a talented but marginally delinquent juvenile in an adult's body—Ruth over-indulged his love of food and drink over the off-season, and at spring training in 1925, he suffered an intestinal abscess that required surgery. Neither he nor the Yankees fully recovered that season, as reporters accused him of being over the hill.

Suspended and fined $5,000 in early September for violating a one a.m. curfew, the gluttonous Ruth learned that Dot, as she was known, had roamed off his farm in Sudbury, Massachusetts, and killed a neighbor's pedigreed cow—not an easy feat for a lone wolf, much less a show dog. The neighbor promised to sue. Speaking to an Associated Press reporter about the run of plaguesome events, Ruth said, "They come in bunches, like bananas. Well, this luck can't last forever." A better prophet than dog owner, the Babe entered his prime the following year and, with Lou Gehrig, led the Yankees to three pennants and two World Series victories over the next three years. Yankees' owner Jacob Ruppert was himself an avid breeder of prizewinning Saint Bernards. He was also a sponsor of Richard Byrd's polar expeditions.[8]

When dogs became stars and heroes, they reinforced noble ideals and became ambassadors for their breed, if not their species. For all their accomplishments, Stubby and other war heroes could not match the renown of a dog found on September 15, 1918, by army corporal Lee Duncan. He and his fellow soldiers were examining an abandoned German war dog station in Lorraine when they encountered a mother with five young puppies. Duncan took the mother and two of the pups, naming them Rin Tin Tin and Nannette, after the finger dolls French children gave the soldiers for good luck, and distributed the other puppies among his comrades. Nannette caught distemper on the way back to America and died before Duncan reached his home in Santa Monica, California.

There he began training Rin Tin Tin and taking him to perform high jumps at local dog shows and events—jumps being popular displays of a dog's physical power.

Determined to make the dog a movie star, Duncan unsuccessfully made the rounds of Hollywood studios until, one day in 1922, he reportedly watched a wolf refuse repeatedly to perform its scene on the set of a Warner Bros. movie, *The Man from Hell's River.* Duncan convinced the frustrated director that his Alsatian wolf dog would do the scene in one take, and from there Rin Tin Tin leaped into stardom, making twenty-six films for Warner Bros. and lifting the studio from bankruptcy to profitability. In silent films, he was directed by Duncan's voice commands. After he began making sound films, according to Peter Shaw Baker in his 1933 book, *Animal War Heroes*, Duncan used toys to cue him—a black velvet cat that sent him into a fury, a stuffed lion that made him bark, and a rabbit that signaled him to wag his tail. For defeating screen desperadoes, Rin Tin Tin received, at the height of his career with Warner Bros., $1,000 a week and had his own chef and chauffeur. But the Depression and changing tastes caused a slump in his box office, and he left Warner Bros. On August 10, 1932, he met a Hollywood death in the arms of Duncan and Duncan's neighbor, the actress Jean Harlow; he was eventually buried in Paris. Heirs of the star have continued to make movies or television programs, including the 1950s television series *The Adventures of Rin Tin Tin*, and today a lively cult surrounds the dog.[9]

Rin Tin Tin's offspring were widely sought during the 1920s and 1930s and are still available today, with various Web sites proudly boasting of their accomplishments. Rin Tin Tin's celebrity coincided with and reinforced selection of the German shepherd as the preferred dog for personal protection, police work, and guide dog service for the blind, all of which catapulted it to the top of the popularity charts. He also contributed to the cult of the dog hero, which grew in strength after the Great War, as if the dog, as an enduring symbol of loyalty, love, and courage, could help heal a shattered civilization and help the weak and the needy.

⚬⁓

THE GERMAN SHEPHERD'S FAME was so great that in 1926 it accounted for 36 percent—21,569—of all dogs registered by the American Kennel Club. But the American version of the shepherd quickly became a poster dog for what happens when too many animals are bred too quickly from a small gene pool. Shepherds had already been created through intense inbreeding; in America, where their numbers were initially small, they were bred that way again to please judges and meet popular demand. Quality went down so precipitously that when Dorothy Harrison Eustis set up the breeding program for her Seeing Eye dogs in 1929, she went to Switzerland, where the stock was better. Her work was documented in an analysis conducted by Elliott Humphrey and Lucien Warner for their 1934 book, *Working Dogs*, which showed a near-complete bifurcation for generations between dogs bred solely to please the shifting taste of show judges and those bred for working. By the time Humphrey and Warner's book was published, German shepherd registrations with the American Kennel Club had fallen, and the fox and Boston terriers and the dachshund, which had been shunned during the war, reigned in the popularity sweepstakes. With few exceptions, like the $20,000 pointer, that split between show dogs and working dogs existed for all breeds, except the non-working toys—and still does.[10]

Members of the fancy regularly imported foreign-bred dogs, believing them better overall than their American counterparts. They generally performed so well in the show ring, in fact, that on December 21, 1929, the American Kennel Club announced its intention to request the federal government to place an embargo on the importation of foreign purebred dogs to protect domestic breeders. The plan went nowhere, although separate prizes were subsequently awarded at the Westminster Kennel Club show in New York to foreign-bred and American-bred dogs.[11]

The Problem of Blood Purity

The notion that pure-blood dogs had inherent value and talent exceeding that of mere mutts or curs continued to gather adherents and sink into the realm of received wisdom, even though with a few exceptions, like the greyhound, a biological sprinting machine with an extraordinary 90 percent fast-twitch muscles—compared with 50 to 60 percent in dogs in general—the brilliant specialist dog never quite lived up to expectations. Experienced dog handlers understood, of course, that mongrels could perform most tasks as well as, if not better than, any of the pure bloods, but they were often ignored. The decades-long habit of attributing superior characteristics to the well-bred dog dovetailed with prevailing attitudes toward race and ethnicity. It was a period of institutionalized racism, of widespread anti-Semitism, of anti-immigrant bills designed to keep "inferior" southern and eastern Europeans and Asians out of America, and of forced sterilization of "mentally deficient" people in the name of improving the human gene pool. Eugenics and racism ultimately ran amok in Germany, but they were widespread at the time.

The bias in favor of "scientific breeding" and Western dogs was so ingrained that it regularly led people to maintain without examination ideas their own experience refuted. In 1930, Captain Vladimir Perfiliaff persuaded *The New York Times* and other American groups to fund an expedition to southwestern Brazil to kill and "study" jaguars. He took with him an ethnographer, a photographer, a writer, and the veteran big-game hunter and explorer Alexander Siemel, whose chief claim to fame was a predilection for killing the big cats with a spear to prove his courage. The expedition enlisted twelve crossbred American hounds—three quarters foxhound and one-quarter bloodhound—to track and bay the big cats. Half the dogs came from Florida, where they had trained hunting black bears, and half from Arizona, where they had tracked black bears and cougars. Because of their breeding, Siemel told the *Times* before leaving for Brazil, the hounds would have a keener sense of smell than the native mongrels, who were specially trained by the tribesmen and older dogs for the task. Without missing a breath, he then went on to reminisce about the genius of Valenté, one of those native mongrels who had been his best friend for two years and helped him kill sixty-four jaguars before being killed himself by the big cats. The American dogs reportedly performed well but not brilliantly in helping Siemel kill more jaguars, including one weighing 307 pounds, which he and his native helpers skewered with spears. Their sense of smell, though, proved no better than that of the local mongrels.[12]

THE MASTERS OF ILLUSION in Hollywood showed greater understanding of dogs and their ability than did explorers like Siemel, who, it must be said in fairness, was not unusual for his time. For several years during the 1920s, the foremost canine star in Hollywood was Lassie, a long-haired cross between a bull terrier and a cocker spaniel. Belonging to Emery Bronte, the little dog—not to be confused with the collie of the same name who achieved fame fifteen years later—earned $15,000 a week in 1927, starring in such forgettable films as *Knockout Riley*, *The Beautiful City*, *Sonny*, and *The Street of Forgotten Men*. By all accounts, Lassie and Bronte were a perfect pair. She was an inquisitive, head-cocking dog, eager to understand and please, and he treated her with total respect, according to a June 16, 1927, article in *The New York Times*. He never whipped or punished her; rather, he trained her by speaking in a conversational voice and explaining what he wanted her to do. She was, as they said in show business and sports, a natural.[13]

By 1930, some 400 dogs were working in the film industry, the majority of them mongrels of the terrier type, trained on food or games. Jules White and Zion Myers figured out how to synchronize human speech with dog barks, inspiring the entire genre of talking-dog movies. "We found out one thing early in the work—mongrel dogs were as a rule cleverer than thoroughbreds," Myers told *The New York Times*. He thought it was because they were not pampered the way purebred dogs were. Other observers believed the apparent superiority of mongrels was due to the fact that they could exercise their minds and perform a variety of tasks denied a show dog, confined to a kennel or to shows. Still others argued that the purebreds were being bred stupid. In a significant shift, the mongrel collie was seen as more intelligent and harder-working than its show cousin.[14]

Dog Heroes

Fortunately, any dog could be a hero, and groups around the country, like the New York Anti-Vivisection Society, hosted awards ceremonies for lifesaving dogs and other animals as well as people. Most of the heroics involved a dog rescuing its family from a burning building by barking, scratching, and sometimes biting, or a dog protecting home, store, or owner from thieves or miscreants. For example, in October 1925 a scrappy little mongrel, Spot, born of a fox terrier and an undifferentiated other dog, who years before had lost a leg defending a child from the attack of a German shepherd, alerted a governess to a fire in the New York house occupied by his owners, actors Dorothy Mackenzie and Ray Raymond, who were then at the theater. Spot led the governess and the couple's child to safety, then dashed back into the house and up to the smoke-filled second floor, where he tried desperately to summon help from behind a closed window. Unsuccessful, he leapt through the glass and crashed to the ground, bruised but alive. The next day Mackenzie and Raymond realized Spot had been trying to save the family lovebird.[15]

Compelling though such stories were, they could not match the drama of Alaskan mushers racing across the interior of Alaska in the depths of a bitterly cold, gale-battered winter. Suspended during World War I while Alaskan and Canadian huskies served the French in the Vosges Mountains, sled dog racing resumed in the 1920s in Nome and Fairbanks, and it quickly attracted the attention of adventurers and writers from Europe as well as other states. In what are now the lower forty-eight states, racing had begun around

1917 in Idaho, and it gained in popularity after the war, especially in New England. But the Alaskan sled dogs achieved their greatest glory in what became known as the Serum Run, a 674-mile relay from Nenana to Nome, involving twenty Anglo-European and native—Athabascan and Inupiat—mushers and their dogs along the frozen Yukon River and across the ice-encrusted Norton Sound to the Seward Peninsula in late January 1925.

Early that month, diphtheria appeared in Nome, and the U.S. Army Signal Corps sent out an urgent call for antitoxin containing the serum needed to stave off an epidemic. On January 27, 300,000 units of serum, enough for 100 to 300 exposed patients, reached Nenana, near Fairbanks, by train from Anchorage and were loaded onto the sled of William "Wild Bill" Shannon. With the world observing through radio and newspaper reports received by telegraph, Shannon started his dogs, led by Blackie, down the Yukon at 11 p.m., the temperature hovering at minus 40-degree Fahrenheit. The last musher, Gunnar Kaasen, pulled into Nome at 5:30 a.m. on February 2—five days, six hours, and thirty minutes later, delivering enough serum to arrest the outbreak that had already claimed five lives. Another shipment arrived by dogsled on February 15; scandalously, the governor of Alaska had refused a request that it be flown from Anchorage to Nome by government plane, choosing to rely on the slower, more reliable dogs.

Among those stricken, though she recovered, was Sigrid, daughter of the Norwegian-born North American sled dog racing champion Leonhard Seppala, who covered 134 miles—pushing the pace—behind his lead dog, Togo. Using mail cabins and native villages as exchange points, nearly all the other mushers covered thirty to forty miles, while Shannon traveled fifty-eight and Kaasen fifty-three. Seppala's run came after he had already raced 121 miles from his home near Nome to Shaktoolik, an Inupiat village on the Norton Sound, where he picked up the serum. He and his team made the always treacherous crossing of the jagged ice of the sound, which rattled the bones of dogs and men, in the raging, bone-numbing, terror-inducing, blinding, wind-driven snow of a gale off the Bering Sea. The man who never took a whip to his dogs—the hu-

manitarian award of the Iditarod dogsled race is named for him—
handed off the precious serum at Golovin to Charles Olson, who
drove it twenty-five miles through the same whiteout, to Bluff,
where Kaasen took over. On the way home, Togo broke out of his
harness and led two team dogs on a caribou hunt, but fortunately
for Seppala, they returned to his cabin on their own after eating
their fill. To the press and public, the champion became "the great
Seppala" for his heroics. Seppala, said Arthur Shield in a laudatory
story for *The New York Times* on February 8, 1925, "might give pause
to the apostles of racial purity," because he represented a mix of all
Nordic types—the Finn, the Swede, and the Norwegian. Indeed,
Shield proclaimed, his Siberian huskies were better bred than he.[16]

But the immediate glory went to Kaasen and his lead dog, Balto,
who drove through the relentless gale and bypassed their relief at
Safety—thinking Kaasen had stopped for the storm to abate, the
musher was sleeping inside—to reach Nome. Having lost his way
in the whiteout, Kaasen said, he simply let Balto lead the team and
the serum home. Although to many observers the tireless Togo deserved top-dog honors, the city of New York, following the dictum
that says "to the winner the spoils," erected a statute of Balto in
Central Park. Known as an indifferent lead dog in Alaska, Balto,
cast in bronze, became the enduring symbol of the devoted, loyal
dog. But his own fate was not nearly so heroic. Kaasen, who liked
to boast that Balto had led his 1915 championship racing team, sold
his leader and the rest of his team to a Hollywood barker, who
resold some and locked the remaining seven, including Balto, in his
roadside zoo catering to car-driving tourists. For a dime, tourists
got a look at the famous, flea-bitten, out-of-shape "wolfdogs." There
they languished until a Cleveland businessman saw them and organized a campaign to save them. The (Cleveland) *Plain Dealer* and
local schoolchildren helped raise $2,000 in ten days to purchase the
dogs and bring them to Cleveland in 1927, where they lived out
their lives under more pleasant circumstances. Upon his death in
1933, Balto was taxidermied and put on display at the Cleveland
Museum. He was eleven—not more than eighteen, as the boastful
Kaasen insisted.

Togo's death by euthanasia in his Maine retirement kennel in December 1929 was widely reported, and he was eulogized as the true hero of the Serum Run. His remains went to the Whitney Collection of dog evolution in the Peabody Museum at Yale University. Writing in *The New York Times* on January 5, 1930, Mildred Adams placed Togo in the pantheon of great dogs, along with Chinook, an old sled dog on Admiral Richard Byrd's Antarctica expedition who had recently vanished. "Every once in a while a dog breaks through the daily routine of feeding and barking and tugging at a leash," she said, "and for some deed of super-canine heroism wins the adoring regard of every one who hears of him." Once that happens, she added, humans imbue the dog with all the noble characteristics they admire but seldom find in themselves—unselfishness, devotion, affection, self-sacrifice.[17]

The Serum Run brought a surge in popularity for sled-dog racing. In Alaska, major championships were held around Fairbanks, featuring a number of now legendary drivers. Many of the Anglo-European drivers used Siberian huskies, while the Inuit and Athabascans relied on their own animals. Siberian huskies also dominated racing in the lower forty-eight states and in Europe, where until recently, in homage to the cult of racial purity, only purebred dogs could compete—rendering the Europeans noncompetitive when they raced against the mutts called Alaskan huskies. The most famous of the native mushers, Johnny Allen, used dogs that were a mix of Irish setter, wolf, and husky; in 1938 he became the first musher to average fifteen miles an hour over thirty miles. In Idaho, mushers experimented with Targhee hounds, crosses between Irish setters and staghounds, and in New England and Canada, they often created their own crossbred dogs, until the Siberian became established.

The sport was so popular that sled dog competition was added to the Lake Placid Winter Olympics in 1932 as a demonstration event, involving teams from Canada and the United States. Seppala headed the American team, which included Eva "Short" Seeley of Wonalancet, New Hampshire, the only woman to compete against the men. The favored Seppala took second place behind Emile St.

Goddard, the Canadian star. Seeley was later instrumental in gaining recognition for the Siberian husky from the American Kennel Club, and the dogs became synonymous with the term *sled dogs* during the 1930s; although after World War II, the Alaskan husky, a purpose-bred mutt that runs fast and pulls hard, began to dominate racing. Purebred Siberian huskies are no longer competitive.

Antarctica with Byrd

Sled dogs again proved their mettle in 1928, when Admiral Richard Evelyn Byrd, riding the glory of his (probably fudged) overflight of the North Pole in a tri-engine Fokker airplane two years earlier—a flight that meant yet another American had "beaten" Amundsen to the Pole—led his "million-dollar expedition" to Antarctica. Amundsen did complete the first unquestionable overflight of the North Pole several months after Byrd, in a dirigible, but few Americans noticed. Byrd was also cashing in on his transatlantic flight in 1927, the third crossing after Lindbergh's solo flight, with a cat on board. As he had in the Arctic, Byrd used a pilot on his transatlantic flight, which would have gone unremarked had he not decided to ditch the plane off the coast of France and row to shore in a raft. That bit of melodrama earned him his first New York ticker-tape parade; he gained another for claiming the North Pole. Now he planned to fly over the South Pole, while his second in command conducted an ambitious 1,500-mile dog sled exploration of the glaciers and geology of the Queen Maud Mountains, whose peaks reached 15,000 feet. Along the way, he intended to explore and map the terra incognita of Antarctica. Following Amundsen's advice to take "lots of dogs," Byrd packed on his ship ninety-four, seventy-eight of them "Greenland huskies" from kennels in Labrador "of the breed and blood with which some of the greatest marches in the polar regions have been made." He also took sixteen "Chinook" dogs, from the Wonalancet, New Hampshire, kennel of Arthur T. Walden, "heavy draught animals, of his own breed, with a splendid record in transport." A brilliant self-promoter with a passion for

the polar regions, Byrd enjoyed the sponsorship of Fords, Rocke-
fellers, Sulzbergers, Rupperts, and others among the richest families
in America, as well as great popular support, and he provided them
all with tales of adventure, exploration, and heroic acts of men and
dogs. He also took with him Russell Owen, a reporter from *The
New York Times*, one of his sponsors, who filed regular dispatches
in Morse code by wireless telegraph that Byrd initially would not
let his men read because some of them were mentioned little, if at
all. He relented only after winter and boredom set in. Later, he reportedly began rewriting Owen's copy to put the best face on his
effort and even "fired" Owen at one point, only to reinstate him.
Not missing any opportunity for publicity and profit, Byrd also
took along two Paramount studio cameramen to film the expedition for what became an Academy Award–winning documentary,
With Byrd at the South Pole.[18]

Byrd knew what was needed to accomplish his task and keep his
name before the public, and he sought and used those tools selectively, especially the dogs, including his own pet dog, Igloo, along
for the ride. Unlike other polar explorers, he named many of the
dogs, especially the leaders of his eleven dog teams, along with their
drivers, in his account of the expedition and related some of their
characteristics and exploits. The book's uncredited ghostwriter was
Byrd's press agent, Charles Murphy. An additional chapter was
written by the second in command and geologist, Laurence Gould.
But for all the drama conveyed in his books and in independent accounts, there was something abstract and ritualistic, almost pedes-
trian, about the whole affair. The South Pole had been conquered
already and, although considerable risk was still involved and past
disasters remained fresh in everyone's mind, the protocols for surviving on the ice continent were well established.

The challenge was to reach the Pole using a different means of
transportation and thus claim some glory, but a larger goal involved
exploration and naming newly discovered physical features for his
patrons. Even the dogs were domestic, born and reared not among
the Inuit of Greenland but in kennels on Labrador and in New
Hampshire. Walden had created his Chinooks by crossing a Saint

Bernard with a "Greenland husky" he had obtained in Alaska, re-portedly a granddaughter of "Polaris," Robert Peary's lead sled dog. He then crossed that dog to German and Belgian shepherds and appears to have used them primarily in local New England events. Although they performed well in Antarctica, their record as draft animals prior to that is as fictive as their heritage: Peary called his favorite leader North Star.

There is little to tell of the actual South Pole, Byrd said: "One gets there, and that is about all there is for the telling. It is the effort to get there that counts." He got there in a Ford plane with a pilot, radioman, and cameraman on November 29, 1929, just a month af-ter the stock market crash that marked the beginning of the De-pression. For that effort, he had forty-two men and, upon landing, ninety-one dogs, including Igloo, having lost four on the passage from New Zealand to Antarctica. Others were killed, in polar tra-dition, to lighten demands for food during the long land expedition, or died, including Walden's twelve-year-old Chinook, the founding stud of his kennel and his favorite lead dog. Around twenty-six puppies were born in Antarctica, with twenty surviving to be put in harness before they were a year old and fully grown.[19]

Chinook's disappearance on his twelfth birthday, in late January 1929, was, Byrd said, "perhaps the saddest incident during our whole stay in Antarctica." Walden was devastated. "The affection between [Chinook] and Walden was a beautiful thing to see," said Byrd. "One sensed that each knew and understood the other per-fectly, and it was Walden's rare boast that he never needed to give Chinook an order: the dog knew exactly what had to be done." Af-ter losing a fight with three younger huskies, the aged leader van-ished without a trace, and Walden speculated that, old and disgraced, he had nobly wandered off to die. Owen suggested in his report on Chinook's death on January 23, 1929, cited as one of his best stories from Antarctica—his reporting won a Pulitzer Prize in 1930—that the old dog probably met his end voluntarily in a crevasse. Indeed, the following spring, one of the explorers, Frank Davies, discov-ered evidence that Chinook had fallen into a thirty-foot-deep cre-vasse, but signs of a struggle to escape indicated he did not commit canine suicide. It is the fate of dogs to know humans, and their curse to believe humans know them.[20]

Byrd worked dogs and men nearly to the breaking point in unloading his ship, *The Spirit of New York*, and establishing his base camp, Little America, packing each sled with 150 pounds of cargo per dog. The teams made two sixteen-mile trips from the ship to the base each day, hauling 700 to 1,000 pounds, depending on the number of dogs, across uncertain terrain. It took twenty-seven dogs to haul to base the fuselage of the tri-engine Ford airplane. The most intriguing driver was Christoffer Braathen, a recent evangelical college graduate with no dog experience, who put together a team of rejects, the halt and the lame, led by one-eyed Moose. He treated them like children, Byrd said, and they responded like champions, making him an exception among a crew that, while reportedly fond of their animals, drove them with whips, liberally applied when they felt it was necessary, following the custom of the day.

For the winter, the dogs lived in Dog Town, an excavated snow tunnel, a place, Byrd said, where the strongest ruled. The dogs fought, fornicated, and downed as much seal meat as they could—more than a thousand pounds. On the other hand, it appears that the men's quarters was a place of dark dissension, where bored, cooped-up young men formed cabals, drank too much laboratory alcohol (Byrd included), played endless hands of poker for a diminishing supply of cigarettes, and had access to a library of 3,000 books that remained largely unread. Some of them found more pleasure at times with the dogs than with one another.

In October, the Antarctic spring, Gould's geology and depot-laying party—the caches were laid in case Byrd's plane had to make an emergency landing—finally got under way, after a few false starts, with five teams of nine dogs each. The initial plan called for the group to return after three months with twenty-one dogs, the others having died or been killed and fed to the healthy. That seems to have been fulfilled, although all participants, including Norman Vaughan, the chief dog handler, who talked about the difficulty involved in deciding which dogs would be killed, were reticent about the numbers. They may not have been as high as planned, for the expedition returned to New York with seventy-five dogs, including puppies, meaning they had lost around forty dogs. The *Eleanor Bolling*, one of the expedition ships, also carried Snow Ball, a jet-black mongrel mascot who charmed New Yorkers with his calm demeanor while waiting out a quarantine period onboard. The expedition also bought home Adélie and Emperor penguins for zoos, but reluctantly, Byrd claimed, after the men watched their captives build pyramids with their bodies to allow a few to escape their holding tank. It was an act of intelligent desperation that impressed and depressed their captors, although not enough for them to free the remaining birds. Nor did Byrd's regret prevent him from bringing back more penguins on his second trip to Antarctica three years later.

The men were welcomed as heroes. Byrd received his third ticker-tape parade in New York, quite an accomplishment for an aviator who never piloted his own planes, and by some accounts was afraid of flying. He deserved credit for overcoming his fear, for leading the transition from the age of exploration to the age of science in Antarctica, and, despite his fondness for dogs, for ushering in the era of the machine. The dogs were essential to his success, but they would be superfluous within several decades, in part because of the human habit of feeding them fresh seal meat, but that would become more clear in the second Byrd polar expedition, launched in 1934 at the height of the Depression, as if in defiance of reality.

The men had helplessly listened to news of the stock market crash, and upon their return home, heroes or not, several of them faced a new reality. Fiscally broken, distraught at the loss of Chinook and his own demotion from the post of chief dog driver—the task had fallen to Vaughan—Walden found his wife in poor health, and, to raise money, sold his share of Chinook Kennels to Eva Seeley and her husband, Milton, who were breeding Siberian huskies. But Walden kept breeding his Chinook dogs, and the week before Christmas 1931, President Herbert Hoover, presiding over the nation's economic free fall, welcomed to the White House Laurence Orne, thirteen, of Melrose Highland, Massachusetts, and his dog, Paugus, descended directly from the incomparable Chinook and, it was reported, Peary's 1909 leader. Orne, a Boy Scout and model-plane builder, and Paugus were the first recipients of the Chappel Kennel Foundation's "America's typical boy and dog" contest. The association of boys and dogs, as an American ideal, continued long past the life of the prize.[21]

BYRD BILLED HIS 1934 EXPEDITION as one of scientific and geographic discovery, and he took with him a Columbia Broadcasting System radio correspondent, Charles Murphy, and equipment for broadcasting to the United States. Long involved in sponsoring polar expeditions, *The New York Times* passed on this one, picking up articles from the radio. Byrd enlisted other corporate sponsors to donate or discount gear and food, airplanes, tractors, ships, tobacco, and money—$150,000 in cash at the height of the Depression, he boasted. The federal government donated scientific equipment, and he sought and obtained dogs—153 in all—from "Quebec Province, Labrador, Manitoba and the pick of American kennels." The man who was pioneering the mechanization of research on Antarctica knew that dogs were popular and for the moment vital: "Planes and tractors are superb instruments, but there is no getting away from dogs. The Eskimo husky still is, as he always has been, the one absolutely reliable means of polar advance. He can overcome terrain, which a tractor can't penetrate and a plane can't land on."[22]

In his book *Discovery: The Story of the Second Byrd Antarctic Expedition*, Byrd played up the dogs, recounting that fifty came from the Seeleys, who had crossed Chinook veterans from the first voyage with Siberian huskies and a wolf to create faster, lighter dogs. He secured seventy-six huskies from the north shore of the St. Lawrence and Labrador, "typical Labrador dogs, motley in coat and blood history with a distant wolf strain, stocky dogs with wide foot pads and strong legs, averaging between 70 and 75 pounds." These "motley" mongrels included Jack, the best leader of all the dogs. During a three-month, 1,400-mile geological expedition, involving three teams of thirteen dogs each, Jack, leading Stuart Paine's sled, broke trail for all but 100 miles—a feat of remarkable endurance given that the dogs were dragging heavy loads through deep snow over broken country, where a crevasse might open under them at any moment. Byrd also brought thirty huge Manitoba huskies, "descendants of the dogs used by Sir Ernest Shackleton's second expedition"—a nice story, but only if they reproduced before sailing. Shackleton killed all of his dogs, as Byrd, a student of polar exploration, surely knew. But the Manitoba huskies—also called Shambouls—performed well, and one of them, Power, leader of Finn Ronne's team, was considered nearly equal to Jack. Power went on strike whenever he felt the team was being mismanaged, Byrd said, literally sitting down and barking "furiously . . . declining to budge until the matter was adjusted then and there."[23]

Whatever their origin, Byrd complained that the dogs were spoiled on the long trip to Antarctica, so that when they finally landed they were pets more than working dogs. Yet in the first voice broadcast from Antarctica, in April, Murphy said that the dogs were essential to getting Little America in shape before winter set in and the temperatures of mid-April—minus 40 degrees Fahrenheit—fell to minus 70 degrees in June's full darkness. Byrd himself was more than a little annoyed at dogs in general by the time they landed, having loaded two of his ninety-pound Shambouls, purchased from a French-Canadian farmer in Quebec for their size and power, onto his seaplane for an advance trip toward the continent only to have them escape their crates and barge through the cabin, scattering gear and bowling over the flight crew, Byrd included. The dogs had been loaded as a safety precaution, to haul supplies in case the plane had to make an emergency landing, but Byrd decided they were the greater hazard and packed them back to the ship. When it finally came time for the dogs to haul freight, Byrd declared "their holiday has ended . . . Polar exploration moves forward and survives mostly by brute force and by its capacity for punishment." Clearly, sentiment concerning dogs was doled out for public consumption; on the ice, they worked until they could work no more.

Byrd had carried along four airplanes and five tractor/snow machines—two Citroëns adapted from desert to snow and ice travel, with treads and skies; two new Ford snow machines; and a Caltrec tractor—but four of them promptly broke down, leaving only one to join the dogs, organized into sixteen teams of nine dogs each, in unloading two ships and dragging tons of supplies, including a small mountain of coal, 100,000 pounds of Ralston's Purina dog chow, 1,500 pounds of pipe tobacco, countless cigarettes, twenty-seven varieties of knives, and everything else fifty-six men, four milk cows, and about 150 dogs would need to endure for a year or more—4.5 miles from the ships' anchorage on the Bay of Whales to base camp. After three chaotic days of runaway and fighting teams, the drivers got themselves in order, and dogs and men were soon near the breaking point, their efforts stalled by crumbling ice, high winds, and crevasses that opened without warning. A fifty-foot-deep crevasse opened directly under seven harnessed dogs, leaving them dangling from their sled until they could be pulled to safety.[24]

Hunters added to the camp's supplies 200 seals to feed the dogs over the long, dark winter. Coal and equipment finally secure, the teams raced to complete their fall schedule, and a race it was, between dogs and the repaired snow machines, which Byrd called tractors, the past and the future of polar land travel. The tractor drivers called the mushers dog catchers, Byrd reported in *Discovery*, the first of his two accounts of the expedition, while the dog men responded with "limousine explorers." The dogs performed in their usual stellar fashion despite being overloaded, overworked, driven with whips, and shut in crates at night so they couldn't move, inactivity that caused some to freeze to death during the winter, even in the tunnels of Dog Town. They regularly traversed terrain that stopped the heavy machines, and at the end of the expedition they were hauling spare parts to the broken-down tractors. But the dogs were beaten. Despite the mechanical unreliability of these early models, the tractor was superior, said Byrd, in terms of its speed, its carrying and hauling capacity, its stability in gales that stopped dog teams, and its range. Within thirty years, the sled dog would be used largely for racing and recreation; the snowmobile, or snow machine, would have thoroughly and loudly supplanted it, the way the car and tractor during this period were driving horses into retirement.

ON MARCH 27, 1934, Byrd secured his Advance Base, 143 miles south of Little America, where he planned to spend seven solitary months of the Antarctic winter, making meteorological observations and sending dispatches to his fifty-five colleagues and the rest of the world. He chose solitude, he explained, for fear that if he shared his close quarters with another man, they would grow to hate each other, and because he wanted to experience monastic discipline. Little America finally battened down two months later, parking 126 dogs in Dog Town, where seven puppies were born over the winter and twelve adults died, usually in fights that erupted after one or more broke free of their leads. The dogs, Byrd said, made short work of the wolf hybrids, to no one's displeasure, because they were aggressive troublemakers. Toby, a 100-pound husky, went AWOL for a week in June, apparently roaming the barrier between land ice and sea ice without much ill effect. In the main, the dogs suffered boredom and ate one seal a day, of 500 to 1,000 pounds, to supplement their dry food. The men also ate seal blubber as protection against scurvy. There were books, movies, electricity, cards, tobacco, and moonshine in Little America, but for some there were also too many people. " 'Stu' Paine used to say that when he grew bored with the interminable controversies and the microscopic issues of humans," Byrd said, "he could always find something amusing, something lovable and fine in the simple society of Dog Town."[25]

Byrd came close to never writing his books. By the beginning of June, poor ventilation for his kerosene heater had brought carbon monoxide to such dangerous levels in his hermitage that he nearly died. He tried to remedy the problem and seemed to recover, but he suffered a relapse of carbon monoxide poisoning in July. Aware of his condition by late June, his men planned to rescue him as soon as it was light enough to travel safely by snow machine, faster and more protected from the bitter winter than dogsled. The expedition's second in command, Thomas C. Poulter, and two other men made the risky journey that reached Byrd on August 11, after sixty-six hours of travel, as good a recommendation as could be made for the snow machine. Finding Byrd too weak for travel, the men remained at the Advance Base, making meteorological observations until a plane could reach them on October 12 and Byrd could be airlifted back to Little America, where he ran the expedition until its completion early in 1935.

In the spring of 1934, Byrd had sent out nine teams of dogs, drivers, and scientists on various mapping expeditions and boasted that few of the animals had died. Attitudes had changed: the public rebelled at the habit of killing dogs, or letting them perish unnecessarily, and its support was necessary if Byrd was to continue his explorations, which he fully hoped to do. Still, there was no way to carry exhausted or injured dogs, so stragglers were shot, whereupon Byrd often recounted their names and the circumstances of their deaths. For example, the white-eyed Siberian husky named Coal, dubbed the assassin for having ambushed and killed four dogs in Dog Town, was, after another unprovoked attack, court-martialed and shot "at the foot of the Queen Maud Range."[26]

BYRD'S ACCOUNTS of his adventures were best-sellers, and his popular following attracted the attention of President Franklin D. Roosevelt, who had already heard the protests, as had Herbert Hoover before him, from England and other nations over Byrd's extravagant claims for the United States of nearly all the land he surveyed, from sea, ground, and air. Roosevelt led the federal government to back Byrd's 1939–41 Antarctic expedition and resume its sponsorship after World War II, to the chagrin of other nations, who felt they had a stake in whatever wealth and strategic importance the icy continent might have. In 1957, twelve interested nations, including the United States, got together for the International Geophysical Year, devoted to mapping and exploration. The same nations signed the Antarctic Treaty of 1959, forsaking additional territorial claims, and in 1991 they signed a new Antarctic Treaty, including strict en-

vironmental protections for seals and penguins and a ban on non-
native species, excepting the most destructive of all. Even dogs were
prohibited, on the grounds that they spread a distemper-like virus
to seals, a claim later proved untrue, and that the tradition of feeding them seals was depleting the population, which was more likely.
The ban took effect on April 1, 1994, closing an era.

Depression

In 1928, Walt Disney introduced his animated, scrappy, proletarian
rodent to the world and spent the next three decades transforming
Mickey Mouse into a very humanlike, desexed, perpetually juvenilized creature, with no tail, a turned-up nose, and eyes facing forward. Some purebred dogs had already been juvenilized in their
appearance, and bringing the dog more fully into human society remained one of the goals of the fast-growing fancy during the 1930s.
Participation in dog shows and various field events grew throughout the decade, with Westminster drawing 2,673 dogs, valued at
$1 million, in 1930; 2,837 in 1935; and 3,070 in 1939. In an effort to
prove their dogs were not mere objects of personal vanity, members
of the fancy expanded the number of canine performance events
and trials they sponsored. Most notably, the American Kennel
Club began offering an obedience competition, designed by Helen
Whitehouse Walker in part to prove her standard poodles could do
something. The end of the 1930s brought another war to Europe
and a halt to the importation of European dogs. At the time, there
were around 14 million dogs in the United States, an estimated
500,000 of them purebred—believed, like the people who owned
them, to be the elite of society.

Confirmation that many of those purebred dogs were what in
evolutionary terms are called "hopeful monsters" (will they survive?), kept alive through human intervention, came from a series
of crossbreedings Charles Stockard made at Cornell University
during the 1930s in an effort to understand the marked differences
between breeds. "Modern dog breeds have been developed entirely

by sportsmen and 'fanciers' who have carefully selected and bred the various strange mutations spontaneously occurring in the stocks," he said in his 1941 monograph *The Genetic and Endocrinic Basis for Differences in Form and Behavior*, for the Wistar Institute in Philadelphia. "Many of the stocks were probably of hybrid origin. After the breeds have once been established, they are perpetuated and perfected by careful selection." Those mutations were for giants, or acromegalic dogs; midgets, or ateliotic dwarfs; and true dwarfs, or achondroplastic animals; not to mention those that were brachycephalic, with the distinctive punched-in nose that Stockard showed was the result of separate mutations for the upper and lower jaw. "Some of the dog breeds are so grossly deformed as to be rendered almost helpless and unable to maintain an independent existence," he said. He observed that nearly all of the sorting had occurred within the past century. Unfortunately, as people bred for extravagant looks, they selected against working ability, for reasons still not fully understood, although scientists analyzing inheritance believe that in many cases the genes for physical oddity might be closely related, if only spatially on a chromosome, to those controlling some types of behavior. Thus, focusing solely on peculiar physical characteristics would have the unintended consequence of limiting or even eliminating desired behavorial traits. Purebred dogs are certainly more prone to cytoskeletal problems and inherited diseases than are mongrels, and as Stockard showed, some of the dogs could not perform physically even if they wanted to.[27]

Whatever their lineage, dogs remained a public health and safety issue of significant concern through the 1920s and 1930s, only now car chasing and death by car were added to the list. In various parts of the country there were still major roundups and kills of strays during rabies scares, despite a growing body of knowledge about that disease. Prosecution of livestock killers, with death the punishment of those convicted, was the norm; the federal Wichenham Commission report of 1930, which gave generally bad marks to 575 state and city police departments, praised the New York State Police for keeping medical and dental charlatans from fleecing rural residents, capturing prison escapees, enforcing fish and game laws, and exterminating sheep-killing and mad dogs. In Florida in the early 1930s, many curs were run off the cattle range because of a screwworm epidemic. Catch dogs caused lesions on the noses of cattle that became prime repositories for the eggs of screwworm flies; once hatched, the voracious larvae ate their host. A few ranchers continued to use and breed dogs throughout the period, but the tradition was damaged.

Rather than filing civil suits or criminal complaints against canine miscreants, many people simply continued the long-standing practice of poisoning them. Sitting in his apartment on East Twenty-first Street in New York, Woody Guthrie saw a dog get run over in the street below and wrote to the historian Alan Lomax about the scene and his own memories, from his childhood in the 1920s in Oklahoma, of his big dog, "old pooch." The dog would chase a baseball, play football, "and stand around with his eyes shot over and his ears stuck about half way up and his tongue running in and out of his mouth, his head cocked over sideways like and watching the kids play marbles." But an "old neighbor lady with something haywire in her head" poisoned the dog one day, and all the heart-broken kids gave him a funeral, laying a rock with his name painted on it as a headstone. "You could write a song about that," Guthrie said, "and it would contain enough of all of the high and low feelings to put over if the blame was properly placed on the old lady that poisoned the pooch."[28]

12

World on Fire:
Hot War, Cold War, Race War, Guerrilla War—Peace

❦

Aᶠᵀᴱᴿ ᴛʜʀᴇᴇ ʏᴇᴀʀs of hard fighting, the hero was returning home to the Wren family of Pleasantville, New York,
accompanied by six reporters and photographers, but at
the crucial moment, when the train doors drew open on that crisp
morning of December 11, 1945, and the flashbulbs popped in his
eyes, his courage flagged and he slunk back in stark contrast to the
teeth-slashing attacks that had brought him fame and glory in Morocco, Sicily, Naples, Rome, France, and Germany. Finally, four-
year-old Johnny Wren threw his arms around Chips's neck and the
family led him home, where he collapsed into deep sleep. *Sic transit
gloria mundi*, or, as an understanding Edward J. Wren told *The
New York Times*, "He doesn't seem to wag his tail as much as before going to war, but I suppose he is suffering from battle fatigue."
Perhaps he was suffering more from the folly of men, for Chips, the
most celebrated canine hero of World War II, the first war in which
the American military deployed its own dogs on a systematic basis,
was also the most controversial—not for his deeds, but because of
people's reactions to them. Lost on the reporters covering his less

than heroic homecoming was the fact that his greatest glory probably arose from the same fear response that caused him to shy from
exploding flashbulbs.

The Wrens had donated three-year-old Chips, a cross between a
husky and German shepherd–collie mix, after he bit at least one
garbageman, and he became one of the first of the new American
war dogs sent to the European front. With his handler, Private John
Rowell, and the rest of the Third Infantry Division, Seventh Army,
then under the command of General George S. Patton, Jr., Chips
saw his first action in North Africa in November 1942, going
ashore at Fedallah, French Morocco, under heavy fire, with three
other dogs—Pal, Watch, and Mena, who later gave birth and was
sent home, to become the darling of the 1944 Westminster Dog
Show. Trained as a sentry dog, meaning he worked on a leash to
find and stop intruders and other miscreants, with his teeth if necessary, Chips, along with his dog comrades, kept the camp free of
sneak thieves, and in January 1943 he helped guard Roosevelt and
Churchill at their meeting in Casablanca. The dogs and their handlers joined the invasion of Sicily in July 1943, hitting the beach under intense fire that caused them to eat sand and Chips to go
wild—a sign that the dog was more than a little gun-shy, a frequent
problem with the first wave of American dogs.

Whether Chips was responding specifically to thunder cracking in counterpoint to the booming guns, or simply the unending bursts of gunfire, is unclear, but overwhelmed by fear and
loathing—not least at being constrained by a leash when his every
instinct told him to take action—the dog tore free of Rowell. A fell
beast, a canine berserker, he raced through the bullets of Italian defenders and dove headfirst into a bunker holding a machine gun and
crew, teeth slashing. Above the din of battle, Rowell and his fellow
soldiers heard the howls of men replace the rattle of the machine
gun and then watched an Italian soldier rise from the bunker with
Chips clamped to his throat. Immediately three more men rose,
hands up in surrender. Chips suffered singed hair and a scalp
wound and settled back to work. While on guard that night, for an

encore, he detected ten Italian soldiers trying to sneak into camp and helped Rowell capture them.

On November 19, 1943, four months later, Major General Lucian Truscott, commander of the Third Infantry Division, citing the "special brand of courage, arising from love of master and duty" that led Chips to take out the machine-gun bunker, awarded the big mongrel a Purple Heart and a Silver Star. For people accustomed to dog heroics—*Lassie Come Home*, with a purebred male collie playing the female rough farm collie of Eric Mowray Knight's original story, was a smash hit movie in 1943—and the men he saved, Chips deserved his honors. But there were in America, as always, men and women who took deep offense and declared it an insult to human heroes that a dog—not to mention a carrier pigeon or horse— should receive the same award. They wanted to add the requirement that the recipient be "human," as well as wounded or brave above and beyond the call of duty, to the selection criteria.

William Thomas, principal of the Lincoln School in New Rochelle and former national commander of the Military Order of the Purple Heart, protested to President Roosevelt, the secretary of war, and whoever else would listen that the honors were demeaned—befouled by a dog. He claimed in his complaint that in addition to Chips, three or four other dogs had been similarly decorated, which was not true. On February 3, 1944, Adjutant General J. A. Ulio declared that only Chips had been so honored and that no other dog could receive human combat awards. He revoked Chips's Purple Heart and Silver Star, although some reports said the dog was allowed to keep his medal of valor. Individual unit commanders were permitted to issue commendations for bravery to dogs in their general orders, and several did, but the effect was not the same; the dog had been put in his place by William Thomas and his dog-phobic compatriots.

Mrs. Wren reacted with equanimity, telling *The New York Times* that she understood "the reasoning of some persons that man is brave through forethought and dog through instinct" and that in any event, Chips probably would have preferred a pound of good beef. Chips's comment went unrecorded, but just a few months earlier, suffering battle fatigue, he had served a stint as a guard at a POW camp behind the lines. Sometime during that assignment, he managed to meet and bite his commanding general, Dwight David Eisenhower, who, violating military protocol, had reached out to pet the working sentry dog. When Chips finally came home, the men with whom he served "unofficially" gave him a Theater Ribbon with eight battle stars for the campaigns in which he had fought, and the Walt Disney Company in 1993 made a movie of the biter and his exploits. But the awards meant little to Chips, whose kidneys failed seven months after his homecoming.[1]

AMERICA'S LACK OF PREPAREDNESS before entering the war is received wisdom by now, as is the corollary that America must remain a garrison state to preserve its freedom from external enemies, whether the Communists of the Cold War or the terrorists of today. Eisenhower himself warned against the unbridled power of the military-industrial complex, and thus the garrison state, at the end of his second term as president, an office that was his because of his success in war, but those who heard his warning lacked the will or the power to stop, much less dismantle, the juggernaut that consumes resources for essential services like health care and perpetuates the forces of inequity. It is not clear how dogs would vote on the matter, were they given the franchise, but it seems unlikely that any self-respecting cur would voluntarily opt for servitude over freedom. That said, the war finally established, though not without continuing institutional resistance, the value of dogs in the military, and ultimately opened for them a wide range of new jobs.

But in the chaos of those first months after Pearl Harbor, the citizenry pitched in to get the war machine moving, as any free people will when they are challenged, exhorted by the man who just a year earlier had broken a tradition established by George Washington and run for and won a third term as president. Of course, the patrician Franklin D. Roosevelt had led the country toward recovery from the Depression and surely felt he had unfinished business. The curiosity here is not only that Eleanor Roosevelt served as surrogate president on so many public occasions, due to her husband's polio—he was struck down the year after Harding and Coolidge trounced the Democratic ticket on which he ran for vice president with James Cox—but also that a black Scottish terrier, Fala, became a highly visible and calming symbol for the nation throughout the war, a sure giveaway that the president was on the move or busy in the White House.

In all, perhaps a quarter of a million dogs saw active service in World War II, in nearly every corner of the globe where there was fighting. The Germans reportedly had 200,000 dogs in service as casualty dogs, sentries, scouts, guards, and intimidators of civilians. The Japanese deployed some 25,000 dogs, obtained from the Germans, to devastating effect in China and Southeast Asia. The Soviet Union put 50,000 into service, including antitank suicide dogs. They pulled half-starved animals from city streets—not too hard to find when humans were starving and dying by the tens of thousands in the siege of Stalingrad—strapped explosives to their backs, and sent them to wander among German tanks and half-tracks, looking for food. The bombs detonated when they tried to climb into or onto the vehicle. The Soviets also began using dogs to help clear minefields, an experiment the Americans and their British allies would undertake with poor results, primarily because of improper training.

Following Pearl Harbor, the American military bought nearly every healthy sled dog in Alaska and, under Byrd's old dog driver, Norman D. Vaughan, set them to work hauling supplies and patrolling in search and rescue operations. That was an easy decision since the dogs had unambiguously proved themselves in the Vosges and on numerous polar expeditions. Outside Alaska, however, the situation was more confused.

Sergeant Robert H. Pearce had set up a small K-9 Command program at Fort MacArthur in San Pedro, California, three months before Pearl Harbor, according to a report by Cecilia Rasmussen in the May 4, 2003, *Los Angeles Times*. Designed to train aggressive sentries capable of bringing down an intruder, the program got fully under way in January 1942 with an appeal to the people of Los

Angeles to donate dogs. Pearce and trainer Carl Spitz, a Hollywood veteran, preferred Doberman pinschers, German shepherds, and various other big aggressive animals, like their first recruit, Bruno, a mongrel chow. Rin, a grandson of Rin Tin Tin, also joined up, Rasmussen reported. In 1943, Pearce started a breeding program designed to create an especially trainable, aggressive sentry, by crossing a German shepherd and pit bull terrier and then crossing that animal to an Airedale. There is no record, Rasmussen said, of whether any dogs trained at Fort MacArthur saw duty overseas.[2]

Despite the obvious advantages of dogs, and that small California effort, the military hemmed and hawed over the issue until a group of New York, New Jersey, and New England dog fanciers began agitating them to get up to speed. Well connected, employing a *New York Sun* writer and dog breeder, Arthur Kilbon, as publicity director—he wrote a column on war dogs under the pseudonym Arthur Roland, rather than his customary Roland Kilbon—the group included Mrs. Milton S. Erlanger (the women were so commonly referred to in this fashion that given names often never appeared in the public record), a New Jersey poodle breeder; Mrs. William H. Long; and Leonard Brumby, president of the Professional Handlers' Association, among others. On March 13, 1942, Dogs for Defense was established to procure and train dogs for the Army Canine Corps—usually shortened to K-9 Corps—for the Quartermaster Corps under Major General Edmund B. Gregory. The group had as its officers several officials from the American Kennel Club and the Westminster Kennel Club, although it was a separate legal, financial, and corporate entity.

The group moved quickly, sending its first three sentry dogs to the Munitions Manufacturing Company in Poughkeepsie, New York, on April 13, and nine to Major General Philip S. Gage's forces defending New York Harbor. They were quickly deployed in increasing numbers by the coast guard as sentries. By the summer, the Quartermaster Corps began training all army dogs itself—adding those for the navy and coast guard in the fall—at Fort Robinson, Nebraska; Front Royal, Virginia; Cat Island, Mississippi; Camp Rimini, Montana; and San Carlos, California. By the end of the war, 140 mine-detection dogs—various spaniels and bloodhounds—had been trained in Beltsville, Maryland, and Fort Belvoir, Virginia, and shipped to North Africa for testing. They failed to locate mines with enough accuracy—more than 90 per-cent—and the program was dropped. Professional trainers spent eight to twelve weeks per dog, following a regime that, according to one participant, involved "beating the crap out of the dog when it did wrong."[3]

On December 30, 1942, the Quartermaster Corps announced that it needed 125,000 dogs for the army, marines, and coast guard and specified that they should be fourteen months to three years old, weigh a minimum of fifty pounds, and stand at least twenty inches at the withers. Desired qualities were endurance, alertness, strength, tractability, speed, ability to withstand exposure to the el-ements, and fearlessness. The Quartermaster Corps initially had a list of thirty-two acceptable breeds, which was cut to seventeen: Airedale, malamute, Belgian sheepdog, boxer, bull mastiff, Chesa-peake Bay retriever, farm-type collie (the purebred dog was deemed worthless), curly-coated retriever, dalmatian (later excluded when efforts to dye them gray failed), Doberman pinscher, Eskimo dog, flat-coated retriever, German shepherd, giant schnauzer, Irish water spaniel, Labrador retriever, and Siberian husky. Notable for their absence were the standard poodle, considered not aggressive enough, and pointers, hounds, and setters, thought not up to the work. By about 1944, the list was narrowed to German shepherds, Belgian sheepdogs, Doberman pinschers, farm collies, giant schnauzers, and "positive crosses between them."[4]

Initial estimates proved wildly high—in part because suitable dogs were limited in number. Between 1942 and 1945, according to Quartermaster Corps statistics, 19,000 dogs were recruited for training—Dogs for Defense obtained 17,000 of them—but only 10,425 actually completed training and were deployed. Fully 45 percent washed out, usually because they could not make the grade physically or psychologically. A few people requested their dogs back before they went through training, including one man whose wife had suffered a nervous collapse after they turned their dog

over to Dogs for Defense, according to Fairfax Downey in his officially sanctioned history of the program. The doctor, he explained,
said that only the return of the dog would restore her to health. At
least one other dog, Duke, a three-year-old collie, went AWOL
from the Dogs for Defense induction center at 111 East Seventy-
seventh Street in New York and fled into Central Park, where the
ASPCA finally nabbed him. Of those who made the cut, 9,300
served as sentries, a third of them with the coast guard, leashed to
handlers to snoop out miscreants, spies, and saboteurs. One of
these was Rolf, a boxer who, patrolling a Boston defense factory
one summer night in 1943, captured a "saboteur," carrying the
blueprints that were taken as proof of his guilt.[5]

Dogs were also trained as messengers, with the traditional two
handlers, and as casualty dogs. As was customary in all wars, they
often accompanied soldiers as mascots. The most famous, of
course, was Willie, Patton's bull terrier. Named for William the
Conqueror, Willie was fifteen months old when he joined Patton on
March 4, 1944. "My bull pup . . . took to me like a duck to water,"
Patton wrote in his diary. At the time, he was still commanding the
Seventh Army, but was under a cloud because he had on several occasions slapped soldiers he felt were slacking off. In July he was
transferred to the Third Army, which he would lead to glory in his
charge across Europe, Willie and his pearl-handled pistols at his
side. Known for his randiness, Willie wore bells, so people would
know when he was around and take extra care. After Patton's accidental death in December 1945, Willie went to live with the general's widow and children.[6]

Slapping had fallen from grace as attitudes toward the proper
handling of humans and beasts had softened. In February 1944 the
American Kennel Club decreed that judges at its events could no
longer slap dogs on the side of the head because it agitated dogs and
spectators, any of whom might attack. The judges had adopted the
practice, they said, as a way to test a dog's temperament—a timid dog
would shy away from the unsolicited blow, while any self-respecting
dog would take offense and bite the judge, earning it immediate dismissal from the ring. Some human crowds also hated the practice,

saying it was abusive; at a show in Baltimore early in 1944, observers became so incensed after several slappings that they, too,
threatened to attack the judges.[7]

The dogs drawing the most attention as heroes were the 1,894
who served abroad as messengers—sometimes actually laying telephone cable—casualty dogs, sentries, and scout dogs. The 436 scout
dogs who actually saw service overseas in fifteen War Dog Platoons
assigned to the army and the marines—seven in Europe and eight in
the Pacific—were trained to work in silence up to 1,000 yards in
front of the main body of soldiers to detect ambushes. They proved
most effective in the dense jungles and broken terrain of the Pacific
Islands, where their keen senses of smell and hearing "saw" more
than any human eyes. But rapid motorized troop movements in
Europe, like those of Patton's Third Army, rendered them fairly superfluous for detecting enemy patrols, unless progress stalled or
they were dropped by parachute, as some were, to work on foot. In
open country, they were clearly visible announcements of the
American presence, and in deep snow and mud, they simply lost
their ability to move freely or detect their prey. Studies showed, as
well, that because tests initially had weeded out as gun-shy only
those dogs that hesitated or cowered at the sound of small arms,
many of the first dogs sent to the front reacted badly to louder, continuous artillery bombardments. After dogs were subjected to that
in training, their performance improved.

The army preferred German shepherd–type dogs, while the
marines favored the Doberman pinscher. They believed its short
coat made it better adapted to the heat and humidity of the tropics,
but equally important, one of the founding commanders of the marine scout dog programs, Lieutenant Clyde Henderson, was a
Doberman pinscher man in civilian life, and he favored the breed he
knew. As the war progressed, however, people working with war
dogs came to see the Doberman as unreliably nervous and aggressive; indeed, for years after the war the breed suffered those temperament problems, although most dog behaviorists say that over
the past decade breeders have gentled them. Controversy over ear
cropping and tail docking, painful practices outlawed in many

countries as inhumane but avidly pursued in the United States, also dogged Dobermans. After the war, the military settled on the German shepherd as its primary working dog but later included the Belgian malinois and assorted other breeds as detector dogs.

The first dog to earn wide recognition in the Pacific was, in fact, a German shepherd and chow mix named Hey, apparently trained for sentry duty in Honolulu. A mean-tempered beast, not fond of sailing, he expressed his displeasure at the long voyage from Hawaii to the South Pacific by biting twenty of the men he was supposed to defend. The marine landing on August 7 on Guadalcanal in the Solomon Islands, the first American land offensive of what became an island-hopping war in the Pacific, was relatively calm. But no sooner had the troops secured Henderson Field, an airstrip already under construction by the Japanese, than the counterattack came from the air and from troops who had retreated to the mountains of the interior. The bloody six-month struggle for the island would cost the lives of some 25,000 Japanese and 1,600 Americans. Hey, the biter, arrived in the fall with army reinforcements and set to work defending the airfield. Stalking the perimeter on a moonless night in December, he detected a Japanese sniper setting up for a morning shoot and nailed him, thereby earning himself forgiveness for past transgressions and giving the Canine Corps a much-needed boost. More significantly, according to most histories victory on Guadalcanal and Tulagi, Papua New Guinea, along with the earlier Navy victories in the Coral Sea and Midway, secured Australia and turned the tide of the war against Japan.[8]

Lieutenant Clyde Henderson led the First Marine dog platoon ashore at Bougainville on November 1, 1943, with the first wave of American troops. The platoon's twenty-one Dobermans and three German shepherds were divided into three squads of eight dogs, each assigned a specialty—scout, messenger, and casualty or first aid—and they immediately proved their value to skeptical commanders. Caesar, a German shepherd trained as a messenger, kept the connection between the field headquarters and his sector open for two days and nights. On the third night, he was moving beyond the front lines with one of his two handlers when they were forced to take cover in a foxhole. Sensing a threat, Caesar leapt up and grabbed the arm of a Japanese soldier preparing to lob a grenade on top of them. During the struggle, the Japanese soldier shot Caesar in the rump and in the side, but his handler, Private Rufus Mayo, was able to kill the attacker and summon a stretcher for Caesar, who, treated at the field hospital, recovered and rejoined the fray. Otto, a Doberman scout dog, detected and pointed a machine-gun nest before it could open fire on his patrol, while Andy warned his patrol of a sniper ambush, which they were then able to surprise and rout.[9]

On New Britain near Cape Gloucester, a scout dog named Dick, like a shell game champion, picked the one hut out of five that contained Japanese soldiers, and his fifteen-man patrol killed them all in what was a war of attrition. From December 1943 to March 1945, Teddy, a Marine Raider Regiment scout dog, led almost daily patrols without being ambushed, while also serving as a messenger. In the same campaign, a messenger dog named Sandy repeatedly ran the gauntlet between his handler, with front-line troops, and his counterpart at field headquarters, keeping communications open under intense fire while passing through thick, high grass, crossing a river and a patch of open beach, and then leaping over barbed wire. The first time he ran it, he had never seen the route and was carrying the coordinates of a Japanese artillery battery that had his men pinned down. An American mortar barrage soon followed and destroyed the Japanese position.[10]

As the war progressed, expectations rose, especially in the Pacific where, on island after island, patrols accompanied by dogs regularly escaped the sorts of ambushes that decimated their dogless comrades. On Morotai in the Netherlands East Indies, for example, Marine scout dogs led a hundred patrols in September and November 1944 without losing a man. They also proved themselves adept at identifying occupied caves; on Luzon, during the retaking of the Philippines, an army scout dog, Duchess—the marines preferred males, although females worked just as well—found on April 30, 1945, a cave holding thirty-three Japanese soldiers, and her patrol filled it with live grenades, killing them all. The dogs also died for their country—twenty-five on Guam alone, where not one of 550 dog-led patrols was ambushed. Leading a patrol in the mountains of Europe on March 10, 1940, Peefke, a German shepherd, showed his handler a trip wire connected to three German mines that the men then destroyed. Later that day a German grenade killed him.[11]

In the tropical Pacific, heartworms were probably more lethal to dogs than bullets and mines. Of the 1,047 dogs serving with the marines abroad, 491 returned and were repatriated to civilians— first their former owners, then people who requested them—and of those, only 19 proved unmanageable. A note is in order here: the canines of the marines are often referred to as devil dogs, and that is fair enough. But the Germans first used the term Teufel Hunden, "devil dogs," to refer to the hard-charging marines they encountered in the bloody battle for Belleau Wood in France in June 1918, long before the marines employed war dogs, and the name stuck.

Meanwhile, in America, at the height of the war, dogs increased their numbers and importance as companions. Elrich Davis reported in the *American Kennel Club Gazette* for January 1944 that in Washington, D.C., "the companionship of dogs has become the next thing to a necessity, if not of life, at least sanity." That summer, a Red Cross volunteer brought a German shepherd puppy to a young air force lieutenant lying in a Pawling, New York, hospital, with two badly broken legs and severe depression, and within four months he walked out of the hospital with his dog, Fritz. Clever doctors and nurses seized on dogs as a way to help veterans with severe mental and physical injuries readjust, and it worked. But the veterans were often choosy, insisting on expensive purebred dogs and rejecting mongrels—a trend that would take hold in middle-class society following the war. The informal program was not continued after demobilization, but by then some 700 dogs had been employed as therapy animals.[12]

Following the war, about 3,000 of the 8,000 dogs still in service were returned to civilian life, the majority of them to their owners and the rest to adoptive homes. All were retrained to tolerate strangers, bicycles, and loud noises. Fewer than fifty of the discharged animals, including the nineteen marine dogs, failed to pass the retraining and were killed; only four of those with homes were returned as unmanageable.

The Presidential Dog

Arguably the most important dog in the war never saw combat; in fact, he was one of the breeds deemed unfit for duty by virtue of his stubby legs and long coat. But he was also of a breed considered suitable for a gentleman to keep in town since the mid-nineteenth century, and in the president he met the perfect human companion. Harding's Laddie Boy, who could have served, was a poseur next to Roosevelt's Scottie, Fala. Roosevelt's cousin Margaret "Daisy" Suckley brought the small, six-month-old black puppy, a gift from Katharine Davies, usually referred to as Mrs. Augustus G. Kellog, of Westport, Connecticut, to the White House on November 10, 1940, just after Roosevelt's historic third victory. Suckley had already trained the terrier, named Big Boy, to sit, roll over, and jump in exchange for food, and those seem to have remained his only tricks. Charm he doubtless learned from the dog-loving Roosevelt, who had long desired a canine companion in the White House after his big dogs were deemed safer in New York at Hyde Park than in Washington, where they might have threatened government employees and diplomats, as his distant cousin Teddy's had a quarter of a century earlier. Roosevelt renamed the Scottie Murray the Outlaw of Falahill, after an ancestral Scottish rogue, and soon shortened that to Fala.

The dog became Roosevelt's inseparable companion, according to Doris Kearns Goodwin in her book on Eleanor and Franklin during the war years, *No Ordinary Time*. He slept in a chair at the foot of the bed, camped out in the study, and traveled around the country and various parts of the world. Around the White House and even on the road, Fala often served as a herald for the president. Goodwin reported that while Roosevelt toured the Midwest and South in 1943, Suckley tended Fala on his walks from the president's private train car, the *Ferdinand Magellan*, and crowds actually watched for the dog. His appearance alone seemed to give many people a sense of security, because it was a sign that Roosevelt was on the move, present and vital, watching over the country and them. Although most Americans were unaware of the extent of Roosevelt's paralysis, he could not walk freely among them, so in a sense Fala, although on a scale much smaller but oddly more intimate than that of the indefatigable Eleanor, was a physical projection of Roosevelt into the world, another small element in the illusion of vigor.[13]

The dog was spoiled from the start. Shortly after joining the White House, he was hospitalized for digestive problems, due, it was said, to a surfeit of rich snacks from the White House staff, not to mention the Roosevelts and their many guests. After Fala's return, Goodwin said, Roosevelt decreed that no one but he could feed the dog, to prevent a relapse and obesity, but the edict must have been largely honored in the breach, for other reports reveal that Eleanor fed Fala cake when he performed, and in the fall of 1942 a movie crew making a film of his life as the "first dog" seduced him with bacon, which made him sick. The crew was not banned as a result. Roosevelt did use "feeding time" and Fala in general as a way to choreograph his entry to meetings—imagine the reaction of dignitaries kept waiting for Fala.[14]

"What is difficult for some folks to understand is that Fala is no longer just a dog; he is a personage," wrote John Crider in the October 15, 1944, *New York Times*, at the height of Roosevelt's final campaign. Fala, he explained, attends international conferences, writes letters, greets guests, and has an "official biographer in the person of Miss Margaret Suckley." A visitor to the White House on at least one occasion saw the door open, heard the steward announce "The President of the United States," and watched Fala enter the room, tail wagging. Fala was friendly toward everyone, Crider said, without adding that the trait is invaluable in a politician. Many of the thousands of letters Fala received involved requests for his services as a stud—politely couched, of course—for the writer's dog. Although Fala's attendants rejected all such requests, in late January 1945, Suckley did mate him successfully with her Scottish terrier Buttons. But there was no postcoital bliss; the two fought so viciously afterward that both ended up in the veterinary hospital for sutures.

Often perched on the backseat of the president's open car, by Roosevelt's shoulder, Fala campaigned in cities around the country. He was aboard the *Prince of Wales* when Roosevelt and Churchill signed the Atlantic Charter in 1941, bringing the United States closer to open war. At the first Quebec Conference, on August 17, 1943, Fala rode in an open car with a Secret Service agent, right behind the car carrying Roosevelt and Canada's governor general and just ahead of the one with Churchill and Canada's prime minister, W. L. Mackenzie-King. The following summer, Roosevelt and Fala traveled by train and ship to Honolulu and on their return stopped at the Aleutians, secured just the year before. Fala then attended, less visibly, the second Quebec Conference, where Roosevelt and Churchill discussed the future of Germany, whose defeat was clearly in sight.[15]

That secret stop at Adak Island in the Aleutians set in train a series of events that led to Fala's finest moment, a speech that opened and arguably ended the 1944 presidential election. Thomas Dewey appeared to be running strongly against Roosevelt, who was tired and was suffering from congestive heart failure, which was kept secret—perhaps even from him—and another ailment that might have been stomach cancer, according to Goodwin. He was also depressed by the death of his longtime secretary and confidante—some would say second wife—Marguerite "Missy" LeHand, who had already left his service because of a stroke. But then the old master formally opened his campaign at the Teamsters Union meeting in Washington's Statler Hotel on September 23. In a concession to his health, he delivered the speech sitting down, and it was a classic. He opened by directly addressing the fact that he was four years older, then quickly switched, in an embrace both of his age and history, to say that everyone was eleven years older than when they began fighting the Depression together.

Time danced through the speech. Roosevelt reminded his audience of teamsters that every four years in the six-month run-up to the election, Republicans became friends of labor, an inconsistency and inconstancy he denounced, before also accusing them of fraud for attempting to blame the Depression on the Democrats. He condemned the Republicans for other hypocrisies, without using the word, including their second-guessing of war strategy and their planting of rumors that men were to be kept in the military after the war because there would not be enough jobs for them—presumably because women and blacks held them. Roosevelt insisted that was not true, but he failed to say or did not recognize that women and blacks were often replaced by demobilized white veterans. Republican lies were the target, and they abounded.

Following the setup, with its warm embrace of labor, Roosevelt cut loose with this salvo: "These Republicans have not been content with attacks on me, my wife, or on my sons. No, not content with that, they now include my little dog, Fala. Well, of course, I don't resent attacks, and my family doesn't resent attacks, but Fala does resent them. You know, Fala is Scotch, and being a Scottie, as soon as he learned that the Republican fiction writers in Congress and out had concocted a story that I had left him behind on the Aleutian Islands and sent a destroyer back to find him—at a cost to taxpayers of two or three, or eight or twenty million dollars—his Scotch soul was furious. He has not been the same dog since. I am accustomed to hearing malicious falsehoods about myself . . . But I think I have a right to resent, to object to libelous statements about my dog."

He closed by listing the things that needed to be done to finish the war and establish "international machinery" for securing the peace. He also promised an efficient demobilization of the troops and a smooth transition from a war to a peace economy, but it is not clear how many people heard that. The comments on Fala had brought down the house and everyone listening on the radio. Although some pundits attempted to keep the election close, it was clear that Roosevelt and Fala had turned the tide, exposing the pettiness of the Republican campaign, making a mockery of Dewey and his minions. In New York's five boroughs, 3 million people (2 million in Manhattan alone) lined the streets on a cold, wet October 21 to greet them and, ignoring his bad health, Roosevelt responded by riding with the top down on his car, Fala and Eleanor beside him, basking in the adulation. He gave a speech at Ebbets Field, home of the Brooklyn Dodgers, that day, and in the evening discussed his vision for a United Nations organization to enforce the peace.

Fala had become not just a "personage," as Crider wrote, but a dignitary, an icon, as well. At a White House conference on rural education that drew 200 educators to the East Room on October 5, Austin R. Meadows of Alabama abruptly laid aside his text in midspeech and said, "The folks back home really only wanted me to say hello to Fala." Not missing a beat, Eleanor slipped out of the room to request a cameo. After fifteen minutes, Fala appeared, accompanied by a steward who gave Eleanor a plate with pieces of sponge cake while the educators scattered chairs, clapped, laughed, and squealed with delight. "A group of dignified school officials had suddenly become a bunch of care-free high school kids," *The New York Times* reported. Fala ignored Eleanor until he got a snort of the cake and then came running. He rolled over and stood up on his legs to beg, but the floor proved too slick for him to jump successfully.[16]

On Election Day, Roosevelt received 53.5 percent of the popular vote, for 432 electoral votes, a smashing victory that Fala, apparently upset by the election night crowd at Hyde Park, did not greet with his usual aplomb. Roosevelt did not live to experience the greater victory in war. He died on April 12, a month before Germany's surrender and four months before the atomic bombs forced Japan's capitulation and ushered in a new age. Fala went briefly to live with Suckley, as Roosevelt had requested before his death, but she soon returned him to Eleanor, who enjoyed his company and ultimately took in one of his grandsons to be his companion in old age. The two lived at Val-Kill, the cottage on the Hyde Park estate she had donated to the government, and Fala appeared periodically in the news. He was present when dignitaries like the victorious Eisenhower and the imperious Charles de Gaulle visited Hyde Park to lay wreaths in homage on Roosevelt's grave.

In December, Fala tangled with Blaze, a 135-pound bull mastiff belonging to Eleanor and Franklin's son, Elliott, and ended up in the hospital suffering from neck wounds and loss of blood. Blaze had gained notoriety the previous January when Elliott had pulled strings and bounced three servicemen to send the dog, as a "high priority" item, on a transcontinental army flight to his new wife in California, the actress Faye Emerson. Fortunately, that trip came after the election. This time, the only high priority was Blaze's execution, which Eleanor ordered, according to published reports she never denied. His brain was tested for rabies but, not surprisingly, the state health department inspectors found none.[17]

In July 1946, Eleanor, the great champion of equal rights and integration, traveling with her dog in the grand American tradition, found herself at a posh Portland, Maine, hotel that refused to let her keep Fala in her room. She promptly canceled the reservation and spent the night in a "tourist cabin." That bit of Fala and Eleanor lore capped the front-page *New York Times* obituary announcing the death on April 5, 1952, of "the rakish little black Scotty who sat in on the making of history . . ." Euthanized just shy of his twelfth birthday, and of the seventh anniversary of Roosevelt's death, Fala was buried in an unmarked grave in the Hyde Park rose garden at the feet of his "master and constant companion for five years."[18]

The language underscores Fala's particular and general significance. Despite people and establishments who refused to welcome dogs, they had made the transition, like America itself, from the country and the yard into the city and the home. They had become not just dogs but personages, and their masters and mistresses were "companions." Fala was an exceptional dog, of course, and the dog wars are not over to this day. People continue to abuse and abandon their animals and to breed dogs to satisfy their own vanity or to make profit. But a shift in perception, long under way, had become fixed in the collective psyche, as surely as America had changed from a predominately rural society through the Depression to an urban and suburbanizing society after World War II.

FALA WAS NOT THE AGENT of that change, of course, just its most visible manifestation. On another level, it was manifest in the image of the boy and his dog—that the girl was generally missing is indicative of how far society still had to go—an image celebrated in scores of books and essays, not to mention national campaigns. Some of these accounts, like Farley Mowat's *The Dog Who Wouldn't Be*, are outrageously funny; others are pompous, bittersweet, or nostalgic. Still others are works of grace, like Willie Morris's *My Dog Skip*. At their best they explore the bond between a dog and a person, regardless of gender, that is as ancient as both species and that has flourished in disparate societies around the world, sometimes defying attempts to stamp it out. "The dog of your boyhood teaches you a great deal about friendship, and love, and death: Old Skip was my brother," said Morris of the fox terrier who came to him in 1943 when he was a nine-year-old in a small Mississippi Delta town, and grew up with him, dying of old age while his friend, then a young man, studied at Oxford.[19]

In the Ashes a Cold War Burns

World War II convulsed the world more thoroughly than had any previous war. More than half the estimated 55 million casualties were civilian: some 11 to 12 million dead in the death camps; at least 7 million out of 20 million total Russian dead; and 3.6 million German and 2 million Japanese dead, more in both cases than military casualties. Firebombing and the atomic bomb had brought war to civilians on a new and terrifying scale. In that light, the United States was fortunate, although to the dead and maimed that word meant nothing—just over 290,000 U.S. troops were killed in battle, with another 115,000 dead from other causes, out of a total of 16,353,659 men in uniform, a monumental mobilization.

Demobilized, victorious, many of them took advantage of the GI Bill and Veterans Administration loans to go to college, often as the first in their families to do so. They wanted new homes, new cars, new appliances, new families for a new world not wracked by war or Depression. Like their shell-shocked, disabled comrades in

New Paltz, they wanted dogs—purebred dogs. They believed that the pedigree stood for quality, and the breed name, like any brand name, identified the appearance and behavior of the dog. Having a purebred dog was no less a sign of success than having the right car or the proper address or brand of appliance, and there were easily as many choices. American Kennel Club registrations track the explosion in purebred dogs. The year after the war ended, the AKC registered 204,957 dogs, a figure that jumped to 251,812 in 1950. From 1960 to 1970, the heart of the baby boom's formative years and a decade that rattled the world, AKC registrations rose from 442,875 to 1,056,225.[20]

Through the late 1940s into the 1960s, gender divides persisted in popular lore, if not reality, as boys had their big dogs or their terriers, and girls had cats or little dogs, lap dogs—even if Mom ended up taking care of all the animals in the house. In the early 1970s, women were still rare in veterinary schools, excluded on the vague grounds that they usually married after graduation and opted for families rather than practice. But with the women's movement, that began to change, and by the millennium, women students were a clear majority in veterinary schools around the nation. The gender gap in the types of animals owned had not ended entirely—men still tended to opt for big, aggressive dogs more frequently than women—but it had narrowed. Women trainers were abundant and successful, and often taught better, more humane techniques than their male counterparts.

The dog made science news, as well, when it was announced that the Roscoe B. Jackson Memorial Laboratory had received a sizable $282,000 grant to settle the relative influences of nature, or genetics, and nurture, or environment, on the dog and, by implication, all organisms. The dog was chosen precisely because the inbreeding of the fancy had served theoretically to concentrate certain characteristics in specific breeds. This ambitious undertaking led John Paul Scott and James L. Fuller to produce the classic work on the subject, *Genetics and the Social Behavior of the Dog*, in 1965. Their research fundamentally altered understanding of dogs, especially of the importance of early socialization and learning to their development, and it underscored that despite generations of intensive breeding, there was often as much difference in behavior within breeds as there was between breeds. Combined with advances in behavioral science and the refinement of training techniques using rewards by dolphin trainers in the commercial aquarium business during the Vietnam era, their work transformed dog training and management.

Concomitant with the explosion in the number of pet dogs during that period were the development of easily administered vaccines for rabies and distemper and nearly universal passage of mandatory vaccination and licensing statutes and fence and leash laws—all ostensibly designed to protect human health. The animals did not always benefit. The number of stray and abandoned dogs and cats reached the millions, with estimates of those killed each year in overtaxed shelters reaching 15 to 17 million at their peak in the late 1980s. The explosive growth of the purebred-dog market created problems as well, with the creation of puppy mills—commercial breeding establishments that mass-produced puppies for pet stores—and a rise in the number of sick and crippled "purebred" animals, due to sloppy breeding and inbreeding.

DEFECTIVE AND ABANDONED dogs were just one of a number of manifestations that the perfect suburban, consumer life was a fragile illusion—and not a very interesting one, even for its creators, although many of them clung to it tenaciously. Fresh from beating Germany and Japan, the Allies turned on each other and divided the world into two nuclear-armed camps, divided by an Iron Curtain, vying for "nonaligned" countries. Dogs saw duty as sentries, guarding atomic weapons sites, missile silos, and military bases, and they served when hot spots in the ashes of World War II burst into flame. When the Korean War flared between 1951 and 1953, the men and dogs of the Twenty-sixth Infantry Scout Dog Platoon drew the grim duty of escorting hundreds of patrols under impossible circumstances. The dogs were commended because they never faltered, they saved lives, and they boosted morale among men who found something human in dogs. Still, the animals reached the peak of their importance as war dogs beginning a decade later, in the jungles of Vietnam.

The "great man" theory of history was battered during the 1960s, as were so many other packets of received wisdom. But the postwar years produced a man, and leader, who embodied much of the ambition, paranoid anti-Communism, idealism, hypocrisy, ravenous consumerism, and paradox of the decades following World War II: Richard M. Nixon. He was the antithesis of everything progressive the period stood for—except upward mobility and, perhaps, meritocracy, the latter said advisedly because Nixon was not above cheating, lying, and buying his way to victory with the aid of rich supporters. From his first run for vice president, the man brought his dogs to the fore, as self-conscious stage props, in a poor evocation of Roosevelt and Fala.

Nixon's inimitable dog moment came on September 23, 1952, when he went on national television—at a time when not every home had a television, much less two or more running on cables or off satellite dishes—in a desperate attempt to salvage his vice presidential candidacy with Eisenhower. A shrewd man, Nixon surely had Fala and Roosevelt in mind when he prepared his defense against charges that he had benefited while serving as senator from California from a secret $18,000 slush fund created by his wealthy Southern California supporters.

He appeared, he said, to defend his honesty and integrity and argued that it would have been legally and morally wrong to take money from the fund, whose existence he admitted. Rather, he was a man of modest means who used the money to pay for expenses relating to "political business," not "official business." It was better, he said, than putting his wife on the government payroll, the way his opponent had, although certainly he could have justified doing so because Pat Nixon was a "wonderful stenographer"—what else could a woman be? In any event, he said he had used the money to print and distribute his speeches exposing Communists in the Truman administration, such as Alger Hiss. Nixon had persecuted Hiss unmercifully to his own political advantage. After giving his "complete financial history" and observing that while Pat did not have a "mink coat," she did have a "respectable Republican cloth coat," this hero of the middle class—later to be portrayed as the "silent majority"—delivered the heartbreaker. A man in Texas had heard Pat say on the radio that "our two youngsters would like to have a dog," so he sent one as a gift by train to Baltimore's Union Station, knowing Nixon would be campaigning there. Tricia, the six-year-old, named the black-and-white and spotted cocker spaniel Checkers. "And you know," Nixon said in his stilted, colloquial style, "the kids, like all kids, love the dog, and I just want to say this, right now, that regardless of what they say about it, we're gonna keep it."[21]

Nixon produced an audit and swayed enough people with his "Checkers Speech" to persuade Eisenhower to leave him on the ticket. It was the first of several comebacks for the man who devised the Republican Party's "Southern strategy" to wrestle Southern white voters alienated by civil rights legislation from the Democrats. Of course, Nixon prosecuted the Vietnam War with fury while claiming to be negotiating peace, only to abandon the South Vietnamese while blaming American peace demonstrators for not supporting the troops—a charge that echoes loudly to this day—and promoted a war on the "1960s" that his heirs in the Republican Party continue to pursue vigorously.

Freedom: That's What I Want, Now!

It was in the 1950s and1960s that the ugly history of slavery and slave-hunting dogs was reprised and segregation was finally exposed for what it was—a manifestation of the rawest form of bigotry and hatred, hypocrisy, fear, and ignorance. Demands for freedom and equality are as old as chattel slavery on this continent, and while emancipation had brought nominal freedom under the Constitution, it had in fact produced neither full freedom nor equality. In the South, segregation was enshrined in law and maintained through custom and terrorism; in the North, custom and bigotry tended to dictate. The result of both was a society of white and black, separate and unequal, that extended to the military through World War II, with black troops usually serving at menial tasks. There were exceptions, like the Tuskegee airmen, who did not lose a single bomber over Europe, and the volunteers who came to the relief of their white comrades at the Battle of the Bulge. Whenever black soldiers did fight in World War II, they fought courageously, as they had in previous conflicts, but their courage did not bring equality. Then, in 1948, President Harry S Truman finally ordered full integration of the armed forces, a move that many people considered long overdue and others vehemently opposed.

Whatever their rank, the returning veterans from World War I, World War II, and Korea wanted their rights and the opportunity to participate fully in society. Together with noncombatants who had made their way North or into Southern industrial cities, they also wanted good educations and jobs. In the 1950s, African-Americans filed lawsuits and organized, forcing an end legally to "separate but equal school systems," which everyone knew were separate and unequal. They also began marching, protesting, sitting in, and demanding change, especially in the South and big, segregated Northern cities, behind an emerging corps of young leaders, including the Reverend Martin Luther King, Jr. White volunteers, often from the North, joined them on "freedom rides," beginning in 1961, intended to register voters and force an end to segregation. The protesters were killed, harassed, beaten, imprisoned, and abused, often in front of television cameras.

In April 1963, with Easter approaching, King and other activists, including the Birmingham preacher Fred Shuttleworth, launched a major campaign of protests and demonstrations aimed at bringing an end to segregation and inequality in Birmingham, an industrial center, in Southern terms. Birmingham whites had badly beaten freedom riders on Mother's Day 1961, and the city had a history of mysterious bombings in the black community. King, it was felt, needed to reclaim some momentum for his own brand of nonviolent protest as well as for the civil rights movement, and Birmingham was a city in need of reform. On Palm Sunday, police dogs attacked a young black protester. On April 12, Good Friday, King was arrested and held incommunicado in solitary confinement until April 20. On Easter Sunday, police German shepherds were again trotted briefly into the fray, their presence barely remarked.

On May 2, the civil rights activists sent schoolchildren into downtown Birmingham to protest nonviolently and, it was hoped, march to city hall, but their route was blocked, and 959 were arrested. The next day the public safety commissioner for Birmingham, Theophilus Eugene "Bull" Connor, ordered high-pressure fire hoses and dogs turned on the students as they again tried to march on city hall. The bone-breaking water tumbled the students down the street, while the dogs, urged on by their white-helmeted police handlers, tore clothes and flesh. Television cameras rolled and flashbulbs popped continuously, capturing an act of brutality toward children that no amount of print journalism could have conveyed and that no self-serving rationalization could counter. Irrational hatred had been turned on children. For a week the ugly confrontations continued, until the city agreed to some desegregation, giving King and the Southern Christian Leadership Conference an important but ultimately costly victory. On September 15, just months after King's success, a bomb at the Sixteenth Street Baptist Church, the center of the protests, killed four young girls and set off two days of riots, in which two more blacks were killed. Only in 2000 were arrests finally made in the bombing case; on May 1, 2001, Thomas Blanton was found guilty and sentenced to life in prison.

Police departments that had created canine (usually called K-9) units because of their proved ability to deter crime began using them to chase down demonstrators, further inflaming much of the nation. The police German shepherd became, like the cattle prod, fire hose, tear gas canister, and gas mask, the visible manifestation of power intent on blocking change. In a double paradox, while American police officers turned dogs first on civil rights protesters and then on antiwar demonstrators, American soldiers used dogs in Vietnam to protect themselves from ambush. Though it is unpopular to say so in some quarters, it is nonetheless true that the Vietcong and North Vietnamese saw those dogs as tools of an imperialist power that killed more than a million Vietnamese men, women, and children. But like human fighters on both sides, the dogs were simply trying to survive.

IF THE 1950S WERE A PERIOD of fragile illusions, consumerism, and alienation, underpinned by rabid anti-Communism and overhung by the mushroom cloud of nuclear destruction, the 1960s, running until about 1972 or 1973, were a time of revolution, much of it unfulfilled, of radical experimentation, a time that remains so complex in its currents and crosscurrents that nearly every observer interprets it differently, usually through an ideological and emotional perspective. Unquestionably, it was the decade of drugs, sex, and rock 'n' roll; civil rights; black power; the New Left; Vietnam and anti-Vietnam; student uprisings around the world; guerrilla wars; repression; the birth of a more expansive environmental movement demanding clean air, clean water, and protection for endangered species; Free Love; brutality; hippies; yippies; thuggery; hypocrisy; racism; the assassinations of John F. Kennedy, Martin Luther King, Jr., and Robert F. Kennedy; urban riots that reshaped cities—not for the best—and women's liberation. A book on any of these topics is bound to set off a firestorm of condemnation and protest, in part because the issues raised then and the forces loosed are still at play in the world, as always happens in periods of great ferment.

Dogs, as always, had no say in how they were deployed or even in their fate, although they were often more dignified than many of the humans ordering them about. Dogs reached their literal apogee in the late 1950s and early 1960s not in America but in the Soviet Union, whence they ascended the firmament before any other of God's creatures, including His chosen one. As usual, the stars of the show were street curs from Moscow, caught and trained to ride rockets into space, chosen because Soviet scientists believed them better suited to long periods of idleness than other animals. The Soviets launched the first human-made craft, *Sputnik I*, into orbit on October 4, 1957, sending shock waves through the smug American establishment, which suddenly found itself losing a technological race it did not know it had entered. A month later, on November 3, the Soviets launched Laika, a little mongrel female the American press liked to call Muttnik, into orbit on *Sputnik II*. The Soviets preferred females for space travel because they peed without lifting their leg—seriously. That mattered little to poor Laika. With no way to return safely to earth, she died in space. At least one Russian scientist later rued the needless loss of the dog.

America started playing catch-up in 1958, and John F. Kennedy defeated Richard Nixon for the presidency in 1960 partly because of the space and missile gap. Moscow street curs Bella and Strelka flew in *Sputnik V* just two months before the American election, and, with forty rats, two mice, and assorted plants, spent a day in orbit before returning safely to earth. Strelka sometime later gave birth to six pups, one of whom was given to the dog-loving President Kennedy, who had committed America to putting a man on the moon before the end of the decade. By then, American dogs and men were being dragged into the morass of Vietnam, proving dogs, too, could move from the heavens to a circle in hell.

Americans began supplying sentry and scout dogs to the South Vietnamese military in 1960, but their keepers, inexperienced in the way of war dogs, often neglected to feed them regularly, or they fed them food that had spoiled in the tropical heat. Heartworm and other parasites, as well as spoiled food, took their toll on dogs throughout the conflict. With increasing American involvement came more dogs—3,747 officially counted, according to the United States War Dogs Association, which estimates that 4,900 might have seen service. The figure is uncertain because the military kept no records on dogs before 1968. The lack of numbers from a war that was always measured in statistics—body counts, primarily—is surprising at first glance, but it reflects the general devaluation of dogs.

Some 10,000 American servicemen, out of 4,368,000 in uniform during the course of the conflict, handled those dogs, largely German shepherd sentries trained to "detect, detain, and destroy" intruders, and scout dogs looking for booby traps, ambushes, tunnels, and caves. The army also employed tracker dogs for finding Vietcong and North Vietnamese fighters—and sometimes missing American soldiers—Labrador retrievers, trained at the British Jungle Warfare School in Malaysia. In some accounts they were actually crossbred Labradors, to withstand the heat. Bloodhounds were tried as trackers around 1965 but were quickly abandoned in favor of the more biddable Labrador, whose nose was just as fine. Composed of five men and one dog, tracker teams were frequently flown by helicopter into regions in advance of search-and-destroy missions.

Sentry dogs regularly patrolled the perimeter of Ton Son Nhut Air Base, the main entry point for American forces. On December 4, 1966, a Vietcong attack killed three dogs and one handler—out of 283 dogs and 235 handlers killed in action during the war. On the second day of the attack, Robert Thorneburg released his dog Nemo with instructions to attack the enemy. Nemo was shot almost immediately, and Thorneburg rushed to his rescue, killing one Vietcong before falling to a gunshot himself. Despite the loss of an eye and other injuries, Nemo crawled over to Thorneburg and shielded him as best he could until both were rescued. Ton Son Nhut came under heavy attack during the Tet Offensive in late January 1968, which gave the lie to claims by President Lyndon Baines Johnson, his generals, and top advisers that the enemy's strength had been severely reduced and that the war of attrition was being won. Although hard-pressed, American defenders managed to beat back the onslaught. Following Tet, and challenged by a growing antiwar movement, Johnson decided not to seek reelection, opening the way for the Democratic National Convention debacle in Chicago, where police rioted, turning dogs, gas, horses, truncheons, and rage against antiwar demonstrators, and setting the stage for Nixon's election as president.[22]

On patrol near Da Nang with handler John Flannely in 1969, Bruiser, a marine sentry dog, alerted, and before he could even identify the target, Flannely opened fire. Lying in ambush, the Vietcong returned fire, wounding Flannely. He ordered Bruiser back, according to the account he gave for a 1999 television documentary, *War Dogs: The Untold Story of Dogs in Combat*, but the dog disobeyed and instead dragged Flannely to safety, despite his own wounds. In all, the dogs of Vietnam saved some 10,000 lives, the American War Dogs Association has estimated. No one knows, but it is well documented that dogs kept their patrols from falling into ambushes more often than not.[23]

The documentary *War Dogs* rode a wave of nostalgia about Vietnam war dogs that crested around the millennium with creation of memorials to canines and handlers at March Air Force Base, California, and Fort Benning, Georgia. It presented a romanticized view of the bond between man and dog more in keeping with the 1990s, when dogs were widely seen as sentient beings, than the 1960s, when working dogs were, like hunting hounds, celebrated for their prowess but more often than not considered expendable. Indeed, in 1949 the military had changed its regulations so that it no longer demobilized dogs, meaning that when they had outlived their usefulness, they were generally killed. The Americans moved only 204 dogs out of Vietnam to other military bases; the rest of the 4,900 who served were killed in action, euthanized by American veterinarians, or turned over to the South Vietnamese army as the Americans withdrew. It is assumed that with the fall of Saigon in 1975, most of them were killed.

The decision to leave the dogs was justified in part on the dubious grounds that they might harbor strange tropical diseases they could pass on to other dogs or animals, including endangered wildlife. But it was grounded as well in the military's classification of them as equipment. When declared surplus, they could be disposed of in just about any fashion. Dogs for Defense had forced a change in that approach at the end of World War II, but no similar organization existed to fight for the war dogs of Vietnam, all of whom had been purchased or bred by the military. Only in 2000 was the policy changed, a result of congressional intervention inspired by the *War Dogs* documentary and the fondness of Americans for their 64 million dogs.

Historians and hounds share a seemingly endless capacity for backtracking and a boundless trust that people will follow their meanderings without growing impatient, the way most drivers do when caught behind a slow-moving recreational vehicle crawling toward the sun, at least one dog onboard. Adlai Stevenson, the man too intellectual to be president, urged his friend John Steinbeck to backtrack around 1959 when he was recovering from a stroke. Stevenson and some of Steinbeck's other friends and supporters wanted him to revisit some of the sites of his dust bowl–masterworks, *Grapes of Wrath* and *Of Mice and Men*, to see what had become of America. Steinbeck managed instead to create one of the first recreational vehicles—a truck with a custom cabin equipped with bed, table, and cookstove—and, in the finest tradition of America's old travelers, set out with his French-bred standard poodle, Charley, who took his commands in that language. Beginning in September 1960, man and dog spent fifteen months driving 10,000 miles through thirty-eight states in the truck Steinbeck named *Rocinante* for Don Quixote's horse. The resulting *Travels with Charley* is a lark of a book. Although the world of the old travelers was gone—driving a custom-built truck 10,000 miles on paved roads was proof enough of that—the book was nonetheless a huge success for its author, who in 1962 was awarded the Nobel Prize in literature.

Less than two years later, Ken Kesey and the Merry Pranksters boarded a 1939 International Harvester bus in California, bound for New York and the publication party for his second novel, *Sometimes a Great Notion*, which contains extended stream-of-consciousness passages by a bear dog. The journey marked the metaphorical, if not the literal, beginning of the long strange trip known as the 1960s.

13

The Good, the Bad, and the Dog; or, New Games for Old Talents, Plus a Lingering Question. What Is the Dog?

❧

IN ONE OF THE PATCHES OF PINE flatwoods that pockmark the cypress stands and freshwater marshes of South Florida's Big Cypress Swamp, the crossbred hounds caught the scent of a panther traveling along the raised bed of an old logging road and took off, their handlers trailing behind, guns ready. A century or even seventy years ago, they would have followed the dogs to the big cat's den, shot her, and clubbed her two kittens—or taken them to a roadside zoo—but these hunters were wildlife biologists out to tranquilize, weigh, measure, and take DNA samples from them all. Tests on those samples confirmed that the kittens were first-generation hybrids born of a female Texas cougar and a male Florida panther, the products of a bold and controversial attempt by scientists to save from extinction the last known breeding population of panther—also called cougar, catamount, puma, painter, and mountain lion—east of the Mississippi River. This particular "subspecies," the Florida panther, ranged throughout Florida, Georgia, Alabama, Mississippi, Louisiana, Arkansas, and southern-most Tennessee before human hunting and development isolated it in the remote expanses of the Big Cypress Swamp by the middle of the last century. A century earlier, the last of Florida's Seminole and Miccosukee Indians had been driven into this wet and remote land of alligators, brightly colored wading birds, orchids, bromeliads, palms, cypress, and raptors wheeling through the sky. Down to approximately thirty animals in 1967, and suffering such signs of inbreeding depression as cryptorchidism (one or both testicles fail to descend), malformed sperm, heart murmurs, kinked tails, and cowlicks, the Florida panther was given fewer than 100 years before it blinked into extinction. If disease or natural disaster did not erase it from the earth, scientists predicted, infertility would.

The panther was proof that setting aside large chunks of land as parks or wild lands, while necessary for preserving landscapes and ecosystems with most of their flora and fauna, was insufficient for saving wide-ranging predators, grazers, and even birds. Isolated in parks, their numbers depleted, these animals became inbred shadows of their former selves, the way some purebred dogs are mere shells of the old rustic working dog, diminished in physiology, psychology, and the genetic variability needed to meet changing circumstances. Some, like the Florida panther, can no longer leave their preserves to find and breed with others of their kind because there is no other population nearby or because they are prevented from reaching a neighboring population by natural or artificial barriers. Biologists must therefore assist in maintaining both their genetic variability and their genetic uniqueness. Although scientists admit that they still have much to learn about the genetics of development and evolution, they now possess a number of tools that, if deployed judiciously, can aid in the effort.

Indeed, in the late 1980s, Stephen J. O'Brien, a geneticist and chief of the National Cancer Institute's genomic diversity laboratory, showed that genetically, the various subspecies of North American puma that taxonomists had identified based on geography and subtle differences in phenotype—size and appearance— actually represented a single population, with gene flow throughout. Armed with that knowledge, federal and state officials launched a program in 1995 to introduce a handful of female cougars from the arid hill country of West Texas to bring some genetic vigor back to the big South Florida cats—males can stretch seven feet from nose to tail tip and weigh 130 to 140 pounds; females are a little shorter and weigh in at 80 to 90 pounds. By 2002, there were 70 to 100 panthers in South Florida, 40 of them hybrids, all vigorous and healthy, without any of the telltale signs of inbreeding. In fact, because of the large territory each of the solitary cats claims, the population was rapidly outgrowing the protected lands in South Florida, and biologists were beginning to look for places to put them. There was scant evidence that they would be tolerated or could survive in more developed areas of the rapidly growing state, including those abutting the Big Cypress.

There is a certain poetic justice and historic irony to employing dogs' natural hunting talents in preserving animals they might once have helped drive to the brink of extinction, but it represents a significant if still small and cautiously applied movement in conservation biology. Roy McBride, a wildlife biologist and expert trapper, used his hounds to track and capture the Texas cats, and has long turned them to studying the Florida panther, as well as big South and Central American cats. In Colorado, black bear biologist Hal Black from Brigham Young University used a trained bear hound for many years to help locate bears for study, not killing. He often asked the dog to backtrack to where the bear had been, a task that ran counter to the dog's training to follow its prey but that it easily accomplished with retraining. Wildlife biologist Carrie Hunt trained Karelian bear dogs from Finland to chase grizzly bears in Glacier National Park and black bears in Yosemite in an effort to teach them not to forage around human habitation and camp sites, where conflicts frequently arise and humans and bears wind up injured or dead, not a happy circumstance for either, but especially not for the increasingly rare grizzly. Following a more unique course in the late 1990s, although one that does tap into one of the dog's favorite occupations—finding feces—Samuel Wasser, a conservation biologist at the University of Washington, began training dogs to detect scat from specific species. DNA can be extracted from scat, and its collection is less invasive and dangerous than baying and tranquilizing an animal in order to draw blood. In related activities, border collies were used on golf courses, beaches, and other areas to haze off large flocks of Canada geese, whose populations had skyrocketed with stricter regulation of hunting and who had begun wintering in the North because of a warming climate. The geese presented a nuisance and a health hazard.

Hunting for sport and for food still exists. Sportsmen and collectors continue to hunt big game, and a number of countries oblige them, issuing permits for killing rare and endangered species, ostensibly as a way to generate income for conservation. A recent survey found that around 7 percent of America's 40.6 million dog-owning households—representing 39 percent of the nation's total households—keep their dogs for hunting. But over the past thirty years the number of people who hunt regularly has steadily declined, as the country has become more suburban and the land available for hunting has been reduced. Attitudes toward vanishing wildlife have changed dramatically, to emphasize conservation. A number of states banned the hunting of bears and cougars with hounds during the 1990s, in response to public campaigns launched by animal welfare advocates who consider the practice cruel. Fox-hunting has also come under attack, although less in the United States than in Britain. But there are a large number of people who still enjoy the sound of hounds on game, or the sight of a top pointer or retriever at work, and many of them—perhaps as many as hunt—now participate in more stylized field trials and no-kill hunting trials. The more significant work of hunting dogs and people is now to keep animals alive.[1]

Dogfights, or Civilize What?

The struggle to preserve endangered species and their habitats represents both the success and the failure of American conservationism, or, more contemporaneously, environmentalism, which burst into the popular imagination with the first Earth Day, April 22, 1970. The tradition of viewing Wild Nature as separate from humans has created a situation in which humans increasingly manage the ecology of big parks and preserves as if they were free-form zoological gardens. They cull species considered dangerous exotics; attempt to reintroduce others, sometimes from captive-bred stocks, like the California condor, Mexican wolf, red wolf, and black-footed ferret, and sometimes from wild stock, like the lynx and gray wolf; and even direct breeding, however lightly, of some native animals by importing prospective mates, such as Texas cougars. Those drastic steps have become necessary because continued human population growth and suburban expansion, combined with mining, ranching, and logging, have over the last century isolated many of those parks and refugia, like the Big Cypress Swamp. Their animal occupants are often corralled and returned, or killed outright, when they wander off the reservation. Dogs are frequently banned from those areas, despite their traditional role as mediators between the wild and the built, and the companionship and protection they provide on the trail. In the Big Cypress Swamp, for example, humans can hunt hogs, an exotic species destructive of indigenous snakes and ground-nesting birds, but not with dogs—curs are the traditional hog-hunting dogs of the region—for fear they will bother other animals or spread diseases to which some of the native species have no immunity.

A radical solution to the problem involves recognizing that there are no more wild places on the planet—there never were—and finding a way to integrate humans with the natural world. That would involve overthrowing the view that humans must conquer and contain nature, which continues to dominate business and government, in favor of a view that sees humans as woven into the fabric of creation. Complicating that effort is a general decline in the number of people who experience nature directly rather than through television programs and movies. Surveys have revealed a steady decline in the number of people who actually go into the backcountry in parks or hike into wilderness areas. Strong physical, philosophical, theological, and cultural walls also continue to separate the human world from Wild Nature, often popularly defined as anything not subjected to human development.

A number of people have worked in recent decades to develop an ethos for living more responsibly on the land, with respect for the variety of life and local environmental conditions. It involves individual and social choices regarding everything from energy to land use and food. On a small scale it takes the form of attempts to reduce or ameliorate conflicts between animals—elephants, tigers, wolves, and bears, for example—and people, so that they can share the same landscape, or efforts to design coffee plantations in such a way that they also provide a habitat for birds. Achieving success at the local level is difficult enough. Effecting meaningful change nationally and internationally is more difficult still, and people involved in these efforts recognize that even their victories are provisional, that the best they can do now is try to preserve as much biodiversity as possible against some future when humans have collectively achieved more wisdom and equanimity.

A long tradition of seeing animals as sentient, feeling beings was overwhelmed during the last decades of the nineteenth and much of the twentieth centuries, when it became more common to view them as stimulus-response machines incapable of feeling pain or thinking. In recent decades, the tide has turned, supported by scientific studies showing that animals possess emotions and minds that allow them to learn and adapt and think. Like other animals, dogs experience a different perceptual universe: their noses are orders of magnitude more sensitive, their hearing is sharper, and their eyesight is more attuned to half-light and shadows than that of humans, which is why they are so useful in extending human reach and understanding. Once dismissed as sentimentalism, it has become more commonly accepted and preferred to speak of dogs not as belonging to a person but as being his or her companion. By the same token, the person is not the "owner" but the companion or guardian of the animal. Of course, legally, people are responsible for the well-being and behavior of their animals, call them what they will, and English still suffers pronoun confusion when it comes to referring to a generic "dog" or "cat," not unlike the problem in finding a gender-neutral third-person-singular pronoun for a "person" whose sex is unknown.

A growing animal rights movement, propped up philosophically by Peter Singer's 1975 book *Animal Liberation*, has also contributed to the shift in perception. Singer argued that species overlap in their mental development, so that in some cases a chimpanzee or a dog is more advanced than a "mentally deficient" human, and for that reason it is not justifiable to kill the chimp or dog for medical research, for example, but not the human. In fact, he said, to the consternation of many people, that killing the human would be more acceptable than killing the more advanced chimp. Making the case another way, Singer argued that because all animals feel pain, the suffering inflicted on them for medical and scientific research or hunting, as well as in breeding, raising, and slaughtering them on factory farms for food, is morally and ethically indefensible. Simply put, animals deserve the same consideration as humans. Bolstered by Singer's arguments, animal rights groups—the largest is People for the Ethical Treatment of Animals (PETA), founded in 1979—advocated granting legal and moral standing to animals. Traditional animal welfare groups—the Humane Society of the United States and various SPCAs—have focused primarily on ending animal suffering caused by humans, rather than on granting rights to animals, but the two movements often advocate the same policies.[2]

The animal rights argument leads inevitably to the conclusion that one should not eat meat or use animal products. Advocates also condemn the maintenance of "breeds" of livestock, dogs, and cats because they are artificial. That argument has yet to make an impact, as is evident in the rising number of purebred dogs and cats in people's homes, and the intensive breeding of livestock—and now cloning—to the point that some groups, including the United Nations Food and Agriculture Organization, warn against the loss of biodiversity among domestic plants and animals. But both animal rights and animal welfare advocates have kept pressure on puppy mills, the commercial breeding facilities that mass-produce puppies for the pet trade. More significant, the argument for the more humane treatment of animals, including livestock, long advanced by animal welfare advocates, had begun to gain sufficient support by the late 1990s to force improvement, through legislation and consumer pressure, in the often deplorable conditions of factory farms and slaughterhouses.

Unfortunately for traditional working dogs, a number of groups, in addition to promoting bans on hunting with hounds, have also criticized the use of stock dogs—a necessity on many cattle and sheep ranches where human labor is scarce—as stressful to livestock and dangerous for all animals concerned. Dogs have been working livestock for thousands of years; in fact, they helped domesticate other animals. Properly used dogs remain the best, least stressful way of working most livestock. In continuing to make these charges, animal protection groups remain true not only to their traditional objection to meat eating but also to their urban, upper-class origins, with their ingrained bias against the dogs of the working class and poor.

IN AN IRONIC SWITCH from the nineteenth century, when many dog people celebrated the dog as more obedient and subservient than even human servants, some animal rights advocates have argued that because dogs and cats are virtual slaves, under the life-and-death control of humans, they should not be kept at all. (Because it is unpopular with the general public, most groups now play down that idea.) Animal welfare and animal rights activists have also concerned themselves with the issue of pet overpopulation, often bolstering their case by overstating the numbers of animals killed in shelters by factors of two or three—the real numbers are a bad enough reflection on the cavalier attitude of many Americans toward their "best friends" and of the problems arising from breeding pure-bred dogs. But the total number of animals euthanized annually—primarily dogs and cats—fell from around 17 million in 1987 to between 5 and 6 million a decade later, and by some estimates is now as low as 3 million. Roughly half are dogs. (By contrast, around 100,000 dogs and cats are killed in the name of science and medicine, with many more maintained alive for experiments.) The decline in shelter deaths parallels a drop in stray dogs from an estimated 30 percent of the total canine population in the 1960s to 2 percent at the end of the millennium, and a marked increase in ster-ilizations. A number of "no kill" shelters, where animals granted refuge are guaranteed life, have also come into prominence, al-though the facilities are frequently criticized for refusing to take overly aggressive, old, or otherwise unadoptable dogs. Those ani-mals are then shunted to shelters that practice euthanasia.

In 2002, one survey estimated that 72 percent of all dogs were spayed or neutered, the result of decades-long educational cam-paigns by animal welfare groups to solve the problem of "overpop-ulation"—that is, to reduce the number of pariah, or ownerless, animals roaming the streets and countryside. Calling those animals unwanted surplus is a cultural decision; there are other societies where pariahs are the norm. But in America, efforts to rein in free-roaming dogs, even in the country, date back to colonial times. With the expansion of suburbs, it became unacceptable, in the minds of many people, for dogs to roam freely—for the public's protection from dog bites and the dogs' protection from cars and thieves and, when they are homeless, from sickness and starvation.

These changes are coincident with the explosion in the number of dogs from 40 million in the mid-1960s to 65 million in 2003, and the steady rise in the number of dogs who are purebred. In a dra-matic reversal from the situation on the eve of World War II, more than half of American dogs were purebred by 2002, although not all are registered, with the Labrador and its variants having replaced the cur as the most common dog. Some experts have speculated that people are less likely to abandon animals they bought for $1,000 or more, but the APPMA National Pet Owners Survey for 2003 showed that the average amount paid for a dog was $210, far less in real dollars than the equivalent animal would have cost before World War II. Fewer animals are entering shelters not only because of widespread sterilization but also because breed clubs and indi-viduals, desiring to keep dogs from being killed in shelters, have formed rescue groups that take in unwanted dogs and find homes for them.[3]

FOLLOWING THE TRADITION established at their inception a century ago of opposing the use of dogs for transport, entertainment, and sport, the vast majority of animal welfare groups, joined by animal rights organizations, launched media campaigns aimed at crushing the Iditarod International Sled Dog Race, a 1,041-mile marathon for humans and dogs from Anchorage to Nome, founded in 1972. The groups argue that because from one to six dogs have died in the race each year from a variety of accidents and illnesses, out of roughly 1,000 dogs that participate, the Iditarod is inherently cruel. The race and other mushing events keep alive the use and breeding of sled dogs, which had fallen into steep decline with the arrival of the snowmobile, as common now as dog yards once were. The Iditarod has evolved in response to the criticism and changing attitudes of its own participants, who, like many other people involved with dogs, have learned that positive attitudes and reinforcement are much better applied to dogs than whips, clubs, and even electric collars—training aids developed in the 1960s that deliver an electric shock by remote control, as punishment for wrong behavior. The race has become one of the best supervised events in the world, from a medical standpoint, with volunteer veterinarians examining each dog at every rest stop. Yet no one can participate or prevent sudden accidents or heart attacks or any of the countless other pathologies that kill dogs.

I have investigated the race and followed it in person across Alaska and have not seen evidence of dog abuse, although I have seen dog teams quit because they are tired or their chemistry with one another or the musher has turned sour. I have also seen the distress a musher feels when his or her dog dies. But opposition groups have not shown an interest in understanding the event or its participants, much less in the findings of veterinarians who have worked with the dogs. Their argument is about morality, politics, and class more than it is about the event itself. Upper-class reformers founded animal welfare groups in England and the United States in the nineteenth century to combat bull and bear baiting and the use of dogs as beasts of burden by ragpickers and ash haulers in urban shantytowns—laborers who were believed by definition to abuse their animals. They succeeded in England, but the use of dogs in transport continued in Europe, America, and throughout the Arctic. There were always people who treated their animals with the utmost kindness, but most followed the prevailing norms of their day, as they still do, and until recently dog driving was hard on dogs.

The Iditarod was a well-established endurance event, testing humans and dogs—males and females alike—when in 1994, Susan Butcher, a popular five-time winner, lost a dog, HC, on the trail. David Wills, vice president for investigations of the Humane Society of the United States, appeared on ABC's *Good Morning America* to announce that his organization, which bills itself as the largest animal welfare group in the world, was opposing the race henceforth because it was inherently cruel and dangerous for the dogs. Butcher, who had worked to put Wills on the Iditarod's animal care committee and to raise the overall level of treatment of dogs, felt doubly betrayed by the sudden announcement, as did the Iditarod Trail Committee, the race's governing board. In a twist, Wills was dismissed from HSUS in 1995 while under investigation for financial improprieties and sexual harassment, but the organization has continued its opposition to the Iditarod. Its luster dimmed in the popular imagination, the race nonetheless survived the loss of major corporate sponsors and television coverage in subsequent years and has recently experienced a resurgence of interest, although not on its former scale.

My investigations for *The Atlantic Monthly* in 1995; *Natural History* in 1996, when I traced the origins of the Alaskan husky; and my 1997 book, *Dog's Best Friend*, indicated that the campaign HSUS launched and maintains was founded on false statements—notably a charge that one leading musher slept on his moving sled while a dead dog was dragged along in its harness by the rest of the team—misinterpreted medical information, and manipulation of the media, if not, as irate mushers claimed, outright deception. In a 1995 interview, Merritt Clifton, editor of *Animal People*, an independent newsletter devoted to animal rights issues, called the HSUS effort against the Iditarod "a bullshit campaign." The Iditarod is run in early March, and each year in the run-up to the race, animal welfare and animal rights groups in the lower forty-eight level their charges. Neither side has sponsored essential research that might finally identify the reasons some dogs die on the trail.[4]

The $2 billion greyhound racing industry has been subjected to even more intense scrutiny, because of a long-standing practice of killing dogs too old or too slow to race. Culling—the killing of un-wanted animals—is an old tradition with dogs, cats, and livestock. It is effectively what humane shelters do with unadoptable animals. In his charges against the Iditarod, Wills claimed that mushers reg-ularly culled dogs, and some do. But culling of surplus animals on a family farm or at a musher's cabin is far different from institution-alized, mass killing of the sort long practiced at dog pounds and greyhound racetracks. Animal shelters initially killed dogs for public health reasons and continued the practice on the debatable grounds that from a humane standpoint, stray dogs were better off meeting a sudden death, if they could not be adopted, than suffer-ing from starvation and injury. No such ambiguity surrounds grey-hounds: thousands of young, healthy dogs were, and are, killed each year simply because they did not win or produce offspring who would win.

Adoption groups formed to find homes for the unwanted racers in the closing decades of the millennium, and the industry began to work more actively with those groups, as pressure on it mounted to reform or be shut down. An industry spokesman told National Public Radio on May 31, 2002, that 85 to 90 percent of the 22,000 greyhounds "retired" each year, usually when they are two to four years old, are now adopted. The rest are killed, putatively by lethal injection. His comments came after the discovery on the farm of Robert Rhodes in Lillian, Alabama, of the remains of thousands of greyhounds from one track in Pensacola, Florida, the bulk of them shot in the jaw or throat. A former guard at the Pensacola dog track, Rhodes said that he had killed 2,000 to 3,000 washed-out greyhounds over thirty years at a price of $10 a dog. Nationally, fifteen states have forty-eight dog tracks, one third of them in Flor-ida. Under pressure from animal welfare and antigambling groups,

DEAR MOM AND DAD, HOW ARE YOU?

I AM FINE.

MY FIRST DAY OF CAMP IS OVER.

I LIVED THROUGH IT.

© Peanuts Worldwide LLC

5 FRIDAY
JUNE

THE DAILY EXTRA

How many common words of four letters or more can you make from the letters in the following word? (You may use each letter only once.)

SEASIDE

(answer to Thursday's puzzle:)

8	3	1	5	4	6	7	9	2
5	7	4	3	9	2	6	8	1
6	2	9	8	1	7	3	4	5
4	5	3	6	8	1	9	2	7
2	9	8	4	7	5	1	6	3
7	1	6	9	2	3	8	5	4
3	4	5	7	6	9	2	1	8
1	6	7	2	5	8	4	3	9
9	8	2	1	3	4	5	7	6

DIFFICULTY RATING: ★ ★ ☆ ☆ ☆

seven states have banned the sport over the past twenty years, with more likely to follow. The demise of racing would probably bring with it the extinction of the greyhound as it currently exists, a dedicated sprinter, capable of reaching speeds in excess of forty miles an hour during a race.[5]

FAR MORE PROBLEMATIC FOR DOGS and their people than radical animal rights activists who oppose pet ownership is the sizable proportion of the population that fights the presence of dogs in parks, other public spaces, condominiums, co-ops, and rental housing— not to mention stores and restaurants. Their fear and loathing of dogs is reinforced every time a hyperaggressive animal, like a pit bull or rottweiler or Presa de Canario, attacks and kills an innocent bystander. Although dogs are no longer rounded up each summer in America and killed to prevent "hydrophobia," thanks to mandatory rabies vaccinations, their bites have become a major public health issue—an epidemic, according to the federal Centers for Disease Control. Researchers at the CDC and the Humane Society of the United States have estimated that 4 to 5 million people are bitten each year, and twenty to twenty-five are killed in fatal attacks. Fully 40 percent of Americans keep big dogs for protection, as well as companionship, as they always have, and not surprisingly, the most popular of those breeds are the most prolific biters—German shepherds, rottweilers, Akitas, chows, Doberman pinschers, malamutes, and Siberian huskies. More than half the fatal attacks since the 1980s have been by pit bulls and rottweilers, but every dog has the capacity to bite. Little Lhasa apsos and Pomeranians were among the thirty breeds involved in fatal attacks between 1977 and 1988. Most of the time, the dog, no matter its breed, bites a family member or friend, especially the elderly and young—the most frail and the smallest of those with whom it has contact.[6]

America's obsession with crime and illicit drugs in the 1980s combined with a furor over fatal attacks involving pit bulls to inspire publicity-driven, inadequate attempts to deal legislatively with the problem of dangerous dogs. In a sense, those campaigns represented a continuation of earlier attempts to curb sheep-killing dogs, only this time the victims were innocent people and the dogs were powerful animals bred for fighting. Kept by drug dealers and drug growers to guard against competitors, thieves, and police, by a cross section of society—rich and poor, black and white suprema- cist—seeking to derive power and ferocity from their dogs, and by people engaged in illegal dogfighting, pit bulls were involved in a number of fatal attacks around the country, some particularly sav- age. Nearly all were recounted in lurid detail in press accounts, which consistently demonized the pit bull as a born killer.

By the end of the decade, the public outcry against the breed had grown so intense that states and municipalities moved to ban the pit bull, despite expert testimony that such breed-specific ordinances failed to address the real problem of dangerous dogs, which could belong to any breed. Reprising arguments made during the nine- teenth century, that only low-born mixed breeds, not purebred sheepdogs, could kill sheep, representatives of the American Ken- nel Club argued that purebred pit bulls were gentle animals inca- pable of such horrors, and that the killers were mongrels. Around the same time, insurance companies began to require extra premi- ums to insure homes with breeds at the top of the bite statistics. But neither legislation nor more costly insurance had an effect. Lovers of hyperaggressive dogs—usually men—turned to rottweilers and similar animals not covered in the legal bans, and ignored insurance strictures.[7]

Perhaps the most gruesome killing involved two Presa de Ca- narios—believed to be descendants of the original Spanish killers brought to the Canary Islands in 1480 for *la montería infernal*— named Hera and Bane. They broke free from their handler and at- tacked and mauled to death a young woman, Diane Whipple, outside the door of her San Francisco apartment on January 26, 2001, in an unprovoked attack remarkable for its ferocity. The woman handling the dogs, Marjorie F. Knoller, an attorney, was convicted of involuntary manslaughter for her failure to restrain dogs known to be dangerous. Her attorney husband, Robert K. Noel, was convicted of the same offense, although he was not present at the killing. The couple claimed they were simply keeping the dogs for someone else, but the court ruled against them. That the dogs belonged to a white supremacist serving a life term in prison—whom Noel and Knoller had represented and adopted—and that charges of bestiality swirled around the couple and the dogs added a sordid element to the tragedy. The owner had planned to have a surrogate breed the pair and sell the puppies to drug dealers as protection. The dogs were destroyed, even while demand for the little-known breed skyrocketed after the killings.

The Healing Dog

The contradictory views of society toward the dog, who embodies unconditional love and cold destruction, domesticity and wildness—opposite forces in continual, dynamic equilibrium—found full expression in the decades following the fall of Vietnam. Relying on increased scientific understanding of behaviorism and of the dog's own physical capabilities, psychology, and development, particularly the importance of early socialization, people have consistently found new, sometimes surprising applications for the dog's innate abilities, the tracking of endangered species not least among them. Researchers also have shown conclusively that dogs and other pets are good for an individual's psychological and physical well-being. Science, in effect, has confirmed what dog owners have always known and what has been enshrined in myth and lore—that dogs are healers—and shown that the dog's usefulness easily outweighs the problems it sometimes causes.

Following the ad hoc experiments with therapy dogs in the New Paltz veterans' hospital during World War II, and the pioneering work of Boris Levinson and Samuel and Elizabeth Corson in the 1950s and 1960s, researchers have thoroughly documented the value of pets in general and dogs in particular—Levinson worked with Jingles, his mongrel—in helping children and adults suffering from stress, anxiety, depression, alienation, and other psychological problems. They can also help some autistic children connect to the world. In his 1969 book, *Pet-Oriented Child Psychology*, Levinson argued that children raised with pets were more cautious around strange animals and less afraid of animals in general than those raised solely among humans. Children learned fear of animals from their parents, he posited, the way a puppy learns fear initially from its mother, with abuse also playing a role. Refuting the argument of Konrad Lorenz, one of the founders of modern ethology, that children were inherently gentle around animals and thus, with their mothers, were the agents of domestication, Levinson documented that children had to learn not to hurt animals. Skepticism greeted Levinson's findings when he first presented them, at the 1961 meeting of the American Psychological Association, and faded slowly. But by 2003, psychologists and psychiatrists were increasingly prescribing pets as part of continuing therapy for children and adults.[8]

The medical establishment responded with equal skepticism in 1980 when Erika Friedmann of Brooklyn College documented that heart attack patients with pets had a better chance of surviving a year or more than those who did not. Stroking a dog lowered a person's blood pressure and heart rate, she showed. Subsequent studies at the Baker Medical Research Institute in Melbourne, Australia, revealed that plasma triglyceride and cholesterol levels were also lower in pet owners, thus reducing their risk of heart attacks. Since then, other studies have confirmed those findings. As if to prove the power not only of dogs but also of cultural stereotypes in perpetuating themselves, studies revealed as well that men often interact more freely and openly with their dogs than with other people, including members of their families. Indeed, both men and women benefit psychologically and physically from pet ownership, especially if they take the time to train and walk their dogs, thereby getting essential exercise for themselves.

Unfortunately, those who do not belong to the homeowning middle class, and those in condominiums and co-ops, often find that their landlords or association boards refuse to allow them to keep a dog. By some estimates, for example, only 10 percent of the apartments in New York City allow dogs, a number that seems high to people who have searched for dog-friendly accommodations in New York and other cities.

THE MEDICAL FINDINGS inspired a movement to bring dogs trained as therapy assistants into nursing homes and hospitals, where they immediately proved effective in reaching patients who were withdrawn or those suffering from Alzheimer's disease. Stories abound of patients speaking for the first time in years when greeted by a therapy dog. Prison officials had long known that dogs were an effective deterrent against uprisings, but they were surprised to learn that the presence of animals among inmates served generally to reduce violence. Everyone, including the dogs, seems to benefit from these encounters.

In 1975, Canine Companions for Independence was founded to train and provide service dogs for people with disabilities other than blindness. The dogs opened doors, retrieved items, pulled wheelchairs, anticipated epileptic seizures, and performed other tasks that extended the capabilities of people. Dogs were also trained to assist deaf people by alerting them to specific sounds. In 1990 the federal Americans with Disabilities Act mandated that trained assistance dogs be admitted with their people into public places, offices, businesses, restaurants, and transport vehicles without requiring proof of training or certification. Previously, only guide dogs had that access. Researchers at the University of Pennsylvania added to the growing portfolio of assistance dogs when they began training them to help people with Parkinson's disease and other movement disorders stand up and stabilize themselves.

Dog Health Declines

The rapid expansion of the purebred dog population to meet consumer demand for dogs that look and behave in a predictable way created a health crisis in many breeds and supported the charge of animal rights and animal welfare groups that the dog is better for human health than humans are for the dog's. Even many people who have refused to attribute validity to racial stereotypes accept the notion that dogs of a certain breed have set and predictable behavioral characteristics, that "function follows form," in a direct reversal of the fundamental rule of evolution that "form follows function." These people also ignore the well-documented fact that there is as much variation in behavior and abilities within breeds as there is between breeds. Genetic ailments are even more problematic, especially those that affect the duration and quality of an animal's life. By 2000, a database at the University of Pennsylvania maintained by the geneticist Donald F. Patterson listed 370 genetic disorders in dogs, with 5 to 10 new ones added each year. Many of them segregate according to breed, and many breeds are prone to more than one affliction. That pattern persists because breeders rely heavily on a "favored sire," a champion bred to many females, thus passing on good and bad characteristics, and inbreeding.

The American Kennel Club and some breed clubs have sponsored research to identify the genes responsible for particular ailments through the Dog Genome Project, for many years a loose-knit group of fifteen researchers from the United States and Europe interested in mapping the dog genome. Jasper Rine, a University of California at Berkeley geneticist, started the project in 1991 in an attempt to understand how genes shape behavioral and physical characteristics of the dog. After he dropped out, the focus shifted to mapping disease genes, especially those found in humans as well as dogs, continuing at a genetic level the types of comparisons of dogs and humans that inspired early vivisectionists. With the human genome complete, scientists decided to sequence the genomes of a number of other animals, and in 2002 they chose the dog. The following year they selected a boxer's genome for sequencing because it was among the most inbred of dogs, and thus its genes would be less variable and easier to define. That project was to be completed at the Whitehead Institute for Biomedical Research as this book went to press.

Working independently, scientists at the Institute for Genomic Research and the Center for Genomics completed a rough gene map of a standard poodle belonging to J. Craig Venter, the geneticist who funded the research, in the fall of 2003. The map showed a fairly significant overlap between the dog and human genomes, which is why the dog is a good model for many genetic ailments in humans, and also revealed that the dog has gene coding for a greater diversity of olfactory receptors than humans and many other animals, which accounts for its keen sense of smell. As with much having to do with dogs and genomics, grandstanding played a role in the Venter team's publication of their incomplete map in *Science* on September 26, 2003. They wanted to prove that their privately funded endeavor could beat the more thorough and deliberate publicly funded effort under way at the Whitehead Institute.[9]

Scientists have long recognized the value of inbred populations of dogs, with their elaborate pedigrees, for genetic study and, when money has been available, have used the dog as a model for equivalent human diseases. For example, in 1999, Emmanuel Mignot at the Stanford University School of Medicine identified the gene and mutations responsible for narcolepsy in Doberman pinschers, Labrador retrievers, and dachshunds. This finding directed researchers toward the biochemical and neurological pathways involved in human narcolepsy. But canine geneticists have also long argued that the knowledge exists now for breeders to breed selectively against many of these ailments, the way in the 1990s the Seeing Eye organization effectively eliminated hip dysplasia from the Labradors and German shepherds it breeds as guide dogs. With few exceptions, the breeders have refused to take action, partly because in some cases they would have to outcross to closely related breeds, thereby giving up their archaic notion of blood purity, and in others because they would have to recognize that the extreme physical forms they desire are unhealthy for the dog and must be surrendered.

But with the huge growth in human and purebred dog populations, animals that once had been objects of conspicuous consumption, affordable only to the wealthy, became mass-produced commodities for the rapidly expanding popular consumer culture. With little regard for quality or early socialization, puppy mills cranked out popular breeds for sale in pet stores, and commercial kennels sold directly to the public. Breeds that became popular because of movies or television shows or a notion that they were rare and unique—for whatever reason—were quickly bred to meet demand, without regard to the quality of the animal. In the 1980s, for example, the wrinkled shar-pei, billed as an ancient Chinese fighting dog, suddenly became prized because of its rarity, and its population soared to an estimated 50,000 from a dozen in 1968, with some dogs fetching $10,000, a bargain by the standards of the 1920s. The dogs became known as genetic disasters, suffering skin problems, eyelids that had to be cut from over the eye, bad hips, and a surly temperament. As anti–pit bull sentiment rose in the 1980s, so did rottweiler ownership, as people sought more aggressive dogs that would escape police scrutiny. Rottweiler registrations with the AKC leapt from 21,207 in 1984 to 102,596 a decade later, with many of the dogs having hip, eye, and temperament problems. Their unpredictable aggressiveness became notorious.

A number of veterinarians specializing in animal behavior—a field that did not exist half a century ago—and trainers have argued that the mass production of purebred dogs and the emphasis on certain aggressive personality features for show dogs has created animals not always well suited to serve as companion animals. They have urged breeders to concentrate more on temperament when they breed their dogs, seeking animals that are not aggressive, highstrung, or hyperactive. Some experts have even tried to categorize and rank the behavioral characteristics of individual breeds, with not very satisfactory results because of the variations within breeds and the human bias of the judges. Other research has suggested that boldness, not aggression, is the essential characteristic of successful working dogs.[10]

In the Nose

Despite those serious problems, dog ownership continued to grow and spread, and people found new employment for dogs' talents, whether playing Frisbee, running agility courses with jumps and tunnels, or competing in flyball; herding trials, which grew in popularity as raising sheep for profit declined because of synthetic fabrics; or field trials to test hunting ability. Other dogs worked as volunteers in hospitals and in search-and-rescue organizations that began to proliferate in the 1980s and saw service everywhere in the aftermath of earthquakes and hurricanes, war and terrorist attacks. Search-and-rescue teams worked the rubble of the Oklahoma City Federal Building after it was bombed in 1995 and that of the twin towers of the World Trade Center after their collapse following the attacks of September 11, 2001.

Dogs have searched battlefields for thousands of years, initially as scavengers. No one knows when their natural hunting ability was first turned to finding survivors, but systematized training of casualty and ambulance dogs was well established in Germany by World War I. During World War II, the British used dogs to find civilian victims of the Blitz. After the war, when recreational skiing mushroomed, the Swiss formally resurrected the old custom of using dogs to hunt for victims of avalanches, in small-scale search-and-rescue operations. In the 1960s, trainers in England and other European countries began to follow the Swiss lead, as did American military trainers in Vietnam. Civilian search-and-rescue squads began to expand in America during the late 1970s. Now the dogs and their handlers are often among the first on a disaster scene; indeed, it is unusual not to see them. But search-and-rescue work has become just one of a rapidly expanding list of tasks to which dogs are being trained to turn their noses.

Faced with an elusive foe engaging in guerrilla warfare in Vietnam, as well as new generations of land mines and plastic explosives, military trainers began experimenting with new ways of training dogs to detect a variety of objects and materials, including explosives and narcotics, that involved rewarding success and not punishing errors. The trainers also learned not to ask scout or guard dogs to perform double and triple duty as detector dogs, but to train specialists who could focus on one task. The trainers' method of "shaping behavior" through rewards of food or play objects, like balls and towels, produced dramatic results and opened a new world of possibilities. On a basic level, they were simply training the dog to apply its natural sense of smell and desire to hunt to a different task and rewarding the effort. Truffle hunters who give their dogs stale bread or cheese for each find have understood the process for centuries, as have their dogs, while pigs have never gotten it. They eat the truffles, if not stopped. Montague Stevens trained his pack of grizzly bear dogs using food in the late nineteenth century, and other people attuned to their animals have long done the same. But they were always in the minority and frequently considered more than a little deluded, if not deranged. Yet science had weighed in on the side of the eccentrics, and the military dog trainers were learning from behavioral scientists who were applying the techniques of operant conditioning to train dolphins to find mines and other underwater objects.

This reward-based approach received a significant boost among civilians from Karen Pryor, a former dolphin trainer who in 1995 published a practicum on "shaping behavior" called *Don't Shoot the Dog,* and began actively promoting "clicker training," which employs a simple toy cricket. The animal is first taught to associate the signal—in this case a click, although a whistle or other consistent simple noise or gesture will do—with its primary reward, generally food. Toys and other objects also are used as rewards. Then, because timing is all-important in this kind of operant conditioning, the signal, which has become something of a substitute for the reward, is given immediately after a desired behavior is performed, allowing the trainer to delay delivery of the food. This is essential if the animal is not right next to the trainer. In most cases, the trainer dispenses with the food and ultimately the signal, once the animal has learned the particular task. In scent-detection work, success is *always* rewarded because the dogs are being asked each time to discriminate between often infinitesimally weak, closely related odors. Nonabusive, reward-based training systems are not universal. Many trainers continue to believe that they must "civilize" the dog with a choke chain or electric collar—modern equivalents of the nineteenth-century boot and whip. Those methods work, but their influence is waning.

In 1970 the U.S. Customs Service began using dogs to detect drug shipments, as part of Nixon's "war on drugs"—really a war on the triumvirate of the 1960s: drugs, sex, and rock 'n' roll. Nixon himself reportedly abused alcohol and prescription drugs, and he enlisted the notorious drug abuser and rock avatar Elvis Presley in his campaign, but the hypocrisy mattered less than exacting vengeance on the people perceived as pulling America down. After its creation, the Drug Enforcement Administration added its own dogs, as have many state and local police forces. Trained to detect heroin, amphetamines, cocaine, hashish, marijuana, and, more recently, ecstasy, the dogs annually account for $2 to $3 billion, street value, in drug seizures, with seizures of the personal property of drug dealers worth even more. The war on drugs has remained controversial since its inception, not least because of indications that it has meted out unequal justice to black and Hispanic males, much the way breed-specific dog legislation was directed at their dogs, and because it has failed to address the problem of addiction. Customs dogs have also been trained to detect money, chemical weapons, and explosives.

In 1984 the Department of Agriculture's Animal and Plant Health Inspection Service organized the Beagle Brigade to patrol airports and international postal depots for contraband meat and fruit. The goal was to keep out of the country invasive pathogens that could threaten citrus, pork, chicken, and other crops and livestock. The beagles, often mongrels, since all the dogs are adopted or donated, are trained to sit when they smell one of a number of banned foods. They receive food for their successes, and, like most detector dogs, are said to be correct more than 90 percent of the time. In 1995 the USDA deployed eight Jack Russell terriers on Guam, trained to seek out and destroy brown tree snakes that had entered the island from Australia, New Guinea, and the Philippines and extirpated nine of its twelve indigenous bird species. The dogs searched cargo pallets bound for Hawaii in effort to keep the snakes, which can grow to ten feet in length, from reaching those islands and wiping out their unique and endangered birds.

With about 220 million mucous-covered scent receptors, forty times the number found in humans, the dog is designed to sniff, picking out more minute quantities of an odor than humans or machines can measure, and they can be readily trained to identify a range of smells that currently seems limited only by human imagination. Significantly in an age of terrorism, dogs have proved to be the most effective detector of explosive yet found, better than any machine. They are maneuverable, quick, and decisive. In the turmoil following the destruction of the World Trade Center, bomb-detector dogs came into such high demand that drug-detector dogs were being converted and new ones trained at a frenetic pace. A number of incompetent trainers entered the fray, producing poorly trained and vetted dogs, who at this writing have not yet failed spectacularly, although the risk is real. Experts worry that a failure could spur a backlash against relying on dogs that would feed into a long-standing bias among many officials who favor machines over dogs.

Building on early success, detector dog programs proliferated through the 1990s. Plagued by settlement claims for arson that were costing companies and consumers several billion dollars and causing hundreds of deaths a year—some people literally had "kitchen fires" every two or three years, so they could remodel—the insurance industry in 1993 began paying local fire departments to take on dogs trained to detect minute traces of weathered gasoline or other flammable chemicals (accelerants) in burned-out buildings. The dogs were trained to sit and point when they smelled something and proved better at the job than any machine yet invented at detecting evidence needed to support a conclusion that a fire had resulted from arson. Soon people were training dogs to detect termites, hidden mold, and gasoline and water leaks in underground pipes. Dogs are reportedly able to detect even some forms of cancer, like melanoma, although no ones knows how. Dogs also continue to be used to identify suspects in crimes, usually after they have been trailed from the scene, but the dogs are sometimes allowed to pick the person out of a scent lineup, as well. The evidence that they can reliably pull off that form of identification or even track a specific person—as opposed to following human scent, the way they follow deer or panthers—remains scant and controversial.

Indeed, by 2003 the deployment of dogs had outstripped basic scientific understanding of their olfactory capabilities and potential, primarily because essential research has gone unfunded. More troubling, the issue of errors has remained almost completely unstudied despite suggestions that a poor handler can make a dog's accuracy rate plummet 30 to 40 percent, and studies showing that various physical problems, some undetected, affect a dog's sniffing ability. Research and experience have repeatedly pointed to the leash as an instrument of error, with handlers transmitting their expectations directly to the dog, but most American handlers consistently refuse to work their dogs off the leash, for fear of lawsuits, should the dog bite, and of relinquishing their "control." The dog, eager to please and anticipating a reward, quite naturally indicates the presence of the desired object—or residual odor from it—with the result that a car is searched for nonexistent explosives, a person for narcotics he or she never carried. Most American law enforcement agencies have refused to address the question of these "false positives," where the dog alerted to a substance that was not present. Officials have testified in public and in court that the dog never makes a mistake, which is, of course, untrue. In short, at the time of this writing, the use of dogs as biological detection systems remains very much a work in progress that is in need of more rigorous analysis to make it more effective and to dispel criticisms.

Increased demand began to create supply problems, as well. Traditionally, detector dogs were adopted from animal shelters or donated. They were selected because of their physical health, their size—large retriever types and diminutive beagles—and their desire to go and seek, their "prey drive," trainers called it. Approximately 30 to 40 percent of the dogs failed to make the grade. As detector-dog programs grew, especially in the aftermath of the World Trade Center attacks, it became harder for trainers to find dogs from their traditional sources. In an attempt to ensure a steady supply of quality dogs and cut down on the failure rate, the U.S. Customs Service—most federal detector-dog programs are now under the Department of Homeland Security—began breeding its own Labrador retrievers. Breeding working dogs is difficult, of course, because of the need to maintain genetic diversity, but the rewards should justify the effort.

Fala's Shadow

Whether they embraced or battled the long shadow of Franklin D. Roosevelt—and they have had to do one or the other—American presidents over the past fifty-five years have had dogs, even Bill Clinton, who entered the White House without one, and Jimmy Carter, who appeared to prefer cats and rabbits. Following a tradition dating to Warren G. Harding's Airedale, Laddie Boy, of presidential dogs "writing" to their public, George H. W. Bush's springer spaniel, Millie, wrote a best-seller, with the help of Bush's wife, Barbara. As befitted the age of semiotics, however, there was something self-consciously self-referential about the effort. Lyndon B. Johnson's habit of picking his beagles up by the ears—a form of abuse apparently born of ignorance and an unbridled lust for power—demonstrated something more genuine but indisputably lacked the magic of Roosevelt and Fala. George W. Bush has a tendency to carry his Scottie, Barney, under his arm, as if to keep him on display—or under control and out of trouble. Barney also stars in live White House–produced videos broadcast over the Internet that are among the most visited Web sites in the Bush administration. The difference between these presidential dogs and Roosevelt's is that Fala was a personality who came along at a historic moment and met a person he could assist. Roosevelt and Fala formed an organic unit, whereas the deployment of subsequent White House dogs has too often appeared, and in fact been, staged for publicity, a political ploy designed to connect to the past and to dog lovers in the electorate. That might change when an inhabitant of the White House takes a stand on off-leash walking in public parks, or takes a walk through the streets of Washington, plastic poop bag in hand, dog walking freely by her side.

Finding a place for the dog to run, swim, and play—in short, to be a dog—remains one of the most difficult problems confronting the sizable minority of people with dogs today. Their desire to provide a quality life for their dogs, and the backlash it triggers, presents local officials with one of their most contentious issues. Many suburbs lack public parks where dogs and people can exercise, and even in cities with good parks, battles often rage over dogs, especially off-leash walking and the cleanup of excrement. The New York City "pooper-scooper law" took effect on August 1, 1978, and drew an immediate court challenge, with opponents charging, among other things, that the law discriminated against Orthodox Jews because it would make them labor on the Sabbath—an argument rejected on the ground that walking the dog would also constitute labor—and that it discriminated against infirm and disabled people. Opponents also argued that many of the million-plus dogs believed to reside in New York would be turned loose to wander the streets. The challenge was dismissed, and the law has been in effect since then, with the result that New York's streets have become relatively free of dog excrement, if not other garbage.

More intense battles have occurred between those people who like to exercise their dogs off leash—the dogs prefer it—and city officials and non–dog owners who insist that leash laws be enforced and obeyed, justifying their demands by saying that wildlife—usually meaning squirrels and opossums—and people must be protected. As usual, dogs are caught in the middle of a human debate over the appropriate use of woefully limited public space and people's relation to the world outside their own illusions. Many communities have constructed "dog parks," also called "bark parks," where off-leash activities are permitted—New York has twenty-six—but they tend to be small, overcrowded havens for fleas and ticks. More enlightened cities and towns have established hours in certain parks or sections of parks for off-leash activities. Still others have attempted to construct agility courses and provide other areas for people to train and play with their dogs. Harmony, a planned community under construction on 11,000 acres in Central Florida, south of Orlando and east of Disney World, has billed itself as the most dog- and animal-friendly community in the nation. Fully 6,000 acres have been set aside as nature sanctuaries, and the built sections are designed to be dog-friendly, with designated off-leash areas and other amenities. How well the community will fare, no one can yet say, but most pet owners cannot afford a home in a new, planned community.

Dogs are here to stay because a great many people could not manage without them. But after thousands of years of mutual companionship and work, we still do not quite know what to make of them, or how to repay them. Solving that problem involves understanding the dog better—perhaps as well as they understand us. In doing so, we might just learn something about ourselves and the world we are constantly creating—with timely assistance from the dog.

Notes

∿

Preface

1. Henry Rowe Schoolcraft, *Journal of a Tour into the Interior of Missouri and Arkansaw, from Potsoi, or Mine on Burton, in Missouri Territory, in a South-West Direction, toward the Rocky Mountains, Performed in the Years 1818 and 1819* (London: Richard Phillips and Company, 1821), entry dated Thursday, December 24, 1818.
2. *2003–2004 APPMA National Pet Owners Survey* (Greenwich, Conn.: American Pet Products Manufacturers Association, 2003), p. 7.

1. First People and Dogs Settle the New World

1. *The Journals of the Lewis and Clark Expedition*, ed. Guy E. Moulton, vol. 4, (Lincoln, Nebr.: University of Nebraska Press, 1983), pp. 246–47. Entry for June 3, 1805.
2. George Catlin, *North American Indians*, 2 vols. (Philadelphia: Leary, Stuart and Company, 1913), vol. 1, p. 258.
3. Alexander Mackenzie, *The Journals and Letters of Sir Alexander Mackenzie*, ed. W. Kaye Lamb (London and New York: Cambridge University Press for the Hakluyt Society, 1970), p. 215.
4. Carles Vilà et al., "Multiple and Ancient Origins of the Domestic Dog," *Science*, vol. 276, June 13, 1997, pp. 1,687–89; Peter Savolainen et al., "Genetic Evidence for an East Asian Origin of Domestic Dogs," *Science*, vol. 298, November 22, 2002, pp. 1,610–13.

5. George C. Frison, "PaleoIndian large mammal hunters on the Plains of North America," *PNAS*, vol. 95, November 1998, pp. 14,576–83. Frison wryly dismisses the common picture of Paleo-Indian hunters killing adult mammoths in bogs, observing that mammoths, like all elephants, spent much of their lives in bogs and therefore could have extricated themselves at will, unless infirm.

6. Marjorie Brooks Lovvorn, George C. Frison, and Larry L. Tieszen, "Paleo-climate and Amerindians: Evidence from stable isotopes and atmospheric circulation," *PNAS*, February 27, 2001, vol. 98, no. 5, pp. 2,485–90.

7. Samuel Hearne, *A Journey from Prince of Wale's Fort in Hudson's Bay to the Northern Ocean: Undertaken By Order of the Hudson's Bay Company for the Discovery of Copper Mines, a North West Passage, &c. In the Years 1769, 1770, 1771, and 1772.* (New York: Da Capo Press, 1969; reprint of 1795 London edition), p. 323.

8. Ibid., p. 289; Richard B. Lee and Irven DeVore, eds., *Man the Hunter* (Chicago: Alden, 1968).

9. Hearne, p. 342.

10. William K. Powers and Marla N. Powers, "Putting on the Dog," *Natural History*, February 1986.

11. Marion Schwartz, *A History of Dogs in the Early Americas* (New Haven: Yale University Press, 1997); Alana Cordy-Collins, "An Unshaggy Dog Story," *Natural History*, February 1994.

12. Cordy-Collins.

13. *The Journals of the Lewis and Clark Expedition*, vol. 4, p. 54.

14. Maximilian, Prince of Wied, *Travels in the Interior of North America,* trans. Hannibal Evans Lloyd, ed. Reuben Gold Thwaites (Cleveland: The Arthur H. Clarke Company, 1905), p. 310.

15. Glover M. Allen, "Dogs of the American Aborigines," *Bulletin of the Museum of Comparative Zoology*, vol. 58, no. 9, March 1920, p. 439.

16. Farley Mowat, *Sea of Slaughter* (Boston and New York: Atlantic Monthly Press, 1984), pp. 150–51.

17. Allen, pp. 442–43.

18. Ibid., p. 463.

19. Ibid., p. 464.; *The Journals of the Lewis and Clark Expedition*, p. 318.

20. Allen, p. 469.

21. Ibid., pp. 481 and 495.

22. Ibid., p. 491.

23. Ibid., p. 492; Schwartz, pp. 43–44.

24. Allen, p. 476.

25. Ibid., pp. 472, 475, and 476.

26. Cordy-Collins.

27. Allen, p. 480.

28. Jennifer K. Leonard et al., "Ancient DNA Evidence for Old World Origin of New World Dogs," *Science*, vol. 298, November 22, 2002, pp. 1,613–16.

2. Deadly Encounters

1. John Grier Varner and Jeannette Johnson Varner, *Dogs of the Conquest* (Norman, Okla.: University of Oklahoma Press, 1983), pp. xiv–xv.

2. Ibid., p. 5.

3. Bartolomé de Las Casas, *Brevísima relación de la destrucción de las Indias;* in English, *The Tears of the Indians being an account of the cruel massacres and slaughters of above twenty millions of innocent people, committed by the Spaniards in the islands of Hispaniola, Cubas, Jamaica &c; as also in the continent of Mexico, Peru & other places of the West Indies, to the total destruction of those countries, written in Spanish by Casaus, an eyewitness of those things; and made English by J.P.* (Ann Arbor, Mich.: Early English Books Online, from the 1656 London edition), p. 10; *Historia de las Indias*, trans. and ed. Andrée Collard (New York: Harper and Row, 1971).

4. Ibid., pp. 6–7.

5. Varner and Varner, pp. 13, 18.

6. Las Casas, p. 5.

7. Ibid., p. 21.

8. Varner and Varner, pp. 25–26.

9. Ibid., p. 26.

10. Gonzalo Fernández de Oviedo y Valdés, *Historia general y natural de las Indias* (Asuscíon del Paraguay: Editorial Guaranta, 1945); Varner and Varner, p. 27.

11. Varner and Varner, pp. 48, 54–56.

12. Alvar Nâuänez Cabeza de Vaca, *Castaways: The Narrative of Núñez Cabeza de Vaca*, trans. Enrique Pupo-Walker (Berkeley, Calif.: University of California Press, 1993, electronic book).

13. Knight of Elvas, *The Hernando de Soto Expedition*, ed. Jerald T. Milanich (New York: Garland Publishing, 1991).

14. Josiah Gregg, *Commerce of the Prairies, or, The Journal of a Santa Fe Trader, 1831–1839* (New York: J. & H. G. Langley, 1845), in Reuben Gold Thwaites, ed., *Early Western Travels*, vol. xix (Cleveland: Arthur H. Clark Company, 1905), p. 322.

15. J. H. Lyman, *American Agriculturist*, vol. 3, issue 8, August 1844.

3. The English Take Hold, Spread Out

1. Thomas Hariot, *A Briefe and True Report of the New Found Land of Virginia* (Amsterdam: Theatrum Orbis Terrarum, and New York: Da Capo Press, 1971; facsimile reproduction of the 1588 London edition).

2. Ralph Lane, *An account of the particularities of the imployments of the English men left in Virginia by Sir Richard Greenevill under the charge of Master Ralph Lane Generall of the same, from the 17. Of August 1585. Until the 18. Of June 1586. At which time they departed the Countrey: sent and directed to Sir Walter Ralegh*, in *The Principal Navigational Voyages Traf-*

fiques & Discoveries of the English Nation Made by Sea Overland to the Remote and Furthesst Distant Quarters of the Earth at any times within the compasse of these 1600 years, Richard Hakluyt, machine-readable version by Peter Brownfeld (Virtual Jamestown Project, Virginia Center for Digital History, University of Virginia, 2000, from New York: Macmillan, 1904; reprint of the 1586 edition, http://jefferson.village.virginia.edu/vcdh/ jamestown).

3. Hariot, p. D3.

4. Giles Milton, *Big Chief Elizabeth: The Adventures and Fate of the First English Colonists in America* (New York: Farrar, Straus and Giroux, 2000), pp. 336 ff.

5. Alexander Whitaker, "Good News from Virginia sent to the Counsell and Company of Virginia, resident in England" (Virtual Jamestown Project, Virginia Center for Digital History, University of Virginia, 2000; original, 1613).

6. George Percy, "A Trewe Relacyon," machine-readable version by Julie Richter (Virtual Jamestown Project, Virginia Center for Digital History, University of Virginia, 2000; from *Tyler's Quarterlly Historical and Genealogical Magazine,* vol. 3, no. 4, April 1922).

7. John Smith, *The Generall Historie of Virginia, New England, and the Summer Isles, with the names of the Adventurers, Planters, and Governours from their first beginning An: 1584 to this present 1624,* in *The Complete Works of Captain John Smith,* ed. Philip L. Barbour (Chapel Hill, N.C.: University of North Carolina Press, for the Institute of Early American History and Culture, 1986), p. 261.

8. *Proceedings of the Virginia Assembly, 1619,* machine-readable version by Paul Grady (Virtual Jamestown Project, Virginia Center for Digital History, University of Virginia, 2001).

9. Crandall Shifflett, Virtual Jamestown Timeline (Virtual Jamestown Project, Virginia Center for Digital History, University of Virginia, 1998).

10. Robert Beverly, *History of Virginia* (Virtual Jamestown Project, Virginia Center for Digital History, University of Virginia, 2001), pp. 88–89.

11. Anonymous, "Narrative of a Voyage to Maryland 1705–1706," *The American Historical Review,* vol. 12, issue 2 (1907), pp. 323–40.

12. Howard M. Chapin, *Dogs in Early New England* (Providence, R.I.: Press of E. A. Johnson and Co., 1920), p. 1; William Bradford, *History of Plymouth Plantation 1606–1646,* vol. 7, in *Original Narratives of Early American History,* ed. William T. Davis (New York: Scribner's, 1908), p. 98; William Bradford, Edward Winslow, and Robert Cushman, *A relation of or journal of the beginning and proceedings of the English Plantation at Plimouth in New England, by certaine English Adventurers both Merchants and others*; Commonly, *Mourt's Relation* (Ann Arbor, Mich.: University of Michigan Early English Books Online; reprint of 1622 London edition), p. 13.

13. *Mourt's Relation*, pp. 21 and 22.

14. Everett Emerson, ed., *Letters from New England: The Massachusetts Bay Colony, 1629–1638* (Amherst, Mass.: University of Massachusetts Press, 1976), p. 17; George Francis Dow, *Every Day Life in the Massachusetts Bay Colony* (New York: Dover Publications, 1988; reprint from Boston: Society for the Preservation of Antiquities, 1935), p. 106.

15. *Collections of the Massachusetts Historical Society,* vol. 6 (Boston: Massachusetts Historical Society, 1863), p. 491; John Winthrop, *The Journal of John Winthrop, 1630–1649,* eds. Richard S. Dunn, James Savage, and Laetitia Yeandle (Cambridge, Mass.: Belknap Press, Harvard University Press, 1996), p. 101; *Letters from New England,* pp. 124–25; Chapin, p. 8.

16. Edward N. Wentworth, *America's Sheep Trails: History, Personalities* (Ames, Iowa: Iowa State College Press, 1948), p. 487; Chapin, p. 6; Alice Morse Earle, *Home Life in Colonial Days* (Stockbridge, Mass.: Berkshire Traveller Press, 1974; reprint of 1898 edition, New York: Grosset and Dunlap), pp. 188–89.

17. Winthrop, pp. 504–505.

18. William Cronon, *Changes in the Land: Indians, Colonists, and the Ecology of New England* (New York: Hill and Wang, 1983), pp. 96–97.

19. *History of the Pequot War: The Contemporary Accounts of Mason, Underhill, Vincent and Gardener,* ed. Charles Orr (Cleveland: Helman-Taylor Co., 1897, from Collections of the Massachusetts Historical Society, vol. 3, 1833).

20. Lion Gardener, *Narrative of the Pequot War,* in *History of the Pequot War,* pp. 129–30.

21. Lion Gardener and John Mason, *A Brief History of the Pequot War: Especially of the Memorable Taking of their Fort at Mistick in Connecticut in 1637* (Boston: S. Kneeland and T. Greene, 1736), pp. 25–26.

22. *The Public Records of the Colony of Connecticut* (Storrs, Conn.: University of Connecticut, 2000–2001, http://www.colonialct.uconn.edu), p. 86.

23. "Cougar hunting tales from New York and Pennsylvania," *Spirit of the Times,* May 19, 1832.

4. Washington, Lafayette, and Jefferson

1. Lafayette to Washington, May 13, 1785, quoted in *The Diaries of George Washington*, vol. 4 of *The Papers of George Washington*, eds. Donald Jackson and Dorothy Twohig (Charlottesville, Va.: University of Virginia Press, 1978; online at the Library of Congress, http://memory.loc.gov/ammem/gwhtml/gwhome.html), p. 186.

2. Washington to Grayson, August 22, 1785, *The Writings of George Washington from the original manuscript sources, 1732–1799*, vol. 28, ed. John Clement Fitzpatrick (Charlottesville, Va.: Electronic Text Center, the University of Virginia, 2001, http://etext.lib.virginia.edu/washington).

3. Common Council Minutes, City of New-York, October 26, 1785.

4. Anonymous, "Dog," *American Turf*, October 1830, from *Boston Tribune*, n.d.

5. Washington to Cochran, August 31, 1785, *Writings*, vol. 28.

6. Washington to Lafayette, September 1, 1785, and Washington to Comte d'Oilliamson, September 1, 1785, *Writings*, vol. 28.

7. Entry for February 1789, *The Diaries of George Washington*, vol. 5, p. 444; T. B. Thorpe, "About the Fox and Fox-hunters," *Harper's New Monthly Magazine*, November 1861.

8. Entry for March 26, 1770, *Diaries*, vol. 2, p. 228; George Washington to William Pearce, December 4, 1796, *Writings*, vol. 34.

9. Washington to James Anderson, January 8, 1792, *Writings*, vol. 35.

10. Bryan Fairfax to George Washington, July 5, 1772, the George Washington Papers at the Library of Congress, 1741–1799, http://memory.loc.gov/ammem/gwhtml/gwhome.html.

11. Fairfax to Washington, August 3, 1772, George Washington Papers.

12. Washington to President of Congress, February 14, 1777; Washington to Lee, February 16, 1777, *Writings*, vol. 7, and note, p. 155.

13. Charles Lee to Washington, June 30, 1778 (misdated July 30), *The Papers of George Washington* (Charlottesville, Va.: University of Virginia, http://www.gwpapers.virginia.edu).

14. Washington to Lee, June 30, 1778; Lee to Washington, June 30, 1778 (misdated June 28), *The Papers of George Washington*. Anonymous, "Character of the American General Lee . . . ," *Child of Pallas*, vol. 1, issue 1, 1800.

15. Washington to Howe, October 6, 1777, *Writings*, vol. 9.

16. Washington to Carter, February 5, 1778, *Writings*, vol. 29.

17. Washington to Newenham, February 24, 1788, *Writings*, vol. 30.

18. Washington to Anthony Whiting, December 16, 1792, *Writings*, vol. 32.

19. Thomas Jefferson to Thomas Mann Randolph, May 17, 1791, the Thomas Jefferson Papers at the Library of Congress, http://memory.loc.gov/ammem/mtjhtml/mtjhome.html.

20. Jefferson to P. S. DuPont Nemours, March 2, 1809, Letters 1743–1826, Thomas Jefferson Digital Archive (Charlottesville, Va.: Electronic Text Center, University of Virginia, http://etext.virginia.edu/jefferson/texts).

21. Jefferson to Marie Joseph Paul Yves Roch Gilbert du Motier, Marquis de Lafayette, November 30, 1813, *The Works of Thomas Jefferson in Twelve Volumes*, collected and edited by Paul Leicester Ford (Washington, D.C.: Library of Congress, Federal Edition, from New York and London: G. P. Putnam's Sons, 1904; http://memory.loc.gov/ammem/mtjhtml/mtjhome.html).

22. Wentworth, p. 407; and Henry S. Randall, *The Practical Shepherd: A complete Treatise on the Breeding, Management and Diseases of Sheep* (New York: The American News Company, 1863, 31st ed., first published 1858), pp. 400–10.

23. Washington to Anthony Whiting, December 16, 1792, *Writings*, vol. 32.

24. T. B. Thorpe and Frederick Jackson Turner, "The Colonization of the West," *The American Historical Review*, vol. 2, issue 2, January 1906, pp. 303–27.

25. Anonymous, "The Faithful Dog," *The Key*, vol. 1, issue 6, February 17, 1798.

26. Common Council Minutes, City of New-York, July 13, 1801, and February 28, 1803.

27. James Turner, *Reckoning with the Beast: Animals, Pain, and Humanity in the Victorian Mind* (Baltimore: Johns Hopkins University Press, 1980), p. 20.

5. Crossing the Great Divide

1. Thomas Jefferson to George Rogers Clark, from Annapolis, December 4, 1783 (New Haven, Conn.: the Avalon Project, Yale University Law School, 1996–2003, http://www.yale.edu/lawweb/avalon/avalon.htm).

2. William Bartram, *The Travels of William Bartram: Naturalist's Edition*, ed. Francis Harper (Athens, Ga.: University of Georgia Press, 1998), pp. 140–41.

3. Hearne, p. 58.

4. Mackenzie, p. 266.

5. Ibid., p. 302.

6. Ibid., pp. 358 and 378.

7. Ibid., p. 389.

8. Ibid.

9. The first edition of the journals of Lewis and Clark was published in 1814, edited by Nicholas Biddle. A definitive edition, edited by Gary E. Moulton, did not appear until the University of Nebraska Press began its monumental project in 1983: *The Journals of Lewis and Clark Expedition* (Lincoln, Nebr.: University of Nebraska Press, 1983). This thirteen-volume edition serves as the basis for this account and is referred to as *The Journals*.

10. *The Journals*, vol. 2, p. 79.

11. Ibid., p. 87.

12. Ibid., p. 391.

13. Ibid., vol. 3, pp. 7, 22, 118.

14. Ibid., vol. 4, p. 60.

15. Ibid., pp. 101, 111.

16. Ibid., p. 118.

17. Ibid., p. 166.

18. Ibid., pp. 309, 336, 338.

19. Ibid., pp. 383, 411, 430.

20. Ibid., vol. 5, p. 112.

21. Ibid., p. 256.

22. Ibid., vol. 6, p. 163.

23. Ibid.

24. Ibid., p. 318.

25. Ibid., vol. 7, pp. 104–105.

26. Ibid., pp. 204, 209.

27. Ibid., p. 210.

28. Ibid., pp. 351, 356.

6. Moving On

1. Alexis de Tocqueville, *Democracy in America* (Charlottesville, Va.: American Studies, University of Virginia, 1996, from http://xroads.virginia.edu/~HYPER/DETOC/home.html), Appendix U.

2. Anonymous, "Sagacity of the Dog," *American Turf Registry and Sporting Magazine*, June 1831.

3. David Crockett, *A Narrative of the Life of David Crockett of the State of Tennessee*, eds. James A. Shackford and Stanley J. Folmsbee (Knoxville, Tenn.: University of Tennessee Press, 1973), p. 190.

4. Material on Crockett from Mark Derr, *The Frontiersman: The Real Life and the Many Legends of Davy Crockett* (New York: William Morrow, 1993).

5. George Norbury Appold, "Chesapeake Duck Dog," *The Century*, May 1885.

6. Maximilian, *Travels in the Interior of North America*, p. 115.

7. John James Audubon, *The Birds of America*, vol. 7, Plate CCCLXVIII-Male, in *Audubon's Birds of America*, HTML version by Richard Buonanno (New York: National Audubon Society, 2003, reprint from first octavo edition, 1840, http://www.audubon.org/bird/BoA/F38_G1f.html).

8. W.I., "Sketch of a Voyage to Labrador, Newfoundland, & C.," *The New-England Magazine*, May 1834.

9. John K. Mahon, *History of the Second Seminole War: 1835–1842* (Gainesville, Fla.: University of Florida Press, 1967), pp. 265–67.

10. *House Journal*, 26th Cong., 1st sess., March 9, 1841, p. 559.

11. Ibid.

12. Catlin, *North American Indians*, vol. 1, p. 23.

13. Ibid., vol. 1, p. 227; vol. 2, p. 72.

14. Maximilian, p. 273.

15. Ibid., p. 34.

16. John E. Baur, *Dogs on the Frontier* (San Antonio: Naylor Press, 1964), p. 124.

17. Richard Henry Dana, Jr., *Two Years Before the Mast* (New York: Dodd, Mead, 1946), p. 124.

18. Ibid., pp. 128–29.

19. Ibid., pp. 323–24.

20. Lansford W. Hastings, *The Emigrant Guide to Oregon and California* (Cincinnati: George Conclin, 1845), pp. 6 and 7.

21. John Muir, *My First Summer in the Sierra* (Boston: Houghton Mifflin, 1911, online at the Library of Congress, http://lcweb2.loc.gov/ammem/amrvhtml/conshome.html).

22. Frank Marryat, *Mountains to Molehills; or, Recollections of a burnt journal* (New York: Harper and Brothers, 1855), p. 111.

23. Ibid., p. 318.

24. J. Ross Brown, "A Trip to Bodie Bluff and the Dead Sea of the West," *Harper's New Monthly Magazine*, September 1865.

25. Malcolm E. Baker, *Bummer & Lazarus: San Francisco's Famous Dogs* (San Francisco: Londonborn Publications, 2001), p. 35.

26. *Daily Alta Californian*, April 12, 1861, in Baker, pp. 21–22.

27. *Daily Evening Bulletin*, June 17, 1862, in Baker, p. 27.

28. "Another Lazarus," *Daily Morning Call*, June 31, 1864.

29. "Exit Bummer," *Californian*, November 11, 1865.

7. Polar Opposites

1. Interview with Will Glass, Born in Slavery: Slave Narratives from the Federal Writers Project, 1936–1938, Library of Congress, Manuscript Division, http://memory.loc.gov/ammem/snhtml/snhome.html.

2. Interview with Uncle Hilliard Johnson, Born in Slavery: Slave Narratives from the Federal Writers Project.

3. Frederick Law Olmsted, *A Journey Through Texas or, A Saddle-Trip on the Southwestern Frontier* (New York: Burt Franklin, 1969; reprint of 1860 edition), p. 257.

4. Thomas R. Gray, *The Confessions of Nat Turner* (Baltimore: Thomas R. Gray, 1831).

5. Olmsted, *Texas*, p. 240.

6. Harriet Beecher Stowe, *Uncle Tom's Cabin* (New York: Modern Library Association, 1996), p. 492; Olmsted, *Texas*, p. 93.

7. Frederick Law Olmsted, *A Journey in the Seaboard Slave States in the Years 1853–1854 With Remarks on Their Economy*, 2 vols. (New York: G. P. Putnam's Sons, 1904; reprint of 1856 edition), p. 178.

8. Frederick Law Olmsted, *A Journey in the Back Country* (New York: Mason Brothers, 1861), pp. 214, 246–47.

9. Olmsted, *Texas*, p. 14.

10. Charles Hallock, "Wild Cattle Hunting on Green Island," *Harper's New Monthly Magazine*, July 1860.

11. Frederic Remington, "Cracker Cowboys of Florida," *Harper's New Monthly Magazine*, August 1895.

12. John McElroy, *Andersonville: A Story of Rebel Military Prisons* (New Haven, Conn.: Avalon Project, at Yale Law School, 1996–2003, http://www.yale.edu/lawweb/avalon/treatise/andersonville/ander.htm).

13. David Dodge, "The Cave-Dwellers of the Confederacy," *Atlantic Monthly*, October 1891.

14. "C," "The pointer, setter, and springer," *American Turf Register and Sporting Magazine*, December 1829.

15. "About Dogs," *Putnam's Monthly Magazine*, March 1857.

16. Randall, *The Practical Shepherd*, p. 401.

17. Ibid., pp. 396, 410; Thomas H. Terry, "The Collie," *Century*, August 1885.

18. "Trip to Newfoundland," *Harper's New Monthly Magazine*, December 1855.

19. Elisha Kent Kane, *Arctic Explorations in 1853, 1854, 1855* (New York: Arno Press, 1971; reprint of 1856 edition), pp. 20, 55–56, 110–11.

20. Charles Darwin, *The Descent of Man, and Selection in Relation to Sex* (Chicago and New York: Rand McNally, 1874), pp. 81, 100.

21. Charles Darwin, *The Variation of Plants and Animals under Domestication* (New York: D. Appleton, 1896), vol. 1, p. 15; vol. 2, pp. 99–100.

22. C. D. Shanly, "New York Dogs," *Atlantic Monthly*, May 1872.

23. Ibid.

24. Ibid.

25. H. C. Bunner, "Shantytown," *Scribner's Monthly*, October 1880.

26. William M. Tileston, "Some American Sporting Dogs," *Scribner's Monthly*, April 1877.

27. Shanly, "New York Dogs."

28. Ibid.

8. Fights Indians; Runs with Dogs

1. Richard Irving Dodge, *The Plains of North America and Their Inhabitants*, ed. Wayne R. Kime (Newark, Del.: University of Delaware Press, and London and Toronto: Associated University Presses, 1989; from 1876 edition), p. 135.

2. Ibid., pp. 135, 196.

3. Ibid., p. 126.

4. Andrew C. Isenberg, *The Destruction of the Bison: An Environmental History, 1750–1920* (Cambridge: Cambridge University Press, 2000), p. 29. While smaller than the previously accepted estimates of 40 to 70 million bison slaughtered during the nineteenth century, Isenberg's numbers are based on more precise science.

5. Connie A. Woodhouse, Jeffrey J. Lukas, and Peter M. Brown, "Drought in the Western Great Plains, 1845–46," BAMS, October 2002.

6. Elizabeth B. Custer, *"Boots and Saddles" or Life in Dakota with General Custer* (New York: Harper and Brothers, 1885), p. 42.

7. George Armstrong Custer, *My Life on the Plains* (New York: Citadel Press, 1962), pp. 79–84.

8. Robert Marshall Utley, *Cavalier in Buckskins: George Armstrong Custer on the Western Military Frontier* (Norman, Okla.: University of Oklahoma, 1991; electronic book, 1998), pp. 107–108.

9. Ibid., p. 310.

10. Ibid., pp. 57–58.

11. Samuel Woodworth Cozzens, *The Marvelous Country, or Three years in Arizona and New Mexico* (Boston: Lee and Shepherd, 1876), pp. 280–81.

12. Ed Dorn, *Recollections of Gran Apacheria* (San Francisco: Turtle Island Foundation, 1974).

13. Charles F. Lummis, *A Tramp Across the Continent* (New York: Charles Scribner's Sons, 1913; reprint of 1892 edition), p. 72.

14. Ibid., pp. 14, 74.

15. Ibid., p. 131.

16. Ibid., p. 225.

17. Ibid., p. 254–55.

18. Ibid., pp. 256, 257.

19. Frederic Remington, "Bear-Chasing in the Rocky Mountains," *Harper's New Monthly Magazine*, July 1895.

20. Montague Stevens, *Meet Mr. Grizzly: A Saga of the Passing of the Grizzly Bear* (Silver City, N.M.: High-Lonesome Books, 1990; reprint of 1943 University of New Mexico edition).

21. Theodore Roosevelt, *Ranch Life and the Hunting Trail*, illustrated by Frederick Remington (New York: Century Company, 1902; reprint of 1888 edition), p. 186.

9. Don't Fence Me In

1. Frederick Jackson Turner, *The Frontier in American History* hypertext by Michael W. Kidd (Charlottesville, Va.: American Studies, University of Virginia, 1996, from New York: Henry Holt, 1935, http://xroads.virginia.edu/~HYPER/TURNER/).

2. Edward N. Wentworth, "Eastward Sheep Drives from California and Oregon," *Mississippi Valley Historical Review*, vol. 28, issue 4, March 1942.

3. Ibid.

4. Muir, *My First Summer in the Sierra.*

5. Wentworth, *America's Sheep Trails*, p. 487.

6. Ibid., p. 525; Jack Gage, *Tensleep and No Rest: A Historical Account of the Range War of the Big Horns in Wyoming* (Casper, Wyo.: Prairie Publishing Company, 1958).

7. Charles Dudley Warner, *In the Wilderness* (The Project Gutenberg Literary Archive Foundation, electronic text #3132, March 2002, http://www.gutenberg.net/etext02/cwitwll.txt).

8. Theodore Roosevelt, "John Muir: An Appreciation," *Outlook*, January 16, 1915 (http://sierraclub.org/john_muir_exhibit/life/appreciation_by_roosevelt.html).

9. John Muir, "An Adventure with a Dog and a Glacier," *Century*, September 1897. All quotes are from the original text.

10. Sir William Francis Butler, *The Wild Northland: being the story of a winter journey, with dogs, across northern North America* (New York: Allerton, 1922; reprint of 1904 edition), p. 24.

11. Jack London, *The Call of the Wild* (Berkeley, Calif.: University of California, 1999, http://sunsite.berkeley.edu/London/Writings/CallOfTheWild/), chap. 1.

12. Ibid., chap. 7.

13. Adolphus W. Greely, *Three Years of the Arctic Service: An Account of the Lady Franklin Bay Expedition of 1881–84 And the Attainment of the Farthest North*, 2 vols. (New York: Charles Scribner's Sons, 1885).

14. Robert E. Peary, *The North Pole: Its Discovery in 1909 under the Auspices of the Peary Arctic Club* (New York: Frederick A. Stokes, 1910), p. 70.

15. Ibid., p. 8.

16. Ibid., p. 170.

17. Ibid., pp. 70, 273, 333. Dr. S. Allen Counter, http://www.people.fas.harvard.edu/~counter/culture.html.

18. Sir Ernest Shackleton, *South: The Story of Shackleton's Last Expedition, 1924–1917* (Project Gutenberg Literary Archive Foundation, electronic text #5199, February 2004, http://www.gutenberg.net/etext04/south12.txt).

10. Civilizing the Dog but Forgetting the Man

1. Charles Dudley Warner, Editor's Study, *Harper's New Monthly Magazine*, January 1896.

2. Gaston Fay, "Typical Dogs," *Century*, May 1885.

3. Hugh Dalziel, "Dogs and Their Management," *Harper's New Monthly Magazine*, March 1886.

4. Thorstein Veblen, *The Theory of the Leisure Class* (New York: Macmillan, 1899), chap. 6.

5. Alfred M. Downer, *Firefighters and Their Pets* (New York and London: Harper and Brothers, 1907), pp. 124, 126.

6. Clyde E. Keeler and Harry C. Trimble, "Inheritance of Position Preference in Coach Dogs," *Journal of Heredity* 31 (1940): 51–54.

7. *Theodore Roosevelt: An Autobiography* (Project Gutenberg Literary Archive Foundation, electronic text #3335, July 2002, http://www.gutenberg.net/etext02/trabi.txt).

8. "Pete the Bulldog Gets a Victim," *New York Times*, May 11, 1907; "Pete the Bulldog Guards Roosevelt," *New York Times*, May 1, 1907.

9. Samuel G. Chapman, *Police Dogs in North America* (Springfield, Ill.: Charles C. Thompson, 1990).

10. Lieutenant-Colonel Edwin Hautenville Richardson, *Forty Years with Dogs* (Philadelphia: David McKay, n.d.), p. 182.

11. Ernest Harold Baynes, *Animal Heroes of the Great War* (New York: Macmillan, 1925), pp. 179–82.

12. Theodore F. Jager, *Scout, Red Cross and Army Dogs: A Historical Sketch of Dogs in the Great War and a Training Guide for the Rank and File of the United States Army* (Rochester, N.Y.: Arrow Printing, 1917), p. 21; Baynes, p. 16.

13. Richardson, p. 225.

14. Peter Shaw Baker, *Animal War Heroes* (London: A&L Black, 1933), p. 67.

15. "Monument Planned to Dog Hero of War; Rags May Be Buried at Fort Hamilton," *New York Times*, March 23, 1936.

16. "Monument Planned . . ."

17. "Perishing Honors Dog Mascot of AEF," *New York Times*, July 7, 1921.

18. Herbert B. Mayes, "Naming of Your Pet Dog Often is Sacred Rite," *New York Times*, January 20, 1924.

11. Twenties Roar, Thirties Crash and Rumble

1. "Westminster Show to Be Gala Event," *New York Times*, February 17, 1918.

2. "Hotel Man Buys Famous Dog," *Cleveland Advocate*, January 13, 1917.

3. Michel de Montaigne, "Apology for Raimond de Sebonde," *The Essays of Michel de Montaigne*, trans. Charles Cotton, ed. W. Carew Hazlitt (New York: A. L. Burt, 1892).

4. "'Dickie Boy' in Trouble," *New York Times*, July 30, 1921; "Laddie Boy's Son Found," August 18, 1922.

5. "Laddie Boy Ends Sitting," *New York Times*, October 1, 1923; "Mrs. Harding Quietly Leaves White House; Laddie Boy Greets Coolidge Warmly," August 18, 1923; "Laddie Boy Locked Up," November 19, 1923.

6. "Daniel G. Reid Dies of Pneumonia at 66," *New York Times*, January 17, 1925.

7. "D. G. Reid Disputes Ex-Wife Over Dog," *New York Times*, July 17, 1921.

8. "More Trouble for Ruth," *New York Times*, September 8, 1925.

9. Baker, *Animal War Heroes*, p. 66.

10. Elliott Humphrey and Lucien Warner, *Working Dogs* (Baltimore: Johns Hopkins University Press, 1934).

11. "AKC to Confer with Government on Placing a Quarantine on Dogs," *New York Times*, December 22, 1929.

12. "Scientists to Take Dog Pack to Brazil," *New York Times*, December 22, 1930.

13. "Famous Screen Dog," *New York Times*, June 16, 1927.

14. "Barking Dogs in Films," *New York Times*, April 20, 1930.

15. "Three-Legged Dog Saves Two in Fire," *New York Times*, October 15, 1925.

16. Arthur Shield, "Men and Dogs Conquer Alaskan Winter," *New York Times*, February 8, 1925.

17. Claire Randolf Murphy and Jane G. Hough, *Gold Rush Dogs* (Anchorage, Ala.: Alaska Northwest Books, 2001), pp. 101 and 104; Mildred Adams,

"Dogs That Rank As Heroes Have a Hall of Fame," *New York Times*, January 5, 1930.

18. Richard Evelyn Byrd, *Little America: Aerial Exploration in the Antarctic and the Flight to the South Pole* (New York: G. P. Putnam's Sons, 1930), p. 79. For the controversy over Owen, see Eugene Rodgers, *Beyond the Barrier* (Annapolis, Md.: Naval Institute Press, 1990).

19. Byrd, p. 342.

20. Ibid., pp. 108 and 109; Russell Owen, "Chinook Vanishes into Antarctica," *New York Times*, January 23, 1929.

21. "'Typical Boy and Dog' Greeted by Hoover," *New York Times*, December 18, 1931.

22. Richard Evelyn Byrd, *Discovery: The Story of the Second Byrd Antarctic Expedition* (New York: G. P. Putnam's Sons, 1935), p. 17.

23. Ibid., pp. 18, 321.

24. Ibid., p. 74.

25. Ibid., p. 177.

26. Ibid., p. 245.

27. Charles Stockard, *The Genetic and Endocrinic Basis for Differences in Form and Behavior*, in *The American Anatomical Memories*, no. 19 (Philadelphia: Press of the Wistar Institute of Anatomy and Biology, 1941), pp. 7 and 10.

28. Letter to Alan Lomax, September 9, 1940, Woody Guthrie and the Archive of American Folk Song: Correspondence, 1940–1950, The Library of Congress.

12. World on Fire

1. "Award of Soldier Medals to Dogs is Barred by Army After Protest," *New York Times*, February 16, 1944.

2. Cecilia Rasmussen, "L.A. Then and Now: The Dogs of War Laid Their Lives on the Line for U.S.," *Los Angeles Times*, May 4, 2003.

3. Fairfax Downey, *Dogs for Defense: American Dogs in the Second World War, 1941–45*, for Dogs for Defense, Inc. (New York: Daniel P. MacDonald, 1955), pp. 14–19.

4. K. M. Born, *Quartermaster Corps War Dog History* (Fort Lee, Va.: Department of the Army, Office of the Quartermaster General, 1999–2002, http://www.qmfound.com/k-9.htm); U.S. War Department, *War Dogs*, Technical Manual 10-396, July 1943.

5. Downey, p. 37; "Dog Evades Draft at Induction Here," *New York Times*, June 24, 1943; Henry R. Isley, "Dogs for Defense Out for Recruits," *New York Times*, August 5, 1943.

6. George S. Patton, Jr., cited at http://www.pattonhq.com/willie.html.

7. Henry R. Isley, "Kennel Club Bans Striking of Dogs," *New York Times*, February 20, 1944.

8. H. L. Brock, "Mentioned in Dispatches," *New York Times*, January 23, 1944.

9. Ibid.

10. Anna M. Waller, *Dogs and National Defense* (Fort Lee, Va.: Department of the Army, Office of the Quartermaster General, 1958, http://www.qmmuseum. lee.army.mil/dogs_and_national_defense.htm).

11. Ibid.

12. Elrich Davis, "Dogtown on the Potomac," *American Kennel Club Gazette*, January 1944, p. 10; Downey, p. 114.

13. Doris Kearns Goodwin, *No Ordinary Time: Franklin and Eleanor Roosevelt: The Home Front in World War II* (New York: Simon & Schuster, 1984), pp. 200 and 528.

14. Ibid., p. 200.

15. John Crider, "Fala, Never in the Doghouse," *New York Times*, October 15, 1944.

16. "Fala Takes Charge of White House Parley," *New York Times*, October 6, 1944.

17. "Blaze Is Killed After Hurting Fala in a Battle of the Roosevelt Dogs," *New York Times*, December 1, 1945; "Fala 'Sleeps Away': Was Roosevelt's Pet," April 6, 1952.

18. "Fala 'Sleeps Away.' "

19. Willie Morris, *My Dog Skip* (New York: Vintage Books, 1996), p. 118.

20. Registration statistics from Charles A. T. O'Neill et al., eds., *The American Kennel Club: 1884–1984* (New York: American Kennel Club, 1985), p. 225.

21. Richard M. Nixon, "Checkers," September 23, 1952, HTML Transcription by Michael E. Eidenmuller, Top 100 American Speeches, Online Speech Bank, http://www.americanrhetoric.com/speeches/richardnixoncheckers. html.

22. Nemo story from Michael G. Lemish, *War Dogs: A History of Loyalty and Heroism* (Washington, D.C.: Brassey's, 1996), p. 176.

23. *War Dogs: The Untold Story of Dogs in Combat* (Studio City, Calif.: Jeffrey Bennett and GRB Entertainment, 1998), television documentary.

13. The Good, the Bad, and the Dog

1. *2003–2004 APPMA National Pet Owners Survey*.

2. Peter Singer, *Animal Liberation: A New Ethic for Our Treatment of Animals* (New York: New York Review of Books, 1975).

3. *2003–2004 APPMA National Pet Owners Survey*.

4. Mark Derr, "The Perilous Iditarod," *Atlantic Monthly*, March 1995; Mark Derr, *Dog's Best Friend: Annals of the Dog-Human Relationship* (New York: Henry Holt, 1997), pp. 255–56.

5. *All Things Considered*, National Public Radio, May 31, 2002.

6. Mark Derr, "It Takes Training and Genes to Make a Mean Dog Mean," *New York Times*, February 6, 2001.

7. Derr, *Dog's Best Friend*, p. 212; Derr, "It Takes Training and Genes . . ."

8. Derr, *Dog's Best Friend*, p. 306.

9. Ewen F. Kirkness et al., "The Dog Genome: Survey Sequencing and Comparative Analysis," *Science*, September 26, 2003, vol. 301, pp. 1,898–1,903.

10. Mark Derr, "What Makes Dogs Tick? The Search for Answers," *New York Times*, August 19, 2003.

Acknowledgments

✑

I WOULD LIKE TO THANK first and foremost my wife, Gina Maranto, without whose support and encouragement this book never would have happened. Others who were instrumental in realizing *A Dog's History of America* are my agent, Alice Fried Martell, a true believer; my editor at Farrar, Straus and Giroux and North Point Press, John Glusman; his able assistant, Aodaoin O'Floinn; Allen Peacock; Barbara Kolk and Ann Sergi at the American Kennel Club Library; Lynne P. Brown; Cornelia Dean; and Nancy Hooper. I owe a special debt to the dogs—Katie and Harley, the Kelpies who keep order in the house, and especially Marlow and Clio, the leopard dogs who, sadly, did not make it to the finish.

Index

❦

A Note About the Author

MARK DERR is the author of *Some Kind of Paradise,* a critically acclaimed social and environmental history of Florida; *The Frontiersman,* a biography of Davy Crockett; and *Dog's Best Friend.*